English Grammar through Jokes

ジョークで楽しむ英文法再入門

豊田一男

開拓社

He who laughs most, learns best.
(John Cleese)

もっともよく笑う者がもっとも良く学ぶ.

まえがき

　本書は中学・高校で一応英語を学んだ人が英語のジョークを楽しみながら英文法の重要な項目を再学習するための主に社会人向けのものです．大人のための，少なくとも 30 歳以上の人を特に意識して編集しましたので，若い人には難解であったり，面白いと思えなかったりするジョークが含まれているかもしれません．仕事の現場で英文法の知識の必要性を強く感じてはいるが，例文の内容の物足りなさから今さら高校レベルの参考書を読む気になれないでいる人をかなり意識して編集しました．

　文法用語の解説は最小限にとどめ，それぞれの文法事項を含むジョークを読みながら英文法を復習し，同時に英語を母語とする人々の「笑いの文化」とでも呼ぶべきものを感じ取っていただきたいというのが編著者の願いです．

　本書は次のような読者を想定しています．
　★ いつも女性に痛めつけられている（主に既婚の）男性
　★ いつも上司に文句や嫌味を言われているサラリーマン諸氏
　★ ジョークを教室で使ってみたいと思っている英語の先生
　★ 医師・弁護士・政治家など社会的地位の高い人々に対する日頃の鬱憤を一瞬でも晴らしたい人
　★ 映画・演劇などで他の人が笑っているのに何がおかしくて笑っているのか分からずみじめな思いをしている人

　逆に，本書の対象外の人は，① ジョークを聞いて［読んで］「そんなバカなことがあるか！」と怒ってしまう人，② そもそもジョークだと分からないでポカンとしてしまう人，です．
　① の人は謹厳実直，真面目を絵に描いたような人．
　② の人はちょっと訓練（？）すれば分かるようになる可能性があるかもしれません．

　先代の落語家林家三平は駄じゃれを言っては「これがなぜ面白いかというと」

と言ってまた笑わせていましたが,「なぜ面白いか」を説明するくらい笑いをそぐことはありません.次の言葉はそれを表現しています.

> You cannot teach humour. If you have to explain it, it is no longer funny.
> (Woolard (1996))
>
> (ユーモアを教えることはできない.もし説明しなければならないなら,それはもはやおかしくなくなってしまう.)
>
> Analyzing humor is like dissecting a frog. Few people are interested and the frog dies.　(E. B. White)
> (ユーモアを分析するのはカエルを解剖するようなものだ.ほとんど誰も興味を持たないしカエルも死んでしまう.)

また,ジョークについても次のような言葉があります.

> A joke is a form of humor enjoyed by some and misunderstood by most.
> (ジョークは一部の人に楽しまれ,大部分の人に誤解されるユーモアの一形式.)

しかし,ジョークにあまり慣れていない人のためにまさに「蛇足」(☞の記号)を付けました.そのジョークが笑えた人はここは飛ばしてください.

　一応和訳をつけてありますが,特に駄じゃれ(pun)を含んでいる翻訳不可能なジョークは表面的な和訳をつけて,注(⇔)でその落ち(punch line)を説明する形にしてあります.和訳可能なジョークを除くと,pun の絡まないジョークを見つけるのは容易ではありません.逆に言うと,ジョークの大多数が何らかの意味で pun になっています.

　また,ジョークは作り話(fiction)であることを忘れずに読み進んでいただきたいと思います.人生・人間を真正面からではなく,斜めから,時に後ろから見る面白さを味わっていただけたら,編著者のこの上ない喜びです.

　ジョークには様々なタイプ,登場人物が現れます.本文から「ジョークの常識」と名付けた囲み記事への参照(★の記号)によってジョークの概略が分かるようにしてあります.

　「ジョークは文脈は無視しても,文法は無視しない」(岩間(2003))という名言があります.本書によって読者諸氏が英文法の概要を再学習されることを期待

しています．

　最後になりましたが，開拓社出版部部長 川田 賢氏には感謝の言葉もありません．あまり整理されないまま，うっかり送ってしまった「見本原稿」という名の「全原稿」に目を通し，出版の可能性を示唆していただいた時の喜びを今も忘れることはできません．本書の体裁・構成には特にお骨折りをいただきました．また内容・記述についても多くの適切なご指摘をいただきました．

　思わぬ解釈の誤りなどについて読者諸賢のご指摘をいただければ幸いです．

　　2015年6月

　　　　　　　　　　　　　　　　　　　　　　　　　　　豊 田 一 男

記号の説明

A ⇔ B： AとBが（何らかの意味で）駄じゃれ（pun）になっていることを表す．
Anon.： Anonymous「作者不明」
attrib.： be attributed to ～「～の作とされる」
do： 原形不定詞を表す．
done： 過去分詞を表す．
（　）： 省略可能・追加説明を表す．
[　]： 前項と入れ替え可能を表す．
＿＿： 節（S+V+...）を表す．

目　次

まえがき .... *iii*

第1章	現在(進行)形・過去(進行)形・未来(進行)形	*1*
第2章	疑問文	*27*
第3章	命令文・感嘆文	*40*
第4章	5文型	*47*
第5章	完了形	*57*
第6章	受動態	*65*
第7章	助動詞	*73*
第8章	名詞	*98*
第9章	代名詞	*119*
第10章	Itの用法	*140*
第11章	形容詞	*154*
第12章	冠詞	*170*
第13章	副詞	*188*
第14章	不定詞	*200*
第15章	分詞	*230*
第16章	動名詞	*250*
第17章	前置詞	*267*
第18章	句と節	*306*

第19章	等位接続詞	313
第20章	名詞節	321
第21章	形容詞節	330
第22章	副詞節	346
第23章	条件・仮定表現	362
第24章	比較表現	376
第25章	否定表現	396
第26章	時制の一致・話法	413
第27章	倒置・強調・挿入・省略	423

あとがき	435
参考書目	437
索　引	441

第1章 現在(進行)形・過去(進行)形・未来(進行)形

> Yesterday I **was** a dog. Today I**'m** a dog. Tomorrow I**'ll** probably still **be** a dog. Sigh! There**'s** so little hope for advancement.
> (Charles M. Schulz, *Snoopy*)
> (昨日は犬だった．今日も犬だ．明日も間違いなく相変わらず犬だろう．ああ．進歩の見込みがあまりにもないじゃないか．―チャールズ M. シュルツ『スヌーピー』)

☞ Charles M. Schulz (1922-2000): アメリカの漫画家．

◆be 動詞の形：be 動詞は人称・数・時制などに応じて次のような形になる．

主語			現在形	過去形	過去分詞形	-ing 形
1人称	単数	I	am	was	been	being
	複数	we	are	were		
2人称	単数	you	are	were		
	複数	you				
3人称	単数	he, she, it, 単数形の名詞	is	was		
	複数	they, 複数形の名詞	are	were		

【注意1】be 動詞が原形 be のままの形で用いられるのはふつう次の場合：

1) 助動詞の後ろ：That *must* **be** true.（それは本当にちがいない．）
2) 不定詞：I want *to* **be** a scientist.（私は科学者になりたい．）
3) 命令文：**Be** careful.（気をつけなさい．）
　　　　　Don't **be** careless.（不注意ではいけません．）

【注意2】時制：時制には次の 12 の形がある．

	現 在	過 去	未 来
基本形	I write	I wrote	I will write
進行形	I am writing	I was writing	I will be writing
完了形	I have written	I had written	I will have written
進行形	I have been writing	I had been writing	I will have been writing

現在（進行）形

1 現在形

"What type of car **does** your dad **drive**?"
"I don't **know** the name, but it **starts** with a 'P.'"
"That's strange. Our car **starts** with a key."
(「きみのお父さんはどんな型の車を運転するの」「名前は知らないけどピーで始まるやつだよ」「それって変だね．家のはキーでエンジンがかかるけどな」)

☞ start with 〜：「〜から始まる」⇔「〜で動き出す」　　☞ P [píː] ⇔ key [kíː]
★ **Pun** → p. 26

◆ 3 人称単数現在形の作り方

主語が 3 人称単数現在のとき，動詞の現在形には **-(e)s** がつく．ただし，下記のような綴りの変化に注意．

原形の語尾の形	-(e)s のつけ方	例
-s, -x, -sh, -ch で終わるもの	-es	pass－pass<u>es</u>,　mix－mix<u>es</u>, finish－finish<u>es</u>, catch－catch<u>es</u>
「子音字＋y」で終わるもの	y を i にかえて -es	carry－carr<u>ies</u>,　cry－cr<u>ies</u>, fly－fl<u>ies</u>,　study－stud<u>ies</u>
「子音字＋o」で終わるもの	-es	go－go<u>es</u>

【注意1】「子音字」とはアルファベットの母音字 (a, e, i, o, u) を除くすべての文字をいう．
【注意2】「母音字＋y」はそのまま -s をつける：stay－stay<u>s</u>, enjoy－enjoy<u>s</u>, buy－buy<u>s</u>

A. 基本用法： (1) 現在の事実—状態動詞
　　　　　　　(2) 現在の習慣—動作動詞
　　　　　　　(3) **have**
　　　　　　　(4) 時に関係のない真理
B. 未来を表す用法： (1) 確定的な未来の行動
　　　　　　　　　　(2) 時・条件の副詞節で

A. 基本用法

(1) 現在の事実—状態動詞：現在だけでなく過去と未来にも及ぶ現在の状態を述べるもので以下のような動詞が含まれる．**ふつう進行形にしない．**

　(a) 状態を表す動詞：be（〜である），belong（属している），contain（含んでいる），resemble（似ている）など
　(b) 好悪・希望などを表す動詞：like（好む），love（愛する），hate（憎む），hope（望む），want（ほしがる）など
　(c) 心理作用を表す動詞：know（知っている），think（思っている），understand（理解する），forget（忘れる）など
　(d) 知覚作用を表す動詞：see（見える），hear（聞こえる），smell（においがする）など
　　cf. look（見る），listen (to)（聞く），smell（においをかぐ）は動作動詞．

I **like** every season. In winter I **like** summer and in summer I **like** winter.
（どの季節も好きだ．冬には夏が好きだし，夏には冬が好きだ．）

"Does this package **belong to** you? The name is blurred."
"Can't be mine. Mine is McGinty."
(「この包みは君のかな．名前が汚れてはっきりしないが」「ぼくののはずはありません．ぼくの名前はマクギンティーです」)
☞ Can't = It can't　　Mine = My name
☞「ぼくの名前は Blurred（ブラード）ではありません．」

"My brother's got dozens of trophies and medals for football."
"Does he play for England?"
"He doesn't play at all. He **owns** a pawnshop."
(「兄はフットボールのトロフィーやメダルを何十個も持ってるよ」「イングランドの代表なのかい」「フットボールはまったくやらないんだ．質屋なんだ」)
☞ 's got = has
☞ もらったトロフィー，メダルなどを質に入れる人は多い．

"Our economic prof talks to himself. Does yours?"
"Yes, but he doesn't **realize** it—he **thinks** we're listening."
(「経済学の教授は独り言を言うんだ．君の先生はどうだい」「言うとも，でも気づいていないよ．ぼくらが聴いていると思っているんだ」)

"How did you break your arm?"
"Well, do you **see** that broken step?"
"Yes."
"Well, I didn't."
(「どうして腕を折ったんだい」「あの壊れた階段が見えるだろう」「見えるよ」「僕には見えなかったんだ」)

(2) 現在の習慣―動作動詞：現在の習慣的動作を表す．状態動詞と異なり自由に進行形を作ることができる．

"Mum, does God **go** to the bathroom?"
"No, son, why do you **ask**?"
"Well, every morning Dad **goes** to the bathroom, **knocks** on the door and **shouts**, 'Oh, God! Are you still in there?'"

(「お母さん，神様はトイレへ行くの」「行かないわよ，お前．でもなぜ聞くの」「だって毎朝お父さんはトイレへ行くとドアをノックして『おお神よ，まだ入っているのか』って叫ぶんだもん」)

☞ Oh, God!:「おやおや，これは驚いた」

"My husband **writes** fiction."
"My husband **speaks** it."
(「夫は小説を書いてますのよ」「宅のはしゃべってますわ」)
☞ fiction:「小説」⇔「作り話」　　★ **Pun** → p. 26

My wife is a careful driver. She always **looks** both ways before hitting somebody.
(妻は運転が慎重だ．いつも両側を見てから誰かをはねる．)

I **take** my pet lion to church every Sunday. He has to eat.

(Marty Pollio)

(ペットのライオンを毎日曜日に教会へ連れて行く．彼は食べなければならないのだ．)
☞ 教会に来ている人を餌にする．
☞ Marty Pollio (1955-　)：アメリカのコメディアン・俳優．
★ **Tall tale** → p. 412

(3) have は「〜を持っている」の意味の状態動詞としてもその他の意味の動作動詞としても用いられる．

"What didn't Adam and Eve **have** that everyone else **has**?"
"Parents."
(「アダムとイブは他のみんなが持っている何を持っていなかったか」「両親」)

☞ 人類の祖に親はいない．

A mother said to her son one day, "Sam, we**'re having** very important dinner guests. Would you go upstairs and **have** a wash, put on clean clothes and make yourself presentable?"
"Why?" said Sam. "Are they going to eat me for dinner?"

（母親がある日息子に言った「サム，とても大事なお客様をお食事にお招きするの．2階へ行って手を洗ってきれいな服を着て身なりをきちんとしておいてちょうだい」「なぜなの」とサムは言った．「夕食にぼくを食べるの」）
☞ presentable「（人前に出て）見苦しくない」⇔「提供に適した」
★ **Pun** → p. 26

Patient: **I'm having** trouble breathing.
Doctor: Well, I think I can give you something to stop that.
（患者「息がなかなかできないんです」医者「なるほど，それを止めるものをあげられると思います」）

(4) 時に関係のない真理

Mother always *said* that honesty **is** the best policy, and money **isn't** everything. She was wrong about other things too. (Gerald Barzan)
（母は正直は最善の策で，お金がすべてではないといつも言っていた．母は他のことについても間違っていた．）（→「第26章 時制の一致・話法」）

☞ Honesty is the best policy.（正直は最善の策），Money isn't everything.（金がすべてではない）はいずれもことわざ．
☞ Gerald Barzan: アメリカのユーモア作家．

"When are you going back to school, Tom?"
"I'm not going back, 'cause my teacher's gone crazy."
"Gone crazy?"
"Yes. One day she *told* us four and one **are** five, and today she *said* that two and three **make** five."
（「いつまた学校へ行くつもりなの，トム」「もう行かないよ，だって先生がおかしくなったんだもの」「おかしくなったって」「そうなんだ．ある日先生はぼくらに4+1は5だと言ったのに，今日は2+3は5になるって言ったんだ」）
☞ 'cause = because

B. 未来を表す用法

(1) 確定的な未来の行動

> "I **begin** to work at the Swan Laundry on Monday."
> "That's wonderful! But tell me, how do you wash a swan?"
> (「月曜に白鳥洗濯店で働き始めるよ」「それはすばらしい．だけど教えろよ，どうやって白鳥を洗濯するんだ」)

Wife to husband who was reluctant to help their small son with his homework: "Help him now while you can. Next year he **goes** into the fourth grade."
(幼い息子の宿題を手伝いたがらない夫に妻が言う「今できる間に手伝ってちょうだい．来年は4年生になるのよ」)
☞ それから先はあなたの学力では無理でしょう．

(2) 時・条件の副詞節で

> A boy was up an apple tree stealing apples. A policeman came along and caught him. He looked up at the boy in the tree and said, "When are you coming down, young man?" "*When* you **go** away!" replied the boy.
> (少年がリンゴを盗もうとリンゴの木に登っていた．警官がやって来て少年を見つけた．警官は木にいる少年を見上げて言った「君はいつ降りてくるんだ」「お巡りさんがいなくなったらさ」と少年．)

"Are you going to the football match this afternoon?"
"Yes. Are you?"
"No, it's a waste of time. I can tell you the score *before* the game **starts**."
"Can you? What is it, then?"
"Nothing to nothing."
(「午後サッカーの試合に行くんだろう」「うん．君は」「時間の無駄だよ．ぼくには試合

が始まる前にスコアーが分かるぞ」「ホントか．じゃあ何対何だ」「0 対 0 さ」）

Teacher: Tommy Russel, you're late again.
Tommy: Sorry, sir. It's my bus—it's always coming late.
Teacher: Well, *if* it**'s** late again tomorrow, catch an earlier one.
（先生とトミーの対話：「トミー・ラッセル，君はまた遅刻だ」「すみません，先生．バスのせいです．いつも遅れて来て困るんです」「じゃあ，明日また遅れたら，もっと早く来るのに乗りなさい」）

★ **Irish bull** → p. 39

cf. 条件を表す節の主語が意志をもつときは「if+S+**will** *do*」になる．
Housewife: You can earn your dinner **if** you**'ll** chop that pile of wood.
　　Tramp: Let me see the menu first.
（主婦「あの薪の山を割ってくれる気があれば夕食にありつけるわよ」浮浪者「まず先にメニューを見せてくださいよ」）

❷ 現在進行形：am [is/are]+*do*ing

My wife's family **is coming** to visit us, and **I'm getting** ready for them. All week long **I've been erasing** letters from the welcome mat.
（妻の家族が我が家へ来ることになっていて，準備をしているところだ．丸 1 週間玄関のドアマットから「ようこそ」の文字を消し続けている．）

☞ 've been erasing: 現在完了進行形（→ p.60）

A. 基本用法：現に進行中の動作を表す
B. たびたび繰り返される現在の動作
C. 近い未来の予定
D. 状態動詞の進行形

-ing は次の表の場合を除き，下記のように原形に **-ing** をつける．
（例）visit−visit**ing**;　wash−wash**ing**;　play−play**ing**

原形の語尾の形	-ing のつけ方	例
「子音字＋e」で終わるもの	e をとって -ing	come—com<u>ing</u>, close—clos<u>ing</u>, have—hav<u>ing</u>, write—writ<u>ing</u>
「1母音字＋1子音字」で終わる1音節のもの	最後の子音字を重ねて -ing	cut—cut<u>ting</u>, get—get<u>ting</u>, run—run<u>ning</u>, stir—stir<u>ring</u>, stop—stop<u>ping</u>
「1母音字＋1子音字」で終わる2音節以上のもので，最後の音節に第1アクセントのあるもの		omít—omit<u>ting</u>, occúr—occur<u>ring</u>, begín—begin<u>ning</u>, prefér—prefer<u>ring</u>
-ie で終わるもの	ie を y にかえて -ing	die—d<u>ying</u>, lie—l<u>ying</u>, tie—t<u>ying</u>

cf. 「子音字＋e で終わるもの」で dye（染める）は dyeing と e をとらないで -ing をつける．(die（死ぬ）の -ing 形 dying と区別するため)

A. 基本用法

現に進行中の**動作**を表す．

> *Teacher:* What **are** you **reading**?
>   *Pupil:* I dunno.
> *Teacher:* But you**'re reading** aloud.
>   *Pupil:* But I**'m** not **listening**.
> （先生と生徒の対話：「何を読んでいるの」「分かりません」「でも声を出して読んでいるじゃありませんか」「でも聞いてないです」）

☞ dunno = don't know

"Come out of the water. Swimming is not allowed here."
"But I**'m** not **swimming**, officer. I**'m drowning**!"
（「水から出なさい．ここは水泳禁止だ」「でも，お巡りさん，僕は泳いでなんかいません．溺れているんです」）

Waiter: You sometimes find a pearl in an oyster stew.
Customer: **I'm looking** for oysters.
(「お客さま，カキのシチューの中にときどき真珠が見つかりますよ」「いや，そのカキを探しているんだ」)
★ **Waiter** → p. 266

Dick: Have you heard that all the busses and trains **are stopping** today?
Nick: No. Is there a strike?
Dick: No. They**'re stopping** to let the passengers off.
(ディックとニックの対話:「バスも電車も全部今日止まりそうだと聞いたか」「いや．ストライキがあるのか」「いいや．乗客を降ろすために止まろうとしてるんだ」)
☞ are stopping に「止まっている」の意味はない．

B. たびたび繰り返される現在の動作

ふつう always（いつも），constantly（絶えず）などの副詞を伴い，話し手の非難・軽蔑・迷惑などの気持ちを表す．

Adults **are** *always* **asking** little kids what they want to be when they grow up because they're looking for ideas.
(大人が幼い子供に大きくなったら何になりたいかをしきりに質問するのはアイデアを欲しがっているからだ．)

"Diane, I could die for your sake."
"You **are** *always* **saying** that, but you never do it."
(「ダイアン，きみのためなら死んでもいい」「あなたいつもそんなこと言っているけど，決してそうしないじゃない」)

Experience is the one perpetual best-seller—everybody **is** *continually* **buying** it.
(経験は唯一売れ続けているベストセラーだ—みんな絶えずそれを買い続けている．)

C. 近い未来の予定

> "I'm sorry, I can't see you Sunday. **I'm expecting** a headache."
> (「ごめんなさい，日曜には会えないわ．頭痛になるはずなの」)

☞ Sunday ＝ on Sunday

Husband: Put your coat on. **I'm going** to the pub.
　Wife: How nice! **Are** you **taking** me out?
Husband: No, **I'm turning** the heating off.
(夫と妻の対話：「コートを着なさい．私はパブへ行く」「まあ素敵．私を連れて行ってくださるの」「そうじゃない．暖房を止めるんだ」)
☞ ひどい夫だが，ジョークの中では例外的．普通は妻が夫をやりこめる．

> "Does your vacation start soon?"
> "Yes, my wife **is leaving** tomorrow."
> (「休暇はすぐ始まるのかい」「そうだ，妻が明日出発するんだ」)
> ☞ 妻がいなくなるのでゆっくり休める．

Bert takes his dog to the vet and says, "Can you cut off my dog's tail?" "Why do you want me to do that?" asks the vet. Bert replies, "My mother-in-law**'s arriving** tomorrow, and I don't want her to think she's welcome."
(バートは犬を獣医のところへ連れて行って言う「犬の尻尾を切ってくれないか」「なぜそんなことをしてほしいのですか」と獣医．バートは答えて「義理の母が明日来ることになっていて母に自分が歓迎されていると思ってほしくないんでね」)
★ **Mother-in-law** → p. 305

D. 状態動詞の進行形

(1) be 動詞：主語の行動・態度の一時的な状態を強調する．

> Angry wife to her husband: "**You're being** deliberately calm."
> (腹を立てた妻が夫に「あなたってわざとらしいくらいおとなしいわね」)

I **am being** frank about myself in this book. I tell of my first mistake on page 850. (Henry Kissinger)
(この本で私は自分自身について率直になっている．850 ページで私の最初の間違いについて述べている．)
☞ それまで間違いを犯していない？
☞ Henry Kissinger (1923-　)：アメリカの国際政治学者・政治家．

cf. 次は過去進行形の例：
"All you have to do is look the lion in the eye and show him you're not afraid."
"Yeah, but the lion would know I **was** just **being** deceitful."
(「君はライオンの目を見て，怖がってはいないことを示せばいいんだよ」「それはそうだろう．しかしライオンはぼくがだまそうとしているだけだと分かるだろう」)

(2) その他の状態動詞：ある状態の一時的な進行を強調する．

> She **is resembling** her mother more and more these days.
> (彼女は最近どんどん母親に似てきている．)

> She**'s thinking** of having her hair dyed back to its original colour — but she can't remember what it is!
> (彼女は髪を元の色に染めてもらおうかと思っているが，どんな色か思い出せないのだ．)
> ☞「have+O+過去分詞」(→「第 15 章　分詞」B. (3))

> **Are**n't we **forgetting** the true meaning of Christmas—the birth of Santa?　(Bart Simpson)
> (クリスマスの真の意味を忘れかけていないか—サンタの誕生だということを．)
> ☞ クリスマスはキリストの誕生日．
> ☞ Bart Simpson：アメリカのテレビアニメの主人公の名．

(3) have，see，smell，feel などが一時的に動作動詞として使われるとき．

> My mother-in-law has come round to our house at Christmas seven years running. This year we**'re having** a change. We're going to let

her in.　(Les Dawson)
（義理の母は7年続けてクリスマスに家へぶらりとやって来る．今年は変更して，入れてあげるつもりだ．）

☞　今まで玄関払いしていた．
☞　Les Dawson (1931–1993)：イギリスのコメディアン・作家．
★ **Mother-in-law** → p. 305

Christmas at my house is always more pleasant than anywhere else. We start drinking early. And while everyone **is seeing** only one Santa Claus, we**'re seeing** six or seven.　(W. C. Fields)
（我が家のクリスマスはいつも他のどこよりも楽しい．早めに飲み始める．だから，みんながサンタが1人しか見えていないときに6, 7人見えているのだ．）

☞　酔っぱらって1人が6人にも7人にもダブって見える．
☞　W. C. Fields (1880–1946)：アメリカのコメディアン．

過去(進行)形

動詞には**規則動詞**と**不規則動詞**がある．
　規則動詞：動詞の原形に **-(e)d** をつけて過去形・過去分詞形をつくる動詞．
　　（例）look－look**ed** [-t],　play－play**ed** [-d],　want－want**ed** [-id]
　不規則動詞：規則動詞以外の方法で過去形・過去分詞形をつくる動詞．

A. 規則動詞の過去形・過去分詞形の作り方

原形の語尾の形	-(e)d のつけ方	例
-e で終わるもの	-d	love—lov<u>ed</u>,　die—di<u>ed</u>, smile—smil<u>ed</u>,　agree—agre<u>ed</u>
「子音字＋y」で終わるもの	y を i にかえて -ed	carry—carr<u>ied</u>,　cry—cr<u>ied</u>, study—stud<u>ied</u>,　try—tr<u>ied</u>
「1母音字＋1子音字」で終わる1音節のもの	最後の子音字を重ねて -ed	stop—stop<u>ped</u>,　nod—nod<u>ded</u>, beg—beg<u>ged</u>,　stir—stir<u>red</u>

「1母音字+1子音字」で終わる2音節以上のもので,最後の音節に第1アクセントのあるもの		omít—omit<u>ted</u>, prefér—prefer<u>red</u>, refér—refer<u>red</u>, regrét—regret<u>ted</u>

【注意】 次の場合は -ed を付けるだけでよい．
1)「母音字+y」：stay—stay<u>ed</u>, enjoy—enjoy<u>ed</u>
2)「1母音字+1子音字」でない：pick—pick<u>ed</u>, watch—watch<u>ed</u>
3)「1母音字+1子音字」で終わる2音節以上のもので，最後の音節に第1アクセントのないもの：óffer—offer<u>ed</u>, vísit—visit<u>ed</u>

B. 不規則動詞は約200語あり，日常しばしば使用されるものが多い．
　変化の類型

型	変化の型	原形	過去形	過去分詞
A−B−B	−, −d, −d	hear say	heard said	heard said
	−, −t, −t	keep send	kept sent	kept sent
	−, −ght, −ght	catch teach	caught taught	caught taught
	−, −a−, −a−	sit	sat	sat
	−, −e−, −e−	meet lead	met led	met led
	−, −o−, −o−	get win	got won	got won
	−, −u−, −u−	dig strike	dug struck	dug struck
	−, −oo−, −oo−	stand	stood	stood
	−, −ou−, −ou−	find bind	found bound	found bound
A−B−A	原形=過去分詞形	run come	ran came	run come

A−B−C	−i−, −a−, −u− など	begin	began	begun
	過去形+n＝過去分詞形	speak break	spoke broke	spoken broken
	原形+n＝過去分詞形	drive know	drove knew	driven known
A−A−B	−, −, −en	beat	beat	beaten
A−A−A	(不変化)	cut shut set spread	cut shut set spread	cut shut set spread

❸ 過去形

What **were** you when you **were** alive? (Henny Youngman)
(おまえは生きていたとき何者だったんだ．)

☞ Henny Youngman (1906–1998)：アメリカのコメディアン・バイオリニスト．
★ **Insulting joke** → p. 97

A. 基本用法：過去の状態・動作を表す
 (1) 過去のある時点での状態・動作
 (2) 過去のある期間にわたる状態・動作
B. 時制の一致のため（→ 第26章 時制の一致・話法）

When I **was** a student I **lived** with a farmer and his wife. The first day I **was** there, one of the chickens **died** and we **had** chicken soup for dinner. The second day a sheep **died** and we **had** lamb chops. The following day a duck **died** and we **had** roast duck. The next day the farmer **died**, so I **decided** to leave.
(学生のとき私は農場主夫妻のところに厄介になった．そこでの初日，鶏が一羽死ぬと夕食はチキンスープだった．2日目に羊が死ぬとラムチョップを食べた．次の日鴨が死んで皆でローストダックを食べた．次の日農場主が死んだ，だから私は去ることに決めた．)

☞ このままいると農場主を食べることになる？

A. 基本用法

(1) 過去のある時点での状態・動作

"My sister **threw** pepper in my face yesterday."
"That's terrible! What **did** you **do**?"
"I **sneezed**."
(「きのう妹がぼくの顔にコショウをひっかけたんだ」「それはひどい. 君はどうしたんだ」「くしゃみをしたさ」)
☞ 仕返しどころではない.

"My mother never **liked** any of my girlfriends. Last week I **invited** my latest girlfriend home. She **looked** like my mother, **talked** like my mother and even **dressed** like her."
"What **did** your mother **think** of her?"
"She **liked** her a lot."
"Well, that's the end of your problems!"
"Not quite. My father **didn't like** her!"
(「母はぼくのどのガールフレンドも決して好きにならなかった. 先週, 最近できたガールフレンドを家へ呼んだんだ. 彼女は外見も母に似ているし, しゃべり方も服装も母に似てたんだ」「お母さんは彼女をどう思ったんだ」「とても気に入ったよ」「じゃあ, 一件落着ってわけだ」「そうでもないんだ. 親父は彼女が気に入らなかったんだ」)
☞ あまりにも妻に似ていてうんざり.

(2) 過去のある期間にわたる状態・動作

For twenty years my wife and I **were** very happy—then we met.
(20年間妻と私は非常に幸福だった―そして2人は出会ったのだ.)
☞ そして結婚した.

My wife went to the beauty shop and got mud pack. For two days she **looked** nice. Then the mud fell off.
(妻は美容院へ行って泥んこ美容パックをしたんだ. 2日間はきれいに見えたよ. その後泥が剥げ落ちてしまったんだ.)
☞ そして元通りになった.

"I **wrote** her a letter every day for three years."
"Then what happened?"
"She married the postman."
(「彼女に毎日 3 年間手紙を書いたんだ」「それでどうなったんだい」「彼女その郵便配達と結婚したよ」)
☞ 手紙より直接会う方が強い.

4 過去進行形：was [were]+*do*ing

過去のある時点における進行中の動作を表す.

> "John, what **were** you **doing** out there in the rain?"
> "I **was getting** wet, mom."
> (「ジョン，雨の中へ出て何してたの」「濡れてたんだよ，お母さん」)

"What **was** he **doing** during the quarrel with his wife?"
"**Listening**."
(「奥さんと口げんかの最中，彼は何していたんだい」「聞いていたよ」)

"I was sorry for your wife in church this morning when she had a terrific attack of coughing and everyone turned to look at her."
"You need not worry about that. She **was wearing** a new spring hat."
(「奥様お気の毒でしたわ．今朝教会でひどくせき込まれて，皆さん振り返って奥様を見ましたわ」「ご心配にはおよびません．新しい春用の帽子をかぶっていたのです」)
☞ 帽子を見せびらかしたかった.

Father: Johnny, I can't hear your prayers.
Johnny: Well, I **was**n't **talking** to you.
(父「ジョニー，お祈りが聞こえないよ」ジョニー「だって，お父さんに話しかけてはいなかったもん」)

未来(進行)形

5 未来形

"What is the future of 'he drinks'?"
"He is drunk."
(「彼は飲む」の未来形は何か」「彼は酔っぱらっている」)

☞ 正解は "He will drink."
★ **Boner** → p. 46

A. will
B. 未来を表すその他の形

A policeman was escorting a prisoner to jail when his hat blew off. "**Shall** I run and get it for you?" asked the prisoner obligingly. "You must think I'm dumb," said the officer. "You stand here and **I'll** get it."
(警官が被告人を刑務所へ護送していると帽子が吹き飛んだ.「走って行って取って来ましょうか」と被告は親切心から言った.「君はきっと私をバカだと思っているな」と警官は言った.「君はここに立っていろ,私が取りに行く」)

英語の動詞には未来形という決まった形がないので, **will/shall/be going to**+動詞の原形などを用いて未来(これからのこと)を表す. **will, shall** が未来を表さないものについてもここで取り上げる.

A. will

---
(1) 単純未来
(2) 意志未来:(a) 話し手の意志
        (b) 主語(2人称・3人称)の意志
        (c) 相手の意志を尋ねる疑問文
---

(3) その他の用法：(a) 現在の推量
(b) 現在の習慣的行為または習性

"Doctor, **will** I be able to read after I get my glasses?"
"Indeed, you **will**."
"Well, that**'ll** be great. I never could read before."
(「先生，メガネをかければ読めるようになりますか」「もちろんですとも」「それはすばらしい．今まで字が読めなかったんで」)

(1) 単純未来：話し手や主語の意志と関係なくこれから生じることを表す．
A fortune-teller said to a man, "You **will** be poor and unhappy until you're thirty."
"And then what?"
The fortune-teller replied, "And then you**'ll** get used to it!"
(占い師が男に言った「30 までは貧乏で不幸でしょう」「その先はどうなりますか」占い師は答えた「それからはそれに慣れるでしょう」)

"I can't sleep, Doctor," said the patient.
"Well, hire a beautiful nurse and kiss her every fifteen minutes," advised the doctor.
"**Will** that put me to sleep?"
"No. But it **will** be a pleasure to keep awake."
(「先生，眠れないんです」と患者が言った．「美人の看護師を雇って 15 分ごとにキスをしなさい」と医者が助言した．「それで私は眠れるのですか」「いいえ．しかし目を覚ましているのが楽しみになるでしょう」)

"Say, Dad, did you go to Sunday school when you were a little boy?"
"Yes, son, regularly."
"Well, I bet it **won't** do me any good either."
(「ねえ，お父さん，小さいころ日曜学校へ行ったの」「行ったよ，おまえ，きちんとね」「じゃあ，きっと僕にも役に立たないんだ」)
☞ I bet = I'm sure

(2) 意志未来：話し手や主語の意志を表す．

> *He:* Darling, **will** you marry me?
> *She:* No, but I **will** always admire your good taste.

（「きみ，僕と結婚してくれないか」「いやよ，でもあなたのすてきな好みはずっとほめてあげるわ」）

☞ わたしの魅力が分かっているのね．

(a) 話し手の意志

"Darling, I want to see the world!"
"**I'll** give you an atlas for your next birthday, then."

（「あなた，わたし世界を見てみたいわ」「じゃあ，今度の誕生日に地図帳を買ってあげるよ」）
☞ 地図帳には世界地図が載っている．

> *Romeo:* Say, cutie, how would you like to go to the mountains with me this weekend?
> *Young Woman:* I don't think my mother would like that.
> *Romeo:* No problem. We **won't** invite her.

（「ねえ，お前，今週末一緒に山登りに行かないか」「母は行きたがらないと思うわ」「問題ないよ．お母さんは誘わないから」）

★ **Mother-in-law** → p. 305

(b) 主語（2人称・3人称）の意志

I'm having awful car trouble—The car **won't** start and the payments **won't** stop.

（車が故障して大変なんだ．車は動こうとしないし払いは待ってくれないんだ．）

I own a hundred and fifty books, but I have no bookcase. Nobody **will** lend me a bookcase.

（私は本を150冊持っていますが本箱がないのです．だれも本箱は貸してくれません．）
☞ 本はすべて借りたものを返さずに持っている．

(c) 相手の意志を尋ねる疑問文

1) Will [Won't] you *do***?**：「＿＿してくれませんか；＿＿しませんか」と依頼・勧誘を表す．

Little girl (to policeman): Please, sir, **will you** take my little brother home? He's lost.
Policeman: Why can't you take him home?
Little girl: Because I'm lost too.

（少女と警官の対話：「お願い，お巡りさん，弟を家まで連れて行ってください．迷子になっちゃったんです」「どうしてきみが連れて帰れないの」「だってわたしも迷子になっちゃったんですもの」）

"Doctor, I'm getting very forgetful."
"I see, Mr. Bloggs. **Won't you** take a chair?"
"Thanks―take a what?"

（「先生，とても忘れっぽくなってるんですが」「分かりました，ブロッグズさん．椅子にお掛けください」「どうも，何に掛けるんですって」）
☞ 今聞いた医者の言葉も忘れてしまう．

2) Shall I [we] *do***?**：「＿＿しましょうか」と相手の意志を尋ねて，申し出・提案を表す．

"Wake up, dear, there's a burglar downstairs in the kitchen eating that pie I made this afternoon! Ring 999!"
"**Shall I** ask for the police or an ambulance?"

（「あなた，目を覚まして．下の台所に強盗がいて午後私が作ったあのパイを食べてるのよ！ 999に電話してちょうだい」「警察か救急車のどっちに頼む」）

☞ 999 (three nines)：イギリスの緊急電話の番号．
☞ 救急車を呼ぶのは食べたパイによる食中毒の恐れを感じたから．

Old Grouch: Waiter, give me two pounds of dog food now!
Salesclerk: Certainly, sir. **Shall I** wrap it up or will you eat it here?

（老不平家「君，今すぐドッグフードを 2 ポンドくれたまえ」店員「かしこまりました，お客様．包みましょうか，それともここでお召し上がりになりますか」）

★ **Insulting joke** → p. 97

"**Shall we** have a friendly game of cards?"
"No, let's play bridge."
(「友好的なトランプでもやりましょうか」「いや,ブリッジをやろう」)
☞ ブリッジは勝つか負けるかの真剣勝負.

cf. 話し手の意志

> *Waiter:* Have another glass of beer, sir.
> *Husband:* Shall I have another glass, Henrietta?
> *Wife:* **Shall he** have another, mother?
>
> (ウェイター「もう一杯ビールをどうぞ,お客様」夫「ヘンリエッタ,もう一杯ビールを飲もうか」妻「もう一杯飲ませてもいいかしら,お母さん」)

★ **Mother-in-law** → p. 305

(3) その他の用法
(a) 現在の推量

"Why is a launderette a really bad place to pick up a woman?"
"Because a woman who can't even afford a washing machine **will** never be able to support you."
(「なぜコインランドリーは女の子のナンパには最悪の場所なんだい」「なぜって,洗濯機も買う余裕がない女の子が君を養うことなんかできないからさ」)

(b) 現在の習慣的行為または習性

> The human body, with proper care, **will** last a lifetime.
> (人間の身体は,きちんと気をつければ,一生もつものだ.)

★ **Irish bull** → p. 39

Money **will** buy a dog, but it **won't** buy the wag of his tail.
(金で犬は買えるがしっぽを振らせることまでは買えない.)

A golf ball **will** always travel furthest when hit in the wrong direction.
(Henry Beard)

（ゴルフボールは見当違いの方向へ打たれると常に最も遠くへ飛ぶものだ.）
☞ Henry Beard (1945-): アメリカのユーモア作家.

B. 未来を表すその他の形

(1) **be going to** *do*: (a) 近い未来の予測
　　　　　　　　　　(b) 前もって考えていた意図
(2) 現在進行形（→ p. 8）
(3) 現在形（→ p. 2）

(1) be going to *do*

"And what **are** you **going to** do when you are big like your mother?"
"Stop eating chocolate!"
（「それで，あなたはお母さんのように大きくなったらどうするつもりなの」「チョコレートを食べるのをやめるわ」）

(a) 近い未来の予測

My watch is three hours fast and I can't fix it. So **I'm going to** move to New York.　(Steven Wright)
（私の時計は3時間進んでいて修理できない．だからニューヨークへ引っ越す予定だ．）
☞ 時差が解消できる．
☞ Steven Wright (1955-): アメリカのコメディアン・作家.

"I think **I'm going to** lose my job in the flower shop tomorrow."
"What for?"
"I sent flowers to a funeral with the wrong card on them."
"What did the card say?"
"HOPE YOU'LL BE HAPPY IN YOUR NEW HOME"
（「あした花屋の仕事をくびになると思うよ」「なぜ」「葬式に間違ったカードを付けて花を送ってしまったんだ」「カードには何て書いてあったんだい」「新居でお幸せに」）
☞ 新居は天国ではなく地獄．

(b) 前もって考えていた意図

When I die, **I'm going to** leave my body to science fiction.

(Steven Wright)

(死んだら身体をサイエンスフィクションにゆだねるつもりだ.)
- ☞ science（科学）にではありません.
- ☞ Steven Wright (1955–): アメリカのコメディアン・作家.

"I have some good news for you and some bad news."
"Tell me the bad news first, doctor."
"**I'm going to** amputate your legs."
"And what is the good news?"
"The man in the next bed wants to buy your shoes."

(「あなたに良い知らせと悪い知らせがあります」「悪い方を先に言ってください,先生」「両足を切断することになります」「じゃあ,良い知らせは何ですか」「隣のベッドの男性があなたの靴を買いたいそうです」)

6 未来進行形：will be *do*ing / *be* going to be *do*ing

A. 未来のある時における進行中の動作
B. 未来の予定・行動

A. 未来のある時における進行中の動作

A famous female film star asked the artist, Pablo Cassells, to paint her. Pablo was talking to his friend about it.

"**Will** you **be painting** her in the nude?" asked the friend.
"Oh no!" said Pablo. "**I'll be keeping** my clothes on!"

(有名な映画女優が画家のパブロ・カセルズに自分を描いてほしいと頼んだ.パブロはそのことについて友人に話していた.「彼女をヌードで描くのかい」と友人は尋ねた.「とんでもない」とパブロ.「服は着たままさ」)
- ☞ her in the nude（裸の彼女）⇔ paint(ing) in the nude（裸で描く）

B. 未来の予定・行動

"Why do you want to learn French, Mr and Mrs Orr?"

"Well, we**'ll be adopting** a little French baby next month and we want to be able to understand it when it begins to talk."

(「オーご夫妻, なぜフランス語を習いたいのですか」「来月可愛いフランス人の赤ちゃんを養子にするので, 赤ちゃんが話し出したら話すことを理解できるようになりたいのです」)

★ **Irish bull** → p. 39

"**Are** you **going to be using** your lawn mower Saturday?"

"Yes."

"Good. I need to borrow your car."

(「土曜には芝刈り機を使っているかい」「うん」「良かった. 君の車を借りる必要があってね」)

ジョークの常識①

★ **Pun:**「1 つの語を 2 つ以上の意味になるように用いたり，意味が異なり同じ音またはほとんど同じ音の 2 つの語を用いてユーモラスな，あるいは，おどけた効果を生むようにするもの」で，日本語の「洒落・駄じゃれ」「地口」「語呂合わせ」に相当する．

発音，綴り，意味によって，大きく 3 種類に分類できる．（○は同一，×は相違，△は類似を表す．）

	Sound（発音）	Spelling（綴り）	Meaning（意味）
(1)	○	○	×
(2)	○	×	×
(3)	△	×	×

(1) は address の「演説」「住所」のように語の多義性に基づくものと，fan の「扇，扇風機」と「(チームなどの) ファン（＜fanatic）」のように語源を異にする同音同綴語に基づくもの．

(2) は sun [sʌn]（太陽）と son [sʌn]（息子），hair [hɛər]（髪）と hare [hɛər]（野ウサギ）のように同音異綴語に基づくもの．

(3) は類似音に基づくもので，いくつかのタイプに下位区分できる．
   (i) *h*aste [heist]（急ぎ），*w*aste [weist]（無駄）のように語頭音転換に基づくもの．**Spoonerism**（→ p. 422）と呼ばれる．
   (ii) ca*ke* [keik]（ケーキ），Ka*te* [keit]（人名）; bliss [blis]（至福），blis*ter* [blistər]（火ぶくれ）のように語尾音転換［追加］に基づくもの．
   (iii) **異分析**（→ p. 375）に基づくもの．

などである．（詳しくは拙書『英語しゃれ辞典　Punctionary』（研究社）参照．）

第 2 章　疑　問　文

> *Drunk:* **Has** Mike **been** here?
> *Man:* Oh, yes, he was here about an hour ago.
> *Drunk:* **Was** I with him?
> (酔っ払いと男の対話:「マイクはここにいたか」「いたとも. 1 時間くらい前にここにいたぞ」「おれはあいつと一緒だったか」)

- **A.** 疑問詞のない疑問文 (1)
- **B.** 疑問詞のない疑問文 (2)：選択疑問文
- **C.** 付加疑問文
- **D.** 疑問詞のある疑問文

A. 疑問詞のない疑問文 (1)：Yes / No で答えることができるもの.

(a) 動詞が be 動詞, その他の助動詞を含む文の場合：主語と (助) 動詞の順序を逆にする.

> "**Is** this one of your abstract paintings?"
> "No, that's a mirror."
> (これはあなたの抽象画ですか」「いいえ, それは鏡です」)

☞ あなたが映っているのです.

> "**Were** there any great men born in this town?"
> "No, only little babies."
> (「この町でだれか偉い人が生まれましたか」「いいえ, 小さな赤ん坊だけです」)

☞ 生まれたときからの偉人はいません.

Fortune teller: I charge five dollars for two questions.
  Man: **Isn't** that expensive?
Fortune teller: I don't think so. Now what is your second question?
(占い師と男の対話:「質問 2 つに 5 ドルいただきます」「それ高くないですか」「そんなことはありません．では，2 つ目の質問をどうぞ」)
☞「それ高くないですか」が 1 つ目の質問．

Mary: I'm sorry—I quite forgot your party the other evening!"
 May: Oh, **weren't** you there?"
(「ごめんなさい．先日の夜のパーティーすっかり忘れてしまって」「あら，あなたいらっしゃらなかったの」)
☞ Mary はいないことに気づかれなかった薄い存在．

Fortune teller: You are going to marry a tall, dark man.
  The girl: **Can't** you be specific? All four of them are tall and dark.
(易者「あなたは背の高い浅黒い男性と結婚することになります」女性「もっとはっきりさせていただけませんか．4 人とも背が高くて浅黒い人なんです」)

(b) 一般動詞の文の場合:「Do [Does, Did] +主語+動詞の原形」の語順になる．

Frank: I went to the dentist yesterday.
Ernest: **Does** your tooth still ache?
Frank: I don't know. He kept it.
(「昨日歯医者へ行ったよ」「歯はまだ痛いのかい」「分からないよ．先生が持ってるんだ」)

"**Did** you take my advice and sleep with the window open to cure your cold?"
"Yes."
"**Did** you lose your cold?"
"No, I lost my watch and pocketbook."
(「言うことを聞いて，風邪を治すのに窓を開けたまま寝たかい」「うん」「で風邪は抜けたかい」「いいや．時計と財布を抜かれた」)

cf. Yes / No の使い分け：問いの文が肯定か否定かに関わりなく，答えの内容が肯定なら Yes で，否定なら No で答える．否定の疑問文の場合，日本語と逆の感じになるので注意が必要．

"I hear your husband tried to get a government job. What's he doing now?"
"Nothing."
"Oh, **didn't** he get the job?"
"**Yes**, he did."

(「ご主人，政府のお仕事に就こうとなさったそうね．今，何をなさってるの」「何もしてませんわ」「あら，お仕事に就かなかったの」「いいえ，就きましたわ」)

☞ ジョークの世界では公務員は働かないことになっている．

  Barber: **Haven't** I shaved you before, sir?
Customer: **No**, I got that scar in France.

(床屋「前にお客さんのひげをおそりしたことありませんか」客「ないよ，その切り傷はフランスでつけられたんだ」)

☞ お前さんのそり方もひどいが．

B. 疑問詞のない疑問文 (2)：選択疑問文

A or B? (A ですかそれとも B ですか) と尋ねる疑問文．or の前では上昇調，or の後ろでは下降調で発音する．

> "Is your baby a boy **or** a girl?"
> "Of course, what else could it be?"
> (「赤ちゃんは男の子，それとも女の子」「もちろん．他の何だと言うの」)

☞ A ↗ or B ↘ 「A ですかそれとも B ですか」⇔ A ↗ or B ↗ 「A とか B とかですか」

Do you have a headache **or** are you single?
(あなたは頭痛持ちですか，それとも独身ですか．)
☞ headache「頭痛」⇔「頭痛の種」 ★ **Pun** → p. 26

"Without you, everything is dark and dreary ... the clouds gather and the wind beats the rain ... then comes the warm sun ... you are like a rainbow."

"Is this a proposal **or** a weather report?"

(「きみなしでは,すべてが暗く陰うつだ.雲は群がり,風は雨を打つ.すると暖かな太陽が現れる.きみはまるで虹のようだ」「これ結婚の申し込みなの天気予報なの」)

C. 付加疑問文

会話で使われる形で,肯定文には否定の,否定文には肯定の疑問をつける.「～ですね」と念を押したり,同意を求めるときにしばしば用いられ,下降調で発音される.質問の気持ちが強い場合は上昇調で発音される.

> *Customer:* There's no turkey in this turkey pie!
> *Waiter:* So what—you don't get a dog in dog food, **do you**?
> (客とウエイターの対話:「この七面鳥パイには七面鳥が入っていないじゃないか」「だから何だとおっしゃるのですか.ドッグフードに犬は入っていませんよね」)

★ **Waiter** → p. 266

"He is a man of few words, **isn't he**?"
"Yes, so he was telling me all morning."
(「あの人無口な人でしょ」「ええ,彼ったら午前中ずっとそう言ってたわ」)
☞ こういう人を無口とは言わない.

> *She* (gushingly): Will you love me when I am old?
> *He:* Love you? I shall idolize you. I shall worship the ground under your little feet. I shall—um—er—you are not going to look like your mother, **are you**?

(彼女(感傷的に)「私がおばあさんになっても愛してくださるわね」「愛するだって.きみを心底あがめるよ.きみのかわいい足元の地面を崇拝するよ.そして,えーと,きみまさかお母さんに似てこないだろうね」)

★ **Mother-in-law** → p. 305

第2章　疑問文　　　　　　　　　　　　　　　　　　*31*

She: Now that we're engaged, dear, you'll give me a ring, **won't you**?
He: Yes dear, certainly. What's your number, darling?
(女「もう婚約したのだから，あなた，指輪をくださるでしょ」男「もちろんだよ，きみ．番号は何番だい」)
☞ ring:「指輪」⇔「電話」(どちらにも番号がある．)　　　★ **Pun** → p. 26

A car knocked a pedestrian down.
"What's the matter with you?" shouted the pedestrian. "Are you blind?"
"What do you mean—blind?" said the driver. "I hit you, **didn't I**?"
(車が歩行者をはねた．「どうしたんだ」と歩行者が叫んだ．「目が見えないのか」「どういう意味です，目が見えないとは」とドライバー．「あなたをはねたんですよね」)
☞ 目が見えていたからはねたんです．

"Say, you couldn't lend me $100, **could you**?"
"How did you guess?"
(「おい，100ドル貸してくれないだろうな」「よく分かったな」)

"Say, what's the idea of wearing my coat?"
"You wouldn't want your new suit to get wet, **would you**?"
(「おい，おれのコートを着るとはどういうことだ」「おまえだって新しいコートを濡らしたくはないだろう」)

cf. 次のように「肯定文＋肯定疑問」の例もある．
"My doctor says I can't play tennis."
"Oh, so he has played with you too, **has he**?"
(「医者は僕にテニスをしてはいけないと言うんだ」「じゃあ，彼も君とテニスをしたことがあるんだね」)
☞ 下手すぎて相手をしていられない．

D. 疑問詞のある疑問文：疑問詞で始まる疑問文．

Where have you been, **who**'ve you been with, **what** have you been doing and **why**?
（どこにいたんだ，誰といたんだ，何してたんだ，そしてなぜなんだ．）

　疑問詞が主語の場合を除いて，疑問詞以下の語順は「A. 疑問詞のない疑問文(1)」と同じ．

(1) what を含むもの

What do you send to a sick florist?
（病気の花屋に何を送るか．）
　☞ 病気の人にはふつう花を送るが．

"**What**'s the cause of Janet's unpopularity?"
"She won a popularity contest."
（「ジャネットが人気がないのはなぜだい」「人気投票で1位になったのさ」）

"I was born in South America."
"**What** part?"
"All of me, of course."
（「ぼくは南米で生まれたんだ」「どこだい」「もちろん，身体全部さ」）

"I dreamed last night that I proposed to the best girl in the world."
"And **what** did I answer?"
（「昨日の晩世界一すばらしい女の子にプロポーズする夢を見たんだ」「それでわたし何と答えたの」）
　☞ 自分が世界一すばらしい女の子だと思っている．

"**What** great event happened in 1809?"
"Abraham Lincoln was born, sir."
"Correct. And **what** great event happened in 1812?"

"Er... Abraham Lincoln had his third birthday?"

(「1809 年にどんな大きな出来事が起きましたか」「アブラハム・リンカーンが生まれました，先生」「その通り．では 1812 年にはどんな大きな事件が起こりましたか」「えーと，リンカーンが 3 歳の誕生日を迎えました」)

☞ 1812: 第 2 次米英戦争始まる．

(2) which を含むもの

> *Wife:* The two things I cook best are meatloaf and apple pie.
> *Husband:* **Which** is this?
>
> (夫婦の対話：「わたしの最も得意な料理はミートローフとアップルパイよ」「これはどっちだい」)

Friend: **Which** of your works of fiction do you consider the best?
Author: My last income tax return.

(友人「君のフィクションの作品の中でどれが最高傑作だと思う」作家「最近書いた所得税の申告書さ」)

☞ サラリーマンはごまかせないが．

"Jane, **which** month of the year has twenty-eight days?"
"All of them, sir!"

(「ジェーン，28 日あるのはどの月ですか」「全部です，先生」)

☞ 2 月だけではありません．

"I hear Susan is a twin."
"That's right."
"How do people know **which** is **which**?"
"Her brother has a mustache."

(「スーザンは双子だそうだね」「そうだよ」「どうやってどっちがどっちだと分かるんだい」「弟は口ひげをはやしているよ」)

☞ 双子は同性とは限らない．

(3) who / whose / whom を含むもの

"I entered a face-making contest."
"Oh, you did—**who** won the second prize?"
(「にらめっこ競争に出たよ」「ああそう，誰が2位だった」)

☞ 君の1位は間違いなし．

Teacher: George, go to the map and find North America.
George: Here it is!
Teacher: Correct. Now, class, **who** discovered America?
Class: George!
(先生「ジョージ，地図のところへ行って北アメリカを見つけなさい」ジョージ「ここにあります」先生「その通り．では，みなさん，アメリカを発見したのは誰ですか」生徒たち「ジョージで〜す」)

"**Who** called the master of ceremonies a monkey?"
"**Who** called that monkey a master of ceremonies?"
(「あの司会者を猿呼ばわりしたのはだれだ」「あの猿を司会者呼ばわりしたのはだれだ」)
☞ call A B（A を B と呼ぶ）⇔ call B A（B を A と呼ぶ）

"**Who** does everyone listen to, but no one ever believe?"
"The weatherman."
(「みんなが聞くのに信じる人はいないのはだあれ」「天気予報官」)

A funeral procession was winding its way down the main street of the town. A stranger asked the man next to him, "**Whose** funeral is it?" The man answered, "The guy in the first car."
(葬儀の列が町の目抜き通りを曲がりくねって進んでいた．見知らぬ男が隣の男に尋ねた．「誰の葬式だい」男は答えた．「先頭の車の奴のだよ」)
☞ 名前を尋ねているのに．

"What was her name before she married?"
"Before she married **whom**?"

(「結婚する前の彼女の名前は何だったの」「だれと結婚する前のことを言ってるの」)
☞ あの人何度も結婚しているのよ.

"Have you ever married before, madam? And if so, **to whom**?"
"What's this, a memory test?"
(「前に結婚なさったことがおありですか,奥様.もしおありなら,どなたとですか」「これってなあに,記憶力テストですの」)

(4) when を含むもの

> "**When** were you born?"
> "April 2nd."
> "A day too late."
> (「いつ生まれたの」「4月2日」「1日遅かった」)

☞ April 1st: April Fools' Day (エープリルフール,万愚節)

"**When** is a door not a door?"
"When it is ajar."
(「ドアがドアでないのはどんな時か」「半開きの時」)
☞ ajar (少し開いて) ⇔ a jar (びん)
★ 異分析 → p. 375; **Riddle** → p. 64

"I never told lies when I was a child."
"**When** did you begin, mother?"
(「子供のころ一度も嘘をつかなかったのよ」「いつ始めたの,お母さん」)

"Father, I want to get married."
"No, my boy, you are not wise enough."
"**When** will I be wise enough?"
"When you get rid of the idea that you want to get married."
(「お父さん,結婚したいと思います」「いや,まだお前は分別が足りない」「いつになったら分別がつくんですか」「結婚したいなんて考えを捨てた時だよ」)

(5) where を含むもの

"**Where** were you born?"
"In a hospital."
(「どこで生まれたの」「病院で」)

Passenger: Conductor, **where** am I?
Conductor: In a train, sir.
(乗客「車掌さん，ここはどこだい」車掌「電車の中です，お客さん」)

"**Where** do you complain about the complaint department?"
(苦情処理課についてはどこで苦情を言うのか．)

"Say, did you see the announcement of my death in the morning paper?"
"Yes, I did. **Where** are you calling from?"
(「朝刊で僕の死亡告知を見たか」「見たとも．どこから電話しているんだ」)
☞ 地獄から電話しているのか．

(6) why を含むもの

"I'm going home."
"**Why**?"
"I live there."
(「家へ帰るよ」「なぜだい」「そこに住んでるからさ」)

"**Why** do gorillas have big nostrils?"
"Because they have big fingers."
(「なぜゴリラの鼻の孔は大きいか」「指が大きいから」)

Kid: Mama, **why** hasn't papa any hair?
Mother: Because he thinks so much, dear.

Kid: **Why** have you so much, mama?
Mother: Because—go away and do your lessons.
(「ママ, なぜパパには髪の毛がないの」「とても頭を使うからよ」「ママはどうしてそんなにたくさんあるの」「なぜって...あっちへ行って勉強しなさい」)

If country air is so good, **why** don't they build cities in the country?
(もし田舎の空気がそんなにいいなら, なぜ田舎に都市を造らないのか.)
★ **Irish bull** → p. 39

cf. why を含む慣用表現：**Why don't you** *do*?/ **Why not** *do*?:「＿したらどうですか」

Fat Man on Bus (to schoolboy): **Why don't you** be a gentleman and give a lady your seat?
Schoolboy: **Why don't you** be a gentleman and give two ladies your seat?
(バスに乗っている太った男（男子生徒に）「紳士らしくご婦人に席を譲ったらどうだね」男子生徒「紳士らしく2人のご婦人に席をお譲りになってはどうですか」)
☞ あなたの席は2人分あります.

"Betting on horses is a funny old game," says a man to his friend. "You win one day and lose the next."
The friend replies, "So **why not** bet every other day?"
(「馬に賭けるのはおかしな古くからのゲームだね」と男が友だちに言った.「1日勝つと次の日には負けるんだよ」「じゃあ, 1日おきに賭ければいい」と友だち.)

(7) how を含むもの

Barber: **How** do you want your hair cut?
Man: In silence!
(床屋「髪はどのようにお刈りしましょうか」男「黙ってやってくれ」)

"**How many** prime ministers does it take to change a light bulb?"
"None. They'll only promise change."

(「電球を取り替えるのに首相が何人必要ですか」「1人もいりません．取り替えを約束するだけです」)
★ **Light-bulb joke** → p. 139

"**How long** can a man live without brains?"
"I don't know. **How old** are you?"
(「頭脳なしで人はどのくらい生きられますか」「分からないね．君は何歳だね」)
☞ 君は脳なしだけど．
★ **Insulting joke** → p. 97

"**How often** do these big jets crash?"
"Once, I imagine!"
(「この大きなジェット機はどのくらいの頻度で墜落するのですか」「1回だと思うよ」)

cf. How を含む慣用表現

(1) **How about ... [*do*ing]?**：「...は［＿しては］どうですか」
   Doctor: I have bad news. You have three minutes to live.
   Patient: Oh, my God! What am I going to do?
   Doctor: **How about** boiling an egg?
   (医師と患者の対話：「悪いお知らせです．あなたはあと3分しか生きられません」「何ということだ．何をすればいいんだ」「卵をゆでてはどうですか」)
   ☞ a three-minute egg ＝ a soft-boiled egg（半熟卵）

(2) **How come ＿?**：「(驚きを表して) どうして＿なのか」
   How come black cows eat green grass and give white milk?
   (どうして黒い牛が緑の草を食べて白いミルクを出すのだろうか．)

ジョークの常識②

★ **Irish bull:**「言った本人が気づいていない一見もっともらしいが滑稽な矛盾のある話」単に bull ともいう．

It was hereditary in his family to have no children.
（遺伝的に彼の家族には子供がいなかった．）

An Irish notice of reward for an escaped convict: Age unknown; but looks older than he is.
（脱走囚逮捕に対する報酬のアイルランドの掲示：年齢不明，ただし，実際より老けて見える．）

An Irish man's wife gave birth to twins. Her husband demanded to know who the other man was.
（アイルランドの男の妻が双子を産んだ．夫はもう一人の男は誰かを教えろと息巻いた．）

第3章　命令文・感嘆文

Teacher: Jim, what is the imperative of the verb "to go"?
　Jim: I don't know, sir.
Teacher: **Go**, Jim, **go**.
　Jim: Thank you very much, sir.
(「ジム,『行く』の命令形は何ですか」「分かりません,先生」「行きなさい,ジム,行きなさい」「ほんとうにありがとうございます,先生」)

☞ もう帰っていいんですね.

A. 命令文

(1) 普通の命令文
(2) 命令文 ～, and [or] ...
(3) let's / let us を用いるもの
(4) 否定命令文

"To get rich in the stock market, **buy** stock, and when it goes up, **sell** it."
"But what if it doesn't go up?"
"**Don't** buy it."
(「株の売買で金持ちになるには,株を買いなさい.そして株が上がったら売りなさい」「しかし,もし上がらなかったらどうします」「買ってはいけません」)

★ **Irish bull** → p. 39

(1) **普通の命令文**：命令や依頼を表す文.主語を省略し動詞の原形を使う.主語（You）を省略しないのは強調表現.

"How can I get to the General Hospital fast?"
"**Stand** in the middle of the street for a while."

(「総合病院へ速く行くにはどうしたらいいですか」「しばらく通りの真ん中に立っていなさい」)
☞ すぐ車にはねられて病院へ行けます．

To improve your memory, **lend** people money.
(記憶力を向上させるには人にお金を貸しなさい．)
☞ 借りた方は忘れても，貸した方は忘れない．

Be nice to your kids—they'll choose your nursing home.
(自分の子にはやさしくしておきなさい，老人ホームを見つけてくれます．)
☞ いずれにせよ直接面倒を見てはもらえない．

Helen: What kind of husband would you advise me to get?
Hazel: *You* **get** a single man and **let** the husbands alone.
(ヘレン「わたしはどんな夫を手に入れたらいいとお思いになるかしら」ヘイゼル「独身の男性にしておきなさい．世間の夫どもはそっとしておいてあげなさい」)

(2) 命令文 ~, and [or] ...:「~しなさい，そうすれば［さもないと］...」の意味を表す．

Be kind to your wife, **and** she may help you with the dishes.
(奥さんにはやさしくしなさい，そうすれば皿洗いを手伝ってくれるかもしれない．)
☞ 普段は夫の仕事．

Warden: We must set you to work. What can you do?
Forger: **Give** me a week's practice, **and** I will sign your checks for you.
(刑務所長「君に働いてもらわなくてはいけないんだが，君は何ができるかね」偽造犯人「1週間練習させてください，そうしたら代わりに小切手にサインしてあげますよ」)
☞ 他人の署名をまねるのは専門分野．

Always **go** to other people's funerals, **or** they won't go to yours.
(常に他人の葬式に行きなさい，さもないと君のには来てもらえない．)
★ Irish bull → p. 39

Support peace **or** I'll kill you.（平和を支持しろ，さもないと殺すぞ．）

cf. 次のように動詞の原形を用いない形もある．

"**One more word and** I go back to mother!" "Taxi!"
（「もう一言言ったら母のところへ帰るわよ」「タクシー！」）
☞ すぐ帰ってよ．

(3) let's / let us を用いるもの：「＿しましょう」と提案や勧誘を表す．

> *Gangster:* Come on! **Let's** figure up how much we made on this job.
> *Accomplice:* Hell, no! I'm tired. **Let's** wait and look in the morning papers.
> （ギャング「さあ早くしろ．今度の仕事でいくら稼いだか計算しようぜ」共犯者「とんでもねえ．俺は疲れたぜ．ちょっと待って明日の朝刊を見ようぜ」）

> *Woman* (to her neighbor): I have the most marvelous recipe for meatloaf—all I have to do is mention it to my husband and he says, "**Let's** eat out."
> （女性が隣人に「ミートローフの最高のレシピがあるわ―夫にミートローフのことを言いさえすればいいの，そうすると「外食しよう」って言うのよ」）
> ☞ この女性のミートローフはまずくて食べられない．食べるには外食しかない．

Let us be grateful to the mirror for revealing to us our appearance only.　(Samuel Butler)
（外見だけしか見せないことに対して鏡に感謝しよう．）
☞ Samuel Butler (1835–1902)：イギリスの小説家．
★ **One-liner** → p. 395

(4) 否定命令文：「＿するな」の意味を表す．don't, never を動詞の原形の前につける．

> Advice to people about to get married: **Don't**.
> （結婚しようとしている人々への忠告：やめておきなさい．）

> **Never** borrow money from an optimist. He always expects to get it back!
> (楽天家から決して金を借りるな．いつも金が戻って来ると思っている．)

☞ だから金を貸したことをいつまでも覚えている．

"I've lost my dog."
"Why don't you put an advertisement in the paper?"
"**Don't be** silly—he can't read."
(「犬がいなくなったんだ」「新聞広告を出せばいいじゃないか」「バカ言うなよ．家の犬は字が読めないんだ」)
☞ 新聞広告を読むのは犬ですか？　　★ **Irish bull** → p. 39

"That monkey looks like Aunt."
"**Don't** say such a thing!"
"**Never** mind! The monkey can't hear you."
(「あのサル伯母さんにそっくりだ」「そんなこと言っちゃだめよ」「気にするな．サルはこっちの言うことは聞こえないから」)
☞ 伯母さんに聞こえても問題はない？

Girls, **never** marry a politician. He'll promise you a lot of things you'll never get.
(女性たちよ，政治家と結婚してはいけません．政治家はあなた方の手に入らないものをたくさん約束するのです．)
★ **Politician** → p. 329

"Keep on fighting, boys," said the general, "**Never** say die. **Never** give up till your last shot is fired. When it is fired, then run. I'm a little lame so I'm starting now."
(「諸君，戦い続けるんだ」と将軍は言った．「決して弱音をはくな．最後の一発を発砲するまで決してあきらめるな．最後の一発を撃ったら，逃げろ．わしは足の具合がちと悪いので，もう行くことにする」)
☞ 正直と言えば正直，ひどいと言えばひどい将軍．

B. 感嘆文

Kill all exclamation points!!!（すべての感嘆符たちを殺せ.）

☞ exclamation point = exclamation mark (!)　殺すべき(!)を3つも付けている.

> 「なんと〜なのだろう」という驚き・喜び・悲しみなどの気持ちを表す文で，特に How と What で始まる文をいい，文尾にふつう感嘆符（exclamation mark）(!) をつける.

普通，次の語順になる：

```
How ＋形容詞／副詞＋主語＋動詞!

What ＋ { a(n)＋形容詞＋単数名詞  }  ＋主語＋動詞!
        { 形容詞＋複数名詞       }

cf.「主語＋動詞」のないものも多い.
```

What a wonderful life I've had! **How** I wish I had realized it sooner!
　　　　　　　　　　　　　　　　　　　　　　　　　　　　　　(Collete)
（なんとすばらしい人生だったことか．もっと早く分かっていたらよかったのに．）

☞ Collete (1873–1954)：フランスの作家．

(1) what を用いるもの

"**What** a strange-looking young man!"
"That happens to be my daughter."
"I'm sorry, I didn't know you were her father."
"I'm her mother!"
（「何て変な顔の若者なの」「あれはたまたまわたしの娘ですの」「ごめんなさい．あなたがお父様とは知りませんでした」「わたしあの子の母親ですわ」）

☞ このあと何と言えばよいか．

"**What** a hospital!"
"What do you mean?"
"Well, at three o'clock in the morning they wake you up to give you a sleeping pill!"
(「何という病院だ」「どういう意味ですか」「朝の3時に起こして睡眠薬をよこすんだ」)
☞ 熟睡しているのに.

Tourist: **What** beautiful scenery! Lived here all your life?
Farmer: Not yet.
(旅行者「なんとみごとな景色でしょう. ずっとここにお住まいですか」農夫「まだです」)
☞ all *one*'s life:「今までずっと」⇔「一生の間」

cf. 感嘆を表す節を導く that ＿:「＿とは！」
What a pity **that** the only way to heaven is in a hearse!
(Stanslaw J. Lec)
(天国へ行くのに霊柩車しかないとは何と残念なことか.)
☞ Stanslaw J. Lec (1909–1966): ポーランドの詩人.

(2) how を用いるもの

> *Gloria:* If you want a date with me, you'll have to wait a million years.
> *Jack:* But I'm the only boy left in town.
> *Gloria:* My, **how** time flies!
> (「あなたがわたしとデートしたいなら, 100万年待たなきゃだめよ」「しかし町で残っているのは僕だけだよ」「まあ, 年月ってなんて早く過ぎ去るんでしょ」)

Customer: Waiter, there's a dead fly in my soup.
Waiter: **How** sad! He was too young to die!
(客「君, スープにハエが入ってるぞ」 ウエイター「悲しいことです. 死ぬには若すぎました」)
★ **Waiter** → p. 266

Jane Gossip: Why did they separate?
Joan Gossip: Nobody knows.
Jane Gossip: Oh, **how** terrible!
(うわさ好きの 2 人の対話:「あの人たちなぜ別れたの」「だれも知らないのよ」「まあ,ひどいこと」)
☞ 誰もが知りたいのに.

How beautiful it is to do nothing and then to rest afterwards.
(Spanish proverb)
(何もしないでその後で休むのは何と素敵なことだろう.)［スペインの俚諺］

ジョークの常識③

★ **Boner:**「生徒・学生の知ったかぶりや,苦し紛れによる試験の答案の大間違い」((英))では howler という.答案に限らずトンチンカンな発言・記述をいうことも多い.

What is the capital of Portugal?
"P."
(「ポルトガルの首都は」「P です」)
☞ capital:「首都」⇔「頭文字」の取り違え.正解は Lisbon.

What is wrong with the sentence: "The ox and cow is in the pasture"?
"You should put the lady first."
(次の文はどこがおかしいか「雄牛と雌牛が牧場にいる」「女性を先にすべきです」)
☞ is は are とすべき.語順の誤りではない.

Name three states in which water may exist.
New York, New Jersey and Pennsylvania.
(「水が存在する3つの状態を言いなさい」「ニューヨーク,ニュージャージー,ペンシルベニアの各州」)
☞ states:「状態」⇔「州」の取り違え.正解は「water(水), ice(氷), steam(水蒸気)」.

第4章　5 文 型

"**Call** me a taxi!" said the fat man.
"Okay," said the doorman. "You're a taxi, but you **look** more like a truck to me."
(「タクシーを呼んでくれたまえ」と太った男．「承知しました．お客様はタクシーです．しかし私にはトラックにもっと似ているように思えますが」とドアマン．)

☞ Call me a taxi.:「私にタクシーを呼んでくれ」((S)VOO) ⇔「私をタクシーと呼んでくれ」((S)VOC)

英語の文（sentence）は「主語（subject）＋述語動詞（predicate verb）」を中心に成り立っている．述語動詞は単に「動詞」と呼ばれることが多い．この動詞の性質によって5つの文型（5文型）に分けることができる．英語のすべての文を5つの型に分けることには当然無理があるが，5文型が英文理解の有力な助けになることは間違いない．ここでは基本的なものだけを取り上げる．（→p.55「7文型について」）

	主部	述部				
	主語 S	動詞 V	（主格）補語 C	間接目的語 IO	（直接）目的語 DO	目的（格）補語 C
第1文型	The car	stopped.				
第2文型	I	am	a student.			
第3文型	We	study			English.	
第4文型	She	gave		me	a book.	
第5文型	I	found			the book	interesting.

cf. O を間接目的語＝IO，直接目的語＝DO と区別することもある．

A. 第 1 文型（S＋V）

"You shouldn't **eat** with your knife."
"But, Ma, my forks **leaks**."
(「ナイフで食べてはだめよ」「でも，ママ，わたしのフォーク漏るんだもん」)

「S は V する」，たとえば，The car stopped.（車は止まった．）のように S と V だけで成り立つ文．これは極めてまれで，ふつうは S, V それぞれに修飾語(句)が付く．

"So your doctor saved your life."
"Yes, I **called** and he didn't **come**."
(「それでお医者が君の命を救ったわけだ」「そうなんだ．電話したのに来なかった」)
☞ 藪医者が来なくて助かった．

A husband bragged, "I **talk**. She **listens**. She **talks**. I **listen**. We both **talk**. The neighbors **listen**."
(ある夫が大げさに自慢した「私が話す．妻が聴く．妻が話す．私が聴く．私たちが 2 人で話す．近所の人たちが耳を澄ます」と．)

The journey of a thousand pounds **begins** with a single burger.
(Chris O'Brien)
(1000 ポンド（約 450 キロ）への旅はたった 1 個のハンバーガーから始まる．)
☞ Chris O'Brien (1952-2009): オーストラリアの脳外科医．

◆ there is [are] ～ 構文は 5 文型の枠外であるが，ここで扱う．there は副詞で主語ではないが主語のように振る舞う．

There are three stages of sickness: (1) ill, (2) pill, (3) bill. And sometimes **there is** another: (4) will.
(病気には 3 段階ある：(1) 病気，(2) 薬，(3) 治療費，である．ときどきもう 1 段階ある：(4) 遺言．)

☞ **i**ll, **p**ill, **b**ill, **w**ill: 語頭音転換のしゃれ．　　★ **Pun** → p. 26

"Waiter, waiter, **there's** a fly in my salad."
"I'm sorry, sir, I didn't know you were a vegetarian."
(「君, サラダにハエが入っているぞ」「申し訳ありません. お客様がベジタリアンとは知りませんでした」)
☞ ハエも動物性たんぱく質.
★ Waiter → p. 266

"How many seconds **are there** in a year?"
"Twelve: second of January, second of February ..."
(「1年は何秒ですか」「12です. 1月2日, 2月2日...」)
☞ second:「秒」⇔「第2日」　★ Pun → p. 26

"What's the difference between a dead skunk and a dead banker on the road?"
"**There are** skid marks near the skunk."
(「道路上の死んだスカンクと死んだ銀行家の違いは何か」「スカンクの近くにはスリップの跡が残っている」)
☞ 銀行家の場合は運転者はブレーキを掛けないのでスリップの跡が残らない.
★ What's-the-difference joke → p. 153

B. 第2文型（S+V+C）

> Love **is** blind—and marriage **is** an eye opener.
> (恋は盲目であり, 結婚は目を開かせてくれるものである.)

「SはCである」,「SはCになる」, 例えば He is a student.（彼は学生です.）のように, 何らかの意味で S (He) ＝ C (student) の関係が成り立つ文型で, be 動詞が代表格. C に当たる語を**補語**（**Complement**）という. この種の（目的語を取らない）動詞を**自動詞**という.

"My husband **is** an angel."
"You**'re** lucky. Mine**'s** still alive!"

(「夫は天使だわ」「あなたは運がいいわ．わたしのはまだ生きてるの」)
☞ Mine ＝ My husband
☞ まだ天国へ行っていないの．

"Your wife **looks** stunning tonight. Her gown **is** a poem."

"What do you mean, a poem?" replied the struggling author. "That gown **is** two poems and a short story."
(「今夜の奥方は実に美しい．イブニングガウンは一編の詩ですなあ」「一編の詩とはどういうことですか」と苦しそうに作家は答えた．「あのガウンは2つの詩と短編小説1本分です」)
☞ 2つの詩と短編の原稿料［印税］でやっと買ってやったのです．

"Do smart men **make** good husbands?"

"Smart men don't **get** married."
(「利口な男性は良い夫になりますか」「利口な男性は結婚しません」)

"This **is** good soup."

"Yes, it **sounds** good."
(「これは美味しいスープですね」「はい，美味しそうに聞こえます」)
☞ slurp（音を立てて飲む［食べる］）はマナー違反．　　★ **Insulting joke** → p. 97

C. 第3文型（S＋V＋O）

> *Teacher:* Give me a sentence with an **object**.
> *Pupil:* You are very beautiful.
> *Teacher:* What is the **object** of that sentence?
> *Pupil:* A good mark.
> (先生と生徒の対話：「目的語のある文を言いなさい」「先生はとてもきれいです」「その文の目的語は何ですか」「いい成績です」)

☞ object:「目的語」⇔「目的」　　★ **Pun** → p. 26

> 「SがOをVする」の意味を表す英語で最も多く使われる文型．動作の対象になる語を目的語 (**Object**) といい，目的語を必要とする動詞を**他動詞**という．

My wife **has** a black belt in shopping.
(妻は買い物では黒帯です．)

☞ 売り出し現場は闘技場．

Optician: You **need** glasses.
Patient: I'm already **wearing** glasses.
Optician: Then I **need** glasses.
(検眼士と患者の対話：「眼鏡が必要ですね」「もう掛けてますよ」「では眼鏡が必要なのは私です」)

I never **stir** my coffee with my right hand. I **use** a spoon.
(わたしは決してコーヒーを右手でかき回さない．スプーンを使う．)

I would never **buy** an encyclopedia. My wife **knows** everything.
(決して百科事典を買わないだろう．妻は何でも知っているから．)

She **lost** the marriage but she **won** the divorce.
(彼女は結婚を失ったが離婚を勝ち取った．)
☞ 慰謝料を勝ち取った．

D. 第4文型 (S+V+IO+DO)

Computers are useless. They can only **give** you answers.

(Pablo Picasso)

(コンピューターは役立たずだ．答えしか教えてくれない．)

☞ Pablo Picasso (1881-1973): スペイン生まれの画家・彫刻家．

「S は〜（だれだれ）(IO) に...(DO) を V する」の意味を表す文型で，「だれだれに」に当たる語を**間接目的語**（**I**ndirect **O**bject），「...を」に当たる語を**直接目的語**（**D**irect **O**bject）という．

直接目的語と間接目的語の位置を入れ替えるときは間接目的語の前に前置詞 **to** または **for** をつける：

(1) **to** をつける動詞：give（与える），hand（手渡す），lend（貸す），pay（払う），send（送る），show（示す），teach（教える），write（書く），tell（話す）など．

(2) **for** をつける動詞：buy（買う），find（見つける），get（手に入れる），make（作る）など．

My uncle is rich. So rich he **bought** his dog a boy.
（伯父は金持ちだ．非常に金持ちなので自分の犬に少年を買ってやったほどだ．）

☞ (= ... he bought a boy **for** his dog.)

I was with my wife and she was reading a magazine and she **showed** me a photograph of a fur coat. She said: "I'd like that." So I cut it out and **gave** it **to** her.　(Tommy Cooper)
（妻と一緒にいて妻は雑誌を読んでいた，そして私に毛皮のコートの写真を見せた．妻は「それが欲しいわ」と言った．そこで私はそれを切り取って彼女に与えた．）
☞ that は photograph とも解釈できる．
☞ Tommy Cooper (1921-1984): イギリスのコメディアン・マジシャン．

Daughter: What happens to a car when it gets too old?
　Mother: Someone **sells** it **to** your father.
（娘「車が古くなりすぎたらどうなるの」母親「誰かがそれをお父さんに売るわ」）
☞ お父さんはガラクタしか買わないから．

"**Hand** me my fiddle. I wanna put it under my chin."
"Put the piano under your chin."
"Okay. **Hand** me the piano."
（「バイオリンを手渡してくれ．顎の下に入れたいんだ」「ピアノを入れろよ」「いいとも．

ピアノを手渡してくれ」)
☞ wanna ＝ want to

"Are you superstitious?"
"No."
"Then **lend** me thirteen dollars."
(「君は迷信深いか」「いいや」「じゃあ 13 ドル貸してくれ」)
☞ 13 は迷信では不吉な数字．

The little boy sitting next to the dignified old lady on the bus was sniffling his head off. Finally she turned to him and said, "Little boy, do you have a handkerchief?"
"Yes," came the quick reply, "but I don't **lend** it **to** strangers."
(男の子がバスで気品のある老婦人の隣に座ってしきりに鼻をすすっていた．とうとう彼女は少年の方を向いて言った．「坊や，ハンカチを持っているでしょう」「うん，持ってるよ」とすぐさま返事．「でも知らない人には貸さないよ」)

I **taught** my son the value of a dollar. This week he wants his allowance in yen!
(息子に 1 ドルの価値を教えた．今週息子は小遣いを円で欲しいと言う．)
☞ 円高で成り立つジョーク．

Wife: I **made** you a lovely meat pie for your dinner, but the dog ate it.
Husband: Never mind, I'll **buy** you another dog.
(妻「夕食においしいミートパイを作ってあげたのよ，それなのに犬が食べちゃったの」夫「気にしなくていいよ，犬ならもう一匹買ってあげるよ」)
☞ たぶん食中毒で死ぬだろうから．

E. 第 5 文型（S+V+O+C）

If an animal does something, we **call** it *instinct*. If we do the same thing for the same reason, we **call** it *intelligence*.　(Will Cuppy)

(動物が何かをすると，それを本能と呼ぶ．人間が同じことを同じ理由ですると，それを知能と呼ぶ．)

☞ Will Cuppy (1884–1949): アメリカのユーモア作家・文芸評論家．

「SはOをCにVする［と呼ぶ］」などの意味を表す文型で，何らかの意味でO＝Cの関係が成り立つ．Cの位置には主として形容詞，名詞がくる．

Money won't **make** you *happy*; it will just **keep** you very *comfortable* while you're unhappy.
(金は人を幸せにはしない．不幸なときにとても快適にしてくれるだけだ．)

"You can **call** it *influenza* if you like," said Mrs Machin. "There was no influenza in my young days. We **called** a cold *a cold*."
(「お好きならそれをインフルエンザとお呼びになっても結構よ」とメイチン夫人が言った．「若い頃にはインフルエンザなどありませんでしたわ．風邪は風邪と呼びましたわ」)

"What did the boy magnet say to the girl magnet?"
"I **find** you really *attractive*."
(「少年の磁石は少女の磁石に何と言ったか」「きみはほんとに人を引きつける」)

"His fan mail **keeps** ten secretaries *busy*."
"Answering it?"
"No, writing it."
(「彼のファンレターで10人の秘書たちはいつも忙しいんだ」「返事をするのにか」「いいや，書くのに」)
☞ 秘書に自分へのファンレターを書かせている．

The irony of modern medicine: Hospitals **make** you *better* and medical bills **make** you *sick*.
(現代医学の皮肉—病院は人の病気を治すのに治療費請求書は人を病気にする．)

All men **think** all men *mortal* but themselves.
（誰もが自分以外は死ぬ運命にあると思っている．）

cf.「**7 文型**」について：
多くの文は5文型で説明がつくが，5文型に次の**太字の2つの文型**を加えると，さらに無理なく説明がつく．

第1文型：S+V
第2文型：**S+V+A**
第3文型：S+V+C
第4文型：S+V+O
第5文型：**S+V+O+A**
第6文型：S+V+O+O
第7文型：S+V+O+C

A： Adjunct（付加詞）　場所・様態などを表す副詞語句で，文中で欠くことができない．以下の例の太字の部分を欠くと文として成り立たない．

⟨**S+V+A**⟩
"Whisky is slow poison."
"I'm **in no hurry**."
（「ウイスキーはゆっくり効いてくる毒です」「おれは急いでないよ」）

I go out on a lot of job interviews. My resume is **in its fourth printing**!
（仕事の面接には何度も出かける．履歴書は第4刷になっている．）

"My father is still **on strike**."
"How long has he been **on strike**?"
"Sixty-five years."
（「親父はまだストをしてるんだ」「どのくらいストをしているんだい」「65年さ」）

⟨S+V+O+A⟩

Young boy explaining why he wasn't putting money in his piggy bank: "It turns kids **into misers** and parents **into robbers**."
(幼い少年がなぜお金を（子豚の形の）貯金箱に入れていないかを説明して「そんなことをすると子供をけちん坊に，両親を強盗にしてしまうよ」)

You've got to compromise when you're married. My wife wanted a fur coat. I wanted an automobile. We compromised. I bought her a fur coat, and we keep it **in the garage**.
(結婚したら妥協しなければならない．妻は毛皮のコートを欲しがった．私は自動車が欲しかった．2人は妥協した．妻に毛皮のコートを買ってやり，それを車庫に入れてある．)

ジョークの常識④

★ **Goldwynism:** アメリカの映画製作者 Samuel Goldwyn (1879–1974) の残した言葉として知られている．矛盾がありおかしな表現だが，言いたいことは分かるところが笑いを誘う．boner（→p. 46）の一種．

Give me a couple of years, and I'll make that actress an overnight success.
(2, 3年くれればあの女優を一夜にして成功させてみせる．)

The scene is dull. Tell him to put more life into his dying.
(その場面はつまらん．あいつに死ぬことにもっと命を注げと言ってやれ．)

If people don't want to go to the picture, nobody can stop him.
(人々が映画に行きたがらないなら，誰も止められない．)
☞ なお，him は them の誤り．

第5章　完了形

> "I've just **come** from the beauty parlor."
> "Too bad they were closed."
> (「美容院からちょうど帰ってきたところですの」「閉まっていたとはお気の毒です」)

☞ その髪は美容院へ行って来たようには見えません．
★ Insulting joke → p. 97

A. 現在完了：have [has] ＋過去分詞

> 過去の動作や状態が，何らかの点で**現在とつながり**をもっていることを表す．以下 (1)〜(4) のように**意味上の区別**をする．
> (1) 現在までの動作の完了
> (2) 現在までの経験
> (3) 現在までの状態・動作の継続
> (4) 未来完了の代用

> **I've been** on a diet for two weeks and all **I've lost** is two weeks.
> (Totie Fields)
> (2週間ダイエットをしています，そして失ったのは2週間だけです．)

☞ 前者は (3) 現在までの継続，後者は (1) 現在までの動作の完了，を表す．
☞ Totie Fields (1930–1978)：アメリカのコメディアン．

(1) **現在までの動作の完了**：**already**（すでに），**just**（ちょうど），**now**（いま），**yet**（(疑問文・否定文で) まだ，もう）などを伴うことが多い．

"I'm sorry that I forgot to invite you to my picnic tomorrow. Won't you come?"
"No, you're too late. **I've** *already* **prayed** for a violent thunder storm tomorrow."

(「あなたを明日のピクニックに招待するのを忘れてしまってごめんなさい．いらっしゃらない」「だめよ．遅すぎたわ．わたし明日激しい雷雨になりますようにと祈ってしまったんですもの」)

Customer: The service here is awful.
  Waiter: How would you know? You **haven't had** any *yet*.
(客とウエイターの対話：「この店のサービスはひどい」「どうして分かるんですか．まだ何もサービスされていないじゃありませんか」)
☞ 料理が遅れるのはサービスが悪いのではない？

"What's the matter, son?"
"I've *just* **had** a fight with your wife!"
(「おまえ，どうしたんだ」「ちょうどお父さんの奥さんと取っ組み合いをしたところなんだ」)
☞ 僕のお母さんとは言えないよ．

(2) 現在までの経験：**ever**（いままでに），**never**（一度として...ない），**often**（しばしば），**once**（一度），**before**（以前）などを伴うことが多い．

"I'm a well-known collector of antiques."
"I know. **I've seen** your wife."
(「私は名の知れた骨董品の収集家です」「知っています．あなたの奥さまにお会いしたことがあります」)
☞ 大した古女房ですね．

"Doctor, I'm very nervous. This is the first time **I've** *ever* **needed** an operation."
"Don't worry, I feel the same. This is the first operation **I've** *ever* **performed**."
(「先生，私とても心配です．手術が必要になったのは初めてなんです」「心配には及びません．私も同じ気持ちです．これが初めての手術ですから」)

"I met a man just now I **haven't seen** in twenty years."
"That's nothing. I met a man just now **I've never seen** *before* in my

life."
(「たった今 20 年会っていなかった男の人と会ったわ」「そんなこと何でもないわ．今まで会ったこともなかった男の人とたった今会ったわよ」)

At the airport a child was admiring the stickers on a man's suitcase. He said to the man, "**Have** you really **been** to all those places?" The man said, "No, but my luggage has."
(空港で子供が男のスーツケースに貼ってあるステッカーを感心して眺めていた．その子は男に言った「ほんとにその場所全部に行ったことがあるの」男は言った「ないよ，でもスーツケースはあるんだよ」)
☞ スーツケースなどの誤送はよくあること．

"My son **has** *never* **been** to a psychiatrist?"
"Why? What's wrong with him?"
(「息子は精神科にかかったことは一度もありません」「なぜですの．どこか具合でも悪いのですか」)
☞ まともな人なら一度は精神科医のお世話になります．

(3) 現在までの状態・動作の継続：for 〜（〜の間），since 〜（〜以来）のような期間を表す語句を伴うことが多い．

> We**'ve been** married ten years and we**'ve had** only one quarrel. It started on our wedding day and **hasn't ended** yet!
> (結婚して 10 年になりますが，たった一度しか口げんかをしたことがしたことがありません．結婚の日に始まり，まだ終わっていません．)

She is one of my best friends. **I've known** her ever *since we were the same age*.
(彼女は親友の一人です．二人が同い年の頃からずっと知っています．)
☞ 今は彼女は年下になっています．

Dr Findlay was passing one of his patients in the street.
"Hello, Mrs Merton. You **have**n't **visited** me *for ages*."
"I know, doctor. **I've been** ill."

(フィンドレイ医師は通りで患者の一人とすれ違っていた.「こんにちわ,マートン夫人.長いことお見えになりませんね」「そうなんです,先生.わたくし病気だったんですの」)
☞ for ages「長い間」
☞ 病気をすると病院へ行けません.

"*How long* **have** you **been** married?"
"This time—or all together?"
(「結婚してどのくらいですか」「今度ですか,全部合わせてですか」)
☞ 何度か離婚を経験しています.

(4) 未来完了の代用:時・条件の副詞節では意味上の未来完了に相当する.

"Do you look in the mirror **after** you**'ve washed** your face?"
"No, I look in a towel!"
(「顔を洗ってしまったあと鏡を見るかい」「いいや,タオルを見るよ」)
☞ 汚れが落ちたかはタオルを見れば分かる.

Friend: And what is your son going to be **when** he**'s passed** his final exam?"
Father: An old man.
(「息子さんは最終試験に合格したら何になるんですか」「老人です」)

A smart woman always asks her husband's opinion **after** she **has made** up her mind.
(頭のいい女性は常に自分が決心してしまったあとで夫の意見を尋ねる.)
☞ 夫は反対できない.

B. 現在完了進行形:have [has] been *doing*

現在までの動作の継続を表す.

"Drinking makes you look beautiful, darling."
"But I **haven**'t **been drinking**."
"No, but I **have**."

（「きみ，お酒を飲むときれいだね」「でもわたし飲んでなんかいないわ」「そうさ，でも僕は飲んでるよ」）

☞ I have ＝ I have been drinking.
☞ だからきみがきれいに見える．

"Sir, I **have been going** out with your daughter for five years now ..."

"So what do you want―a pension?"

（「お嬢さんとはもう 5 年付き合っています」「だから何が欲しいんだね．年金かね」）

☞ お前なんかに娘をやれるか！

"I**'ve been singing** since I was two years old."

"No wonder you've lost your voice."

（「2 歳の時からずっと歌っています」「道理で声が出なくなったんですね」）

★ Insulting joke → p. 97

"He**'s been sitting** there all day, doing nothing but wasting his time."

"How do you know?"

"Because I**'ve been watching** him."

（「あいつはあそこに一日中座って何もしないで時間を無駄にしてるんだ」「どうして分かるんだい」「ずっとあいつを見ているからさ」）

C. 過去完了：had＋過去分詞

"What made you quarrel with Conrad?"

"Well, he proposed to me again last night."

"Where was the harm in that?"

"My dear, I **had accepted** him the night before."

（「コンラッドとなぜ口げんかしたの」「彼ったら昨日の晩またわたしにプロポーズしたの」「そのどこが悪いの」「あなた，わたし一昨日の晩に承知してたのよ」）

(1) 過去のある時から過去のある時までの完了・経験・継続を表す．

"Mom, mom! Dad's fallen over a cliff."
"Is he okay?"
"I don't know. He **hadn't stopped** falling when I left."
(「ママ，ママ，パパが崖から落ちちゃった」「お父さん大丈夫なの」「分かんない．ぼくが来るときまだ落ち終わっていなかったもん」)

Today three girls introduced themselves to me. **I had met** all of them before.
(今日3人の若い女性が私に自己紹介した．3人とも以前会ったことがあったのに．)
☞ 悲しいことに彼女らは私を覚えていなかった．

(2) 過去のある時より前に起こったことを表す．

"My uncle was finally put to rest last week."
"We didn't know he **had passed** away."
"He didn't, but my aunt did."
(「伯父はやっと先週安眠できたよ」「亡くなったとは知らなかった」「亡くなりはしないよ．亡くなったのは伯母だよ」)
☞ 口うるさいのがやっといなくなって．

Last Sunday that girl was standing in my uncle's corn field and the birds took her for a scarecrow. She frightened the crows so much they brought back the corn they **had stolen** three days before.
(この前の日曜あの娘が伯父のトウモロコシ畑に立っていると，鳥たちは彼女を案山子と間違えたんだ．彼女あんまり怖がらせたんでカラスは3日前に盗んだトウモロコシを返しに来たんだ．)
★ **Tall tale** → p. 412

D. 過去完了進行形：had been＋*do*ing

過去のある時から過去のある時までの動作の継続を表す．

(Motor Insurance Claim)
I had been driving for 40 years when I fell asleep at the wheel and

had an accident.
((自動車保険支払い請求書から) 40 年間運転してきて運転中に眠ってしまい事故が起きたのです.)

Doris **had been talking** on the phone for about half an hour before she hung up. Her father said, "Wow! That was short. You usually talk for an hour. What happened?"
Doris replied, "It was a wrong number."
(ドリスは約 30 分電話で話をしてから電話を切った. 父親が言った「うわあ, 短かったね. おまえはたいてい 1 時間話すのに, どうしたんだい」ドリスは答えた「間違い電話だったの」)

A theatergoer **had been waiting** for a year to get a ticket to a big Broadway hit, and finally the great day arrived. As he sat down in the theater he was surprised to see an empty seat between him and a little old man. When he commented on it to the old man, he was told that the seat had been reserved for his late wife.
"Couldn't a relative have used it?" asked the theatergoer.
"Oh, no," said the old man. "They're all at the funeral."
(ある芝居の常連がブロードウェイで大ヒットの出し物の切符を手に入れるのに 1 年待ってやっとその日がやってきた. 劇場で席につくと, 彼と小柄な老人の間に空席があるのに気づいて驚いた. 彼が老人にその空席について言うと, その席が老人の亡くなった奥さんのための予約席だったと教えられた.「親戚の方かだれかがお使いになれなかったのですか」と彼は尋ねた.「とんでもない」と老人は言った.「彼らはみんな葬式に出ています」)

E. 未来完了:will have+過去分詞

未来のある時までの動作の完了・経験を表す.

Remember that by fifty you **will have spent** over sixteen years in bed and three years eating.
(忘れてはいけないことは 50 歳までには 16 年以上ベッドで 3 年以上食べて過ごしてしまっているだろうということだ.)

By the age of 6, the average child **will have completed** the basic American education. From television, the child **will have learned** how to pick a lock, commit a fairly elaborate hold-up, prevent wetness all day long, get the laundry twice as white, and kill people with a variety of sophisticated armaments.
(6歳までに，普通の子供は基本的なアメリカの教育を完了してしまっていることになるだろう．テレビから，子供は錠を（鍵以外のもので）開ける方法，かなり手の込んだ強盗のやり方，一日中おもらししない方法，洗濯ものを2倍の白さにする方法，多様な洗練された兵器での殺人法を覚えてしまっているだろう．）
☞ 子供はすべてをテレビから学んでしまう．

F. 未来完了進行形：**will have been** *doing*（めったに用いられない．）

By the time they go to bed tonight, they **will** probably **have been arguing** for several hours. 　（マーク・ピーターセン）
(今夜床に就くまでには，2人はおそらく何時間も口げんかしていることになるだろう．)
☞ マーク・ピーターセン：日本近代文学研究家・明治大学教授．

ジョークの常識⑤

★ **Riddle**：「なぞなぞ」Conundrum ともいう．「普通は答えるのがほとんど不可能な，しばしば面白おかしい問いに対して機転をきかせて答えを推測する言葉遊び」答えを聞いて［見て］なるほどと思わせるものが大半を占める．

Why is the letter U the happiest in the alphabet?
(アルファベットの中でUが一番幸せなのはなぜか．)
—Because it is in the middle of fun.
(Uは fun（おもしろさ）の真ん中にあるから．)

What did the big chimney say to the little chimney?
(大きい煙突は小さい煙突に何と言ったか．)
—You are too young to smoke.（おまえはタバコを吸うには若すぎる．）
☞ smoke:「煙をはく」⇔「タバコを吸う」の駄じゃれ．

第6章　受動態

"Give the **passive** of "John shot my dog."
"My dog shot John."
(「『ジョンがぼくの犬を撃った.』の受動態を言いなさい」「僕の犬がジョンを撃った」)

☞　正解は "My dog was shot by John."

★ **Boner** → p. 46

「XがYを＿する」という主語が（目的語に対して）働きかける動詞の形を**能動態**（Active Voice），「Yが（Xに）＿される」という主語が働きかけられる動詞の形を**受動態**（Passive Voice）といい，ふつう**受け身**ともいう．次のような形がある．

A. be＋過去分詞
B. get＋過去分詞
C. have [get]＋O（物）＋過去分詞

時制・完了形・進行形に応じて次のような形になる．

時制	現　在	過　去	未　来
基本形	It *is written*	It *was written*	It *will be written*
完了形	I *has been written*	It *had been written*	It *will have been written*
進行形	It *is being written*	It *was being written*	It *will be being written*

Everything that can be invented has been invented.
(Charles Duell)

（発明可能なものはすべて発明されてしまっている.）

☞　Charles Duell (1850-1920)：アメリカ特許庁長官・連邦判事.

A. be＋過去分詞：「＿される；＿されている」

(1)「**S＋V＋O**」の受動態

> "What **is** always **broken** before it **is used**?"
> "An egg."
> (「使われる前に必ずこわされる物はなあに」「卵」)
>
> ★ **Riddle** → p. 64

I think the world **is run by** C students.　(Anon.)
(世の中は成績Ｃの学生の言いなりになっていると思う.)
☞ 政界・財界いずこも同じ（？）

The first half of your life **is dominated by** your parents; the second half **is dominated by** your children.
(人生の前半は両親に支配され, 後半は子供たちに支配される.)

"Where **was** the Declaration of Independence **signed**?"
"At the bottom."
(「独立宣言はどこで署名されましたか」「一番下です」)
☞ Where:「どこで」⇔「どこに」　　★ **Boner** → p. 46

A businessman can't win these days. If he does something wrong, he**'s fined**; if he does something right, he**'s taxed**.
(近ごろビジネスマンに勝ち目はない. 何か間違ったことをすると罰金を科せられ, 正しいことをすると税金を課せられる.)

(2)「**S＋V＋O＋O**」の受動態

At six I **was left** an orphan. What on earth is a six-year-old supposed to do with an orphan?
(6歳のとき孤児を残された. 6歳児は一体孤児をどうすべきだというのか.)
☞ I was left an orphan:「孤児を残された」⇔「孤児にされた」
　　Someone left me an orphan（誰かが私に孤児を残した）［S＋V＋O＋O の受動態］

⇔ My parents left me an orphan（両親は私を孤児の状態にして死んだ）[S+V+O+C の受動態]

(3)「S+V+O+C」の受動態

Why **is** it **called** a "building" when it **is** already **built**?
（すでに建てられているのになぜ「建（てている）物」と呼ばれるのか.）

A debut is the first time a young girl **is seen** drunk in public.
(F. Scott Fitzgerald)
（デビューとは若い女性が初めて人前で酔っているのを見られるとき.）
☞ 人前でなければとっくに飲んでいる.
☞ F. Scott Fitzgerald (1986–1940): アメリカの小説家.

(4) be surprised など

> 日本語では「驚く」,「怪我をする」などと言うが, 英語では surprise は「驚かす」, injure は「怪我をさせる」の意味であるから, be surprised, be injured のように受動態にする.

(a) 感情などを表す動詞: **be surprised / be astonished**（驚く）, **be delighted**（喜ぶ）, **be disappointed**（がっかりする）, **be excited**（興奮する）, **be satisfied**（満足する）など.

I **was** so **surprised by** my birth I was speechless for a year and a half.
（私は自分の誕生にあまりにも驚いたので, 1年半口がきけなかった.）

☞ 驚かなくても1年半くらいは口がきけないのが普通.

"My mother **was** terribly **disappointed** when I was born."
"Did she want a boy?"
"No, she wanted a divorce."
（「わたしが生まれたとき母はとてもがっかりしたの」「男の子がほしかったの」「ちがうわ. 離婚したかったのよ」）

"John, I wish you would go out in the kitchen and gave Bridget a good talking-to before you go to business."

"How's that? I thought you **were** very **satisfied with** her."

"So I am, dear, but she's beating some carpets for me this morning, and she does it better when she's angry."

(「ジョン，お願いだから台所へ行って，仕事に行く前に，ブリジットにたっぷり小言を言ってちょうだい」「またどうして．おまえはてっきり彼女に満足していると思ったよ」「もちろんよ，あなた．でもあの子に今朝絨毯をたたいてもらうことになってるの．そしてあの子は怒っているときの方が上手にたたくのよ」)

☞ So I am = Yes, I am

(b) 被害を表す動詞：**be injured [hurt]**（怪我をする），**be killed**（殺される，死ぬ）など．

Drive carefully. Children should **be** seen and not **hurt**.

(注意して運転せよ．子供は見られるべきで，怪我をさせられるべきではない．)

☞ hurt [hə:rt] ⇔ heard [hə:rd]
☞ Children should be seen and not heard. (子供は姿を見せても口をきいてはならない．)（ことわざ）のもじり．「子供は大人たちの前にいてもよいが，口を出してはならない」の意．　★ **Pun** → p. 26; **Parody** → p. 199

There used to be thirteen kids, but one **was killed**. Father was superstitious.

(以前は13人子供がいましたが，1人死にました．父は迷信家だったのです．)

☞ 「13」は迷信では不吉な数．　★ **Black humor** → p. 118

"My brother fell off a ten-story building."

"**Was** he **injured**?"

"No. He fell through a manhole into the subway and **was killed** by an underground train."

(「兄は10階建てのビルから落ちたんだ」「怪我したのか」「いいや．マンホールを突き抜けて地下道に落ちて地下鉄に殺されたんだ」)

★ **Tall tale** → p. 412

(5) 自動詞＋前置詞の受動態：「自動詞＋前置詞」を１つの他動詞と考えればよい．

A man **was run over** by a steamroller. He was in the hospital in rooms 38 to 44.
（男が地ならし用のスチームローラーに轢かれた．彼は病院の 38 号室から 44 号室にいた．）
☞ ぺちゃんこに引き伸ばされて．　　★ **Tall tale** → p. 412

Village idiot: man who used to **be laughed at**, but now elected.
（村のバカ者：昔は笑い者にされていたが今は選挙で選ばれている男．）

(6) It is said that ___「___と言われている」＝ People [They] say ___

It is said that swimming develops poise and grace, but have you seen how the duck walks?
（水泳をすると上品な姿勢や優雅さが身につくと言われているが，アヒルの歩き方を見たことがあるか．）

It's been said that a pretty face is a passport. But it's not, it's a visa, and it runs out fast.
（可愛い顔はパスポートだと言われている．しかし，そうではない．それはビザであって急速に期限切れになるのである．）

B. get＋過去分詞：「＿される」の意味で用いられる．

> I nearly **got killed** yesterday. I went to an antique shop and asked: "What's new?"
> （昨日は危うく殺されるところだった．骨董屋に行って「何か新しいものないか」と聞いたんだ．）

☞ What's new? ＝ How are you?

"Your uncle is always drunk. I'd think he'd **get run over** crossing the streets."
"He'll never **get run over**. He always carries the box marked DYNAMITE and no one ever hit him."

(「きみの叔父さんはいつも酔っぱらっている．通りを横断して車にひかれるぞ」「絶対ひかれないよ．いつも「ダイナマイト」と印のある箱をかかえているから，誰も彼をはねたことはないさ」)

Teacher: Let us learn from the example of the busy ant. He works all the time, night and day. Then what happens?
Edward: He **gets stepped** on.
(先生「忙しいアリの例から学びましょう．アリは昼も夜もいつも働いています．するとどうなるでしょう」エドワード「踏みつけられます」)

My brother-in-law wrote an unusual murder story. The victim **got killed** by a man from another story.　　(Robert Sylvester)
(義理の弟は異常な殺人の話を書いた．被害者は別の話から来た男に殺されたのだ．)
☞ Robert Sylvester (1967–): アメリカのシンガーソング・ライター，レコード制作者．

C．have [get]＋O（物）＋過去分詞：「O が＿＿される」cf. 一種の受動態構文と考えることができる．（→「第 15 章　分詞」p. 242）

First Kangaroo: Annabelle, where's the baby?
Second Kangaroo: My goodness. I've **had** my pocket **picked**.
(カンガルーの対話：「アナベル，赤ちゃんはどこにいるの」「あらまあ，ポケットの中すられちゃったわ」)

Kissing is dangerous. I once kissed a married woman and **got** my nose **flattened**.
(キスは危険だ．かつて既婚の女性にキスして鼻をぺちゃんこにされた．)

D．進行形の受動態：**be＋being＋過去分詞**

Barber: And how did you find the razor?
Customer: Didn't know I **was being shaved**.

Barber: Very glad, I'm sure, sir.
Customer: Thought I **was being sandpapered**.
(床屋と客の対話：「剃刀の当たり具合はどうですか」「ひげを剃ってもらっているとは知らなかったよ」「そう言ってもらうとほんとにうれしいです」「紙やすりでも当てられているのかと思った」)

Mrs Able: I went on a one-man bus for the first time today.
Mrs Cable: How was it?
Mrs Able: I spent the whole journey wondering who was driving the bus when the fare **was being collected** upstairs.
(2人の夫人の対話：「今日初めてワンマンバスに乗りましたの」「いかがでしたか」「乗っている間ずっと，2階で乗車賃が集められているとき誰が運転しているのかしらと思ってましたわ」)

A local politician **is being investigated** because he saved a quarter of a million in ten years. The investigating committee wants to know why it took him so long!
(ある地元の政治家が10年で25万ドル貯め込んだという理由で調査されている．調査委員会はなぜそんなに長くかかったのか知りたがっている．)
★ **Politician** → p. 329

"What's the matter with Briggs?"
"He **was getting shaved** by a lady barber when a mouse ran across the floor?"
(「ブリッグスは一体どうしたんだ」「女性の床屋さんにひげをそってもらっているとネズミが1匹床を駆け抜けたんだ」)

E. 完了形の受動態：have [has / had] been＋過去分詞

"**I've been asked** to get married lots of times."
"Who asked you?"
"Mother and Father."

（「何度も結婚してくれと頼まれているんだ」「誰に」「おふくろと親父にさ」）

"Poor old Perkins has completely lost his hearing. I'm afraid he'll lose his job."
"Nonsense! He**'s been transferred** to the Complaint Department."
（「かわいそうにパーキンスのやつ完全に耳が聞こえなくなってしまった．失業するんじゃないかな」「バカな．やつは苦情処理課へ配転になったよ」）
☞ どんなに苦情を言われても聞こえない．

Of course America **had** often **been discovered** before Columbus, but it **had** always **been hushed** up.
（もちろんアメリカはコロンブス以前にたびたび発見されていた．しかしそのことは常に内密にされていたのだった．）
☞ 助動詞を含む受動態については「第7章　助動詞」H 参照．

ジョークの常識⑥

★ **Elephant joke:**「象が登場する子供っぽいナンセンスなジョーク」日本人にとってはあまり面白くはないかもしれない．Tall tale (→ p. 413) の一種．

Q: Why is it dangerous to go into the jungle between two and four in the afternoon?
A: Because that's when elephants are jumping out of trees.
（「午後2時から4時の間にジャングルへ入って行くとなぜ危険か」「象たちが木から飛び降りている時だから」）

第7章　助動詞

"Where **can** happiness always be found?"
"In the dictionary."
(「幸福をいつも見つけられるのはどこか」「辞書の中」)

　助動詞には be, do, have の他に，動詞の表す内容についての文の主語の心的態度（意志・能力・義務・可能性など）を表すものがある．ここでは以下の助動詞を取り上げる．

　　A. would，　B. should，　C. can / could，　D. may，　E. might，　F. must，
　　G. have to / ought to / used to / dare

cf. **will / shall** については「第1章　未来（進行形）」pp. 18, 21 参照．

A. would

"I **would** go to the end of the world for you!"
"Yes, but **would** you stay there?"
(「きみのためなら世界の果てまで行くよ」「いいわ，でもずっとそこにいてくださらない」)

- **(1)** 依頼：**Would you** *do*?
- **(2)** **would like [love] to** *do*
- **(3)** 過去の習慣的動作
- **(4)** 過去の強い意志
- **(5)** 仮定法（→ 第23章　条件・仮定表現）
- **(6)** 慣用表現：**would rather [sooner] A (than B)**

(1) 依頼：**Would you** *do*?「＿してくださいませんか」

(*Man in street*)

"Excuse me, sir. **Would you** give me twenty pence for a cup of tea?"

"I don't know. Let me see the cup of tea first!"

（通りの男「すみません，旦那．紅茶一杯に 20 ペンスお恵みを」「どうかな．最初に紅茶を見せてくれ」）

☞ for:「〜のために」⇔「〜と交換に」　　★ **Pun** → p. 26

(2) would like to *do*：「＿したいのですが」（want to *do* よりていねい）

Lady in post office: **I'd like to** send a telegram to Washington, please.

　Post office clerk: You can't do that, madam—he's dead.

（郵便局での対話：「ワシントンに電報を打ちたいんですけど」「それはできません，奥さん．もう死んでます」）

☞ Washington: 地名 ⇔ 人名　　★ **Pun** → p. 26

"What **would** you **like to** be when you grow up, Tommy?"

"**I'd like to** be a teacher."

"Would you, indeed? And why **would** you **like to** be a teacher?"

"'Cause I wouldn't have to do any more learning—I'd know everything by then!"

（「大きくなったら何になりたいの，トミー」「先生になりたいです」「ほんとにそうなの．で，なぜ先生になりたいの」「もうこれ以上勉強する必要がないからです—それまでには何でも知っているでしょう」）

(3) 過去の習慣的動作：「＿したものだった」

I used to think that when people said that their legs had fallen asleep, it meant that their leg was resting. When mine fell asleep, I **would** try not to disturb it.

（人が脚が眠ってしまったと言うとき，それは脚が休んでいるという意味だと昔は思っていた．自分の脚が眠ってしまうと，起こさないようにしたものだった．）

☞ My legs have fallen asleep.（脚がしびれた．）

"Our town used to have a curfew law, but we repealed it."
"How come?"
"Every time that bell rang at nine o'clock, it**'d** wake everybody up."
(「昔，町には夜間外出禁止の法律がありましたが廃止しました」「どうしてですか」「9時に鐘が鳴るたびにみんなを起こしたからです」)
☞ 'd ＝ would

(4) 過去の強い意志：「(否定文で) どうしても__しようとしなかった」

I worked in a building that was so high the elevator boy **wouldn't** go up without a weather report.
(私が働いていたのはとても高いビルだったのでエレベーターボーイは天気予報を聞かないと上へ行こうとしなかった．)
★ **Tall tale** → p. 412

She joined the bowling team but quit. Her first ball knocked down four pins, but they **wouldn't** count it because they were in the next alley.
(彼女はボーリングのチームに入ったがやめた．最初投げたボールはピンを4本倒したが彼らはそれを数えようともしなかった．なぜならそのピンは隣のレーンにあったからだ．)

(5) 仮定法（→ 第23章　条件・仮定表現）

I never argue with my wife. I might win and then I **would** be in real trouble.
(妻とは言い争いを決してしない．ひょっとして勝ったりすると本当に困ったことになるからだ．)

(6) 慣用表現：**would rather [sooner] A (than B)**「(Bよりも) むしろAしたい」

The man who **would rather** play golf **than** eat should marry the woman who **would rather** play **than** cook.
(食べるよりむしろゴルフをしたいと思う男性は料理よりもむしろ遊びたいと思う女性と結婚すべきだ．)

"Are you taking the medicine regularly?"
"I tasted it and decided that **I'd rather** have the cough."
(「きちんと薬を飲んでいますか」「味をみて,これなら咳をしている方がましだと決めました」)

Wife: **Would** you **sooner** lose your life or your money?
Husband: My life, of course. I'll need money for my old age.
(夫婦の対話:「あなたは自分の命とお金とどちらを失くしたいの」「もちろん命のほうさ.金は老後に必要だもの」)
★ **Irish bull** → p. 39

The other day a suit salesman said to me, "Shall I measure your waist, or **would** you **rather not** know?"
(先日服のセールスマンが私に言った.「ウエストを測りましょうか,それとも知りたくないですか」)

B. should

Teacher: Now Dan, you **shouldn't** fight, you **should** learn to give and take.
　Dan: I did. I gave him a black eye and took his orange.
(先生と生徒の対話:「いいですか,ダン,取っ組み合いのケンカをしてはだめ.ギブアンドテイクを覚えなきゃいけませんよ」「そうしました.目のまわりを真っ黒にしてやって,あいつのオレンジを取りました」)

☞ black eye:「(殴られてできる) 目のまわりのあざ」

---

(1) 義務・当然
(2) 確実な推定・期待
(3) 驚き・遺憾
(4) **it is** ～ **that S should** *do*
(5) **should have**＋過去分詞

(1) 義務・当然:「＿するべきだ［したほうがよい］」

"Why do you eat in the cafeteria and not in the grill?"
"Oh, the doctor said I **should** take a long walk before meals."
(「なぜカフェテリアで食べてグリルで食べないんだい」「お医者が食事の前には充分歩けと言ったからさ」)
☞ 長い列に並んで歩くことになる．

A smile is a wrinkle that **shouldn't** be removed.
(ほほ笑みは取り除いてはならない皺である．)
★ **One-liner** → p. 395

Mother to son: "Come on, you'll be late for school." "Shan't," came the reply from the bedroom. "Why, what's wrong?" "The teachers hate me and the kids despise me." "I'll give you two good reasons why you **should** go. One—you're forty-one, and two—you're the headmaster."
(母が息子に向かって，「さあさあ，早くしないと学校に遅れますよ」「遅れるもんか」と寝室から返事．「まあ，どうしたっていうの」「先生たちは僕を嫌っているし，子供たちは僕を軽蔑しているんだ」「学校へ行かねばならない2つの理由があるのよ．第1，あなたはもう41よ，そして第2，あなたは校長先生なのよ」)
☞ shan't＝shall not
★ **Jewish mother** → p. 312

Why **should** we do anything for posterity? What has posterity ever done for us? (Joseph Addison)
(なぜ我々は後世の連中のために何かすべきなのか．後世は我々に何かしてくれたか．)
★ **Irish bull** → p. 39
☞ Joseph Addison (1672-1719): イギリスのエッセイスト・評論家．

(2) 確実な推定・期待:「きっと＿だろう」

Boy: I think I **should** be a really tricky player next season, Dad.
Dad: Why's that?
Boy: Our coach says that by next season I **should have grown**

another foot.

(息子と父の対話:「来シーズンにはぼくはほんとにやっかいな選手になるはずだよ」「それはなぜだい」「コーチが来シーズンまでにもう一本足が生えているだろうと言うんだ」)
☞ foot:「足」⇔「(長さの単位の) フィート」　　★ **Pun** → p. 26

"Is my dinner hot?" asked the excessively late husband.
"It **should** be," said his furious wife. "It's been on the fire since seven o'clock!"

(「僕の夕食はまだ熱いかい」と極端に遅く帰宅した夫が尋ねた.「そのはずよ」と妻が怒って言った.「7 時から火にかかってるわよ」)

(3) 驚き・遺憾:「(疑問詞とともに用いて) どうして＿するのだろうか」

Rethel: Dearest, will you still love me when my hair has all gone grey?

Richard: Of course, dear. If I loved you when your hair was blonde then brunette then black and red—why **should** grey make any difference?

(夫婦の対話:「あなた, 髪が真っ白になってしまってもまだ私を愛してくださる」「もちろんだよ, おまえの髪がブロンド, ブルーネットそれから黒, 赤と変わってもお前を愛していたのなら, 白髪にどんな違いがあると言うんだい」)

"Why are you so sad, Bill?"
"My wife said she wouldn't talk to me for 30 days."
"Why **should** that make you sad?"
"Today is her last day!"

(「なぜそんなに悲しいんだ, ビル」「家内が 30 日間僕に話し掛けないと言ったんだ」「いったいなぜそんなことで悲しいんだ」「今日がその最後の日なんだ」)

(4) **it is ～ that S should** *do*:「S が＿するのは～だ」
Bachelors should be heavily taxed. **It is** not fair **that** some men **should** be happier than others.

(独身者は重税を課されるべきだ. 男によって幸福に違いがあるのは公平とは言えない.)

It isn't enough for you to love money—**it's** also necessary **that** money **should** love you.　(Baron Rothchild)
（金を愛するのでは十分ではない．金が君を愛することも必要だ．）
☞ Baron Rothchild (1840–1915): イギリスの銀行家・政治家．

(5) should have＋過去分詞：「＿すべきだったのに」

> *Customer:* My juice is warm. I want it cold.
>   *Waiter:* If you wanted something cold, sir, you **should have ordered** soup.
> （客とウエイターの対話：「私のジュースはぬるい．冷たいのがほしい」「お客様が冷たいものをお望みでしたら，スープを注文なさればよかったのです」）

★ **Waiter** → p. 266

She: I had to marry you to find out how stupid you are.
He: You **should have known** that the moment I asked you.
（「あなたがどんなにバカかを知るために結婚したようなものだわ」「僕が申し込んだ瞬間にそんなことは気づくべきだったね」）

Daughter: Oops! Mom, I just dropped the baby's blanket out the window!
Mother: You **shouldn't have done** that. He'll catch cold.
Daughter: No, he won't. He was in it.
（「まあ困った．お母さん，赤ちゃんの毛布を窓の外へ落としちゃった」「なんてことしてくれるの．赤ちゃんが風邪をひくじゃありませんか」「大丈夫よ．赤ちゃんは毛布の中だから」）

He **should have been warned** when he saw her previous husband in the coffin. The corpse looked relieved!
（彼が棺の中の彼女の前の夫を見るとき前もって注意を受けておくべきだった．死体はほっとしているようだった．）

C. can / could

"My daughter **can** do anything with the piano."
"**Could** she lock it up and drop the key in the river?"
(「宅の娘はピアノで何でもできますのよ」「ピアノにカギをかけてカギは川に落としていただけませんこと」)

- (1) 能力・可能
- (2) 可能性
- (3) 許可
- (4) **cannot have** ＋過去分詞
- (5) **cannot [can never]** *do* **too** 〜
- (6) **cannot help but** *do*（＝**cannot help** *doing* →「第 16 章　動名詞」C (6)）

(1) 能力・可能：「＿することができる」

(In a library)
"Please be quiet. The other people **can't** read."
"Oh, what a pity. I **could** read when I was six."
((図書館で)「どうぞ静かにしてください．他の人が読めません」「おお，それはお気の毒．おれは6つのとき読めたぜ」)

You **can't** win. His first wife **could** cook but wouldn't. His second wife **can't** cook but she does.
(どうしようもないよ．彼の最初の奥さんは料理ができるのにやろうとしなかった．2度目の奥さんは料理ができないのにやるんだ．)
☞ You can't win:「勝ち目はない」

"I see strength, courage, kindness and despair in your face."
"But how **can** you see all that in my face."
"**I can** read between the lines."
(「あなたの顔に力と勇気と親切さと絶望が見えます」「しかしどうやって私の顔の中に

そんなものが全部見えるのですか」「私は行間が読めるのです」)
☞ line:「(文章の) 行」⇔「(顔の) しわ」　　★ **Pun** → p. 26

Teacher: When I was your age I **could** answer any question in arithmetic.
Tommy: Yes, miss, but you had a different teacher.
(先生と生徒の対話:「あなたの年頃には算数のどんな問題でも答えられたわ」「はい,先生,でも先生が違います」)

"When I was a child I used to bite my fingernails; and the doctor told me if I didn't quit it I'd grow up to be an idiot."
"And you **couldn't** stop?"
(「子供のころ指の爪を咬んでいて,お医者はやめないと大きくなったらバカになるよと言ったんだ」「じゃあ,やめられなかったんだな」)
★ **Insulting joke** → p. 97

Patient: The appendix is a useless part of us. We **could** do well without it.
Doctor: You **could**—but we doctors **couldn't**.
(患者「盲腸は何の役にも立ちません。なくても何も困らないですよ」医師「患者さんは困らないでしょう。我々医者は困るのです」)
☞ You could = You could do well without it (それがなくてもうまくいく)
☞ 収入が断たれます.

cf. 未来・完了を表すときは **will be able to** *do* / **have [has] been able to** *do* の形になる.

A music student asked her teacher, "Do you think **I'll be able to** use my voice?"
The teacher said, "Only in case of fire!"
(音楽の学生が先生に尋ねて「私の声使い物になるでしょうか」先生は言った「火事の場合だけはね」)

Husband: In our six years of marriage we **haven't been able to** agree on anything.

Wife: It's been seven years, dear.

(夫婦の対話:「結婚して6年どんなことにも意見が一致できなかったね」「7年よ,あなた」)

(2) 可能性:「(否定文で「__するはずがない」;(疑問文で) 一体__だろうか」

"That **can't** be my ball, caddie. It looks far too old," said the player looking at a ball deep in the trees.
"It's a long time since we started, sir."

(「あれは私のボールのはずはないよ,キャディー君.どう見ても古すぎるよ」とプレーヤーは木立の中に深く入り込んだボールを見ながら言った.「私たちがスタートしてからずいぶん時間が経ちました,お客さん」)

Teacher: Well, at least there's one thing I can say about your son.
Father: What's that?
Teacher: With grades like these, he **couldn't** be cheating.

(先生と父親の対話:「あなたのご子息について言えることが少なくとも1つあります」「何ですか」「こんな成績ですとカンニングをしているはずはありません」)

Conductor: You will have to pay fare for that child, lady. He's over twelve.
Passenger: How **can** he be over twelve when I've only been married ten years?
Conductor: Lady, I just collect fares—not confessions.

(車掌と乗客の対話:「奥さん,その子の料金を払ってもらいます.12歳以上ですね」「結婚して10年しか経っていないのに,どうしてこの子が12歳以上などということがあると言うの」「奥さん,私は乗車賃を集めているだけで,懺悔を集めているのではありません」)

(3) 許可:「＿してもよい」

> *Professor:* You **can't** sleep in my class.
> *Student:* I could if you didn't talk so loud.
> (教授「君，授業中眠ってはいかんよ」学生「先生がそんな大声で話さなければ眠れます」）

☞ can't *do*:「＿してはいけない」⇔「＿できない」　★ **Pun** → p. 26

> *Monty:* My wife is mad at me again.
> *Bartender:* Why is that?
> *Monty:* When I opened the front door this morning, her mother was on the step with her suitcases. She said, "**Can** I stay here for a few days?" I said, "No problem," and shut the door.
> （男とバーテンの対話：「家内がまた私に腹を立てているんだ」「なぜですか」「今朝玄関のドアを開けると，家内の母親がスーツケースを持って階段のところにいたんだ．「2,3日ここにいていいかしら」と言うから，「いいですよ」と言ってドアを閉めたんだ」）
>
> ★ **Mother-in-law** → p. 305

"**Could** I have a day off, sir, to help my wife with the spring cleaning?"
"No, I'm afraid not—"
"Thank you, sir. I knew I **could** rely on you."
（「1日休暇をいただけませんか，家内が春の掃除をするのを手伝うんで」「残念だがだめだな」「ありがとうございます．あなたが頼りになることは知っていました」）
☞ お陰で掃除の手伝いをしなくてすみます．

(4) cannot have＋過去分詞:「＿だった［した］はずがない」

> *Customer:* Waiter! How long have you been working here?
> *Waiter:* Six months, sir.
> *Customer:* Well, it **can't have been** you who took my order.
> （客とウエイターの対話：「君，ここでどのくらい働いているんだい」「6か月です，お

客様」「じゃあ，私の注文を取ったのは君だったはずはないな」)
☞ 注文したのはもっと前だった．

He **can't have taken** my umbrella by mistake. He is an umbrella collector.
(僕の傘を間違えて持っていったはずはないよ．あいつは傘を集めている奴なんだ．)
☞ 集めた傘を売って生計を立てている．

(5) **cannot [can never]** *do* **too** 〜：「いくら〜しても＿しすぎることはない」

> You **can never** know **too** many jokes.　(Geoff Tibballs)
> (ジョークはいくら知っていても多すぎることはない．)

☞ Geoff Tibballs (1945-)：アメリカのユーモア作家．

As usual, the woman was the last to arrive and quite tardy at that. "I beg your pardon for coming so late," she told the host.
"My dear," said the gentleman. "No pardons are needed. You **can never** come **too** late."
(いつものように，その女性は最後にしかも非常に遅れてやってきた．「遅れてしまってごめんなさい」と彼女は主人に言った．「いえいえ」と主人は言った．「お謝りになる必要はありません．あなたはいくら遅れて来られても遅れすぎることはありません」)
☞ at that:「しかも，おまけに」

You **can't** learn **too** soon that the most useful thing about a principle is that it can always be sacrificed to expediency.　(Somerset Maugham)
(どんなに早く学んでも早すぎないことは原理原則についてもっとも役に立つのは原理原則は常にご都合主義の犠牲になるということだ．)
☞ Somerset Maugham (1874-1965)：イギリスの小説家・劇作家．
★ **One-liner** → p. 395

You **cannot under**estimate the intelligence of the American people.
　　　　　　　　　　　　　　　　　　　　　　　　　(H. L. Mencken)
(アメリカ人の知性をいくら低く評価してもしすぎることはない．)
☞ **cannot** *under*estimate＝**cannot** estimate **too** low

☞ H. L. Mencken (1880–1956): アメリカの批評家・ジャーナリスト．

(6) cannot help but *do*:「__せざるをえない」

Paul: I live on garlic alone.

Saul: I'm not surprised. Anyone who lives on garlic **can't help but** live alone.

(「ニンニクだけで生活しているよ」「別に驚かないね．ニンニクを常に食べていれば誰だって一人で生きざるをえないさ」)

☞ alone:「ひとりで」⇔「ただ〜だけで」 ★ **Pun** → p. 26
☞ 臭くてだれも近づかない．
(☞ cannot help *doing* →「第 16 章　動名詞」C (6))

D. may

"**May** I sit on your right hand at dinner?"
"I **may** need it to eat with, but you **may** hold it awhile."
(「ディナーではあなたの右手に座ってもよろしいかしら」「食べるのに必要かもしれませんが少しの間なら押さえていても結構です」)

☞ on your right hand:「右側に」⇔「右手の上に」

---
(1) 許可
(2) 可能性
(3) 祈願
(4) may have＋過去分詞
(5) may well *do*
(6) may as well *do*

---

(1) 許可:「__してもよい」

"**May** I go swimming, Mommy?"
"No, you **may not**. There are sharks here."
"But Daddy's swimming."

"He's insured."
(「泳ぎに行っていい,お母さん」「いけません.ここにはサメがいるのよ」「でも,お父さんは泳いでるよ」「お父さんには保険が掛かってるの」)

Wife: I dreamed you gave me $100 for summer clothes last night. You wouldn't spoil that dream, would you, Dear?
Husband: Of course not, Darling. You **may** keep the $100.
(夫婦の対話:「昨夜あなたが夏服のために私に 100 ドルくれた夢を見たわ.夢を台無しになんかしないわよね,あなた」「もちろんさ,おまえ.その 100 ドル取っといていいよ」)

"Mom, now that I'm fifteen, can I wear lipstick and mascara and perfume and pluck my eyebrows and get my hair waved?"
"No, James, you **may not**."
(「お母さん,15 になったから,口紅,マスカラ,香水をつけて,眉毛を抜いて,パーマをかけていいでしょう」「だめよ,ジェームズ,いけません」)
☞ James は男性名.

(2) 可能性:「__するかもしれない」

A sign on a florist truck:
Drive carefully—The next delivery **may** be yours.
(花屋のトラックに:「運転注意—次の配送はあなたのものかもしれません」)
☞ 花は葬儀につきもの.

Always laugh heartily about your boss's jokes. He **may** be giving you a loyalty test.
(ボスの冗談についてはいつも心から笑え.彼は忠実度テストをしているかもしれない.)

A woman **may** put on a golf suit and not play golf—she **may** put on a bathing suit and never go near the water—but when she puts on a wedding gown, she means business.
(女性はゴルフ服を着てゴルフをしないかもしれない.水着を着て水に近寄らないかもし

れない．しかし結婚衣裳を着たら，本気である．）
☞ mean business:「本気である」

cf.「may + must」は不可であるから「may have to」を用いる：
It's a privilege to be able to pay taxes. If they keep going up, I **may have to** give up the privilege!
（税金を払えることは特権である．税金が上がり続けるとこの特権を放棄しなければならないかもしれないのだ．）

(3) 祈願：「__しますように」

May your troubles in the New Year be as short-lived as your resolutions.
（あなたの新年の悩み事が新年の決意のようにはかないものでありますように．）
☞ New Year('s) resolutions:「年頭の決意」

To the newlyweds: **May** we all be invited to your Golden Wedding Anniversary.
（新婚夫婦に：私たちがみなあなたたちの金婚式に招かれますように．）

(4) may have＋過去分詞：「__したかもしれない」

> *John:* Miss, I eaten seven sausages for dinner.
> *Teacher:* Ate, John, ate.
> *John:* It **may have been** eight, Miss. I know I eaten an awful lot.
> （「夕食にソーセージ7本食ったよ，先生」「食ったじゃなくて食べたでしょ，ジョン」「8本だったかもしれないよ，先生．とにかくたくさん食ったんだ」）

☞ ate [eit] ⇔ eight [eit]　★ **Pun** → p. 26

Benjamin Franklin **may have discovered** electricity—but it was the man who invented the meter who made the money.
（ベンジャミン・フランクリンは電気を発見したかもしれない．しかし，金儲けをしたのは電気のメーターを発明した男だった．）
☞ Benjamin Franklin (1706–1790): アメリカの政治家・科学者・著述家．

"Isn't this a good chicken?"

"It **may have been** good morally, but physically it's a wreck."

(「これは良い鶏ではありませんか」「道徳的には善良だったかもしれませんが, 肉体的には衰弱しています」)

(5) may well *do*:「〜するのはもっともだ」;「たぶん〜だろう」

She **may** very **well** pass for 43 in the dusk with the light behind her.

(W. S. Gilbert)

(彼女が薄暗がりの中で明りを背にして 43 歳で通るのはまったく当然だ.)

☞ W. S. Gilbert (1836-1911): イギリスの劇作家・オペラ台本作家・詩人.

Banking **may well** be a career from which no man really recover.

(J. K. Galbraith)

(銀行業はおそらく誰もそこから本当には正常な状態に戻れない職業であろう.)

☞ J. K. Galbraith (1908-2006): アメリカの経済学者.

(6) may as well *do*:「＿しても悪くない」

An old lady stepped up to the ticket window in the railway station and asked, "How much is a ticket to Cleveland?"

"That's ten dollars and seventy-nine cents," replied the agent.

The old lady turned to the little girl beside her and said, "I guess we **may as well** buy our tickets here. I've asked at all these windows, and they are the same price everywhere."

(老婦人が駅の切符の窓口へ歩いて行って尋ねた.「クリーブランドまでの切符はおいくら」「10 ドル 79 セントです」と係の者が答えた. 老婦人は側にいる小さな女の子の方を向いて言った.「切符はここで買ってもいいと思うわ. ここの窓口全部で聞いたけどどでも同じ値段だから」)

★ **Irish bull** → p. 39

E. might

"I'm glad I'm not a bird. I **might** get hurt."
"Why?"

"I can't fly."
(「鳥でなくてよかったよ. ひょっとすると怪我をするかもしれないから」「なぜだい」「ぼくは飛べないんだ」)

★ **Irish bull** → p. 39

- **(1)** 許可
- **(2)** 推量・可能性
- **(3)** 非難・遺憾
- **(4)** might as well *do*
---

(1) 許可:「__してもよい」(may よりていねい)

 "I expect to be able to see the sea."
 "You *can* see the sea. It's over there between the land and the sky."
 "I'd need a telescope to see that."
 "Well, **might** I suggest you move to a hotel closer to the sea? [under his breath] Or preferably in it."
(「海を見ることができると期待しているんだ」「確かに海を見ることはできます. あそこの陸と空の間です」「見るには望遠鏡がいるだろうね」「海にもっと近いホテルにお移りになってはいかがでしょうか. [声をひそめて] あるいはむしろ海の中へ」)

(2) 推量・可能性:「__かもしれない」

 "Listen, I need fifty dollars."
 "Fifty dollars?"
 "Yeah, and I have no idea where I can get it."
 "That's a relief! I was afraid you **might** have an idea you could borrow it from me."
(「ちょっと, 50ドル要るんだけど」「50ドル」「そうなんだ. でもどこで手に入れられるか分からないんだ」「それを聞いてほっとしたよ. 僕から借りられると思ったのかと心配したよ」)

The waitress stared at the actor. Finally she asked, "Have I ever seen you before?"

The actor said, "You **might have seen** me in the movies."
The waitress said, "It's possible. Where do you like to sit?"
（ウエイトレスは俳優をじろじろ見た．最後に彼女は尋ねた．「以前あなたに会ったことがあるかしら」俳優は「ひょっとすると映画で私を見たかもしれません」と言った．ウエイトレスは言った「ありえますわ．どこに座るのがお好きなの」）

☞ movies：「映画」⇔「映画館」　　★ **Pun** → p. 26

(3) 非難・遺憾：「＿してもよさそうなものだ」

Forest warden: Miss, I'm going to have to arrest you for swimming in the lake.
Young lady: Well! You **might have told** me before I changed into my swimsuit.
Forest warden: There's no law against *that*, miss.

（森林監視員と若い女性の対話：「お嬢さん，湖で泳ぐとあなたを逮捕しなければならなくなりますよ」「まあ，水着に着替える前に言ってくだされればよかったのに」「それを禁止する法律はないんです，お嬢さん」）

(4) might as well *do*：「＿しても悪くない」（may as well *do* より控えめな表現）

One woman advised other women, "There's so little difference between husbands, you **might as well** keep the first."
（ある女性が他の女性たちに忠告して言った．「旦那なんて大した違いはないから最初のを取っておくほうがいいわよ」）

We're fools whether we dance or not, so we **might as well** dance.
(Japanese proverb)
（踊るあほうに見るあほう，同じあほなら踊らにゃ損損．）（日本の俚諺）

F. must

Mother: Now, Donnie, you **must not** be selfish. You **must** let your little brother have the sled half the time."
Donnie: But mother, I do. I have it going down the hill and he has it coming up.

(「ドニー，お前わがままはいけませんよ．弟にも半分はソリを使わせてあげなくてはいけないよ」「でも母さん，そうしているよ．下りはぼくが使って，上りは弟に使わせてやっているもん」）

---
(1) 義務・命令
(2) 推量
(3) must have＋過去分詞

---

(1) **義務・命令**：「__しなければならない」; **must not** *do*「～してはならない」
  Q: What's the difference between a mental institution and a college?
  A: In the mental institution you **must** show improvement to get out.
  （「精神病院と大学の違いは何か」「精神病院を出るためには良くなったことを示さなければならない」）
  ★ **What's-the-difference joke** → p. 153

"Daddy," said the bright boy, accompanying his father on a round of golf, "Why **mustn't** the ball go into the little hole?"
（「お父さん」と頭のいい少年がゴルフのラウンドで父に同伴しながら言った．「なぜボールは小さい穴に入ってはいけないの」）

(2) **推量**：「__にちがいない」

"I wonder why so many marriages are failures."
"It **must** be because so many inexperienced people go into it."
（「なぜこんなに多くの結婚が失敗に終るんだろう」「きっとあまりに多くの未経験者が結婚するからだよ」）

A thief gave his girlfriend a lovely mink coat. Putting it on, she purred, "It's magnificent. It **must** be worth at least ten years!"
（泥棒がガールフレンドにかわいいミンクのコートをやった．それを着ながら彼女は猫なで声で満足そうに言った．「素敵だわ．きっと10年の値打ちがあるわ」）
☞ ten years = ten years in prison（10年の刑）

Diner: This restaurant **must** have a very clean kitchen.
Owner: Thank you, sir, but how did you know?
Diner: Everything tastes of soap.
(食事の客と店主の対話:「このレストランの台所はきっと清潔にちがいない」「ありがとうございます,お客様.しかしどうしてお分かりになったんですか」「ぜんぶ石けんのにおいがするからさ」)

(3) must have＋過去分詞:「＿したにちがいない」

"Yes, travel broadens one."
"She **must have been** around the world."
(「確かに,旅行は人間の幅を広げるものです」「彼女は世界一周したにちがいない」)

☞ あの身体の幅なら.

Pretty Girl: It **must have taken** a lot of courage to rescue me as you did.
Fireman: Yes. I had to knock down three guys who wanted to do it.
(かわいい女性と消防士の対話:「あなたのように私を救出するには大変な勇気が必要だったにちがいありませんわ」「そうです.あなたを救いたい奴らを3人殴り倒さなければなりませんでした」)

If your efforts are criticized, you **must have done** something worthwhile.
(もし努力の結果が批判されたら,君は価値のあることをしたに違いないのだ.)

★ **One-liner** → p. 395

G. have to / ought to / used to / dare

(1) have to *do*:「＿しなければならない」

"Most famous artists die in poverty."
"Yeah, but I **have to** live in it."
(「たいていの有名な芸術家は貧困の中で死ぬ」「そのとおりだ,しかしぼくは貧困の中

で生きなきゃならない」)
☞ 自分を有名な芸術家だと思っている．

If you want to make a living, you **have to** work for it. If you want to become rich, you **have to** find another way.
(生計を立てたければ，そのために働かなければいけません．お金持ちになりたければ，別の方法を見つけなければいけません．)

(*Tattooed sailor has operation*)
Doctor: Sorry, son, but I **had to** sink three battleships before I could get to your appendix.
((刺青(いれずみ)の水夫が手術を受ける)
医師「申しわけない，君，しかし盲腸に着くまでに3隻の軍艦を沈めなければならなかったよ」)
☞ 軍艦の刺青を台無しにしてしまった．

Dentist: My good man, you **don't have to** pay me now.
Patient: Pay you? I'm counting my money before you give me the gas.
(歯科医「あなた，今支払いをする必要はありませんよ」患者「支払いをするですって．先生が麻酔ガスをかがせる前にお金を数えているんです」)

A teacher took her class to a museum. As they walked in, one youngster told the others, "Don't look at too much. If you do, we**'ll have to talk** about it in class later!"
(先生が生徒たちを博物館へ連れて行った．彼らが入って行くとき1人の子供が他の子たちに言った「あんまり見過ぎちゃだめだよ．そんなことをすると，後で授業中に話し合わなければならなくなるよ」)

cf. have to be ...は「...であるに違いない」の意味になることがある．
My wife **has to be** the worst cook. In my house, we pray after we eat.
(妻はきっと最悪の料理人に違いない．家では食後にお祈りをする．)
☞ 食前に祈るのがふつう．

(2) ought to *do*: (a) 当然の推量 (b) 義務・望ましさ

She: I dreamed about the funniest thing last night. Wasn't it a funny dream?
He: How do I know what your dream was about?
She: You **ought to** know. You were in it.
(「昨夜とてもおかしな夢を見たわ.おかしな夢だったわね」「きみの夢が何の夢だったかどうして僕に分かるんだい」「分かるはずよ.あなたも夢の中に出てきたのよ」)

★ **Irish bull** → p. 39

(a) 当然の推量:「__するはずである」

"What number is this?"
"You **ought to** know. You dialed it."
(「そちらは何番ですか」「知ってるはずでしょう.あなたがダイヤルしたんですよ」)

"Young man, do you think you can handle a variety of work?"
"I **ought to** be able to. I've had 12 different jobs in four months."
(「君,いろんな仕事を扱えると思うかね」「できるはずです.4か月で12の違う仕事をしてきましたから」)

(b) 義務・望ましさ:「__すべきだ」

Parents are the last people on earth who **ought to** have children.
                                            (Samuel Butler)
(親はこの世で子供を持つべきではない人々である.)
☞ Samuel Butler (1612-1680): イギリスの風刺詩人.
★ **One-liner** → p. 395

We **ought** never **to** do wrong when people are looking. (Mark Twain)
(他人が見ているときは決して間違ったことをすべきではない.)
☞ Mark Twain (1835-1910): アメリカの(ユーモア)小説家.

(3) used to *do*: (a) 過去の状態 (b) 過去の習慣的動作

"I **used to** be with the circus."

"What cage were you in?"
（「昔はサーカスにいたんだ」「何の檻にいたんだい」）

★ **Insulting joke** → p. 97

(a) 過去の状態：「以前は＿＿だった」

He **used to** be a tree surgeon, but one day he fell out of a patient!
（彼は以前樹木医をしていたが，ある日患者から落ちてしまった．）

I **used to** think that the cold war took place in Siberia or Alaska.
（冷戦はシベリアかアラスカで起こると思っていた．）
★ **Irish bull** → p. 39

(b) 過去の習慣的動作：「よく＿＿した」

"Daddy, can you still do tricks?"
"What do you mean, son, 'do tricks'?"
"Well, Mamma says that when you were young, you **used to** drink like a fish."
（「お父ちゃん，今でも芸当できるの」「お前，「芸当」ってどういう意味だい」「お母ちゃんが，お父ちゃんは若いころには魚みたいに飲んだって言ってるもん」）
☞ drink like a fish：「大酒を飲む」

She **used to** work for her husband until she got him.
（彼女は夫のために働いていたがついに彼を手に入れた．）

(4) dare:「思い切って＿＿する」

> *Passenger:* Fourth floor, please.
> *Elevator Operator:* Here you are, son.
> *Passenger:* How **dare** you call me son? You're not my father.
> *Elevator Operator:* I brought you up, didn't I?
> （エレベーター係と乗客の対話：「4階お願いします」「着いたよ，お前」「よくもおれをお前なんて呼ぶな．おれの親父じゃないぞ」「ここまで上げて来たでしょう」）

☞ bring up：「連れて上がる」⇔「（子供を）育てる」　★ **Pun** → p. 26

"You're stupid!"
"How **dare** you! Say you're sorry!"
"All right, I'm sorry you're stupid."
(「お前はバカだ」「よくもそんなことを．ごめんなさいと言え」「いいとも，おまえがバカでごめんなさい」)

There are many who **dare** not kill themselves for fear of what the neighbours will say.　(Cyril Connolly)
(近所の人たちが何と言うかを恐れて思い切って自殺できない人も多い．)
☞ Cyril Connolly (1903-1974): イギリスの文芸評論家・作家．

H. 助動詞を含む受動態：助動詞＋**be**＋過去分詞

"What question **can** never **be** *answered* by Yes?"
"I don't know."
"Are you asleep?"
(「イエスでは決して答えられない質問は何か」「分からない」「眠っているのか」)

Manners **will** never **be** *observed* until someone invents self-winding spaghetti and invisible toothpicks.
(誰かが自然に巻きつくスパゲティーと見えない爪楊枝を発見するまではテーブルマナーは守られないだろう．)

Teacher: Well, Tom, what are you going to be when you are grown up?
　Tom: I'm going to be a soldier.
Teacher: But then you **may be** *killed* by the enemy. Are you not afraid?
Tom (After thinking for a while): Well, I will be one of the enemies then.
(「トム，君は大きくなったら何になるつもりだい」「軍人になるつもりです」「しかし，そうすると敵に殺されるかもしれないぞ．こわくないのか」トム（しばし考えて）「じゃあ敵になります」)
★ **Irish bull** → p. 39

Did you hear about the man who spent all afternoon trying to go up the escalator in the department store? The sign said, "Dogs **must be** *carried*" and it took him hours to find one.
（デパートのエスカレーターを上ろうとして午後中過ごした男のことを聞いたか．掲示に「犬を乗せなければいけません」とあったので見つけるのに何時間も掛かったんだ．）
☞ must be carried:「乗せて行かねばならない」⇔「持って［抱いて］行かねばならない」

Politicians are like diapers—they **should be** *changed* regularly and for the same reason.
（政治家は赤ん坊のおむつに似ている—一定期的にしかも同じ理由で替えられるべきだ．）
★ **One-liner** → p. 395

ジョークの常識⑦

★ **Insulting joke**：「ジョークの攻撃性が強まって相手を侮辱するジョーク」

Is that your head, or are you carrying a watermelon on your shoulders?
（それは君の頭かね，それともスイカを両肩に載せているのかね．）

When he goes to the zoo, the monkeys throw peanuts at *him*.
（彼が動物園へ行くと猿たちが彼にピーナツを投げつける．）

I hear you're famous. A costume company is using your face as a model for its Halloween masks.
（君は有名だそうだね．コスチューム会社が君の顔をハロウィーンの仮面のモデルに使っているんだってね．）

第8章　名　詞

Teacher: What is a **noun**?
　Pupil: Name of an animal, person, place or thing.
Teacher: Am I a **noun**?
　Pupil: Yes, sir.
Teacher: Are you a **noun**?
　Pupil: Yes, sir.
Teacher: Are all the boys in the class **nouns**?
Pupil (a little doubtfully): Yes, sir.
Teacher: Are all the boys running about the playground **nouns**?
Pupil (brightening up): Please, sir, they are not. When they are running about, they are verbs.

（先生と生徒の対話：「名詞とは何だね」「動物，人，場所，物の名前です」「私は名詞かな」「はい，先生」「クラスの男の子はみんな名詞かな」「（ちょっと迷いながら）はい，先生」「運動場を走りまわっている男の子もみんな名詞かな」「（顔を明るくしながら）ちがいます．先生．走りまわっているときは動詞です」）

名詞は人・動物・事物の名前を表す語で，文の中で**単数形**または**複数形**で用いられ，**主語・目的語・補語**などの働きをする．

A. 名詞の種類

名詞は意味によって(1) 普通名詞, (2) 集合名詞, (3) 物質名詞, (4) 抽象名詞, (5) 固有名詞に分けられる．また，用法によって，1つ2つと数えられる名詞（可算名詞）と数えられない名詞（不可算名詞）に分けられる．

第 8 章　名　詞

可算名詞	不可算名詞
1. **普通名詞**: book, cat, tree, student, house, village 2. **集合名詞**: family, class, team, people	3. **物質名詞**: air, water, tea, sugar, iron 4. **抽象名詞**: kindness, beauty, peace, experience 5. **固有名詞**: Lucy, Tom, London, Japan, Christmas

B. 可算名詞（数えられる名詞）

(1) 普通名詞：一般的な人や物を表す名詞

(a) 単数形：可算名詞の単数形はふつう単独では用いられず，a, an, one, the, this, that, 名詞・代名詞の所有格などのいずれか 1 つをつけて用いられる．

"Right here in *this* one **city** *a* **man** is knocked down by *a* **car** every five minutes."
"I should think he would be worn out."
(「まさにこの町のここだけで 5 分ごとに 1 人の男が車にはねられているんだ」「その男もうくたくただろうな」)
★ **Irish bull** → p. 39

Today's **president** is *tomorrow's* five-cent **stamp**.
（今日の大統領は明日の 5 セント切手．）

"I'm afraid Alice will not be at school today."
"Who's calling?"
"It's *my* **mother**."
(「すみませんがアリスは今日学校へ行けません」「どなたですか」「私のお母さんです」)

(b) 複数形

> The plural of spouse is spice.　(Christopher Morley)
> (spouse（配偶者）の複数形は spice（香辛料）である．)

☞ mouse（ハツカネズミ）の複数形は mice であることからの類推の誤り．「配偶者は互いにとって香辛料」ともとれる．spouse の複数形は spouses．
☞ Christopher Morley (1890-1957): アメリカのジャーナリスト・エッセイスト．

◆ 複数形のつくり方

A little girl came home from school and said to her mother, "Mom, guess what! We learned how to make **babies** today." The mother, more than a little surprised, asked fearfully, "That's interesting. How do you make **babies**?" "It's simple," replied the little girl. "You just change 'y' to 'i' and add 'es'!"
（少女が学校から帰ると母親に言った「ママ，ねえねえ．今日赤ちゃんの作り方を習ったわ」母親は少なからず驚いて，恐る恐る尋ねた．「それは面白いわね．どうやって赤ちゃんを作るの」「簡単よ」と少女は答えた．「ただ y を i に変えて es を足せばいいのよ」）

1) 規則変化

単数語尾	変化	発音	例	例外
無声音	—s	[s]	books, caps, rats, months	
有声音	—s	[z]	dogs, cabs, beds, hills, things, stars, bees, doors	
[s] [z] [ʃ] [tʃ] [dʒ]	—(e)s	[iz]	buses, dishes, boxes, benches, places, carriages, roses	
子音字+y	y → i —ies	[iz]	city—cities, lady—ladies, baby—babies, lily—lilies（ゆり）	
母音字+y	—s	[z]	boy—boys, key—keys, guy—guys（男）	
子音字+o	—es	[z]	heroes（英雄，主人公），potatoes, tomatoes	pianos
f, fe	f → v —ves	[vz]	shelf—shelves（たな），knife—knives, wife—wives	roofs chiefs

2) 不規則変化

- 母音変化などによるもの：
  man−men（男）, woman−women [wímin]（女）, foot−feet（足, フィート）, tooth−teeth（歯）, mouse−mice（ハツカネズミ）, child−children（子供）など
- 単数・複数同形：
  deer（鹿）, sheep（羊）, trout（鱒）, salmon [sǽmən]（鮭）, Japanese（日本人）, Swiss（スイス人）など
- 複合名詞の複数形：その中の主要な語を複数形にするのが原則.
  brothers-in-law（義理の兄弟）, passers-by（通行人）など

Teacher: Give me the plural of 'mouse'.
　Pupil: **Mice**.
Teacher: Very good! And now give me the plural of 'baby.'
　Pupil: **Twins**.
（先生と生徒の対話：「mouse（ハツカネズミ）の複数形を言いなさい」「Mice です」「その通り. では baby（赤ちゃん）の複数形は」「Twins（双子）です」）
☞ 正解は babies.

He was a weird child. At the age of six he was abandoned by an orphanage and raised by **wolves**.
（彼は気味の悪い子供だった. 6歳のとき孤児院から捨てられ狼たちに育てられたのだ.）

"Why do **women** live longer than **men**?" "Because they don't have **wives**."
（「なぜ女性は男性より長生きか」「女性には妻がいないから」）

"How many feet are there in a field with three hundred **sheep**, three **dogs**, two **horses**, and a **farmer**?"
"Two, because all the rest are **hooves** and **paws**."
（「300頭の羊, 3匹の犬, 2頭の馬, 1人の農場主のいる牧草地には足が何本あるか」「2本, なぜなら残り全部ひづめと犬の足だから」）

☞ hooves: hoof（ひづめ）の複数形　　☞ paw:（犬・猫などの）足
★ **Riddle** → p. 64

"How many **fish** have you caught so far?"
"Well, when I've caught another, I'll have one."
(「今までで何匹魚を釣ったんだい」「ええと，もう 1 匹釣ると，1 匹になるよ」)

(c) 文字・数字の複数形

My son is shrewd. When he got **D's** and **F's** on his report card, he swore they were vitamin deficiencies.
(私の息子は抜け目がない．成績通知表で D や F をもらうと，それはビタミン不足だと断言したのだ．)

☞ **Ds**, **Fs** とも綴る．

Patient:　My wife thinks I'm crazy because I like sausages.
Psychiatrist:　Nonsense, I like sausages too.
Patient:　Great—you should come and see my collection. I've got **hundreds of** them.
(患者と精神科医の対話：「妻は私がソーセージが好きだから気がふれていると思っているんです」「バカな，私もソーセージは好きですよ」「それはすばらしい．ぜひ私のコレクションを見に来たほうがいいです．何百本も持ってます」)

In our **twenties** we don't care what the world thinks of us. In our **thirties** we worry about what the world thinks of us. In our **forties** we realize that nobody actually gives a damn about us.
(20 代には世間が自分たちをどう思っているかなど気にしない．30 代には世間が自分たちをどう思っているか気にかかる．40 代になると自分たちのことなど実際は誰も気にしていないことが分かる．)

☞ not give a damn:「まったく興味がない」

(d) 分数とその複数形：分子は基数（1, 2, 3, ...），分母は序数（1st, 2nd, 3rd, ...）で読む．

Five out of four people have trouble with fractions.
(4人中5人が分数で苦労する.)

Ten years ago, only **a third** of schoolchildren went on to higher education. Now it is 33 per cent. (Teachers' spokesman)
(10年前には学童の3分の1しか高等教育へ進めませんでした. 今やその数字は33パーセントになっています.（教員の広報担当者))
★ **Irish bull** → p. 39

One fifth of the people are against everything all the time.
(Robert Kennedy)
(国民の5分の1はいつでもあらゆることに反対するものだ.)
☞ Robert Kennedy (1925–1968): アメリカの政治家. 連邦司法長官(1961–1964). 第35代大統領 John F. Kennedy の弟.
★ **One-liner** → p. 395

Teacher: If I cut a beefsteak in two, and then the **halves** in two, what do I get?
Pupil: **Quarters**, sir.
Teacher: Good! And then again?
Pupil: **Eighths**.
Teacher: All right! And then again?
Pupil: **Sixteenths**.
Teacher: Exactly. And then?
Pupil: **Thirty-seconds**.
Teacher: And then?
Pupil (impatiently): Hash!
(先生と生徒の対話:「もし私がビフテキを2つに切り, それをまた2つに切ると, どうなるかな」「4分の1です」「よろしい」「また切ると」「8分の1です」「そのとおり. でまた切ると」「16分の1です」「そのとおり」「それから」「32分の1です」「それから」「(いらいらしながら) こま切れです」)

Doctor (to portly patient)*:* Follow this diet, and in a couple of months I want to see **three-fourths** of you back here for a checkup.
（医師がかっぷくのいい患者に：「この食事療法に従ってください．そして 2, 3 カ月後にここへ 4 分の 3 になったあなたが検診に戻って来るのを見たいですね」）

(e)　常に複数形で用いる名詞

1)　対になっている衣類・器具：shoes, gloves（手袋），socks, stockings, scissors（はさみ），glasses（めがね），など．数えるときは「**a pair of 〜，two pairs of 〜**」のように表す．

"Are you good at grammar?"
"Now that was my best study."
"Is **trousers** singular or plural?"
"I know that one—singular at the top and plural at the bottom."
（「君は文法は得意かい」「いちばん得意な科目だったよ」「ズボンは単数かい複数かい」「それは知っているよ．上の方が単数で下が複数さ」）

"Do you wear **suspenders**?"
"No. Why should I wear suspenders?"
"To support your **pants**."
"Why should I support my **pants**? They never did anything for me."
（「ズボンつりをしないのか」「しないさ．なぜ必要があるんだ」「ズボンを支えるためさ」「なぜズボンを支えなきゃならないんだ．何もしてくれなかったぞ」）
☞ support：「支える」⇔「（財政的に）援助する」　　★ **Pun** → p. 26

Women's underwear confuses me. Why do they wear ***a pair of panties*** and only one bra?
（女性の下着には面食らう．なぜパンティーは複数でブラジャーは単数で身につけるんだ．）

The young girl student was puzzled why the ageing college professor needed **three pairs of glasses**.

He explained: "I have **one pair** for long sight, **one pair** for short sight, and **the third pair** to look for the other two."
(その若い女子学生はなぜ老齢の大学教授がメガネを3つ必要なのか不思議に思った. 彼はこう説明した「1つは遠くを見るため, 1つは近くを見るため, もう1つは他の2つを探すためだよ」)

"Can I have **a pair of** crocodile **shoes**, please?"
"Sure. What size does your crocodile take?"
(「ワニの靴を1足いただけませんこと」「もちろんです. ワニの靴のサイズはいくつでしょうか」)

The best way to remove coffee stains from a silk blouse is with **a pair of scissors**.
(シルクのブラウスからコーヒーのしみを取る最善の方法はハサミを一丁使うことだ.)
☞ しみは取れないから切るしかない.

2) 学問の名称

> ふつうは単数扱いであるが, 単・複どちらにもなることがある.
> physics（物理学）, politics（政治学）, mathematics（数学）, economics（経済学）, electronics（電子工学）など

"Is **politics** singular?"
"Nothing is more singular than politics."
(「politics（政治）は単数ですか」「政治ほど奇妙なものはありません」)

☞ singular:「単数の」⇔「奇妙な」　　★ **Pun** → p. 26

Politics *is* far more complicated than **physics**.　(Albert Einstein)
(政治は物理学よりはるかに複雑である.)
☞ Albert Einstein (1879-1955): ドイツ生まれの理論物理学者.

All **politics** *are* based on the indifference of the majority.
(James Reston)

（すべての政策は大多数の無関心に基づいている.）
☞ James Reston (1909-1995):ドイツ生まれのアメリカのジャーナリスト.

"**Statistics** *prove* that marriage is a preventive of suicide."
"Yes, and **statistics** also *prove* that suicide is a preventive of marriage."
（「統計は結婚が自殺の予防手段であることを証明している」「その通り，しかし，統計は自殺が結婚の予防手段であることも証明している」）
☞ 自殺すれば結婚しないですむ.

3) **相互複数**：交換・交友関係を示すもので常に複数形を使う.

"That's a nice coat. Did your husband change **jobs**?"
"No, I changed **husbands**."
（「それすてきなコートね．ご主人転職なさったの」「いいえ，夫を替えましたの」）

Interviewer: And when you had your big success in Paris, did you manage to see some sights? The Venus de Milo, for instance?
Silly celebrity: See her! I shook **hands** with her!
（インタビューアーとばかセレブの対話：「それで，パリで大成功なさったとき，何とか観光なさいましたか．例えば，ミロのビーナスとか」「彼女に会ったですって．握手までしましたわ」）

Today medicine is very specialized—I had a head cold and when it went to my chest I had to change **doctors**.
（今日医学は非常に専門化している．鼻風邪に罹ってそれが胸に行ったとき医者を替えなければならなかった.）

(2) 集合名詞

Teacher: Give me an example of a **collective noun**.
　Pupil: Garbage can.
（「集合名詞の例を1つ挙げてごらん」「生ごみ入れです」）

> 同じような性質をもつものが集まった 1 つの集合体を表す名詞．(a) と (b) の 2 つの考え方で単数・複数の区別をする．
> (a) 集合体を 1 単位と考える：単数
> (b) 集合体の個々の構成を考える：複数
> (a) は普通名詞と全く違いはない．(b) の場合は単数にも複数にも扱われる．

Our **family** *was* so poor our Christmas dinner was the leftovers from our last Christmas dinner.
(我々一家はとても貧しかったのでクリスマスの夕食は前の年のクリスマスの残り物だった．)
★ **Tall tale** → p. 412

Tom: Dick's **family** *are* sending their son to his pen friend for summer.
Harry: Does he need a holiday?
Tom: No, but his parents do.
(トムとハリーの対話：「ディックのところでは息子を夏はペン・フレンドのところへ送るんだ」「息子は休暇が必要なのか」「いいや，両親が必要なんだ」)

At my most recent performance the **audience** *were* so tightly packed they could not applaud horizontally; they had to applaud vertically.
(W. C. Fields)
(つい最近の出演では観客があまりにも混み合っていて彼らは水平に拍手できないので垂直に拍手しなければならないほどだった．)
☞ W. C. Fields (1880–1946)：アメリカのコメディアン．

There are no passengers on Spaceship Earth. We are all **crew.**
(Marshall McLuhan)
(宇宙船地球号には乗客はいない．皆が乗組員だ．)
☞ Marshall McLuhan (1911–1980)：カナダの社会学者・情報科学者．
★ **One-liner** → p. 395

The **crowd** *were* behind me all the way, but I shook them off at the

railway station.　(Tom O'Connor)
（群衆がずっと私の後について来た，しかし駅で彼らを振り払った．）
☞ Tom O'Connor (1939–　):イギリスの俳優・コメディアン．

I gave up trying to understand **people** long ago. Now I just let *them* try to understand me.　(Snoopy, *Peanuts*)
（ぼくはとっくに人々を理解しようとすることをあきらめた．今は彼らがぼくを理解するに任せているだけだ．）（スヌーピー『ピーナッツ』）

cf.「国民，民族」の意味では (a) となり普通名詞と同じように扱う：
The Irish are **a** fair **people**; they never speak well of one another.
(Samuel Johnson)
（アイルランド人は公平な国民である．決してお互いをほめない．）
☞ Samuel Johnson (1709-1784):イギリスの詩人・批評家・辞書編纂家．

C. 不可算名詞 （数えられない名詞）

I used to sell **furniture** for a living. The trouble was, it's my own.
(Les Dawson)
（生計を立てるために家具を売ったものだ．困ったことはそれが私自身の物だったことだ．）

☞ Les Dawson (1931-1993):イギリスのコメディアン・作家．

(1) 物質名詞

> 材料・液体・気体・食物などを表す名詞．原則として a / an をつけず，複数形にもしない．

Men worry more about losing their **hair** than their heads.
（男たちは頭を失うことより髪の毛を失うことを心配する．）

☞ lose *one*'s head:「首を切って殺される」

cf. 「1本の髪の毛」はa hair.

 Jackie: Oh, mother! Just look at that man! He hasn't **a hair** on his head.

 Mother: Hush, dear, he will hear you.

 Jackie: Oh, doesn't he know it?

（娘と母親の対話：「お母さん，ちょっとあの男の人を見て．頭に一本も毛がないわよ」「しっ，聞こえるわよ，おまえ」「あの人このこと知らないの」）

"If you make the **toast** and **coffee**, dear," said the newly married girl, "breakfast will be ready."

"What're we gonna have for breakfast?"

"**Toast** and **coffee**."

（「あなたがトーストとコーヒーを作ってくだされば，朝食は準備オーケーよ」と新婚の妻が言った．「朝食は何だい」「トーストとコーヒーよ」）

☞ gonna ＝ going to

 Mistress: Mary, these balusters seem always dusty. I was at Mrs. Brown's today, and her stair rails are clean and as smooth as **glass**.

 Servant: Yes, ma'am, but she has three small boys.

（女主人「メアリー，この手すりはいつも埃っぽいわね．ブラウン夫人のお宅に今日お邪魔したとき，階段の手すりはガラスみたいにきれいですべすべしてたわよ」お手伝い「そうですわ，奥様，小さな男の子が3人いらっしゃいますもの」）

☞ いつも滑り降りて磨いている．

(2) 物質名詞の普通名詞化：製品化した品物・種類を表すときは普通名詞のように単数形・複数形が現れる．

Age is something that doesn't matter unless you are **a cheese**.

(Billie Burke)

（年齢は大して重要なものではない，あなたがチーズでなければ．）

☞ チーズは熟成に時間がかかる．

☞ Billie Burke (1884–1970): アメリカの女優．

"Do you want **a beer**?"
"It's seven o'clock in the morning. Scotch?"

(Jack Butler and Ron Richardson)

(「ビールを1杯飲みたくないか」「朝の7時だぜ．スコッチは」)
☞ Jack Butler (1927-2012): アメリカンフットボールの名選手．
☞ Ron Richardson (1952-1995): アメリカのミュージカル俳優．

I love everything that's old—old friends, old times, old manners, old books, old **wines**. (Oliver Goldsmith)
(私は古いものが何でも好きだ，古い友だち，古い時代，古い行儀作法，古い書物，古いワイン．)
☞ Oliver Goldsmith (1728-1774): イギリスの詩人・劇作家・小説家．

(3) **物質名詞の数量の示し方**：容器・形状などを表す語などを使って数える．単数は「**a ～ of**」，複数は「～の複数形＋**of**」で表す．

On the first day of springtime, my true love gave to me: five **packs of** seed, four **sacks of** fertilizer, three **cans of** weed killer, two **bottles of** insect spray, and a pruning knife for pear trees.
(春の初日に恋人が私にくれたものは種5包み，肥料3袋，除草剤3缶，除虫スプレー2瓶，そして梨の木用の刈り込みナイフだった．)

When I went on knocking on doors asking for donations for a new school swimming pool, one peculiar person gave me **a bucket of** water.
(新しい学校のプールの寄付を求めて一軒一軒ドアをノックし続けていると，一風変わった男が私にバケツ1杯の水をくれた．)

She wanted something for her neck, so I bought her **a cake of** soap.
(彼女は首に何かほしがったので，石鹸1個買ってやった．)
☞ 石鹸を贈るのは，日本と異なり，失礼な行為．

A bum asked me, "Can you give me twelve hundred dollars for **a cup**

of coffee?"
I said, "**A cup of** coffee doesn't cost twelve hundred dollars!"
He said, "I want to have it in Brazil!"
(ホームレスが「コーヒー1杯のために1,200ドルくれませんか」と聞いたので，言ってやった「コーヒー1杯で1,200ドルはしないぞ」すると彼は言った「ブラジルで飲みたいんで」)

You know you're in an expensive restaurant when you ask for **a glass of** water and the waiter asks, "What year?"
(高級なレストランにいると分かるのは水を1杯頼むとウエイターが「何年ものにいたしましょうか」と尋ねるときだ．)

The most expensive **piece of** furniture in the world is a ringside table at a night club.
(世界で最も高価な家具はナイトクラブの最前列のテーブルである．)

Mother: Why were you kept after school today, Johnny?
Johnny: Our teacher told us to write an essay on 'The Result of Laziness,' and I turned in **a** blank **sheet of** paper.
(母と息子の対話：「なぜ今日学校に居残りさせられたの，ジョニー」「先生がぼくたちに「怠惰の結果」について作文を書きなさいって言ったんだ，だからぼくは白紙を出したんだ」)

(4) 抽象名詞

"What is it that you can't see when you are looking at it?"
"An **abstract noun**."
(「見ているときに見えないものは」「抽象名詞」)

目に見えない抽象的な概念を表す名詞．

We all admire the **wisdom** of people who ask us for **advice**.
(我々はみな我々に助言を求める人々の賢明さを称賛する．)

The noun '**honesty**' is usually preceded by 'old-fashioned.'
(「正直」という名詞は通常「流行遅れの」という語が前に付く.)

The search for **happiness** is one of the chief sources of **unhappiness**.
(幸福の探求は不幸の主要原因の１つである.)
★ **One-liner** → p. 395

Everybody gets so much **information** all day long that they lose their common sense. (Gertrude Stein)
(誰もが一日中あまりに多くの情報を得るので常識を失くしてしまう.)
☞ Gertrude Stein (1874-1946): アメリカの作家・詩人・美術収集家.

(5) 抽象名詞の普通名詞化：具体的事例・種類を表すときは普通名詞化する.

"My wife used to play the piano a lot, but since the children came she doesn't have time."
"Children are **a comfort**, aren't they?"
(「妻は以前よくピアノを弾いたのですが子供が生まれて暇がなくなりました」「子供はほっとさせてくれますね」)
☞ 下手なピアノを聞かなくてすむ.

For years I thought I was **a failure**. Then they told me to be positive and it worked. Now I'm positive I'm **a failure**.
(何年も自分は失敗者だと思っていた. すると彼らは私に前向きになれと言った, そしてそれは効果があった. 今は前向きに自分は失敗者だと確信している.)

Nowadays we spend so much on **luxuries** we can't afford the **necessities**.
(今日我々はあまりにも贅沢品に金を使うので生活必需品を買う余裕がない.)
★ **One-liner** → p. 395

(6) 固有名詞

> Definition of the jet age: breakfast in **Rome**, lunch in **Paris**, dinner in **London**, bags in **Singapore**.
> (ジェット機時代の定義：ローマで朝食，パリで昼食，ロンドンで夕食，バッグはシンガポール．)

☞ 預けたバッグの誤送はよくあること．

地名・人名・その他の名前を表す名詞．

I asked my good friend, **Arnold Palmer**, how I could improve my game, he advised me to cheat. (Bob Hope)
(親友のアーノルド・パーマーにどうやったらうまくなるかを尋ねると，インチキしろと助言をもらった．)
☞ Arnold Palmer (1929–): アメリカの往年のプロゴルファー．
☞ Bob Hope (1903–2003): イギリス生まれのアメリカのコメディアン．

"It was so romantic, Mr. Rigsby: champagne, soft lights, **Tchaikovsky** in the background ..."
"Oh, was he there, too?"
(「とてもロマンチックでしたわ，リグズビーさん．シャンペン，柔らかな明かり，チャイコフスキーがバックグラウンドで…」「おや，彼もいたのか」)
★ Irish bull → p. 39

I think they should move **Christmas** to **July** when the stores aren't so crowded. (Goldie Hawn)
(クリスマスは店があまり混んでいない7月に動かした方がいいと思う．)
★ Irish bull → p. 39
☞ Goldie Hawn (1945–): アメリカの女優・ダンサー．

(7) 固有名詞の普通名詞化：製品・家族の一人［全員］などを表すとき普通名詞化する．（→「第12章 冠詞」A 不定冠詞 (5)）

A skeleton walked into a bar and said, "I'll have **a Budweiser** and a mop, please."
(骸骨が歩いてバーに入って「バドワイザー1杯とモップを頼む」と言った.)

The sweet young thing was upset when her boyfriend did not help her into his car. "Where," she asked "is your chivalry?"
And the young man said, "Didn't you notice? I traded it in for **a Ford**."
(かわい子ちゃんはボーイフレンドが車に乗るのを手伝ってくれなかったので取り乱してしまった.「あなたの騎士道はどこへ行っちゃったの」と彼女は尋ねた. すると若者は言った「気がつかなかったかい. それを下取りに出してフォードと取り替えたんだよ」)
☞ chivalry [ʃívəlri]（騎士道）⇔ Chevrolet [ʃévrəlei]（シボレー（車種名））
★ **Pun** → p. 26

The key to success? Work hard, stay focused and marry **a Kennedy**.
(Arnold Schwarzenegger)
(成功の鍵だって. 懸命に働き, 集中し続け, ケネディー家の娘と結婚することさ.)
☞ Arnold Schwarzenegger (1947-): アメリカの映画俳優・政治家.

"Why are there so many **Johnsons** in the phone book?"
"They all have phones."
(「電話帳にはなぜこんなにジョンソンが多いのか」「みんな電話を持っているから」)
☞ Johnson という姓は Smith と並んで極めて多い.

D. 名詞の所有格

The **world's** greatest water power is **women's** tears. (J. K. Morley)
(世界最大の水力は女性の涙だ.)

☞ J. K. Morley (1956-): イギリスの写真家.

第8章　名　詞

◆ 所有格 (Possessive Case) の作り方

名詞	変化	例
単数	—'s	a *cat's* tail,　my *wife's* father, the *girl's* mother,　*Tom's* car, a *spider's* web（くもの巣） a *judge's* seat（審判者の席）
複数	—s' —'s	a *girls'* school（女子校） the *boys'* caps（男児用の帽子） *men's* clothing（紳士服） *children's* shoes（子供靴）
複合名詞	最後の語+'s	my *brother-in-law's* house（義兄[弟]の家） cf. *John and William's* books（共有）

(1) 所有格は所有のほか，主格関係，目的関係などを表す．
(a)「～の」（所有）

> **Men's** troubles are due to three things: women, money, and both.
> （男のトラブルは3つのことのためである：女性，金，そして両方．）

"Do you sell **cat's** meat?"
"Only if they're accompanied by a human being."
（「ネコの肉を売ってくれるかい」「人間同伴の場合に限ります」）
☞ cat's [kæts]（ネコの）⇔ cats [kæts]（ネコに）　　★ 異分析 → p. 375

　　Clerk: What size collar does your husband wear, madam?
Lady Customer: Dear me, I've forgotten! But I know it's larger than **Fido's**.
（「奥様，ご主人の襟のサイズはおいくつでしょうか」「あらまあ，忘れてしまったわ．ファイドーよりは大きいことは分かっているんだけど」）
☞ Fido's＝Fido's size.　Fido: 犬によくある名前．

cf. 無生物の場合

Today is **tomorrow's** yesterday.
（今日は明日の昨日．）

I have the **world's** oldest globe. It's flat.
（世界最古の地球儀を持っている．それは平らだ．）

One of **life's** difficult decisions is picking the supermarket check-out line that will move fastest.
（人生の困難な決断の1つはスーパーの最速のレジの列を見つけること．）

(b) 主格関係　A's B:「AがBすること」

(An actual extract from nurses' exam papers)
—What can be done to aid the **patient's** recovery?
—Artificial restoration may help the patient to recover.
((看護師試験の答案から)
問「どうすれば患者が回復するのを助けることができるか」答「人工修復が患者の回復を助けるかもしれません」)

☞ restoration（修復）⇔ respiration（呼吸）　★ **Boner** → p. 46
☞ the patient recovers（患者が回復する）(S+V)

Avoid waiting for a **doctor's** appointment by making one for nine o'clock every morning. If you wake up feeling well, simply phone up and cancel it.　(*Viz*, Top Tips)
（医者が予約時間を指定するのを待つのを避けるには毎朝9時に予約することです．気分良く目が覚めたら，ちょっと電話してキャンセルすればいいのです．）

☞ a doctor appoints（医師が指定する）(S+V)
☞ *Viz*, Top Tips: *Viz*（イギリスの大人向けのユーモア漫画雑誌）；top tip:「最高の助言」

(c) 目的関係　A's B:「AをBすること」

Don't accept your **dog's** admiration as conclusive proof that you are wonderful.　(Ann Landers)

（犬をほめられたことがあなたがすばらしいという決定的な証拠だと考えてはいけません。）

☞ admire your dog（あなたの犬をほめる）（V+O）
☞ Ann Landers (1918-2002): アメリカの人生相談回答者．

My father wanted me to have all the educational opportunities he never had, so he sent me to a **girls'** school. (Eric Morecambe)
（父は自分が持てなかった教育の機会を私に与えたいと思った，だから私を女子校に入れたのだ．）

☞ a girls' school ＝ a school for girls（女子のための学校）
☞ Eric Morecambe (1926-1984): イギリスのコメディアン．　★ **Tall tale** → p. 412

(2) 名詞の反復を避ける

Professor: This essay on our dog is, word for word, the same as your **brother's**.
Student: Yes, sir, it's the same dog.
（教授「犬に関するこの論文は一語一句君の兄さんの論文と同じではないか」学生「そうなんです，先生．同じ犬ですから」）

☞ brother's ＝ brother's essay

A linguist is a man who has mastered every tongue but his **wife's**.
（語学に堪能な人とは奥方の言語以外のあらゆる言語をものにした人である．）

☞ wife's ＝ wife's tongue

(3) office，shop，store などは慣用的に省略される．

"Did you have a good time at the **dentist's**?"
"I was bored to tears."
（「歯医者さんでは楽しかったかい」「涙が出るほど退屈したよ」）

☞ bore「穴をあける」⇔「退屈させる」　★ **Pun** → p. 26

A man walked into the **barber's** and asked for a shave. The barber's young assistant spoke up: "May I try shaving him? It will be a good practice."

"All right—go ahead," replied his boss doubtfully. "But be careful. Don't cut yourself."
(男が床屋に入って行って髭剃りを頼んだ．床屋の若い助手が大きな声で「あの人の髭剃りをやってみてもいいですか．いい練習になると思います」と言った．「いいよ，やってごらん」と親方は大丈夫かなという態度で答えた．「気をつけな，自分を切るんじゃないぞ」)

My wife is just crazy about **Macy's**. She spent some of the happiest pages of my checkbook on the third floor.
(妻はメーシーズに無我夢中だ．3階で私の小切手帳の最もうれしい数ページを使ってしまった．)
☞ Macy's = Macy's department store　アメリカのチェーン百貨店．

ジョークの常識⑧

★ **Black humor:**「死・災害・恐怖などに関する，時に不快で気味の悪いユーモア」 cf.「黒人についてのユーモア」の意味で用いることも多い．

"Now, how much would *you* like to contribute to the Indian Relief Fund, Mrs. Custer?"
(「さて，カスター夫人，あなたならインディアン救援基金にいくら寄附なさいますか」)
☞ Custer: George A. Custer (1839–1876): アメリカ南北戦争時の北軍の将校．スー (Sioux) 族との戦いで部下全員と共に戦死した．

第 9 章　代名詞

"Name two **pronouns**."
"**Who**, **me**?"
"Correct."
(「代名詞を２つ言いなさい」「だれ，ぼくですか」「そのとおり」)

代名詞は名詞や名詞句［節］または文の代わりの働きをする．

◆ 代名詞の種類：代名詞には以下のようなものがある．

種　類	例
人称代名詞	I, you, they, we, he, she, it
指示代名詞	this, that, these, those
不定代名詞	one, any, some, another, both, all
再帰代名詞	myself, yourself, herself, ourselves
疑問代名詞	who, what, which
関係代名詞	who, which, that, what

cf. 疑問代名詞 what, which, who については「第 2 章 疑問文」参照．関係代名詞については「第 21 章 形容詞節」参照．関係代名詞 what については「第 20 章 名詞節」参照．

A. 人称代名詞

The objective of '**he**' is '**she**'. (he の目的格は she である．)

☞ objective:「(文法) 目的格」⇔「目的」　　★ **Pun** → p. 26

119

人称			「〜が」「〜は」（主格）	「〜の」（所有格）	「〜を」「〜に」（目的格）	「〜のもの」（独立所有格）
1人称	単数	私	I	my	me	mine
	複数	私たち	we	our	us	ours
2人称	単数	あなた	you	your	you	yours
	複数	あなたたち	you	your	you	yours
3人称	単数	彼	he	his	him	his
		彼女	she	her	her	hers
		それ	it	its	it	—
	複数	彼(女)ら・それら	they	their	them	theirs
	単数	代名詞以外	Ken	Ken's	Ken	Ken's
	複数	代名詞以外	teachers	teachers'	teachers	teachers'

cf.「独立所有格」は「所有代名詞」ともいう．

"They say **him** and **her**'s gonna get married."
"Don't say **him** and **her**. Say **her** and **him**. Always put ladies first."
(「彼と彼女結婚するんだってさ」「彼と彼女じゃない．彼女と彼と言えよ．いつも女性優先だぞ」)

☞ いずれにせよ文法的に間違っている．

Between **you** and **I**, case is important.
(ここだけの話だけど，格は重要だよ．)

☞ 正しくは Between you and **me**.

(1) 普通の用法

> "Why did **you** call the hero of **your** story 'Adam'?"
> "**You** said to write it in the first person."
> (「君はなぜ物語の主人公をアダムと呼んだんだね」「最初の人間で書けとおっしゃったからです」)

☞ the first person:「最初の人」⇔「(文法) 1 人称」　　★ **Pun** → p. 26

Teacher: Andy, say something beginning with '**I**'.
　Andy: **I** is ...
Teacher: No, Andy, you must say **I** am.
　Andy: All right, **I** am the ninth letter of the alphabet.
(「アンディ, I で始まる文を何か言ってごらん」「I is ...」「ちがう. 「わたしは〜」と言いなさい」「はい. わたしはアルファベットの 9 番目の文字です」)

"Mary, why do **you** yell and scream so? Play quietly like Tommy. See, **he** doesn't make a sound."
"Of course **he** doesn't. That's **our** game. **He**'s papa coming home late, and **I** am **you**."
(「メアリー, あなたはなぜそんなに叫んだり悲鳴を上げたりするの. トミーのように静かに遊びなさい. ごらん, 音も立てないわよ」「もちろん立てないわよ. わたしたちの遊びよ. トミーは遅く帰って来るパパで, わたしはお母さんなの」)

Quiet reigned in the neighborhood when a family of ten went on vacation. A few days later the family next door received a postcard asking, "How are **you** enjoying **our** vacation?"
(10 人家族が休暇で出かけると近所は静けさが支配した. 数日後隣の家族は葉書を受け取った. そこにはこうあった「私たちの休暇をいかがお楽しみですか」)

Cuthbert: Darling, if **we** get married, do **you** think **you** will be able to live on **my** income?
　Ethel: Of course, darling. But what are *you* going to live on?
(「きみ, 僕たちが結婚したら, きみは僕の収入で生活できると思うかい」「もちろんよ,

あなた．でもあなたは何の収入で生活するの」）

As soon as the doctor felt **his** wallet, **he** admitted there was nothing more **he** could do.
（医師はその男の財布に触れた途端にこれ以上何もできないと認めた．）
★ Doctor → p. 329

Jessie and Bessie went into a diner and ordered two glasses of water. Then **they** each unwrapped a tuna sandwich and started to eat. The waitress told **them**, "**You** can't eat **your own** sandwiches in here!" So **they** shrugged **their** shoulders and exchanged sandwiches.
（ジェシーとベシーは食堂車に入って行き，水をグラスに2杯注文した．そして各自ツナサンドの包みを開けて食べ始めた．ウエイトレスが彼女たちに「ご自分のサンドイッチはここで召し上がってはいけません」と言った．そこで，彼女たちは肩をすくめ，サンドイッチを交換した．）

When your first baby drops **its** pacifier, you sterilize **it**. When your second baby drops **its** pacifier, you tell the dog 'Fetch'.

(Bruce Lansky)

（最初の赤ん坊がおしゃぶりを落とすと，それを消毒する．2番目の赤ん坊がおしゃぶりを落とすと，犬に行って取っておいでと言う．）
☞ Bruce Lansky (1941-)：アメリカのユーモア詩人・児童文学作家．
☞ it について詳しくは「第10章 It の用法」参照．

(2) we, you, they: ばくぜんと人をさす場合．

> Most politicians don't believe a word of what they say. They're surprised that *we* do!
> （たいていの政治家は自分の言うことを一言も信じていない．私たちが信じるのに驚くのだ．）

Teacher: Martin, how do **you** spell *crocodile*?
Martin: KROKODIL.
Teacher: The dictionary spells it CROCODILE.

Martin: But, sir, you asked me how *I* spell it, not how the dictionary spells it.
(「マーチン，君は crocodile(ワニ)をどう綴る」「K-R-O-K-O-D-I-L です」「辞書には C-R-O-C-O-D-I-L-E とあるよ」「でも先生，先生はぼくがどう綴るか聞いたんです．辞書がどうかは聞きませんでした」)

Why do **they** sterilize the needles for lethal injections?
(なぜ致死注射のために針を消毒するのか．)

(3) 親身の we：親と子・医師と患者のような場合，前者が2人の一体感を示すのに you の代わりに we を用いる．

> Little Johnny's father said, "Let me see **our** report card."
> Johnny replied, "I don't have it."
> "Why not?" his father asked.
> "My friend just borrowed it. He wants to scare his parents."
> (ジョニーの父親が「通知表を見せなさい」と言った．ジョニーは「持っていないんだ」と答えた．「なぜだい」と父．「友だちが借りて行っちゃたんだ．親を脅したいんだよ」)

☞ こんなひどい成績になったのは両親のせいだと他人の通知表で脅すのに使う．

I don't understand that nurse. She keeps saying to me: 'How are **we** today?' and 'Have **we** eaten this morning?' But when I put my hand on her knee, she slapped **our** face.'
(あの看護師がよく分からない．彼女いつも「私たちの具合はどう」とか「私たちは今朝食べたの」とか言い続けるんだ．だけど，僕が彼女の膝に手をのせたら，自分たちの顔をピシャッとたたいたんだ」)

☞ How are we today? = How are you today?

B. 独立所有格

> A woman placed an ad in the classifieds:
> 'Husband Wanted.'
> The next day she got hundreds of replies:

'You can have **mine**!'
(ある女性が案内広告に広告を出した:「夫を求む」翌日何百もの返事が来た:「わたしのをあげるわ」)

(1) 前の名詞を受けて,「所有格+名詞」の代用をする.

Father: Do you think our son gets all his brains from me?
Mother: Probably. I still have **mine**.
(父と母の対話:「息子は頭を全部私から受け継いでいると思わないかい」「きっとそうね. 私のはまだあるから」)

Two little boys were walking by a house that had a high wall when the owner suddenly ran up to them.
'Is this your ball?' he asked.
'Has it done any damage?' asked one of the boys.
'No,' said the owner.
'Then it's **ours**,' said the other boy.
(2人の少年が高い塀のある家の側を歩いてると家主が突然走ってやって来た.「これは君たちのボールか」「何か壊しましたか」と1人が尋ねた.「いいや」と家主.「じゃあぼくらのです」ともう1人が言った.)

Teacher: Poppy! What would you say if I came to school with hands as dirty as **yours**?
Soppy Poppy: I'd be too polite to mention it, Miss.
(先生「ポピー,私があなたのように手が汚れたまま学校へ来たらあなたは何と言うでしょう」センチなポピー「それを口に出して言うほど失礼にはなれません,先生」)

A real woman has a special attitude to money. If she earns money, it is **hers**; if her husband earns it, it is **theirs**. (Joyce Jillsons)
(真の女性は金銭に対して特別な態度を持っています. 金を稼ぐとそれは自分のもの,夫が稼ぐと自分たちのものなのです.)
☞ Joyce Jillsons (1945-2004): アメリカのコラムニスト・作家・女優・占星術師.

Woman (to Marriage Counselor): That's my side of the story—now let me tell you **his**.
（女性が結婚カウンセラーに「これが私の側の言い分です．じゃあ，彼の側の言い分を話させてください」）
☞ これも彼女の言い分．

My wife is the most wonderful woman in the world, and that's not just my opinion—it's **hers**.
（妻は世界中で最もすばらしい女性だ，そしてこれは私だけの意見ではない．彼女の意見だ．）

(2) a / this / that / some(thing)＋名詞＋of＋独立所有格

> The doctor operated on **a friend of mine** for a constant ringing in his ears before they found out he was a bellhop.
> （医師は絶えず耳鳴りがする私の友人の1人の手術をして彼がホテルのボーイだと分かった．）

☞ bellhop＝((米)) bellboy（ホテルのボーイ）ベルが鳴ると跳んで行って仕事をする．

"Did **that** millionaire grandfather **of yours** remember you when he made his will?"
"He must have—he left me out."
（「君のあの億万長者のお祖父さんは遺言を書くとき君を覚えていたか」「覚えていたにちがいないよ．ぼくを除外したんだから」）
☞ お前なんかに遺産をやるものか．

"Daughter," said the father, "your young man, Ferdinand, stays until a very late hour. Hasn't your mother said something to you about **this habit of his**?" "Yes, father," replied the daughter sweetly. "Mother says men haven't altered a bit."
（「おまえ」と父が娘に言った．「あの若者ファーディナンドはずいぶん遅くまで家にいるね．お母さんは彼のこの習慣について何か言わなかったかい」「言ったわ，お父さん」と娘は愛らしく言った．「お母さんは男の人はちっとも変わってないって」）

A composer of movie background music was entertaining some guests in his house. After dinner, he sat down at the piano and played his newest score. A guest said, "You play Brahms beautifully. Now play **something of yours**!"

(映画のバックグラウンド・ミュージックの作曲家が自宅で数人の客をもてなしていた．ディナーのあとで彼はピアノに向かって座り，最新の曲を演奏した．客の 1 人が言った「君はブラームスをみごとに弾くね．今度は何か自分の曲を弾いてくれよ」)

★ **Insulting joke** → p. 97

C. 再帰代名詞

We looked into each other's eyes. I saw **myself**, she saw **herself**.
(Stanislaw J. Lec)
(私たちはお互いの目をのぞき込んだ．私には自分自身が彼女には彼女自身が見えた．)

☞ Stanislaw J. Lec (1909–1966): ポーランドの詩人．

(1) 他動詞・前置詞の目的語／自動詞の補語

(a) 他動詞・前置詞の目的語

Patient (on phone): Doctor, I've decided to kill **myself**.
Psychiatrist: Don't do anything rush until you answer one question for me.
Patient: What's that?
Psychiatrist: Is your bill paid?

(患者と精神科医の対話：「先生，私自殺することに決めました」「早まったことをしてはいけません．私の質問に答えるまでは」「何ですか」「支払いは済んでますね」)

★ **Doctor** → p. 329

Stout Lady: I'm putting on too much weight, Doctor. What shall I do?
Doctor: I prescribe regular exercise. Just push **yourself** away from the table three times a day.

(太った女性と医師の対話：「先生，体重が増えすぎているんです．どうしたらいいでしょうか」「規則正しい運動を指示しましょう．1 日に 3 度ご自分を食卓から押しのけさえすれば結構です」)

My auntie's so modest, she blindfolds **herself** in the shower.
(わたしのおばちゃんはとても慎み深い人でシャワーを浴びていても目隠しをします．)

"Which is the poorest plant?"
"A vine—it can't support **itself**."
(「もっとも貧しい植物は何か」「ブドウの木—自分を養えないから」)
☞ support:「養う」⇔「支える」　　★ **Pun** → p. 26; **Riddle** → p. 64

When the bosses talk about improving productivity, they are never talking *about* **themselves**.
(ボスたちが生産性の向上について語るとき，彼らは決して自分自身については語っていない．)

(b) 補語

The best thing to save for your old life is **yourself**.
(老後のために最もよく蓄えておくべきものは君自身だ．)

You're not **yourself** today. Enjoy it while you can.
(今日君は君らしくない．できる間はそれを楽しみたまえ．)
☞ 君らしい君は見たくない．　　★ **Insulting joke** → p. 97

(2) 強調用法

"What a delicious meal," said the husband to his wife as he cleared the plate. "Did you thaw it **yourself**?"
(「何とおいしい食事だ」と夫は皿をきれいに平らげながら言った．「自分で解凍したのかい」)

Butler: Professor, there's a bill collector at the door. I told him you were out, but he wouldn't believe me.
Absent-minded Professor: No? Then I suppose I'll have to go out and tell him **myself**.
(執事「先生，借金取りが玄関に来ております．先生はお留守だと申したのですが私の言

うことを信じようといたしません」「信じないって．じゃあ私自身が出て行って言ってやらねばならんか」）

★ **Absent-minded professor** → p. 320

(3) 慣用句

> **by** *oneself* (＝**alone**)（ひとりで，独力で），**for** *oneself*（独力で，自分のために），**in itself [themselves]**（それ自体で［は］），**beside** *oneself*（我を忘れて），**in spite of** *oneself*（思わず）　　など

Uncle Zeke: Did you catch all those fish **by yourself**?
Smart Alex: Oh, no, I had a worm to help me.
（「この魚全部一人で釣ったのか」「違うよ，ミミズが助けてくれたよ」）
☞ Smart Alex:「うぬぼれ屋，利口ぶる人」Alec(k), Alick などとも綴る．

Why don't efficiency experts go into business **for themselves** and make fortunes?
（なぜ能率向上の専門家は自分で事業を始めて財産作りをしないのか．）

Adventure is worthwhile **in itself**.　(Amelia Earhart)
（冒険はそれ自体やりがいのあることです．）
☞ Amelia Earhart (1897–1937): 先駆的なアメリカの女性飛行家．

D. 指示代名詞

> **this**（これ），**these**（これら）；**that**（それ，あれ），**those**（それら，あれら）；**so**（そのこと）

"I saw Esan sitting on a see-saw. How many Ss in **that**?"
"There aren't any in '**that**.'"
（「I saw Esan sitting on a see-saw. この中に S はいくつありますか」「that には S は入っていません」）
☞ I saw Esan sitting on a see-saw. で s は 5 つと答えさせたかった．

The doctor answered the phone to hear an excited voice say: "Quick, send an ambulance. My wife Bredget is about to have a baby."
"Calm down," said the Doc. "Is **this** her first baby?"
"No, **this** is her husband Pat speaking."
(医者が電話に出ると興奮した声が聞こえた.「急いでください.救急車を送ってください.妻のブレジェットが今にも赤ん坊を産みそうなんです」「落ち着いて」と医者.「これは最初の赤ちゃんですか」「いいえ,私は夫のパットです」)

☞ Is this Mr. Brown?「(電話で) そちらはブラウンさんですか」
☞ Pat: Patrick の愛称.「アイルランド人」の意味もある. ★ **Irish bull** → p. 39

(1) this, these; that, those

> "Get out of here! **This** isn't your house."
> "**That**'s Okay. I'm not myself tonight."
> (「ここから出ていって.ここはあなたの家じゃないわ」「気にしなくていいよ.今夜は自分が自分でないんだ」)

Policeman: Hey, you! You're crossing the street when the light says, 'Don't Walk.'
Pedestrian: Sorry, officer, I thought **that** was an ad for the bus company.
(警官「おい,君.信号が「止まれ」なのに通りを横断してるぞ」歩行者「すみません,お巡りさん.あれはバス会社の広告だと思ったんで」)

Waiter: **These** are the best eggs we've had for years.
Customer: Well, bring me some you haven't had around for that long.
(ウエイター「これは何年もの中で最上の卵です」客「じゃあ,そんなに長く出回っていなかったやつを頼む」)

My wife wanted beautiful roses like **those** next door, so I waited until it got dark ...
(妻が隣のと同じようなきれいなバラを欲しがったので,暗くなるまで待った...)

Did you hear about the guide who told his visitors: "**These** are the highest mountain in the world, apart from **those** in other countries."?
(観光客にこんなことを言うガイドのことを聞いたか「これらは世界一高い山です，他の国のは別にすればですが」)
★ **Irish bull** → p. 39

(2) **those** は **people**（人々）の意味になることがある．

Those who can, do. **Those** who cannot, teach. (George Bernard Shaw)
(できる人は行う．できない人は教える．)
☞ George Bernard Shaw (1856-1950): アイルランド出身のイギリスの劇作家．

Golf is a game in which the slowest people in the world are **those** in front of you, and the fastest are **those** behind.
(ゴルフは世界で最も遅いのが前でプレーしている連中，最も速いのが後ろの連中というゲームである．)
★ **One-liner** → p. 395

To **those** of you who received honors, awards and distinction, I say, 'Well done.' And to the 'C' students, I say, 'You, too, can be President of the United States.' (George W. Bush, address to Yale University)
(諸君の中で優等賞，何かの賞，名誉賞を受けた人たちには「よくやった」と言う．そして成績 C だった学生諸君には「諸君も合衆国大統領になれる」と言う．)（ブッシュ大統領のエール大学での演説）
☞ George W. Bush (1946-): アメリカの政治家．第 43 代大統領．
★ **Bushism** → p. 169

(3) **so** は前に出た語句を指す代名詞の働きをする．

"Do you think your son'll forget everything he learned in college?"
"I hope **so**!"
(「君の息子さんは大学で学んだことを全部忘れると思うか」「そうであってほしいよ」)
☞ どうせ碌なことを学んでいない．

A husband said to his wife: "Darling, let's go out and have some fun tonight."

"I suppose **so**," she said, "but if you get home before I do, leave the hallway light on."

（夫が妻に「おまえ，今夜は外へ行って楽しもうよ」「それがいいわね」と妻は言った．「でも私より先に帰って来たら，玄関の電気は点けておいてね」）

☞ **So** do I. などについては（→ 第27章 倒置）

E. 不定代名詞

Mother: Did you eat all the cookies, Tom?
 Tom: I didn't touch **one**.
Mother: That's strange. There's **one** left.
 Tom: That's the **one** I didn't touch.
（「トム，クッキーを全部食べたの」「クッキー1つ触らなかったよ」「それは変ね．1つだけ残ってるじゃない」「それが触らなかったクッキーだよ」）

漠然と人または物を指す代名詞で次のようなものがある：
one(s), other(s), some, another, each, *every,* **anybody, everybody, somebody,** *nobody,* **no one, anyone, everyone, someone, anything, everything, something,** *nothing, none,* **any, all, both, half, most, either,** *neither* など

cf. *every* は名詞の前にくる形容詞としてのみ用いられる．*nobody, no one, nothing, none, neither* については「第25章 否定表現」参照．

(1) one(s)

(a) 名詞の代用語

Lady (in theater): Pardon me, sir, does my hat bother you?
Gentleman behind: No, but it bothers my wife. She wants **one** like it.
（婦人（映画館で）：「失礼ですけど，私の帽子目ざわりじゃないかしら」後ろの紳士「そんなことはありません．しかし妻には目ざわりです．そんな帽子がほしいのです」）

Customer: I don't like the flies in here.

Waiter: Well, come around tomorrow, we'll have some new **ones**.

(客とウエイターの対話:「ここに入っているハエが気に入らないね」「では,明日お出でください.何匹か新しいやつが手に入ると思います」)

★ **Waiter** → p. 266

"How do you identify people who can't count to ten?"

"Simple. They're **the ones** in front of you in the supermarket express lane."

(「10 まで数えられない人をどうやって見分けるか」「簡単さ.スーパーの特急レジで君の前にいる連中さ」)

☞ 君も含めて.express lane は fast lane ともいう.　　★ **Insulting joke** → p. 97

(b) (ばくぜんと) 人を表す

> *Mother:* Were you **the one** who saved my little boy from drowning?
>
> *Lifeguard:* Yes.
>
> *Mother:* (*angrily*) Well, where's his cap?

(母親と海水浴場の監視員の対話:「あなたが私の坊やが溺れるのを救ってくれた方なの」「そうです」(怒って)「じゃあ,坊やの帽子はどこにやってしまったの」)

Q: Two men are in love with me, Murray and George. Who will be the lucky **one**?

A: Murray will marry you. George will be the lucky **one**.

(「2 人の男の人がわたしに恋してるの,マレーとジョージなの.運がいいのは誰かしら」「マレーはきみと結婚するだろう.運がいいのはジョージさ」)

(c) one 〜 the other ...:「1つ [1人] は〜もう1つ [1人] は...」

> "What did **one** ghost say to **the other**?
>
> "Do you believe in people?"

(「1人の幽霊はもう1人に何と言ったか」「人の存在を信じるか」)

He has two sons. **One** is a politician and **the other** isn't very good either.
(彼には息子が2人いる．1人は政治家でもう1人もあまり良くない．)
★ **Insulting joke** → p. 97; **Politician** → p. 329

"Doctor, I have a pain in my left foot."
"Try using **the other**."
(「先生，左足が痛むのですが」「もう片方の足を使ってみなさい」)

(2) another（もう1つ [1人]）; **other(s)**（ほかのもの [人]）

> *Friend:* So sorry I couldn't be present at your party.
> *Movie Actress:* Never mind. I'll have **another** soon.
> (友人「ほんとうにごめんなさい，あなたのパーティーに出られなかったの」映画女優「気にしなくていいわ，すぐまたやるから」)

☞ 結婚披露パーティー？

cf. 形容詞として
You know what's embarrassing! When you look through a keyhole and you see **another** eye.
(何が恥ずかしくて極まりが悪いか分かるだろう．カギ穴を覗くともう1つ別の眼が見えるときさ．)

cf. another＋複数名詞：複数名詞をひとかたまりと見る使い方．
(*Phone from a weight loss camp*)
   Wife: I've lost half my weight in four weeks. Can I stay on?
   Husband: Sure, at least stay on **another** *four weeks*!
((ダイエット・キャンプからの電話) 夫婦の対話：「4週間で体重が半分に減ったわ．このままここにいていいかしら」「もちろんさ．少なくともあと4週間いていいよ」)
☞ weight loss camp = diet camp

cf. some ～ others ...:「～もあれば［いれば］…もある［いる］」

Some people have tact and **others** tell the truth.
（機転のきく人もいれば本当のことを言う人もいる．）

Some girls think those new bathing suits are indecent. **Others** have good figures.
（その新しい水着は下品だと思う女の子たちがいる．スタイルがいい女の子たちもいる．）
☞ スタイルがいい女の子たちは下品だと思わない．

cf. some ～ the others ...:「いくつか［いく人か］は～残りは...」
It's true that all men are born free and equal, but **some** of them get married!
（すべての男性は自由平等に生まれるのは確かだ，しかし結婚する男性もいる．）

Willie: Teachers say we're here to help **others**.
　Pa: Of course we are.
Willie: Well, what are **the others** here for?
（息子と父親の対話：「先生たちはぼくたちは他の人たちを助けるためにこの世にいると言うんだ」「もちろんそうだよ」「じゃあ，残りの人たちはなぜいるの」）

I was once thrown out of a mental hospital. For depressing **the other** patients.　(Oscar Levant)
（私はかつて精神病院から追い出された．残りの患者たちを憂鬱にするという理由で．）
☞ Oscar Levant (1906-1972): アメリカのピアニスト・作家・コメディアン・俳優．

(3) each（それぞれ），**every**（どの～もみな）［every は形容詞用法のみ］

I sent my mother-in-law to the Thousand Islands and suggested she spend a week on **each**!
（義理の母をサウザンドアイランズに送り，1つの島で1週間ずつ過ごしてはどうかと言ったのだ．）
☞ Thousand Islands: アメリカとカナダの国境にある Saint Laurence（セントローレ

ンス）川上流の約 1,500 の島々；避暑地で有名.
★ **Mother-in-law** → p. 305

Doctor: Take three teaspoonfuls of medicine after **each** meal.
Patient: But I've only got two teaspoons.
（医師「毎食後薬を茶さじ3杯飲んでください」患者「でも茶さじが2本しかないんです」）
★ **Irish bull** → p. 39

There is only one beautiful child in the world, and **every** parent has it!
（世界には美しい子供が1人だけいる，そしてどの親にもいるのだ．）

cf. every＋複数名詞：複数名詞をひとかたまりと見る使い方．
Women are around all the time, but the World Cup comes only once in **every** *four years*.　(Peter Osgood)
（女性はいつもその辺にいるが，ワールドカップは4年ごとに1回しか来ない．）
☞ Peter Osgood (1947–2006)：イギリスのサッカー選手．

(4) each other / one another:「お互いを［に］」
代名詞であることに注意．他動詞・前置詞の目的語になるが，主語にはなれない．どちらも区別なく用いられる．

(a) each other

> History repeats itself; historians repeat **each other**.
> 　　　　　　　　　　　　　　　　　　　　　(Phillip Guedalla)
> （歴史は繰り返す．歴史家は互いの言い分を繰り返す．）

★ **One-liner** → p. 395
☞ Phillip Guedalla (1889–1944)：イギリスの法廷弁護士・歴史紀行作家．

There are so few books in our house that if the TV set breaks down, we'll have to talk to **each other**.　(Groucho Marx)
（我が家にはほとんど本がないので，もしテレビがこわれたら，お互い同士しゃべらなけ

ればならなくなる.)
☞ Groucho Marx (1890-1977): アメリカのコメディアン. Marx Brothers (マルクス兄弟) の中心.

(b) one another

If we had no faith in **one another**, all of us would have to live within our incomes.
(お互いを信用しないと,みな収入の範囲内で生活しなければならないだろう.)
☞ 借金ができなくなる.

A lawyer was walking down the street and saw two cars smash into **one another**. Rushing over, he said, "I saw everything and I'll take either side!"
(弁護士が通りを歩いていると2台の車が互いにぶつかるのを見た. 大急ぎで走って行って彼は言った「すべてを見ました, ですからどちらの側にもつきますよ」)
★ **Lawyer** → p. 329

(5) ～thing, ～body [one]

Celebrity match: where **everybody** is **somebody**, so **nobody** is **anybody**.
(有名人競技会:誰もが有名人なので,誰も有名人ではない場所.)

What a strange world! **Everybody** wants to go to Heaven, but **nobody** wants to die!
(何とおかしな世の中だ. 皆が天国へ行きたいのに誰も死にたがらないとは.)

Women tell **everybody** not to tell **anybody**.
(女性は誰にでも誰にも言わないでと言う.)

Anyone who supports capital punishment should be shot.
(Colin Crompton)

(死刑を支持する人はだれでも射殺されるべきだ.)
☞ Colin Crompton (1931-1985): イギリスのコメディアン.

"Who introduced you to your wife?"
"We just met. I can't blame **anyone**."
(「誰が君に奥さんを紹介したんだ」「たまたま会ったのさ. 誰のせいにもできないんだ」)

"How are you doing in school?"
"I'm doing well in **everything** except classes."
(「学校での具合はどうだい」「すべてうまくやってるよ, 授業以外は」)

Mrs Clark went out for the day. She left a note on the door for the milkman.
NOBODY AT HOME―DON'T LEAVE **ANYTHING**.
When she got home the door of the house was open. There was a new note on the door. It said: THANKS. WE HAVEN'T LEFT **ANYTHING**!
(クラーク夫人はその日外出した. ドアに牛乳配達のためにメモを残した. 「家には誰もいません. 何も置いていかないでください」家に帰ってみると家のドアが開いていた. ドアには新しいメモがあった. そこに書かれていたのは「ありがとさん. 何も残さなかったよ」)

(6) both(両方とも), **all**(すべて), **half**(半分), **most**(ほとんど)
いずれも形容詞としても用いられる.

> "Loan me a quarter; I want to call one of my fans."
> "Here's fifty cents. Call **both** of them."
> (「25セント貸してくれ. ファンの1人に電話したいんだ」「50セントある. 両方に掛けろよ」)

☞ どうせファンは2人しかいないだろうから.　★ **Insulting joke** → p. 97

"Will you join me a bowl of soup?"
"Is there enough room for **both** of us?"

(「スープご一緒にいかがですか」「2 人とも入れる余地がありますか」)
☞ join A B:「A を B に加える」

cf. 形容詞としての **both**

"You say your son plays the piano like Paderewski?"
"Yes. He uses **both** hands."
(「息子さんはパデレフスキーのようにピアノを弾くのか」「そうさ．両手を使うぞ」)
☞ Paderewski: ポーランドのピアニスト・作曲家・政治家・外交官．

"I just graduated from skydiving school."
"How many successful jumps did you have to make?"
"**All** of them."
(「スカイダイビングの学校を卒業したところだ」「何回うまく飛ばなくてはならなかったんだい」「全部だ」)
☞ 形容詞としての all については「第 11 章　形容詞」A 2. cf. 参照．

"What is **half** of infinity?"
"nity."
(「無限の半分は」「nity」)
☞ infi＋nity　★ 異分析 → p. 375

cf. 形容詞としての **half**

"Are you saving **half** the money you earn?"
"Naw, I don't earn that much."
(「稼ぐ金を半分貯金しているか」「とんでもない．そんなに稼いでないよ」)

"Doctor, can you give me something for my hands—they are shaking all the time."
"Do you drink a lot?"
"No, doctor, I spill **most** of it."
(「先生，手に効くものをくれませんか．いつも震えているんです」「たくさん飲みますか」「いいえ，先生，ほとんどこぼしてしまいます」)
☞ それを「アル中」という．

cf. 形容詞としての **most**

The one thing that **most** people can do better than anybody else is to read their own writing.
(ほとんどの人が他のだれよりも良くできることの一つは自分の書いたものを読むことだ.)

(7) either, neither（→ 第 19 章 等位接続詞, 第 25 章 否定表現）

> "Which end of the train should I get off?"
> **"Either** will do. It stops at both ends."
> (「列車のどちらの端から降りたらいいでしょうか」「どちらでも大丈夫. 両端とも止まります」)

The boss caught the female filing clerk and the stockboy in the back of the supply closet during a coffee break. Angrily, the boss said, "Explain this."
The filing clerk said, "Well, **neither** of us likes coffee!"
(ボスが書類整理係の女性と在庫品係の若い男がコーヒーブレイクの間に在庫品置き場の裏にいるのを見つけた. 怒ってボスは言った「説明したまえ」女性は答えた「あら, 2人ともコーヒーが嫌いですの」)

ジョークの常識⑨

★ **Light-bulb joke**（電球の取り替え）: ほとんど常に "How many Ss does it take to change a light bulb?" の質問で始まり, それに対する答えが何らかの皮肉, からかいを含んでいる.

> "How many civil servants does it take to change a light bulb?"
> "Twenty-eight. One to change the bulb and twenty-seven to do the paperwork."
> (「電球を取り替えるのに公務員が何人必要か」「28 人. 1 人が電球を取り替え, 27 人がその書類を作る」)

第10章　It の用法

> *Professor:* Oxygen is essential to all animal existence. There could be no life without **it**. **It** was discovered only a century ago.
> *Student:* What did they do before **it** was discovered?
>
> （教授「酸素はすべての動物が生きていくのに欠くことができない．酸素なしでは生命はありえない．酸素はほんの100年前に発見されたばかりです」学生「発見される前はどうしたんですか」）

★ Irish bull → p. 39

A. 普通の用法：先行する語句・内容を受ける it
B. 時間・天候・距離・状況などを表わす it
C. 形式主語としての it
D. 形式目的語としての it：S＋V＋it＋形容詞[名詞]＋to *do* [that ＿＿＿]
E. 強調構文の it is ～ that [who] ＿＿＿

A. 普通の用法：先行する語句・内容を受ける it

> *Father:* Where's tonight's paper?
> *Son:* I wrapped the garbage in **it** and threw **it** out.
> *Father:* I wanted to see **it**.
> *Son:* There wasn't much to see. Only an orange peel, two lamb-chop bones and some coffee grounds.
>
> （父と息子の対話：「夕刊はどこだい」「生ごみを包んですてちゃったよ」「見たかったんだ」「たいして見るものはなかったよ．オレンジの皮1枚と羊のチョップの骨2本とコーヒーのかすだけだもん」）
>
> ☞ it: the garbage ⇔ tonight's paper

"I want you to keep that dog out of the house. **It**'s full of fleas."

"Fido! Don't go in the house. **It**'s full of fleas!"

(「その犬を家に入れないでちょうだい．ノミだらけだから」「ファイドー，家に入っちゃだめよ．ノミだらけだから」)
- ☞ It: that dog ⇔ the house
- ☞ Fido: 犬によくある名前．

"What do you think of my latest sculpture? I'd value your opinion."
"**It**'s useless."
"I know, but I'd like to hear **it** all the same."

(「私の最新の彫刻をどう思う．君の意見を大事にしたいんだ」「無用の長物だよ」「分かってる．でもやはり聞きたいんだ」)
- ☞ It [it]: my latest sculpture（私の最新の彫刻）⇔ your opinion（君の意見）

B. 時間・天候・距離・状況などを表わす it

> When **it** is three o'clock in New York, **it**'s still 1998 in London.
> (Bette Midler)
> (ニューヨークが3時のときロンドンはまだ1998年．)

- ☞ Bette Midler (1945-): アメリカの歌手・女優．

"**It**'s twelve o'clock—You can take care of the restaurant. I'm going out to eat."
"Don't you eat lunch here?"
"Do you think I'm crazy?"

(レストランの店主と店員の対話：「12時だ，店を頼むぞ．外で食事をしてくる」「ここで食べないんですか」「気が狂っているとでも思っているのか」)
- ☞ こんな店で食えるか．

Waiter: Here's your wine, sir.
Diner: Thank you. What year is **it**?
Waiter: **It**'s 2010, sir. **It**'s on the top of all the newspapers.

(ウエイターと客の対話：「ワインでございます，お客様」「ありがとう，何年だね」「2010年でございます．どの新聞でも一番上に出ています」)

☞ What year:「(ワインが) 何年もの」⇔「(今年は) 何年」　　★ **Waiter** → p. 266

The other morning, the garbage truck went past my house and I started chasing it down the street.
"Is **it** too late for garbage?" I shouted. "No," called the garbage man, "jump in!"
(先日の朝, ごみのトラックが家の前を通り過ぎたので, 私は通りを追いかけ始めました.「ごみを出すのもう遅すぎますか」と私は叫びました.「いいや」とごみ集めの人が言いました.「飛び乗んな」)
☞ あんたもごみみたいなもんだ.

Paul: Why did you wake me up? **It**'s still dark.
Saul: Open your eyes, then.
(「なぜ起こしたんだ. まだ暗いじゃないか」「じゃあ目を開けろ」)

Mother: Please close the window, son. **It**'s cold outside.
　Son: If I close the window, will **it** be warm outside?
(母と息子の対話:「窓を閉めておくれ. 外は寒いから」「窓を閉めると外は暖かくなるの」)

"Mammy, why does **it** rain?"
"To make things grow. To give us apples, pears, corn, flowers …"
"Then why does **it** rain on the pavement?"
(「お母さん, なぜ雨が降るの」「物を成長させるためよ. わたしたちに与えてくれるためよ, リンゴやナシやトウモロコシや花や…」「じゃあ, なぜ歩道に降るの」)

"Mummy, I don't want to go to Japan! I like **it** here, in Vancouver."
"Don't talk so much—swim!"
(「お母ちゃん, ぼく日本になんか行きたくない. このバンクーバーが好きなんだ」「そんなにしゃべっちゃだめ, 泳ぎなさい!」)
★ **Tall tale** → p. 412

A mother kangaroo complained to a friend, "I hate **it** when **it**'s raining and the children have to play inside!"

（母親カンガルーが友だちにこぼした「雨降りは大嫌いなの．子供たちが中で遊ばなくてはならないんですもの」）

I don't know how old you are, but you don't look **it**.
（あなたがおいくつかは分かりませんが，どう見てもその歳には見えません．）

I have never been in any situation where having money made **it** worse.　(Clinton Jones)
（金を持っていることが状況を悪化させたような場面にいたことは決してない．）
☞ Clinton Jones (1945-): アメリカンフットボールの選手．

C. 形式主語としての **it**

(1) it is 〜 to *do*:「＿することは〜だ」

> **It is** difficult **to** *see* why lace should be so expensive; it is mostly holes.　(Mary Wilson Little)
> （なぜ（細紐で編んだ）レースがこんなに高価なのかを理解するのは難しい．大部分穴ばかりじゃないの．）

☞ Mary Wilson Little (1944-): アメリカの歌手・ボーカリスト．

It's very easy **to** find something you were not looking for.
　　　　　　　　　　　　　　　　　　　　　　　　(Leo Rosten)
（探していなかったものを見つけるのは非常に簡単だ．）
☞ Leo Rosten (1908-1997): ポーランド出身のアメリカのユダヤ系作家・政治学者・ユーモア作家．
★ **One-liner** → p. 395

It is easy **to** *be* beautiful, if you listen to the TV commercials.
（美しくなるのは簡単だ，テレビのコマーシャルを聴けば．）

It's easy the night before **to** *get* up early the next morning.
（前の晩には翌朝早起きすることは簡単だ．）

Mrs. Mouse was taking her babies out for a little stroll when they were startled by a large cat.

"Bow-wow!" shouted Mrs. Mouse and the cat turned and ran away.

"See, children," said the mother, "how important **it** is **to** *speak* another language!"

(母さんネズミが赤ん坊たちを連れて散歩していると大きなネコに出喰わしてみんなびっくり.「ワンワン」と母さんネズミ. ネコは向きを変えて逃げ去った.「分かるだろう, お前たち, 別の言葉をしゃべることがどんなに大切か」と母さんネズミ.)

I've decided to stop voting. **It**'ll be great not **to** *feel* that I'm responsible for what goes on in Washington.

(投票するのをやめることにした. ワシントンで行われていることに責任があると感じないのはすばらしいことだ.)

(2) it is ～ for ... to *do*:「...が＿することは～だ」

> *Teacher* (looking over Teddy's homework): I don't see how **it**'s possible **for** a single person **to** *make* so many mistakes.
>
> *Teddy* (proudly): It isn't a single person, teacher. Father helped me.
>
> (先生(テディの宿題に目を通しながら)「どうして 1 人でこんなにたくさん間違えられるのか私には分からないわ」テディ(誇らしげに)「先生, 1 人じゃないです. お父さんが手伝ってくれました」)

It's hard **for** a teenager **to** *concede* that someday he'll be as stupid as his father.

(10代にとっていずれは父親と同じように愚かになることを認めるのはむずかしい.)
☞ hard:「むずかしい」⇔「つらい」　　★ **Pun** → p. 26

"Once a friend of mine and I agreed **it** would be helpful **for** us **to** *tell* the other all our faults."

"How did it work?"

"We haven't spoken for five years."

(「かつて友だちと僕はお互い相手の欠点をすべて言い合うのがいいだろうと意見が一致

したんだ」「どんな具合だった」「5年も口をきいていないよ」）

Sunday school teacher asked her young class: "Why **is it** necessary **to** *be* quiet in church?"
One boy answered, "Because people are sleeping."
（日曜学校の先生が幼い生徒たちに尋ねた「なぜ教会では静かにしている必要があるの」
1人の男の子が答えた「みんな眠っているからです」）
★ 教会 → p. 345

(3) **It is ～ of ... to** *do*:「...が__するとは～だ」
　この構文の「～」には人の特定の行為を評価する次のような形容詞がくる．

> brave（勇敢な），careless（不注意な），clever（りこうな），foolish（愚かな），good (=kind)（親切な），kind，nice (=kind)，polite（礼儀正しい），rude（失礼な），silly（ばかな），stupid (=silly)，wise（賢い）　など

> *He* (awkward dancer): **It** was nice **of** you **to** *give* me that dance.
> 　　　*She* (sweetly): Not at all—this is a charity ball.
> （ダンスが下手な男「あのダンスを教えてくれてあなたは優しい人だ」彼女（優しく）
> 「とんでもありませんわ，これって慈善舞踏会ですもの」）

Girl: When we get married, I want to share all your worries and troubles and lighten your burden.
Boy: **It**'s very kind **of** you, darling. But I don't have any worries or troubles.
Girl: Well, that is because we aren't married yet.
（若い2人の対話：「結婚したらあなたの心配や苦労をともにして心の重荷を軽くしてあげたいわ」「ありがとう，きみ．でも僕には心配も苦労もないよ」「あら，それはまだ結婚してないからよ」）

"**It** was grand **of** you **to** *dive* from that height fully clothed, to effect such a magnificent rescue," exclaimed the onlooker, patting the hero.

"That's all very well," replied the hero, "but what I want to know is, who pushed me in?"
(「服を着たままあんな高いところから飛び込んですばらしい救助をなさるとはほんとにご立派です」と見物人が勇士の肩をたたきながら叫んだ.「それはそれでいいんですが」と彼は答えた.「しかし知りたいのは誰が私を突き落としたかです」)

"On your picnic, I thought **it was** very considerate **of** your husband **to** *warn* your mother to stay back from that cliff."
"Mother was carrying the lunch basket."
(「ピクニックでご主人があなたのお母様にあの崖から下がっているように注意されたのはとっても思いやりがおありだと思いましたわ」「母がお弁当の籠を持ってましたの」)
★ **Mother-in-law** → p. 305

"Tell me, my dear, how do you manage to get the maid up so early in the morning?" "**It** was rather clever **of** me. I introduced her to the milkman."
(「おまえ,どうやってうまくお手伝いさんに朝早く起きてもらえるんだい」「ちょっと頭を使ったのよ.牛乳配達の男の子を紹介したの」)

(4) 形式主語 **it is** ～ **(that)** ＿＿＿：「＿＿＿は～だ」（～は形容詞・名詞）

> **It** is true **that** I was born in 1962. And the room next to it was 1963.　(Joan Rivers)
> (わたしが 1962 に生まれたのはほんとうよ. そしてその隣の部屋は 1963 だったわ.)

☞ 1962, 1963: 年号 ⇔ 部屋番号
☞ Joan Rivers (1933-): アメリカのコメディアン・作家・映画監督.

Melba: I can't decide whether to be a palmist or a mind reader.
　Ken: Go to a palmist. **It**'s obvious **that** you have a palm.
(メルバ「手相占い師になるか読心術師になるか決められないの」ケン「手相占いのところへ行きなよ.きみに手のひらがあることは明らかだもん」)
★ **Insulting joke** → p. 97

"Is **it** possible **that** you are teaching the parrot to use slang?"

"No, mama, I was just telling him what not to say."
(「オウムに下品なことばを教えるなんてことしていいと思っているの」「ちがうよ，お母さん，ぼくは何を言っちゃいけないか教えていただけだよ」)

Isn't **it** an amazing contradiction **that** guys will jog ten miles a day and then ride the elevator to the balcony?
(人々が 1 日に 10 マイルジョギングをし，それからバルコニーへエレベーターに乗るのは驚くべき矛盾ではなかろうか．)

cf. that の省略

"Isn't **it** funny, when I stand on my head, the blood rushes to my head, but when I stand on my feet the blood doesn't rush to my feet?"
"Your feet aren't empty."
(「おかしいと思わないか，僕が逆立ちすると血液が頭にどっと流れ込むのに，ふつうに立っていると血液は足に流れ込まないなんて」「君の足は空っぽじゃないんだよ」)
★ **Insulting joke** → p. 97

(5) it takes [costs] 〜 to do 「__するのに〜（時間［費用］）がかかる」

> **It** will **take** time **to** *restore* chaos and order.　(George W. Bush)
> (混沌と秩序を回復するには時間がかかるのです．)

☞ law and order（法と秩序）を言い間違えた．　★ **Bushism** → p. 169
☞ George W. Bush: アメリカの政治家．第 43 代大統領．

It takes twenty years **to** *make* an overnight success.
　　　　　　　　　　　　　　　　　　(Eddie Cantor (attributed.))
(一夜にして成功を収めるには 20 年掛かる．)
☞ Eddie Cantor (1892-1964): アメリカの俳優・コメディアン・ダンサー・歌手・作家．
★ **Irish bull** → p. 39

I won't let my girl go to the movies because every time she sees Robert Redford **it takes** her three or four days *to get* used to me again.
(僕は恋人には映画に行かせないつもりだ，なぜって，彼女，ロバート・レッドフォード

を見るたびに，また僕に慣れるのに 3 日も 4 日もかかるんだ．）

It took me seventeen years *to get* three thousand hits in baseball. I did it in one afternoon on the golf course.　(Henry Aaron)
（野球で 3,000 本安打に達するのに 17 年かかった．それをゴルフコースではある午後 1 回でやりとげた．）
☞　Henry "Hank" Aaron (1934-　):　アメリカメジャーリーグ野球選手．

It takes no brain *to be* idealistic.　(Leo Rosten)
（理想主義者でいるのに頭脳はいらない．）
☞　Leo Rosten (1908-1997):　ポーランド出身のアメリカの（ユーモア）作家．
★ **One-liner** → p. 395

"How much does **it cost** *to get* married, Pop?"
"I don't know. I'm still paying for it."
（「結婚するのにどのくらいかかるの，お父さん」「分からん．まだ払っているんだ」）

The most expensive jewelry is the wedding ring. **It**'s already **cost** me $200 a month alimony.
（最も高価な宝石は結婚指輪だ．すでに月 200 ドルの慰謝料が掛かっている．）

(6) It seems (to ～) that ＿＿:「（～には）＿＿のように思われる」; **It occurs (to ～) that ＿＿:**「～（人）に）ふと＿＿が心に浮かぶ」

"**It seems** that everything I say to you goes in one ear and out the other."
"Well, I guess that's why I've got two ears."
（「わたしがあなたに言うことは全部一方の耳からもう一方の耳へ出ていくようね」「まあ，だから耳が 2 つあるんだと思うよ」）

"**It seems** to me I've seen your face somewhere before."
"How odd!"
"It certainly is."

(「以前どこかであなたの顔を見たような気がします」「変ですね」「確かに変です」)
☞ It は your face と取れる.

It seems as though this year the usual unusual weather has been more unusual than usual.
(今年はいつもの異常な天候がいつもよりもっと異常に思えます.)

A famous scientist had two openings made in the bottom panel of his front door. One was for the "mother cat," the other for the "daughter cat." **It** did not **occur to** him **that** the smaller cat could also have used the larger opening.
(有名な科学者が玄関のドアの一番下の羽目板に2つの出入り口を付けさせた. 1つは母ネコ用, もう1つは娘ネコ用だった. 小さいほうのネコも大きいほうの出入り口を使えたであろうことが彼には思いもよらなかったのだ.)

D. 形式目的語としての it: S＋V＋it＋形容詞[名詞]＋to *do* [that ＿＿]

When I was younger I made **it** a rule **never to take** a strong drink before lunch. It is now my rule never to do so before breakfast.
(Sir Winston Churchill)
(若い頃, 昼食前に強い酒を飲まないことにしていた. 今は朝食前には絶対そうしないことにしている.)

☞ Sir Winston Churchill (1874–1965): イギリスの政治家・首相(1940–45, 1951–55).

I find **it** much easier **to be** a good mum in public.
(人前でいいお母さんでいる方がずっと簡単です.)
(＝ I find (that) it is easier to be a good mum in public.)
★ **One-liner** → p. 395

The purpose of drive-in banks is to make **it** possible **for** cars **to meet** their real owners.
(ドライブイン銀行の目的は車が自分の真の所有者に会うことを可能にすることであ

☞ 車を買うために銀行から借金している → 車の真の所有者は銀行

My wife reads the obituary column and thinks **it** very odd **that** people keep dying in alphabetical order.
(妻は死亡欄を読んで人がアルファベット順に死に続けているのはとても変だと思っている.)

E. 強調構文の **it is** ～ **that [who]** ___:「___ は～だ」(「～」の部分を強調する.)

> *Man in a restaurant:* Waiter, there's a dead fly in my soup!
> *Waiter:* Yes, sir, **it's** *the hot water* **that** kills them.
> (レストランでの対話:「君, スープの中に死んだハエが入っているぞ」「そうなんです, お客さま. ハエは熱湯で死ぬんです」)

★ **Waiter** → p. 266

(1) 語句を強める

> **It's** *not the people who are in prison* **that** worry me; **it's** *the people who aren't.*　(Arthur Gore)
> (心配なのは刑務所に入っている人たちではない, 入っていない人たちだ.)

☞ Arthur Gore (1868-1928): イギリスの男子テニス選手.

Augusta and Brenda, both nine, were sitting beside each other.
"Don't you just hate this long bus ride to school every morning?" asked Augusta.
"Oh, I don't mind the bus ride," replied Brenda. "**It's** *getting there* **that** I don't like."
(9歳のオーガスタとブレンダが隣り合って座っていた.「毎朝学校へこんなに長い間バスに乗ってるのいやにならないの」とオーガスタ.「バスに乗るのは平気よ」とブレンダ.「わたしがいやなのはバスが学校に着くことなの」)

Don't worry, I can keep a secret. **It's** *the people I tell it to* **who** can't.
（心配しないで．私は秘密を守れるわ．守れないのは私がそれを教えた人たちよ．）

Absent-minded professor (to ex-student): Remind me, **was it** *you or your brother* **who** was killed in the war?
（心ここにあらずの教授が以前の教え子に「思い出したが，戦死したのは君だったかね君の兄弟だったかね」）
★ **Absent-minded professor** → p. 320

cf. that を省略することもある．（/ は that が省略されている位置）
My job is very secure—**it's** *me* / they can do without.
（私の仕事は極めて安全だ．私がいなくても彼らは困らないのだ．）

I love mankind; it's *people* / I can't stand.　　(Charles Schulz)
（ぼくは人類を愛している．我慢ならないのは（周りの）人たちだ．）
☞ Charles Schulz (1922-2000): アメリカの漫画家．

(2) 節を強める

It is *after you have lost your teeth* **that** you can afford to buy steaks.
　　　　　　　　　　　　　　　　　　　　　　　　(Pierre Renoir)
（ステーキを買う余裕ができるのは歯を失くしてしまった後である．）

☞ Pierre Renoir (1841-1919): フランス印象派の画家．

It's *only when the tide goes out* **that** you learn who's been swimming naked.　　(Warren Buffett)
（潮が引いて初めて誰が真っ裸で泳いでいたかが分かる．）
☞ Warren Buffett (1930-): アメリカの投資家・経営者．

cf. that を省略することもある．（/ は that が省略されている位置）
Sister Peters says that newborn babies mostly sleep well. **It** is *only when they get home* / they start bawling their heads off.
　　　　　　　　　　　　　　　　　　　　　　　　(Elizabeth Jolly)

（シスターのピーターズさんは生れたばかりの赤ん坊はたいていよく眠ると言います．しかし赤ん坊は家に帰って初めて大声で泣き始めるのです．）

☞ Elizabeth Jolly (1923-2007): イギリス生まれのオーストラリアの作家．

(3) 疑問詞を強める

"*What* **is it that** the person who makes does not need, the person who buys does not use, and the person who uses does so without knowing it?"

"A coffin."

（「作る人には必要がなく，買う人は使わず，使う人はそれと知らずに使うものは」「棺桶」）

★ **Riddle** → p. 64

"*Why* **is it that** you are late this morning?" the clerk was asked by his manager.

"I overslept," was the reply.

"What? So you sleep at home as well?" inquired the manager.

（「今朝はなぜ遅刻したんだね」店員が支配人に聞かれた．「寝坊です」と彼は答えた．「何だと．じゃあ 君は家でも寝るのかね」と支配人．）

How **is it that** a man push a lawnmower for an hour and call it work, and when he pushes a golf cart all day he calls it a recreation?

（人が芝刈り機を1時間押すとそれを仕事と呼び，ゴルフ・カートを1日中押してもレクリエーションと呼ぶのは一体どうしてなのか．）

第10章　It の用法

> **ジョークの常識⑩**

★ **What's-the-difference joke**

　AとBの違いというとき，それは何らかの共通点をもつもの同士を比較して違いを明らかにすることである．しかしこのタイプのジョークは普通似ても似つかぬものを比較するもので，その答えがほとんど語頭音転換（Spoonerism（→ p.422）という）の Pun（駄じゃれ）になっている．

"What is the difference between a mouse and a beautiful girl?"
"The mouse harms the cheese and the girl charms the he's."
(「ハツカネズミと美少女の違いは何か」「ハツカネズミはチーズを傷つけ，少女は男の子を魅了する」)
☞ *h*arms [hɑːrmz] ⇔ *ch*arms [tʃɑːrmz]; *ch*eese ⇔ *h*e's（he（男（の子））の複数形）の駄じゃれ．

"What is the difference between a super policeman and a traffic light?"
"One is a star copper; the other is a car stopper."
(「スーパー警官と交通信号の違いは何か」「一方はスター警官，もう一方は車止め」)
☞ *st*ar（花形）⇔ *c*ar（車）; *c*opper（((俗語)) 警官）⇔ *st*opper（止めるもの［人］）の駄じゃれ．

第11章　形 容 詞

The man who first called it the 'easy' payment plan was mighty careless with his **adjectives**.
（それを「楽な」支払い計画と最初に呼んだ人は形容詞の扱いがひどく不注意だった．）

☞ easy payment plan:「分割払い」

Weather forecast for tonight: **dark**.　(George Carlin)
（今夜の天気予報：「暗い」）

☞ George Carlin (1937-2008): アメリカのコメディアン．

> 形容詞は主として名詞の前に置いてその名詞を修飾する用法（**A. 限定用法**）と文の中で補語として働く用法（**B. 叙述用法**）をもつ．ほとんどの形容詞が **-er**, **-est**，または **more**, **most** をつけて，それぞれ比較級・最上級を作る．
> （→ 第24章 比較表現）

A. 限定用法

English is a **funny** language. A **fat** chance and a **slim** chance are the **same** thing.　(Jack Herbert)
（英語はおかしな言語だ．太ったチャンスとやせたチャンスが同じことなのだ．）

☞ a fat chance = a slim chance:「わずかな見込み」
☞ Jack Herbert: 経歴不詳．

(1) 形容詞の位置：ふつう修飾する名詞の前に置かれる．

"How can you win a **small** fortune in Las Vegas?"
"Spend a **large** fortune."
（「ラスベガスで小金を儲けるにはどうすればいい」「大金を使うことさ」）

Sign on an Antique Shop: Stop in and see our **new old** stuff.
(骨董店の掲示：立ち寄って新しい古い物をご覧ください．)
★ **Irish bull** → p. 39

"Oh, I finally found a **perfect** doctor. Every time I go to him, he finds *something* **wrong** with me."
(「やっと申し分のない医者を見つけた．診てもらいに行くたびにどこかおかしいところを見つけてくれる」)

cf. 上例のように *some*thing, *some*body などを修飾する形容詞は後ろに置かれる．
  Driver: What do I do if the brakes suddenly fail?
 Mechanic: Hit *something* **cheap**.
(運転者「ブレーキが急に効かなくなったらどうすればいい」修理工「何か安いものにぶつかることです」)

Some persons never say *anything* **bad** about the dead—or *anything* **good** about the living.
(死んだ人については決して悪口を言わない，あるいは，生きている人については決してほめない人もいる．)

The best thing about reincarnation is that everybody used to be *somebody* **famous**!
(生まれ変わりの最も良い点はみな誰でもかつては有名人だったことである．)

For her birthday, a wife told her husband that she wanted him to take her *somewhere* **expensive**. So he took her to the local gas station.
(自分の誕生日に，妻が夫にどこか値段の高い所へ連れて行ってほしいと言った．そこで彼は妻を地元のガソリンスタンドへ連れて行った．)

(2) 形容詞の語順：形容詞が2つ以上名詞の前に置かれるときは，原則として次の順になる．

判断を示す語*＋大小・長短・形状＋色（＋分詞形容詞**）
---

*expensive（高価な），good（良い），pretty（かわいい），useful（役に立つ），valuable（貴重な）などの「主観的判断を表す形容詞」
** exci**ting**（興奮させる），exci**ted**（興奮した）のような現在分詞，過去分詞が形容詞として使われるもの（→C. -ing / -ed で終わる形容詞）

Mr Goldsmith was shopping in an **expensive London** store. He was talking to a **young male shop** assistant. "I want something **unusual** to give my **beautiful eighteen-year-old** daughter for her birthday." The young man thought for a second, then said, "Here's my phone number, sir!"
（ゴールドスミス氏はロンドンの高級店で買い物をしていた．彼は若い男子店員に話しかけていた．「美人の 18 になる娘の誕生日に何か風変わりなものがほしいのだが」若い店員はちょっと考えて言った「これが私の電話番号です，お客様」）

You know that **little indestructible black** box that is used on planes? Why can't they make the **whole** plane out of the **same** substance?
（飛行機で使われているあの小さい壊れない黒い箱を知ってるだろう．なぜ飛行機全体を同じ物質で作れないんだ．）
☞ black box ＝ flight recorder（フライトレコーダー）

cf. 形容詞 **all** の位置：the，所有格，独立所有格［所有代名詞］の前

America is the only nation in the world where *all* *our* poor people are fat. （Al Franken）
（アメリカは世界で唯一貧しい人たちがみな太っている国である．）
☞ Al Franken (1951-)：アメリカの政治家・政治評論家・コメディアン・作家．

A rich uncle died, and a line in his will read as follows: "I leave to my beloved nephew **all** *the* money he owes me."
（金持ちの伯父が死んだ，そして遺言の一行は次のようになっていた「愛する甥（おい）に私に借りている金を全額残してやる」）

Money talks—**all** *mine* says is 'Goodbye!'
(金は物を言う．私の金は全部「さよなら」と言う．)
★ **Parody** → p. 199

(3) 形容詞的名詞：「名詞＋名詞」で前の名詞が形容詞の役割をする．

> *Customer:* I want to buy a mirror.
> *Shopkeeper:* A **hand** mirror?
> *Customer:* No, I want to see my face.
> (客「鏡を買いたいんです」店主「手鏡ですか」「いいえ，顔を見たいんですの」)

Sister: I've made the **chicken** soup.
Brother: Thank goodness for that. I thought it was for us!
(姉と弟の対話：「チキンスープを作ったわよ」「ああよかった．僕たちが食べるのかと思ったよ」)
☞ make the chicken soup:「チキンスープを作る」(V+O) ⇔「鶏にスープを作ってやる」(V+O+O)

Lady: My pet is sick. Can you recommend a good **animal** doctor?
Nurse: I'm sorry, lady, all the doctors I know are people.
(婦人と看護師の対話：「ペットが病気なの，よい動物のお医者さんを教えてくれませんか」「申し訳ありません．私の知っているお医者様はみな人間です」)
☞ animal doctor:「獣医」⇔「動物の医者」
☞「名詞＋名詞」の表現の間には修飾語を入れない．an animal *good* doctor とはならない．

(4) 名詞の前にのみ用いる形容詞

> **minor**（より小さい），**major**（より大きい），**only**（唯一の），**chief**（主な），**main**（主要な），**wooden**（木製の）など

> Earth: a **minor** planet with **major** problems.
> (地球：大問題を抱えた小惑星．)

Clergyman: Ah! How are you, Mr. Jones? And is this your most charming wife?
Jones: This is my **only** wife.
(牧師「ああ，ジョーンズさん，お元気ですか．この方があなたのとても魅力的な奥様ですか」ジョーンズ「これは私のたった一人の妻です」)
☞ most:「まことに（＝very）」⇔「（最上級を作って）最も」

The **chief** business of the American people is business.
（アメリカ人の主要なビジネスはビジネスである．）

The **main** reason people drive more than they once did is because it is cheaper to drive than park.
（人々が昔より車を運転する主な理由は駐車するより運転するほうが安上がりだからだ．）

Fred: There is a man outside with a **wooden** leg named Martin.
Jed: What is the name of the other leg?
（「マーチンという名前の木の義足の人が外にいるよ」「もう一方の脚は何という名だ」）
☞ a man named Martin（マーチンという名の男）⇔ a wooden leg named Martin（マーチンという名の木の義足）

B. 叙述用法

(1) 次の2つの文型で，動詞の補語（C）になる．（→第4章　5文型）

(a) S+V+**C**

It's always **good** when the TV weatherman is **pessimistic** about the weather. People feel so **good** when he's **wrong**.
（天気予報官が天候について悲観的であることは常に良いことだ．予報がはずれると人々は非常に良い気分になる．）

(b) S+V+O+**C**

"What do you use for washing dishes?"
"Oh, I tried many things, but found my husband **best**."

(「お皿を洗うのに何を使うの」「いろいろ試したけど夫が最高だと分かったわ」)

(2) 名詞の前に用いない形容詞

> **(a) alive**（生きて）, **asleep**（眠って）, **awake**（目が覚めて）, **content**（満足して）, **afraid**（恐れて）, **ashamed**（恥じて）など

> "Say Harry, are you **awake**? There's a burglar downstairs."
> "No, I'm **asleep**!"
> (「ねえ，ハリー，起きてるの．下に泥棒がいるわ」「いや，眠ってるよ」)

Do not take life too seriously; you will never get out of it **alive**.
(Elbert Hubbard)
(人生をあまり真面目に考えすぎるな．生きて脱出することは決してないのだから．)
☞ Elbert Hubbard (1856-1915)：アメリカの作家・画家・哲学者．

We call our baby "Coffee" because he keeps us **awake** all night.
(私たちが赤ん坊を「コーヒー」と呼んでいるのは一晩中眠れないからだ．)

Most persons are **content** with what they have, but they are not **content** with what they don't have.
(ほとんどの人は自分の持っているもので一応満足しているが自分の持っていないものには満足していない．)

A friend of mine was **afraid** of flying. So he went by boat—and a plane fell on it.
(友だちの1人は飛行機を怖がっていた．だから船で行った，そして飛行機が船の上に落ちた．)

Juggler: **Are**n't you **afraid to** put your hand in the lion's mouth?
Lion tamer: Yes. I'**m afraid of** the dark.
(ジャグラー「手をライオンの口の中へ突っ込むのは怖くないのか」ライオン使い「怖い

さ.暗闇が怖いんだ」)

"Your son is making good progress with his violin. He is beginning to play quite nice tunes."
"Do you really think so? We **were afraid that** we'd merely got used to it."
(「息子さんのバイオリンはずいぶん上達していますね.ほんとに良い音色を出し始めていますよ」「本当にそう思いますか.私たちはただあれに慣れただけだと心配していたんです」)

My wife must really **be ashamed of** my looks. For Christmas, she knitted me a turtleneck sweater with no hole!
(妻は私の顔をほんとうに恥ずかしく思っているに違いない.クリスマスに穴のないタートルネックのセーターを編んでくれた.)
★ **Tall tale** → p. 412

(b) be＋形容詞＋to do など:**glad**(喜んで),**likely**(＿しそうで),**ready**(準備ができた),**sorry**(気の毒で),**sure**(確信して),**willing**(＿する用意がある)など.
　cf. (a)とは異なり名詞の前に用いることもある.

"Did the new play have a happy ending?"
"Sure, everybody **was glad** it was over."
(「新しい芝居はハッピーエンドだったかい」「そうさ.みんな終わって喜んでたよ」)

"I'm **glad** I wasn't born in France."
"Why?"
"I can't speak French."
(「フランスで生まれなくてよかったよ」「なぜだい」「フランス語をしゃべれないんだ」)
★ **Irish bull** → p. 39

Some fellows will **be glad to** show you how to get rich, if you'll only lend them a pencil.
（鉛筆を1本貸してやりさえすれば，金持ちになる法を喜んで教えてくれる連中がいる．）
☞ 財テクコンサルタントのような．

"I can't marry you as I don't love you, but I will be a sister to you."
"Fine. How much do you think our father **is likely to** leave us?"
（「愛していないからあなたと結婚はできないわ，でもあなたの妹にならなってもいいわ」「いいとも，ところでぼくたちのおやじさんはいくら残してくれそうだと思う」）

A patriot **is** always **ready to** lay down your life for his country.
（愛国者は国のためにいつでも進んで君の命を投げ出すのだ．）
★ **One-liner** → p. 395

"**I'm sorry to** disturb you at two o'clock in the morning, doctor."
"Oh, that's all right. I had to get up to answer the telephone!"
（「先生，夜中の2時にご迷惑を掛けて申し訳ありません」「いいんですよ．電話に出るのに起きなければならなかったんですから」）
★ **Irish bull** → p. 39

Mother Pig: Why do you want to be a football when you grow up?
　Little Pig: They'll **be sure to** pass me when I go to college.
（母豚「なぜ大きくなったらフットボールになりたいの」子豚「大学へ行くときっとぼくを合格させてくれるからだよ」）
☞ ボールは豚の皮製．pass：「合格させる」⇔「（ボールを）パスする」
★ **Pun** → p. 26

She took her husband to the psychiatrist. "He says he is suffering from hallucinations, but **I'm sure** he is only imagining it," she said.
（彼女は夫を精神科医へ連れて行った．「主人は幻覚に苦しんでいると言うんです．でもわたくし主人はきっとただそう思っているだけだと思いますわ」と彼女は言った．）
☞ それを幻覚という．

cf. 限定用法

There's only one **sure** cure for snoring—insomnia.
(いびきの確実な治し方が一つだけある—不眠症だ.)

Aren't they a lovely couple? He**'s willing to** die for her and she**'s willing to** let him.
(彼らはすてきな夫婦じゃないか. 彼は奥さんのために死んでもいいと思っているし, 奥さんはそうすればいいと思っているんだから.)

cf. (a) 限定用法 と **(b)** 叙述用法では意味の異なる形容詞

> **certain** ((a) ある；(b) 確かな), **late** ((a) 前の；(b) 遅い), **present** ((a) 現在の；(b) 出席して)

"A **certain** young man sent me some flowers this morning."
"Don't say 'a **certain** young man,' my dear. There is none of them **certain** until you've got them."
(「ある若い男の人が今朝わたしに花を送ってくれたわ」「おまえ,「確かな男の人」なんて言ってはダメ. おまえが手に入れるまでは確かな若い男性なんて誰もいないのよ」)
☞ certain:（名詞の前に置いて）「ある」⇔「確かな」　★ **Pun** → p. 26

"Were you in the **late** war?"
"Yeah, I was two years **late**."
(「この前の戦争で戦ったのか」「そうさ, 2年遅れたがね」)
☞ late:「（名詞の前に置いて）前の, この前の」⇔「遅い, 遅れて」　★ **Pun** → p. 26

"There's something wrong with **present**-day marriage."
"How's that?"
"The best man doesn't get the bride."
(「今時の結婚はどこかおかしいよ」「またどうして」「最良の男が花嫁を手に入れられないんだぞ」)
☞ present:「（名詞の前に置いて）現在の」
☞ the best man:「最良の男」⇔「（結婚式の）新郎の付き添い役」　★ **Pun** → p. 26

"You are called as a witness of the quarrel between your friend and his wife. Were you **present** at the beginning of the trouble?"
"Certainly! I was a witness at the wedding."
(「あなたはお友だちとその奥さんの間の口論の証人として呼ばれています．もめごとの始まりに立ち会っていましたか」「もちろんです．結婚式に立ち会っていました」)
☞ present:「出席して」

C. -ing / -ed で終わる形容詞：現在分詞・過去分詞が形容詞として使われるもの．-ing は「＿させる」，-ed は「＿される」の意味になる．

"Why are you looking so **depressed**?"
"I've just been to the doctor and he told me I would have to take a pill every day for the rest of my life."
"Why is that so **depressing**?"
"He only gave me twenty-five pills."
(「なぜそんなに落ち込んだ顔をしてるんだい」「ちょうど医者へ行ってきたんだが，医者はこれから一生毎日薬を1錠飲まなければならないだろうと言うんだ」「それがなぜ君を落ち込ませるんだい」「25錠しかくれなかったからさ」)

"I was extremely **embarrassed** yesterday. I called my wife Sue."
"What's **embarrassing** about that?"
"Her name's Edwina!"
(「昨日はまったく恥ずかしかったよ．妻をスーと呼んでしまったんだ」「その何が恥ずかしいんだ」「妻の名はエドウィナなんだ」)

What a wonderful wedding! The bride looked **stunning** and the groom looked **stunned**!
(何とすばらしい結婚式だったことか．花嫁は驚くほど美しく見え，花婿はただただ驚いているようだった．)

In the old days, if a person missed the stagecoach, he was content to wait a day or two for the next one. Nowadays, we feel **frustrated** if

we miss one section of a revolving door.
(むかし，駅馬車に乗りそこなうと次のが来るまで 1 日 2 日文句も言わずに待ったものだった．今では回転ドアの1区画に入りそこねてもいらいらする．)

D. 数量形容詞：**many, few; much, little; some, any**

cf. 単独で名詞として用いられることも多い．

◆ **many, much, few, little** の用法と意味

意味＼用法	①「数えられる名詞」につけて「数」を表す． ② 名詞の複数形につく．	①「数えられない名詞」につけて「量」「程度」を表す． ② 名詞の単数形につく．
たくさんの	many	much
ほとんど〜ない（否定的）	few	little
少しの（肯定的）	a few	a little
少なくない	not a few / quite a few	not a little / quite a little

To **many** girls, the word "marriage" has a nice ring to it.
(多くの若い女性にとって「結婚」という言葉は素敵な指輪を伴っている．)

☞ ring「指輪」⇔「響き」　★ **Pun** → p. 26

Strange that **some** of us are satisfied with so **little** in ourselves but demand so **much** from others.
(自分のことではほんのわずかなものでも満足するのに，他人からはあまりにも多くを要求する人たちがいるのは不思議だ．)

(1) a few, few; a little, little

The psychiatric nurse said she considered the world to be like a fruit cake ... incomplete without **a few** nuts.
(精神科の看護師は世の中はフルーツケーキのようだと思うと言った...ナッツが少し

入っていないと不完全だと.）

☞ nut(s):「（硬い）木の実」⇔「変人，奇人」　　★ **Pun** → p. 26

Inspector: How many teachers work at this school?
　Pupil: Very **few**!
（指導主事「この学校では何人の先生が働いているのかな」生徒「ほとんどいません」）

Few women admit their age. **Few** men act theirs.
（自分の年齢を認める女性はほとんどいない．年齢相応に行動する男性はほとんどいない．）

cf. quite a few は「（かなり）多くの」
"There were **quite a few** cakes in the cupboard last night when I went out. Now there's only one left. Why is that, John?"
"I didn't put the light on so I missed it!"
（「夕べ出かけるときには食器戸棚にかなりたくさんケーキがあったのに，今は 1 つしか残ってないわ．なぜなの，ジョン」「電気をつけなかったんで見落としたんだ」）

Carol is sitting alone in a restaurant. A man leaves his table and comes over to her table.
"Would you like **a little** company?"
"Why? Do you have one to sell?"
（キャロルはレストランに一人で座っている．男がテーブルを離れ彼女のテーブルにやって来る．「ちょっとご一緒してよろしいですか」「なぜですの．お売りになるのですか」
☞ company:「同席」⇔「会社」　　★ **Pun** → p. 26

Colleges are a storehouse of knowledge, but that's because the students take so **little** of it out!
（大学は知識の倉庫だ，しかしそれは学生がそこからほとんど何も持ち出さないからだ．）
☞ だから知識がどんどんたまる．
☞ **few**, **little** →「第 25 章　否定表現」(9) 準否定

(2) many, much

"Why are **many** artists Italian?"
"I don't know."
"Because they were born in Italy!"
(「なぜ多くの画家がイタリア人なのか」「さあ」「イタリア生まれだからさ」)

"Why were the early days of history called the Dark Ages?"
"Because there were so **many** knights."
(「なぜ歴史の初期の時代が暗黒時代と呼ばれたのですか」「あまりにも多くの騎士がいたからです」)
☞ knight [nait]（騎士）⇔ night [nait]（夜）　　★ **Pun** → p. 26

"Taxi driver, I haven't got **much** money. What's the fare to the railway station?"
"Five pounds, sir."
"Oh! And how **much** for my large suitcase?"
"Fifty pence, sir."
"Right. Take my suitcase to the station. I'll walk."
(「運転手さん，お金をあまり持っていないんだ．駅までいくらだい」「5ポンドです」「おおそうかい．じゃあこの大きなスーツケースはいくらだい」「5ペンスです」「よし．スーツケースを駅へ運んでくれたまえ．私は歩く」)

A sharp nose indicates curiosity. A flattened nose indicates too **much** curiosity.
(とがった鼻は好奇心を示す．ぺちゃんこの鼻は過剰な好奇心を示す．)
☞ 殴られてぺちゃんこになっている．

I read this article. It said the typical symptoms of stress are eating too **much**, smoking too **much**, impulse buying, and driving too fast. Are they kidding? This is my idea of a great day!　(Monica Piper)
(こんな記事を読んだわ．ストレスの典型的な兆候は食べ過ぎ，吸い過ぎ，衝動買い，車のスピードの出し過ぎ，とあったの．冗談でも言ってるの．これこそ私がすばらしい一

日だと思うことよ.)
☞ Monica Piper: アメリカのコメディアン・作家.

慣用表現

many a ～:「(単数扱いで) 多くの」(「many＋複数名詞」に比べて多数の中の個々を強調する.)

　Many a man has lost his best friend by marrying her!
　(多くの男が親友と結婚して親友を失うのだ.)

(3) some, any: some は肯定文に, any は疑問文・否定文に用いるのが原則.

> "Waiter, I'd like **some** coffee. Why isn't there **any** on the menu?"
> "Because I wiped it off."
> (「君,コーヒーが欲しいんだが.なぜメニューにないんだね」「拭き取ったからです」)

☞ on the menu:「メニューに載って」⇔「メニューの上にこぼれて」
★ Waiter → p. 266

"Do you have **any** cheap rooms?"
"Sure, but you have to make your own bed."
"I'll take one!"
"Right. Here's a hammer, **some** nails and **some** wood."
(「安い部屋があるかね」「ありますとも,でもベッド・メークはご自分でお願いします」「それにするよ」「結構です.金づちとクギと板をどうぞ」)

"Doctor, I need **some** advice. I seem to get fat in certain places. What can I do?"
"Stay away from those places!"
(「先生,ご意見をいただきたいんですの.ある場所が太ってきているようなんです.どうしたらいいでしょうか」「その場所から離れていることです」)

"I've got **some** good news for you, Mrs Smith."
"It's Miss Smith, doctor."
"Well, Miss Smith. I've got **some** bad news for you."

(「スミス夫人，良いお知らせがあります」「スミス嬢です，先生」「では，スミス嬢，悪いお知らせがあります」)

"Have you got **any** brothers?"
"No, but my sister does."
(「兄弟はいるの」「いえ，いません．でも妹にはいます」)

"Now, class, are there **any** questions?"
"Yes, where do these words go when you rub them off the blackboard?"
(「みなさん，何か質問がありますか」「はい，黒板から消してしまうとこの単語たちはどこへ行くんですか」)

A man goes up to a politician at a party and says, "I've heard a lot about you." The politician replies, "But you can't prove **any** of it."
(男がパーティーで政治家のところへ行き「あなたのことはたくさん聞いています」と言う．政治家は答える「しかしそのどれも証明できないでしょう」)
☞ 政治家は証明できない汚職に励む． ★ **Politician** → p. 329

cf. 肯定文の中の **any**:「どんな〜でも，だれでも」
Two small boys were discussing the capabilities of their mothers, who were active members.
"My mother can talk on just about **any** subject," one lad declared proudly.
"Aw, shucks," retorted the other, "My mother can talk without **any** subject at all."
(2人の少年が活動的な会員である母親の能力について話し合っていた．「お母さんはまったくどんな話題でも話せるよ」と1人が誇らしげに断言した．「ちぇっ，バカな」ともう1人が言い返した．「ぼくのお母さんなんか全然話題がなくても話せるさ」)

"Why don't you go to a lawyer?"
"My brother said **any** fool could advise me—so I came to you."
(「弁護士のところへ行けばいいじゃないか」「兄がどんなバカでも僕にアドバイスできる

と言ったんだ，だから君のところへ来たんだよ」)
★ **Insulting joke** → p. 97

Any man who thinks he's more intelligent than his wife is married to a smart woman.
(妻より自分の方が頭がいいと思っているどんな男も頭の良い妻と結婚している．)
★ **One-liner** → p. 395

ジョークの常識⑪

★ **Bushism**（ブッシュ語法）:「アメリカ合衆国第 43 代大統領 George W. Bush の非慣用的・非文法的表現」Irish bull（→ p. 39），Boner（→ p. 46）の一種．

"Rarely is the question asked: *Is* our children learning?"
(めったにされない質問は「家の子供たちは学んでいるか」だ．)

"Laura and I really don't realize how bright our children *is* sometimes until we get an objective analysis."
(ローラと私には家の子供たちがときどきどれほど頭がいいかは客観的な分析を得るまでは本当のところは分からない．)
☞ 上の2つの例からブッシュ氏は children が単数だと思っているらしいことが分かる．

"They misunderestimated me."（彼らは私を低く評価しそこなった．)
☞ misunderestimate という英語の単語はない．

It is no exaggeration to say that the undecideds could go one way or the other.
(決心のついていない連中はどっちにでも行きかねないというのは誇張ではない．)
☞ undecided は形容詞としてはあるが名詞としてはない．the undecided＝undecided people のつもりだったと思われる．cf. the＋形容詞＝複数の人

第 12 章　冠　詞

To use "**a**" or "**the**"; that is the question.
(「a」を使うか「the」を使うか,それが問題だ.)

冠詞には**不定冠詞**(**a, an**)と**定冠詞**(**the**)がある.

(1) In April, I introduced **the** coach of my tennis club to **an** ex-wife of my brother, and by June the two were already married.
(2) In April, I introduced **a** coach of my tennis club to **the** ex-wife of my brother, and by June the two were already married.
(4月に,私のテニスクラブのコーチを弟の離婚した妻に紹介したが,6月になったら,2人はもう結婚していた.)
　　　　　　　　　　(マーク・ピーターセン (1988)『日本人の英語』(岩波書店))

☞ (1) テニスクラブのコーチは1人;弟は少なくとも2度離婚している.
　　(2) テニスクラブのコーチは2人以上いる;弟は1度離婚している.

A. 不定冠詞:**a / an**

Teacher: Don't use '**a**' before a plural. Don't say '**a** books.'
Patrick: But, miss, the minister always says, '**A**-men!'
(先生「複数形の前に a を使ってはいけません.a books と言ってはいけません」パトリック「でも,先生,牧師さんはいつも A-men とおっしゃいます」)

☞ amen [èimén / àːmén]:「(キリスト教) ((間投詞)) アーメン」

"What did you get for Christmas?"
"**A** harmonica. It's the best present I ever got."
"Why?"
"My mom gives me **a** quarter **a** week not to blow it."

(「クリスマスに何をもらったの」「ハーモニカさ. 今までで最高のプレゼントだよ」「なぜだい」「母さんはそれを吹かないようにって週に 25 セントくれるんだ」)

不定冠詞は次のような場合に用いられる：
- **(1)** 初めて話題にのぼる単数名詞の前
- **(2)** 一般的な意味での人〔物〕
- **(3)** 「1 人の／1 つの」
- **(4)** 「～につき」
- **(5)** 固有名詞につく場合

---

(1) 初めて話題にのぼる単数名詞の前

A teenage girl was taking singing lessons and was practicing at home. Her younger brother said, "Sis, I wish you'd only sing Christmas carols." "Why?" she asked. "Then you'd only have to sing once a year."
(10 代の娘が歌のレッスンを受けていて家で練習していた. 弟が言った「姉さん, クリスマス・キャロルだけを歌ってくれたらいいなあ」「なぜ」「そうすれば, 1 年に 1 回歌えばすむじゃないか」)

An Albertan visited the Eiffel Tower. The first question he asked the tour guide was: "How many barrels a day do you get out of her?"
((カナダの) アルバータ州の男がエッフェル塔へ行った. ガイドに最初に聞いた質問は「あそこから日に何バレル取れるんだい」だった.)
☞ Albertan: カナダ, アルバータ州の人. アルバータ州は石油産業で知られる.

cf. a か an か： **a** は子音で始まる語の前に, **an** は母音で始まる語の前に置く. (綴り字とは無関係)

Once I thought I saw **a** UFO but it turned out I just rubbed my eyes too hard.　(Midge Pinciotti)
(かつて私は UFO を見たと思ったがただ眼を強くこすり過ぎただけだと判明した.)
☞ UFO [jùːefóu / júːfou]: U [juː]は子音で始まる.
☞ Midge Pinciotti: アメリカテレビネットワーク Fox の連続ホームコメディーの主人

公の 1 人.

An X-ray specialist married one of his patients. Everybody wondered what he saw in her.
（X 線の専門医が患者と結婚した．みんな彼女の中に何が見えたのかしらと思った．）
☞ X [eks] は母音で始まる．

(2) 一般的な意味での人［物］

A woman is always buying something.　(Ovid)
（女はいつも何か買い物をしている．）

☞ Ovid (43 B.C. – A.D. 17?): 古代ローマの詩人．

To remain **a** woman's ideal, **a** man must die a bachelor.
（女性の理想であり続けるには，男は独身で死なねばならない．）

A leader is a dealer in hope.　(Napoleon Bonaparte)
（指導者は希望のディーラーだ．）
☞ dealer in ～ ＜ deal in ～「～（商品）を扱う」; leader [líːdər] ⇔ dealer [díːlər]
★ **Pun** → p. 26
☞ Napoleon Bonaparte (1769–1821): フランス第一帝政の皇帝（在位 1804–1814）

(3)「1 人の／1 つの」

Statistics show that every four seconds **a** woman gives birth to **a** baby. Our problem is to find this woman and stop her.
（統計は 4 秒ごとに 1 人の女性が赤ん坊を 1 人産むことを示している．問題はこの女性を見つけてやめさせることである．）

★ **Irish bull** → p. 39

"Waiter, waiter, there's **a** hair in my sandwich."
"Don't shout, sir, or everyone will want one."
（「君，サンドイッチに髪の毛が 1 本入ってるぞ」「叫ばないでください，お客さま，みな

　　　　　　　　第12章　冠　詞

さん欲しがります」)
☞ 髪の毛もたんぱく質.　★ **Waiter** → p. 266

(4)「～につき」

> We were so poor I bought one shoe at **a** time.
> (私たちは非常に貧しかったので一度に片方ずつ靴を買ったほどです.)

★ **Tall tale** → p. 412

If you work eight hours **a** day faithfully, you can become the boss and works sixteen hours **a** day!
(1日8時間忠実に仕事をすればボスになれて1日16時間働くことになる.)

　　Woman: How much do you charge for taking children's photographs?
Photographer: Ten dollars **a** dozen.
　　Woman: I'll have to come back later. So far, I only have ten.
(写真屋と女性の対話:「子供たちの写真を撮るのはおいくらですか」「12枚で10ドルです」「あとで来なきゃいけませんわ. 今のところ, 10人しかいませんから」)
★ **Irish bull** → p. 39

(5) 固有名詞につく場合（→「第8章　名詞」C (7) 固有名詞の普通名詞化）

> I can't afford **a Ford**.（フォード車を買う余裕はない.）

☞ afford ⇔ a Ford　★ 異分析 → p. 375

　　Man (to Mechanic): Excuse me, sir. Are you familiar with driving **a Mercedes**?
　　　　Mechanic: If I was familiar with **a Mercedes**, would I be working here?
(男と自動車工の対話:「すみませんがね, メルセデスを運転するのに慣れていますか」「慣れていたらこんなところで働いてるでしょうかね」)
☞ Mercedes [məséidis]: ドイツ製の高級車.

You can get along without formal education like Henry Ford and Thomas A. Edison, if you are **a Ford** or **an Edison**.
(ヘンリー・フォードやトマス・エジソンのように正規の教育を受けなくても何とかやっていける，もしフォードやエジソンのような人なら．)
☞ Henry Ford (1863-1947): アメリカの実業家．自動車会社 Ford 社の創業者．
☞ Thomas A. Edison (1847-1931): アメリカの発明家．

B. 定冠詞：the

"What was Alexander the Great's middle name?" "**The**!"
(「アレキサンダー大王のミドルネームは」「The」)

Next to '**the**', the most common word in all nations today is 'deficit.'
(すべての国で今日「the」の次にくるもっともありふれた語は「赤字」である．)

定冠詞は次のような場合に用いられる：
(1) 前に出た名詞を指す
(2) その場の状況・前後関係から相手に分かっているものを指す
(3) 常識的に考えて「唯一のもの」を指す
(4) 最上級，**only**，**last** などで修飾された名詞につける
(5) 句・節によって特定化された名詞につける（→ 第 21 章　形容詞節）
(6) 固有名詞につける
(7) 総称的用法：種類一般を表す
(8) 慣用的な用法

(1) 前に出た名詞を指す

A lion and a rabbit walked into a restaurant. **The** rabbit ordered a nice salad. **The** lion shook his head. He didn't want anything. **The** rabbit explained to the waiter, "Look, if he was hungry, do you think I'd be sitting here?"

(ライオンとウサギがレストランへ歩いて入った．ウサギはおいしそうなサラダを注文した．ライオンは首を振った．彼は何も食べたくなかった．ウサギはウエイターにこう説明した「ほらね，もし彼が腹をすかしていたら，ぼくがこんな所に座っていると思うかい」）

(2) その場の状況・前後関係から相手に分かっているものを指す

"What's on **the** television tonight, son?"

"Same as usual, dad, **the** goldfish bowl and lamp."

(「今夜のテレビには何があるかな」「いつもと同じさ，お父さん．金魚ばちとランプだよ」)
☞ television（テレビ（放送））⇔ the television（テレビ受像機）

A man walked into a grocery store. "I want all **the** rotten eggs you have," he demanded.

"What do you want with stale eggs?" asked **the** clerk. "Are you going to see **the** new comedian at **the** theater tonight?"

"Sh-sh-sh," hissed **the** buyer nervously, "I am *the* new comedian."

(男が食料品店に入って行った．「腐った卵をありったけほしい」と彼は頼んだ．「腐った卵をどうしたいんですか」と店員は尋ねた．「今夜劇場で新人コメディアンを見る予定ですか」「シー」と買い手は小声で言った．「私がそのコメディアンだ」)
☞ ひどい演技には腐った卵をぶつける．買い占めればぶつけられないですむ．

(3) 常識的に考えて「唯一のもの」を指す

Teacher: It's clear you haven't studied your geography. What's your excuse?

Pupil: Well, my dad says **the world** is changing every day, so I've decided to wait till it settles down.

(先生「君が地理の勉強をしなかったことははっきりしている．言いわけは何だい」生徒「あの，お父さんが世界は毎日変化していると言うので落ち着くまで待つことにしたんです」)

"What's the shape of **the earth**?" the teacher asked Willie.

"Round."

"How do you know it's round?"

"All right, it's square. I don't want to start an argument."
(「地球はどんな形だい」と先生はウイリーに尋ねた.「丸です」「丸いとどうして分かるんだい」「いいです, 四角です. 喧嘩を始めたくはありません」)

It was a magical night. **The moon** was out, and so were her parents.
(魅惑的な夜だった. 月は出ていたし, 彼女の両親も出ていた.)

"What colours would you paint **the sun** and **the wind**?"
"**The sun** rose, and **the wind** blue."
(「太陽と風を何色で描きますか」「太陽はバラ色, 風は青です」)
☞ rose:「ばら（色）」⇔「rise（上る）の過去形」; blue:「青」⇔「blew（blow（吹く）の過去形）」
★ **Pun** → p. 26

I always begin at **the left** with the opening word of the sentence and read toward **the right** and I recommend this method.

(James Thurber)

(私は文の出だしの語を左から始めて右の方へ読んでいく, そしてこのやり方を勧める.)
☞ Arabic（アラビア語）は右から左へ読む［書く］. 日本でもかつて横書きは右から左に書いた.
☞ James Thurber (1894–1961): アメリカの小説家.

(4) 最上級, only, last などで修飾された名詞につける

"What is **the hardest** thing about learning to ride a bike?"
"The pavement."
(「自転車に乗るのに一番難しいことは何か」「舗道」)
☞ hard:「難しい」⇔「硬い」　　★ **Pun** → p. 26

"Who succeeded **the first** president of the USA?"
"**The second** one."
(「誰が合衆国初代大統領を継いだか」「第2代大統領」)
☞ 正解は John Adams.　★ **Boner** → p. 46

"Did your previous employer give you a reference?"

"Yes, but I left it at home."
"What does it say?"
"Er, well, it says I was one of **the best** employees he had ever fired ..."
(「前の雇い主は君に人物証明書をくれましたか」「はい，しかし家に置いてきました」「何と書いてありますか」「ええと，今までくびにした中で最も優れた従業員の1人だと書いてあります」)

Movie director: Now, here's where you jump off the cliff.
Nervous actor: Yeah, but suppose I get injured or killed?
Movie director: Oh, that's all right. It's **the last** scene in the picture.
(映画監督と不安そうな俳優の対話：「さて，ここが君が崖から飛び降りる場所だ」「はい，でも怪我をしたり死にでもしたら」「ああ，それは大丈夫だ，映画の最後のシーンだ」)

The only certainty is that nothing is certain.　(Pliny the Elder)
(ただ1つ確かなことは確かなことは何もないということである.)
☞ Pliny the Elder (22 A.D. – 79): 古代ローマの博物学者・政治家・軍人.

(5) 句・節によって特定化された名詞につける（→ 第21章　形容詞節）

Julie was saying her bedtime prayers. "Please, God," she said, "Make Naples **the** capital *of Italy*. Make Naples **the** capital *of Italy*—"
Her mother interrupted and said, "Julie, why do you want God to make Naples **the** capital *of Italy*?"
And Julie replies, "Because that's what I put on my geography exam!"
(ジュリーがおやすみ前のお祈りをしていた.「どうぞ，神様」と彼女は言った.「ナポリをイタリアの首都にしてください，ナポリをイタリアの首都に...」母がさえぎって言った「なぜ神様にナポリをイタリアの首都にしてほしいの」するとジュリーは答えた.「地理の試験にそう書いてしまったんだもの」)

Paul: Is this **the** other side *of the street*?
Saul: No, **the** other side *of the street* is over there.
Paul: Well! **The** policeman *over there* said it was over here.

(ポールとサウルの対話:「ここは通りの向かい側ですか」「いや,通りの向かい側はあっちだよ」「なんと.あそこの警官はこっちだと言ったんだけど」)
★ **Irish bull** → p. 39

Laughter is **the** shock absorber *that cushions the blows of life.*
(笑いは人生の打撃を和らげる緩衝装置である.)
★ **One-liner** → p. 395

(6) 固有名詞につける
(a) 単数形の固有名詞

"Which is correct: **the** Amazon issues into **the** Pacific or **the** Amazon flows into **the** Pacific?"
"Neither. **The** Amazon flows into **the** Atlantic."
(「どちらが正しいですか:アマゾン河は太平洋へ出て行くですか,アマゾン河は太平洋へ流れ込むですか」「どっちでもありません.アマゾン河は大西洋に流れ込みます」)

Teacher: Did you know Henry Hudson discovered **the** Hudson River?
Student: Wow! What a coincidence!
(先生と生徒の対話:「ヘンリー・ハドソンがハドソン川を発見したのを知っていましたか」「わあ.何て偶然の一致なんだろう」)

Turn first right after **the Picasso**. (Jeffrey Archer directing someone to the bathroom, in his London penthouse)
(ピカソの絵を通り過ぎたらすぐ右に曲がりたまえ.)(ジェフリー・アーチャーがロンドンの自分のペントハウスでトイレを案内して)
☞ Jeffrey Archer (1940–):イギリスの小説家・保守党政治家.

cf. 駅・空港・公園・橋の名前にはふつう the をつけない.

"Hello, **Grand Central**? Do you have a sleeping car? You do? Well, wake it up!"
(「もしもし,グランドセントラル駅.眠っている車両があるか.ある.じゃあ,起こしてくれ」)
☞ sleeping:「眠っている」(現在分詞) ⇔「眠るための」(動名詞)

"Where did Dr. Jekyll find his best friend?"
"In **Hyde Park**."
(「ジキル博士はどこで親友を見つけたか」「ハイドパークで」)
☞ Hyde Park: イギリスのロンドンにある公園. *Dr. Jekyll and Mr. Hyde* (『ジキル博士とハイド氏』) は R. L. Stevenson の小説名. ここから「二重人格者」の意味が生まれた.

"Did he find anything wrong with you?"
"My teeth. They were all good except one bridge which was put in by a dentist in London."
"I get it. **London Bridge** is falling down."
(「彼は君のどこか悪いところを見つけたか」「歯だよ. ロンドンの歯医者で付けられたブリッジ以外は全部いいんだが」「なるほど. ロンドン橋が落ちかかってるんだな」)
☞ bridge:「橋」⇔「(義歯の) ブリッジ」　　★ **Pun** → p. 26
☞ 『マザーグース童謡』の中でも有名な唄 *London Bridge* の出だし "London Bridge's falling down" のもじり.　★ **Parody** → p. 199

(b) 複数形の固有名詞

"What is the national flower of **the** United State**s**?"
"A carnation."
(「合衆国の国花は何か」「カーネーション」)
☞ carnation ⇔ car-nation (車の国)　　★ 異分析 → p. 375

"Dad, where are **the** Himalaya**s**?"
"Ask your mother. She puts everything away!"
(「お父さん, ヒマラヤ山脈はどこにあるの」「お母さんに聞きなさい. 何でも片づけてしまうからね」)

cf. 複数形の人名:「〜さんの家族 (全員) ／〜さん夫妻」
　Manager:　I think it's a good time to sell **the** Smith**s** a new car.
　Salesman:　What makes you think so, manager?
　Manager:　Their neighbors bought a new car.
　(支配人とセールスマンの対話:「スミス家に新車を売るのに今がいい時だと思う」「どう

してそう思うのですか」「近所の人たちが新車を買ったからさ」）

(7) 総称的用法：種類一般を表す．（cf. 文章体で用いることが多い．）

 Professor: **The** geologist thinks nothing of a thousand years.
  Student: Great guns! And I loaned a geologist ten dollars yesterday.

（教授「地質学者というものは 1000 年など何とも思わないものです」学生「わあっ! 昨日地質学者に 10 ドル貸しちゃったよ」）

The average person thinks he isn't.　（Larry Lorenzoni）
（普通の人は自分は違うと思っている．）
 ☞ isn't ＝ isn't average
 ☞ Larry Lorenzoni (1923–)：アメリカ，サンフランシスコのサレジオ会の神父．

The merchant has no country.　（Thomas Jefferson）
（商人は国を持たない．）
 ☞ Thomas Jefferson (1743–1826)：アメリカの政治家・思想家．第 3 代大統領．

(8) 慣用的な用法
(a) the＋形容詞
1) 複数の人々

> Q: Why did Robin Hood only rob **the rich**?
> A: Because **the poor** had no money.

（「ロビンフッドはなぜ金持ちだけから金を奪ったのですか」「貧乏な人は金を持っていなかったからです」）

 ☞ the rich [poor] ＝ rich [poor] people
 ☞ Robin Hood: 12 世紀ごろシャーウッドの森に住んでいたと言われる伝説的義賊．

When we're young, we want to change the world. When we're old, we want to change **the young**.
（若い頃は世の中を変えたいと思う．年を取ると若者たちを変えたくなる．）
 ★ **One-liner** → p. 395

There are three types of women; **the intelligent**, **the beautiful**, and the majority.
（女性には3つのタイプがある：知的な人，美しい人，その他大勢．）

cf. 個人を表すこともある．

"I asked **the deceased** before she became unconscious what caused her death, and she feebly replied …" (from the deposition of a police constable in an assault case in which the victim later died)
（「私は故人が意識を失う前に彼女の死因を尋ねました，すると彼女は弱々しく答えました…」（被害者が後に死んだ暴力事件の警官の書いた証言録取書から））
★ **Irish bull** → p. 39

Jury Foreman: We find **the accused** not guilty by reason of insanity.
　　Judge: What, all 12 of you?
（陪審員長「私たちは被告は精神障害の理由で無罪といたします」裁判長「何ですって，あなた方全員がですか」）
☞「精神障害」は陪審員全員？

2) 抽象名詞

If one does not understand the usefulness of **the** useless and the uselessness of **the** useful, one cannot understand art.
　　　　　　　　　　　　　　　　　　　　　　　(Eugene Ionesco)
（もし無用なものの有用性，有用なものの無用性を理解できなければ，芸術は理解できない．）

☞ Eugene Ionesco (1909–1994): フランスの劇作家．　★ **One-liner** → p. 395

An intelligent person is one who understands **the** obvious.
（頭のいい人とは明らかなことは分かる人である．）

(b) 前置詞＋the＋身体の一部

> **look** ～ **in the face**（～の顔をじっと見る），**catch** ～ **by the arm**（～の腕をつかむ），**pat** ～ **on the shoulder**（～の肩を軽くたたく），**kiss** ～ **on the cheek**（～の頬にキスする），**strike** ～ **on the head**（～の頭を殴る）など．

"Why did you *kick* your brother **in the stomach**?"
"Because he turned around."
(「なぜ弟のお腹を蹴ったんだ」「振り返ったからさ」)
☞ いずれにせよ蹴ろうとしていた．

"Last time I went hunting, a bird flew right into my hiding place."
"Duck?"
"No, *hit* me right **in the face**."
(「この前猟に行ったとき，鳥がぼくの隠れているところに飛び込んで来たんだ」「カモかい」「いや，顔の真正面に当たったんだ」)
☞ duck:「(鳥) カモ」⇔「頭をひょいと下げる」　　★ **Pun** → p. 26

Mother: Kate, why are you crying?
　Kate: My new dolly—Tom broke it.
Mother: How did he break it?
　Kate: I *hit* him **on the head** with it.
(母と娘の対話：「ケート，なぜ泣いているの」「わたしの新しいお人形，トムが壊したの」「どうやって壊したの」「トムの頭をお人形で叩いたの」)

High heels were invented by a woman who had been *kissed* **on the forehead**.　(Christopher Marley)
(ハイヒールはおでこにキスされていた女性によって発明された．)
☞ Christopher Marley: 昆虫・チョウなどの映像・造形作家．

C. 無冠詞（冠詞を付けずに用いる場合）

---
(1) **go to bed [school / college]** などそのもの本来の目的を表すとき
(2) 慣用的な表現
   (a) 交通・通信などの手段を表す **by** ～
   (b) 対句
   (c) その他
(3) **chairman, president** など普通 1 人しかいない職名が補語になる場合
(4) その他：食事の名前，家族同士の呼び名など

---

(1) **go to bed [school / college]** など

Q: Why do people go to **bed**?
A: Because the bed won't come to them.
（「なぜ人は（ベッドへ行って）寝るのか」「ベッドが人の方へ来ないから」）

When I went to **college**, my parents threw a going-away party for me, according to the letter. (Emo Philips)
（大学へ行くと両親は私のために送別会をしてくれた，手紙によると．）
☞ 本人は送別会には出ていない．
☞ Emo Philips (1956-)：アメリカのコメディアン．

A little girl was playing in the park when a kindly old lady started talking to her.
"And do you go to **school**?" she asked.
"No," was the sulky answer, "I'm sent!"
（少女が公園で遊んでいると親切そうな老婦人が話し掛け始めた．「それであなたは学校へ行ってるの」と尋ねた．「違うわ」とすねた答．「行かされてるのよ」）

"I'm afraid Alice will not be able to come to **school** today."
"Who's calling?"
"It's my mother."
（「アリスは今日学校に行けないと思います」「どなた」「私のおかあさんです」）

My uncle went to **jail** for something he didn't do. He didn't pay his taxes!
（叔父はやらなかったことのために刑務所行きになった．税金を払わなかったのだ．）

(2) 慣用的な表現
(a) 交通・通信などの手段を表す **by** 〜

"How did I get to Hollywood?" "**By train**."　(John Ford)
（「ハリウッドへはどうやったら行けますか」「電車で」）
☞ John Ford (1895–1973): アメリカの映画監督．

"Oh, my dear, how can I ever leave you?"
"**By bus, taxi, plane or subway**."
（「おまえ，どうやっておまえと別れられるというんだ」「バス，タクシー，飛行機，地下鉄のどれでもいいわよ」）

(b) 対句

Anyone can be heroic **from time to time**, but a gentleman is something you have to be all the time.
（誰でもときどきは英雄のようになれる，しかし紳士は常にそうあらねばならないものだ．）

Little Johnny shouts, "Mummy, Mummy! Do you know the beautiful vase in the dining room that's been handed down **from generation to generation**?"
"Yes," says his mother. "What about it?"
Johnny replies, "Well, the last generation just dropped it."
（幼いジョニーが叫んだ「お母ちゃん，お母ちゃん，食堂の家代々のきれいな花瓶を知ってるでしょう」「知ってるわよ，それがどうしたの」と母親が言う．ジョニーは答える「あの，最後の世代が落としちゃった」）

I used to sell doorbells **door to door**. But when I rang, people who needed my product didn't know I was there!

(以前は玄関のベルを一軒一軒売り歩いていた．しかしベルを鳴らしても私の製品を必要とする人たちは私が玄関にいるのに気付かなかった．)

What's it like to be a mom?
—You have to look young, act young and think young while doing the same old things **day after day**.
(「母であるってどんな感じですか」「毎日毎日相変わらずの同じことをしながら，若く見えなきゃいけないし，行動も考えも若くなくてはいけないって感じね」)

(c) その他

I met my wife at a dance. It was really embarrassing. I thought she was **at home** with the kids.
(妻にダンスパーティーで出会った．まったくばつの悪いことだった．子供たちと家にいると思っていたのだ．)

He heard the country was **at war**—so he moved to the city.
(彼は田舎が戦争中だと聞いた，そこで町に引っ越した．)
☞ country:「田舎」⇔「国」　　★ Pun → p. 26

The teacher asked, "How many of you children want to go to heaven?" All but one boy raised their hands. He said, "I can't. I have to go home right **after school**."
(先生は尋ねた「天国へ行きたいと思っている人は何人いますか」1人を除いて全員が手を上げた．その1人はこう言った「ぼくは行けません．放課後すぐ家に帰らなければいけないんです」)

　Mother: What was the first thing you learned **in class**?
Daughter: How to talk without moving my lips.
(母と娘の対話：「授業で最初に覚えたことはなあに」「唇を動かさないしゃべり方よ」)

(3) chairman, president など普通1人しかいない職名が補語になる場合
Being **president** is like running a cemetery. You've got a lot of people under you, but none of them are listening.　(William J. Clinton)

（大統領であることは共同墓地を経営しているようなものだ．下に多くの人々がいるが，誰ひとり言うことを聴いていない．）
☞ William J. Clinton (1946–)：アメリカの政治家．第42代大統領．

God knew from all eternity that I was going to be **Pope**. You think he would have made me more photogenic. (Pope John XXIII)
（神は気の遠くなるような昔から私が法王になることを知っておられた．皆さんは私をもっと写真写りの良いようになさってくだされればよかったのにと思うでしょう．）
☞ Pope John XXIII (1881–1963)：ローマ法王ヨハネス23世（1958–1963）

(4) その他：食事の名前，家族同士の呼び名など
"What are two things you cannot have for **breakfast**?"
"**Lunch** and **dinner**."
（「朝食に食べられない2つのものは何か」「昼食と夕食」）
★ **Riddle** → p. 64

Never work before **breakfast**; if you have to work before **breakfast**, eat your **breakfast** first. (Josh Billings)
（朝食前に決して仕事をするな．もし朝食前に仕事をしなければならないなら，先ず朝食を食べろ．）
★ **Irish bull** → p. 39
☞ Josh Billings (1818–1885)：アメリカのユーモア作家．

cf. 特定の食事または種類を言うときは冠詞をつける．
All happiness depends on **a** *leisurely* **breakfast**. (John Gunther)
（すべての幸せはゆったりとした朝食に懸かっている．）
☞ John Gunther (1901–1976)：アメリカのジャーナリスト・ノンフィクション作家．

Mother was Irish and proud of it. **Father** was Scotch ... and fond of it.
（母はアイルランド人でそれを誇りにしていた．父はスコットランド人で...それが好きだった．）
☞ Scotch:「スコットランド人」⇔「スコッチウイスキー」（スコットランド人は自分をScotchではなくScotと呼ぶ．）

"**Doctor, doctor**, I've only got 59 seconds to live."
"Wait a minute, please."
(「先生，先生，わたしあと59秒しか生きられないんです」「1分待ってください」)
☞ Wait a minute.:「1分待って」⇔「ちょっと待って」　　★ **Pun** → p. 26

ジョークの常識⑫

★ **misprint:**「誤植・自書の意識しない誤り」その中で笑いを誘うものをいう．Boner [Howler]（p. 46）の一種．

The motorist approached the coroner at 90 mph.
（ドライバーは時速90マイルで検死官に接近した．）
☞ corner（曲がり角）の誤植．

Try our homemade pies—they are a real threat.
（私どもの自家製パイをお試しください―本当の脅迫でございます．）
☞ treat（ごちそう）の誤植．

And now, the Superstore—unequalled, in size, unmatched in variety, unrivalled inconvenience.
（さて今度は「スーパーストアー」です―大きさは匹敵するものなし，品揃えも比べるものなし，不便なことこの上なしです．）
☞ in convenience（便利さの点で）の誤植．

第13章　副　詞

"Is there a word in the English language that contains all vowels?"
"**Unquestionably**."
(「英語にはすべての母音を含んでいる単語がありますか」「もちろん」)

☞ unquestionably にはすべての母音字が含まれている.

> 副詞は (1) 動詞, (2) 形容詞, (3) 他の副詞(句), (4) 文全体 などを修飾する.

◆ 副詞には「形容詞＋ly」の形が非常に多い.

  Man: Do you love me?
 Woman: *Mad***ly**.
  Man: Do you need me?
 Woman: *Bad***ly**.
  Man: Will you marry me?
 Woman: *Glad***ly**.
  Man: Will you take care of this check?
 Woman: *Sad***ly**.

(「僕を愛しているかい」「熱烈に」「僕が必要かい」「とっても」「僕と結婚してくれるかい」「喜んで」「この勘定を何とかしてくれるかい」「悲しんで」)

(1) 動詞を修飾

You'll always stay young if you *live* **honestly**, *eat* **slowly**, *sleep* **sufficiently**, *work* **industriously**, *worship* **faithfully**, and lie about your age.
(常に若くいるには，正直に生活し，ゆっくり食べ，十分に眠り，勤勉に働き，信心深く神を拝み，年齢を偽ることだ.)

A philanthropist is a man who *gives away* **publicly** the fortune he *stole* **privately**.
（慈善家とは密かに盗んだ財産を大っぴらにただで与える人.）
★ **One-liner** → p. 395

"That medicine tastes sour," *said* the boy **bitterly**.
（「その薬はすっぱい」と少年は苦々しく言った.）
★ **Tom Swifties** → p. 229

You have to admire Madonna. She *hides* her lack of talent so **well**.
(Manolo Blahnik)
（マドンナをほめなきゃだめよ．才能がないのを実にうまく隠しているもの．）
☞ Manolo Blahnik (1942–)：スペイン出身のファッションデザイナー．
★ **Insulting joke** → p. 97

Politician: Well, dear, I've been reelected.
　Wife: **Honestly**?
Politician: I don't see that there's any need for you to bring that up.
（政治家と妻の対話：「おまえ，再選されたよ」「ほんとなの」「おまえがそれを蒸し返す必要はないと思うよ」）
☞ honestly:「ほんとに」⇔「正直に」
★ **Politician** → p. 329

(2) 形容詞を修飾

"Are you married?"
"No, but I'm **happily** *divorced*."
（「結婚していますか」「いいえ，離婚して幸せです」）

"I heard your mother-in-law was **dangerously** *ill* last week."
"Yes, but this week she is **dangerously** *well* again."
（「君の義理のお母さんは先週危篤だったそうだね」「そうなんだ，でも今週は危険なほど元気だよ」）
★ **Mother-in-law** → p. 305

"What do you do when you see an **unusually** *beautiful* girl?"
"Oh, I look for a while, and then I get tired and put my mirror down."
(「並はずれて美しい女性を見たらきみはどうする」「しばらく見て，それから見飽きて鏡を置くわ」)
☞ 自分を「並はずれて美しい女性」だと自惚(うぬぼ)れている．

It is always the best policy to tell the truth, unless of course you happen to be an **exceptionally** *good* liar.　(Jerome K. Jerome)
(真実を語ることは常に最善策である，もちろんあなたがたまたま例外的に嘘をつくのがうまい場合を除いて．)
☞ Jerome K. Jerome (1859–1927): イギリスのユーモア作家．

cf. 副詞としての **enough** はふつう後ろから前の形容詞・副詞を修飾する．
"I suppose I'll never get married."
"Why do you say that?"
"Well, I'm not *old* **enough** for the young man, and I'm not *young* **enough** for the old man."
(「わたし決して結婚しないと思うわ」「なぜそんなこと言うの」「そうね，若い男の人と結婚するほどの年でもないし，ご老人と結婚するほど若くないんですもの」)

"My wife kisses me only when she needs money."
"Isn't it *often* **enough**?"
(「妻は金が必要なときだけ私にキスをするんだ」「それで十分じゃないのか」)

"Honest, weren't you ever homesick?"
"Not me, I never stay there *long* **enough**.
(「ほんとに，ホームシックになったことがないのか」「ぼくはないよ，それほど長く家にいることは全くないんだ」)

cf. 形容詞としての **enough** は修飾する名詞の前にも後ろにもくる．
They turned me down for a travel loan. I only wanted **enough** *money* for a one-way ticket to Europe.
(旅行ローンを断られた．ヨーロッパへの片道切符分が必要だっただけなのに．)

Don: She's a bright girl ... she has *brains* **enough** for two.
Art: Then she's just the girl for you.
(「あの人は頭のいい女性だ．2人分の頭脳の持ち主だ」「じゃあ君にピッタリだ」)

(3) 副詞（句）を修飾

Patient: How much to have a tooth pulled?
Dentist: 80 dollars.
Patient: 80 dollars for a few minutes' work?
Dentist: I can extract it **very** *slowly* if you like.
(歯科医と患者の対話：「歯を1本抜くのはいくらですか」「80ドルです」「2,3分の仕事で80ドルですか」「お望みなら非常にゆっくり抜くこともできますが」)

Mother: Don't eat your chips **so** *quickly*, Sam.
Sam: But I might lose my appetite unless I do.
(「ポテトチップをそんなに急いで食べてはだめよ，サム」「でもそうしないと食欲がなくなっちゃうもん」)
☞ chips:「((米)) ポテトチップ；((英)) ポテトフライ」

Anyone who has been to an English public school will always feel **comfortably** *at home* in prison.　(Evelyn Waugh)
(イギリスのパブリックスクールへ行った人は誰でもいつも刑務所で心地よく寛いだ気分になれるものだ．)
☞ public school: イギリスで（かつては）上流階級の子弟を教育する全寮制の私立男子中等学校（日本の中学・高校にあたる）．アメリカでは「公立学校（小学校から高校まで）をいう．
☞ Evelyn Waugh (1903-1966): イギリスの小説家．
☞ Public schools are the nurseries of all vice and immorality. (Henry Fielding (1707-1751))（パブリックスクールはあらゆる悪徳・不道徳の温床である．）という言葉もある．

"Waiter, waiter, this lobster's only got one claw."
"It was **probably** *in a fight*, sir."
"Well, bring me the winner!"

(「君，このイセエビははさみが一本しかないぞ」「おそらく取っ組み合いをしたんだと思います，お客様」「じゃあ，勝った方を出してくれたまえ」)

cf.「名詞＋**ly**」は副詞ではなく形容詞:
"Did the music teacher actually say your voice was *heaven***ly**?"
"Well, she did say it was *unearth***ly**."
(「音楽の先生はほんとにあなたの声が天国のようにすばらしいと言ったの」「そうね，この世のものとは思えないとは確かに言ったわ」)

"If I saw a man beating a donkey and I stopped him, what virtue would I be showing?"
"*Brother***ly** love."
(「もし男がロバを叩いているのを見てやめさせたら，私はどんな美徳を示しているでしょうか」「兄弟愛です」)
☞ donkey:「ロバ」⇔「バカ者」

(4) 文修飾の副詞：文全体を修飾する副詞で，文頭に置かれることが多い．

I went skiing and broke a leg. **Fortunately**, it wasn't mine.
(Mark Twain)
(スキーに行って脚を折った．運よく私のではなかった．)

☞ ＝ it was *fortunate* that it wasn't mine.
☞ Mark Twain (1835-1910): アメリカの（ユーモア）小説家．

The child next door can't play the piano, and **frankly**, we wish he'd stop trying.
(隣の子はピアノが弾けない，そして率直なところ，弾くのをやめてくれればと思う．)

"The play ended**, happily**," recently wrote a local critic. What a difference a comma can make!
(「幸いなことに芝居は終わった」と最近地元の批評家が書いた．1つのコンマが何という違いをもたらすことか．)
☞ The play ended **happily**.（芝居はハッピーエンドだった．）

A man tried to hijack a busload of Japanese tourists. **Luckily** the police had 500 photos of the suspect.
（男が日本人観光客で満員のバスを乗っ取ろうとした．幸いなことに警察は容疑者の写真を 500 枚手に入れていた．）
★ **Ethnic joke [humor]** → p. 361

Harry Smith was sent to Central Africa by his company. He sent a postcard to his wife as soon as he arrived. **Unfortunately** it was delivered to another Mrs Smith whose husband had died the day before. The postcard read: ARRIVED SAFELY THIS MORNING. THE HEAT IS TERRIBLE.
（ハリー・スミスは会社から中央アフリカへ派遣された．着くとすぐ妻に葉書を送った．不幸なことに，それはその前の日に夫を亡くした別のスミス夫人に送られた．葉書には次のように書いてあった「今朝無事到着．熱さがひどい」）

(5) 頻度の副詞

> **always** （いつも），**usually** （たいてい），**often** （しばしば），**sometimes** （ときどき），**rarely** （まれにしか〜ない），**seldom** （めったに〜ない），**never** （どんな場合も〜ない）

cf. 位置はたいてい動詞の前．ただし be 動詞の場合はその後ろが原則．

> I **always** *tell* a young man not to use the word '**always**'.
> (Robert Walpole)

（私は若者に「いつも」という言葉を使うなといつもいう．）

☞ Robert Walpole (1676–1745): イギリス初代の首相とされる政治家．

Paul: Do you **always** *snore*?
Saul: Only when I'm asleep.
（ポール「いつもいびきをかくのか」サウル「眠っているときだけさ」）

Boy (at dentist's): Oh, I wish we were born without teeth.
　　Dentist: We **usually** *are*.
（少年（歯科医院で）「歯がなくて生まれてくればよかったなあ」歯科医「ふつうはそうだよ」）
☞ We *are* **usually** born without teeth. が普通の語順.

"Do boats *sink* **often**?"
"Only once!"
（「船はよく沈みますか」「1 回だけです」）

"Doctor, when I'm tired I **sometimes** *see* two of everything."
"Sit on the sofa, please."
"Which one?"
（「先生, 疲れるとときどき何でも 2 つに見えるんです」「ソファーにお座りなさい」「どっちのですか」）

Gratitude: Something **rarely** *found* outside the dictionary.
（感謝の念：辞書以外ではめったに見つからないもの.）

One of the advantages bowling has over golf is that you **seldom** lose a bowling ball.
（ボーリングがゴルフより有利な点はボーリングのボールはめったになくすことがないことだ.）
☞ **seldom** →「第 25 章　否定表現」(9) 準否定

A: I **never** *boast*.
B: It's certainly worth bragging about.
（「わたしは決して自慢したりはしない」「それは確かに鼻にかける価値はあるな」）
☞ brag の方が boast より意味が強い.
☞ **never** →「第 25 章　否定表現」(3) never

第13章 副詞

(6) 注意すべき時を表す副詞

> **already**:「(肯定文で)「すでに(__した)」;「(疑問文で)(驚き・意外を表して)もう！？」
> **yet**:「(否定文で) まだ(__してない)」;「(疑問文で) もう(__しましたか)」
> **ago**:「(期間を表す語句とともに用いて)(今から)〜前に」
> **before**:「(ふつう完了形とともに用いて)(その時より) 前に」

"There's a man at the door with a moustache."
"Tell him I've **already** got one."
(「口ひげの男が玄関に来てます」「もう持っていると言いなさい」)
☞ with 〜:「〜を付けた」⇔「〜を持って」

Johnny: My two-year-old brother tore up my composition.
Teacher: What? Can he read **already**?
(ジョニー「2歳の弟がぼくの作文破っちゃったんです」先生「なんだって．もう字が読めるのかい」)

"This book has a great ending."
"How about the beginning?"
"I haven't got to it **yet**."
(「この本の結末はすばらしい」「出だしは」「まだそこまで行ってないよ」)

"Has your baby called you daddy **yet**?"
"No, my wife isn't going to tell him who I am until he gets a little stronger."
(「君の赤ちゃんはもう君をお父ちゃんと呼んだかい」「いいや，妻は赤ん坊がもう少し丈夫になるまで僕が誰かを言うつもりがないんだ」)

"Is this milk fresh?"
"You bet. Just three hours **ago**, it was grass!"
(「この牛乳は新鮮なの」「もちろんです．ほんの3時間前は草でした」)
★ **Irish bull** → p. 39

"I want to get him something he's never had **before**."
"How about a job?"
(「あの子が以前持ったことがないものを持たせたいんです」「仕事はどうですか」)
☞ 過去完了の例 → p. 61 「第 5 章　完了形」C　過去完了

(7) 強めの副詞

> Never use "**real**" when you mean "**very**." Therefore: "She is **real** stupid" shows that you are **very** stupid. (This point is **real** important.)
> (very の意味で real を使ってはいけない。だから，「彼女はほんとバカ」はあなたが非常にバカであることを示している。（この点はほんと重要である．））

(a) very と much

1) very は形容詞・副詞の原級を，**much** は主に動詞または形容詞・副詞の比較級・最上級を修飾する．(cf. 最上級はふつう **by far** を用いる；**much** を用いることは少ない．)

I'm going to see my doctor. He's a **very** *sick* man.
(ボストンの掛かりつけの医者に診てもらいに行くつもりだ．ひどい病人なのだ．)
☞ see: 「診てもらう」⇔「会う」　　★ Pun → p. 26

Computers make **very** *fast*, **very** *accurate* mistakes.
(コンピューターは非常に速い，非常に正確な間違いをする．)

A divorce court judge said to the husband: "Mr. Geraghty, I have reviewed this case **very** *carefully* and I've decided to give your wife 800 dollars a week."
"That's **very** *fair*, your honor," he replied. "And every now and then I'll try to send her a few bucks myself."
(離婚裁判所の判事が夫に言った「ジェラフティーさん，この件を非常に注意深く再検討した結果，奥さんに週 800 ドル与えることに決めました」「判事さん，それは実に公平なことです」と彼は答えた．「それでは時々は何ドルかは彼女に自分で送るようにします」)

I don't think my wife *likes* me very **much**. When I had a heart attack she wrote for an ambulance.　　(Frank Carson)
(妻は私をあまり好きではないと思う．心臓発作が起きたとき，救急車を手紙を書いて呼んだんだ．)
☞　Frank Carson (1926-2012): イギリス北アイルランドのコメディアン・俳優．
★ **Tall tale** → p. 412

Excuse me, I didn't recognize you. I*'ve changed* so **much**.
　　　　　　　　　　　　　　　　　　　　　　　　　(Oscar Wilde)
(すみません，あなただと分かりませんでした．私があまりにも変わってしまったので．)
☞　Oscar Wilde (1854-1900): アイルランド生まれのイギリスの詩人・小説家・劇作家．

It's **much** *easier* to get up at 6 a.m. to play golf than at 11 a.m. to mow the lawn.
(午前 6 時に起きてゴルフをする方が 11 時に起きて芝刈りをするよりずっと楽である．)

"But, darling, this isn't our baby!"
"I know, but it's a **much** *nicer* pram!"
(「でも，おまえ，これは家の赤ん坊じゃないぞ」「分かってるわ，でもずっといい乳母車よ」)

"How tragic when a great singer realizes her voice is gone!"
"**Much** *worse* when she doesn't realize."
(「すばらしい歌手が声が出なくなったと分かったら何と悲劇的でしょう」「それと気づかない方がもっとひどいです」)

"I had trouble with my eyes—I saw spots in front of my eyes."
"Do your glasses help?"
"Yeah—now I can see the spots **much** *better*."
(「眼の具合が悪かったんだ．眼の前に斑点が見えたんだ」「メガネは役に立つか」「立つとも―斑点がもっと良く見えるよ」)

cf. by far は主に最上級を修飾する：

The person **by far** *the most likely* to kill you is yourself.　(Jock Young)
(自分を断然最も殺しそうなのは自分自身だ.)
☞ Jock Young (1942–2013): イギリスの社会学者・犯罪学者.

(b) その他の比較級を強める副詞：**a lot**, **even**, **far**, **still**

I keep telling my wife that I like her mother-in-law **a lot** *better* than I like mine!
(妻には彼女の義母の方が私の義母よりずっと好きだと言い続けている.)
☞「彼女の義母」は自分の母親.

They say that a diamond is forever. The payments are **even** *longer*.
(ダイアモンドは永遠だという. 支払いはさらに長い.)
☞ "A diamond is forever."（ダイアモンドは永遠です.）：婚約指輪の宣伝に使われた有名なコピー.

Don't tell your friends your problems. Tell your enemies your problems. They are **far** *more interested* in hearing about it.
(友だちに自分の問題をしゃべるな. それは敵にしゃべれ. 彼らの方がそれを聞くことにはるかに興味を持っているのだ.)

It was wonderful to find America, but it would have been **still** *more wonderful* to miss it.　(Mark Twain)
(アメリカを見つけたのはすばらしいことだった，しかし見つけそこなっていたらさらにすばらしかっただろう.)
☞ Mark Twain (1835–1910): アメリカの（ユーモア）小説家.

cf. 疑問副詞については「第 2 章　疑問文」参照. 関係副詞については「第 21 章　形容詞節」参照.

ジョークの常識⑬

★ **Parody**:「もじり」ジョークにはことわざ・名句・名言などのもじりが頻出する．英語・英米文化などに関する知識が要求されるので，日本人には難解なものが多い．

以下はシェイクスピア『ハムレット』にある有名な台詞 "To be or not to be, that is the question."（「生きるか，死ぬか，それが問題だ」）のもじり：

TV or not TV, that is the question.
（テレビを見るか見ないか，それが問題だ．）

To drink or not to drink, that is the question.
（飲むか飲まぬか，それが問題だ．）

"What did the confused bee say?" "To bee or not to bee."
（「うろたえたミツバチは何と言ったか」「ミツバチでいるべきか，ミツバチでいてはいけないのか」）

第14章 不定詞

The best way **to get** somebody **to live** is **to lean** over and **whisper** the cost of a funeral in his ear.
（人を生きさせる最善の方法は身体を乗り出してその人の耳元に葬式の費用をささやくことだ．）

文の主語が1人称か3人称か，単数か複数か，などによって変化を受けない［特定されない（つまり不定の）］動詞の形を不定詞という．不定詞には「to+動詞の原形」の **to** 不定詞と「動詞の原形」のみの **to** なし不定詞がある．本書では後者を原形不定詞と呼ぶ．

A. **to** 不定詞は文の中で，名詞・形容詞・副詞のいずれかの働きをする．
B. 原形不定詞は助動詞や知覚動詞・使役動詞などとともに用いられる．

A. **to** 不定詞

(1) 名詞用法

to 不定詞は文中で，(1) 文の主語として，(2) 動詞の目的語として，(3) be 動詞の補語として用いられる．また (4)「疑問詞［whether］+to 不定詞」で名詞の役割をする．

(a) 文の主語として

To do nothing is sometimes a good remedy.　(Hippocrates)
（何もしないことがときには良い治療になる．）

☞ Hippocrates [hipákrəti:z]（ヒポクラテス (460?-377? B.C.)）：古代ギリシャの医師で「医学の父」といわれる．

To live is the rarest thing in the world. Most people exist, that is all.
(Oscar Wilde)
(生きることはこの世で極めてまれなことだ．ほとんどの人は存在している，ただそれだけだ．)
☞ Oscar Wilde (1854–1900): アイルランド生まれのイギリスの詩人・小説家・劇作家．

To be interested in the changing seasons is happier state of mind than to be always in love with spring.　(George Santayana)
(季節の変化に興味を覚えることはいつも春を愛していることより幸せな心の状態である．)
☞ George Santayana (1863–1952): アメリカの哲学者・詩人・批評家．
☞ **It is** ～ **to** *do* の形については「第10章　It の用法」C 参照．

(b) 動詞の目的語として

I don't *want* **to be** a millionaire, I only *want* **to live** like one.
(Walter Hagen)
(百万長者になりたくはない，百万長者のように生活したいだけだ．)

☞ Walter Hagen (1892–1969): アメリカのプロゴルファー．

"What three letters do people *hate* **to write**?"
"I, O, and U."
(「人が書くのを嫌がる3つの文字は何か」「I と O と U」)
☞ IOU または I.O.U. は I owe you (あなたに借りがある)，つまり「借用証書」のこと．

"Just do as I say and you'll be another man."
"Okay and, Doctor, don't *forget* **to send** your bill to the other man."
(「私の言うとおりにしていれば別人のようになりますよ」「もちろんそうします．ついでに先生，治療費の請求書も忘れずにその別人に送ってください」)

"Your school report is very disappointing. I *promised* **to buy** you a bicycle if you passed your exams. What have you been doing with your time?"
"*Learning* **to ride** a bicycle!"

(「お前の成績にはほんとにがっかりだ．試験に受かったら自転車を買ってやるって約束したのに．時間を何に使っていたんだ」「自転車に乗る練習をしてたんだよ」)

In general my children *refuse* **to eat** anything that hasn't danced on television.　(Erma Bombeck)
(概して私の子供たちはテレビで踊ったことのないものはどれも食べるのを拒否する．)
☞ テレビのコマーシャルの影響力は大きい．
☞ Erma Bombeck (1927-1996): アメリカのユーモア作家．

Life is like a B-movie. You don't *want* **to leave** in the middle of it, but you don't *want* **to see** it again.　(Ted Turner)
(人生はB級映画のようなものだ．途中で出たくはないが，また見たいとは思わない．)
☞ Ted Turner (1938–): アメリカの実業家・メディア業界人．CNN の創業者．
★ **One-liner** → p. 395

(c) be 動詞の補語として

True terror is **to wake** up one morning and discover that your high-school class is running the country.　(Kurt Vonnegut)
(真の恐怖は朝目が覚めて，高校の同期生が国を動かしているのを知ることだ．)
☞ Kurt Vonnegut (1922-2007): アメリカの小説家．

The best way to avoid a car accident is **to travel** by bus.
(自動車事故を避ける最善の方法はバスで移動することである．)

One of the first duties of the physician is **to educate** the masses not to take medicine.
(医師の最も重要な義務のひとつは大衆に薬を飲まないように教育することである．)
★ **One-liner** → p. 395

(d) 疑問詞［whether］＋to 不定詞

Mother: What did you learn in school today?
　Son: **How to** write.

> *Mother:* What did you write?
> *Son:* I don't know, they haven't taught us **how to** read yet!
>
> (母と息子の対話:「今日学校で何を習ったの」「書き方だよ」「お前は何を書いたの」「分からないよ．先生はまだ読み方を教えてくれていないもん」)

"I don't know **what to** do with my hands while I'm talking."
"Why don't you hold them over your mouth?"
(「わたくしお話ししているとき両手をどうしていいか分かりませんのよ」「口をおおったらどうですか」)
★ **Insulting joke** → p. 97

I finally figured out why surgeons wear masks over their faces. If something goes wrong, you don't know **whom to** blame!
(なぜ外科医が顔にマスクをするのかがやっと分かった．何かうまくいかないときでも，誰を責めていいのか分からないのだ．)

"My wife and I had an argument over **where to** go last night. She wanted to go to the ballet and I wanted to go to a rock concert. But we soon came to an agreement."
"And what was the ballet like?"
(「家内と昨日の晩どこへ行くかでもめたんだ．家内はバレエに行きたかったし，僕はロックのコンサートに行きたかったんだ．でもすぐ意見が合ったよ」「それで，バレエはどうだった」)
☞ 奥方の意見が通るに決まっている．

The most welcome guest is the one who knows **when to** go home.
(もっとも歓迎される客は帰る潮時を知っている客である．)
★ **One-liner** → p. 395

When I was born, they didn't know **whether to** buy a crib or a cage.
(私が生まれたとき，両親はベッドを買うか檻を買うか迷ったのだ．)

(2) 形容詞用法

> to 不定詞が名詞の直後に置かれてその名詞を修飾する形. 意味の上では, (1) 名詞が意味上の主語, (2) 名詞が意味上の目的語, (3) 名詞の内容を説明するもの, がある.

(a) 名詞が意味上の主語

"What are the last teeth **to appear** in the mouth?"
"False teeth."
(「口の中に最後に現れる歯は何といいますか」「入れ歯です」)

☞ the last teeth appear (S+V)

Father (to son): I hear you skipped school to play football.
　　　　　Son: No, I didn't, and I have the fish **to prove** it.
(父「学校をサボってサッカーをしたそうだな」息子「そんなことしないよ, 証明する魚を持ってるもん」)
☞ the fish prove it. (S+V+O)

A cheerleader told her friend, "I'm knitting something **to make** boys happy." Her friend asked, "Oh, a sweater for a player?" The cheerleader replied, "No, a bathing suit for me!"
(チアリーダーと友達の対話:「男の子たちを喜ばせるものを編んでるのよ」「選手のセーターかい」「違うわ. 私の水着よ」)
☞ something makes boys happy (S+V+O+C)

(b) 名詞が意味上の目的語

A bathing beauty these days wears nothing **to speak** *of*, but plenty **to talk** *about*.
(最近の水着美人は取り立てて言うほどのものを着てはいないが十分噂の種になるものは着ている.)

☞ to speak *of* nothing / to talk *about* plenty: いずれも「動詞＋前置詞」の目的語.

Work is the refuge of people who have nothing better **to do**.

(Oscar Wilde)

(仕事は他にもっと楽しめることを何も持っていない人々の逃げ場である.)
- ☞ to do nothing（V+O）　workaholic（仕事中毒の人）を皮肉っている.
- ☞ Oscar Wilde (1854-1900): アイルランド生まれのイギリスの詩人・小説家・劇作家.

"I suppose you played bridge last night?"
"No—our bridge club broke up."
"Why?"
"We had to break up because everybody attended every meeting and there was no one **to talk** *about*."

(「昨夜はブリッジをおやりになったんでしょ」「いいえ，私どものブリッジクラブは解散しましたの」「またどうしてですか」「みんな毎回出席するものですから，話題にする人がいなくなってしまったんですわ」)
- ☞ to talk about no one（V+O）

My husband has given me something **to live** *for*—revenge!

(夫は私に生きがいをくれた—復讐よ.)
- ☞ to live for something（V+O）

(c) 名詞の内容を説明する

> "What is the best way **to see** flying saucers?"
> "Pinch the waitress."
> (「空飛ぶ円盤を見るいちばんいい方法は何ですか」「ウエイトレスをつねることです」)

- ☞ saucer:「円盤」⇔「(カップの) 受け皿」　★ **Pun** → p. 26
- ☞ ウエイトレスが運んでいたカップの受け皿が飛んで行く.

This is a free country. Folks have a right **to send** me letters, and I have a right **not to read** them.　(William Falkner)

(ここは自由な国だ．人々は私に手紙を送る権利があり，そして私はそれらを読まない権利がある．)
- ☞ William Falkner (1897-1962): アメリカの小説家.

My most brilliant achievement was my ability **to persuade** my wife to marry me.　(Sir Winston Churchill)
（私の最も輝かしい成功は妻に私と結婚することを説得できたことだ．）
☞ Sir Winston Churchill (1874–1965): イギリスの政治家・首相（1940–45, 1951–55）

Patience in coaching may often be the inability **to make** a decision.
（コーチをするときの忍耐力とはしばしば決断する能力がないことかもしれない．）

(3) 副詞用法

> to 不定詞は，副詞として，(1) 目的，(2) 結果，(3) 感情の原因，(4) 形容詞の修飾語，として用いられる．

(a) 目的

To make a million, start with $900,000.　(Morton Shulman)
（100万ドル作るには90万ドルから始めろ．）

☞ Morton Shulman (1925–2000): カナダの政治家・実業家・コラムニスト・医師．

To make your dream come true, you have to stay awake.
（夢を実現させるためには目を覚ましていなければならない．）

He drinks **to forget** he drinks.
（彼は自分が飲むことを忘れるために飲む．）

You have to be pretty well off *not* **to be ashamed** to ask the clerk for something cheaper.
（店員に何かそれより安いものを求めて恥ずかしい思いをしないためにはかなり裕福である必要がある．）

★ **One-liner** → p. 395

(b) 結果

If you drink a glass of milk every morning for 1,200 months, you will live **to be** a hundred years old.
（1200ヶ月間毎日コップ1杯の牛乳を飲めば，100まで生きることになる．）

Little boys who never tell the truth grow up **to work** for the weather bureau.
（決して本当のことを言わない少年は成長して気象庁に勤めることになる．）

You spend your whole life believing that you're on the right track, **only to discover** that you're on the wrong train.
（人は正しい道をたどっていると信じて一生を送るが，結局は電車を乗り間違えたことに気づくにすぎない．）

On quiet nights, when he's alone, Fred runs their wedding video backwards, just **to watch** himself walk out of the church a free man.
（静かな夜など一人でいるとき，フレッドは結婚式のビデオを逆回転させて自分が自由人として教会から歩いて出るのをじっと見るのだ．）

(c) 感情の原因

"I seem to have two heartbeats."
"Oh, I'm *relieved* **to hear** that. Now I know where my Rolex is!"
（「心臓の鼓動が2つあるみたいだ」「ああ，それを聞いてほっとしたよ．やっとローレックスのありかが分かった」）

Editor: Did you write this poem yourself?
Contributor: Yes, every line of it.
Editor: Then I'm *glad* **to meet** you, Edgar Allan Poe, I thought you were dead long ago."
（編集者と寄稿者の対話：「この詩はあなたご自身でお書きになったのですか」「そうです，全ての行を書きました」「それなら，エドガー・アラン・ポーさん，お初にお目にかかれ

て何よりです．もうとっくに亡くなられたと思っていました」）
☞ Edgar Alan Poe (1809-1849): アメリカの詩人・小説家．
★ **Insulting joke** → p. 97

"What's the difference between a new husband and a new dog?"
"After a year, the dog will still be *excited* **to see** you."
（「新しい夫と新しい犬の違いは」「1 年後でも犬は君を見てまだ興奮している」）

I was *surprised* **to see** they had a picture of me in the National Portrait Gallery—then I realized it was a mirror.
（ナショナル・ポートレート・ギャラリーには私の肖像画があることを知って驚いた，そしてその後それは鏡だと分かったのだ．）
☞ National Portrait Gallery: ロンドンにある肖像画の美術館．

(d) 形容詞の修飾語

"What's the difference between a hill and a pill?"
"A hill is *hard* **to get up** and a pill is *hard* **to get down**."
（「ヒル（丘）とピル（丸薬）の違いは何か」「ヒルは登るのがむずかしく，ピルは飲み下すのがむずかしい」）

★ **What's-the-difference joke** → p. 153

"What's *easy* **to get** into but *hard* **to get** out of?"
"Trouble."
（「巻き込まれるのは簡単だが抜け出すのは容易でないものは何か」「トラブル」）

"What do money and a secret have in common?"
"They're very *hard* **to keep**."
（「金と秘密の共通点は何か」「どちらも保持するのが難しい」）

"Is your husband *hard* **to please**?"
"I don't know. I never tried!"
（「ご主人は気難しい方ですの」「さあ，どうかしら．試したことがありませんのよ」）
☞ hard to please:「喜ばすのがむずかしい」

(e) 独立の語句として

> **to tell (you) the truth**（本当のことを言うと），**to begin [start] with**（まず第一に），**to be frank with you**（率直に言えば），**to make a long story short**（手短に言えば），**strange to say**（妙な話だが），**needless to say**（言うまでもなく），**to be honest**（正直に言うと），**to be sure**（確かに），**so to speak**（言わば）　など

> The maid was called by her best friend. What were they going to do on the weekend?
> The maid said, "**To tell you the truth**, I'm afraid to leave the baby with its mother!"
> （お手伝いが親友から電話をもらった．週末には何をしようかと言う．彼女は言った「実を言うと，赤ちゃんを奥さんに怖くて預けられないの」）

The advantage of whiskey over a dog as a companion is legion. **To begin with**, whiskey does not need to be periodically wormed.
（ウイスキーが仲間として犬より優位な点は非常に多い．まず第一に，ウイスキーは定期的に寄生虫を除去する必要がない．）

When a fellow says, "Well, **to make a long story short**," it's too late.
　　　　　　　　　　　　　　　　　　　　　　　　　　　　　(Don Herold)
（男が「簡単に言えば」と言ったら，それは手遅れだ．）
☞ 話は簡単にはすまない．
☞ Don Herold (1889–1966): アメリカのユーモア作家・イラストレーター・漫画家．

A teacher was telling a friend about one of her students. "He cheats, he steals, he hits, and **to make it even worse**, he's the only kid in the class with a perfect attendance record!"
（先生が友だちに生徒の1人について話していた．「カンニングはする，盗みはする，人を叩く，それにさらに悪いことに，クラスでこの子だけなの，皆勤は」）

A young boy sat gazing into space. His father said, "Penny for your thoughts, son?"

"Well, **to be honest**, Dad," said the boy, "I was thinking of a pound."
(少年が宙をじっと見ていた．父親が「お前，何を考えているんだい」と言った．「ええと，正直に言うと，お父さん」と少年は言った「1 ポンドのことを考えていたんだ」)
☞ A penny for your thoughts:「何を考えているんだ」＜「1 ペニーあげるから考えていることを教えてくれ」

A manufacturer of patent medicines received this testimonial: "Since taking your tablets regularly, I am another woman. **Needless to say**, my husband is delighted."
(特許薬の製造業者が次の感謝状を受け取った：「そちらの錠剤を飲んで以来わたくしは人が変わりました．言うまでもなく，夫は喜んでおります」)

Girls worry too much about their clothes, but this is only much ado about nothing, **so to speak**.
(若い女性たちは服のことを心配し過ぎる，しかしこれは，言ってみれば，から騒ぎに過ぎない．)
☞ much ado about nothing:「から騒ぎ（シェイクスピアの喜劇の1つの題名になっている）」

(4) tell [ask / want / enable / expect / teach など] ＋O＋to 不定詞

次のように考えるとよい．

	[S]	[V]	[O]		
1.	I ＋	want ＋	him	to come	(彼に来てもらいたい．)
			S'	V'	
2. a)	I ＋	heard ＋	her	sing	(彼女が歌うのを聞いた．)
			S'	V'	
b)	I ＋	made ＋	him	go	(彼を行かせた．)
			S'	V'	

つまり him to come をまとめて want の目的語と考えるが，him to come 自体

は he＋will come という S＋V の意味をもつ．同様に 2. a) → she sang, b) → he went．

(a) O が to 不定詞の意味上の主語

> "I don't think the gentleman next door knows much about music."
> "Why?"
> "Well, he **told** *me* **to** *cut* my drum open and *see* what was inside it."
> (「隣の紳士は音楽のことをあまり知らないらしい」「なぜ」「今朝僕に大鼓を切り開いて中に何が入っているか見てみろと言ったもの」)

I'm not saying my wife is a bad cook, but my doctor **advised** *me* **to** *eat* out more often.
(妻が料理下手とは言っていません，しかし医者はもっと外食しろと勧めたのです．)

Human beings are the only creatures on earth that **allow** *their children* **to** *come* back home.　(Bill Cosby)
(子供たちが家に帰ってくることを許す生きものはこの世で人類だけである．)
☞ Bill Cosby (1937-　)：アメリカのコメディアン・作家・俳優．

"Tell me that you love me."
"Sure, but don't **ask** *me* **to** *write* it."
(「私を愛してるって言って」「いいとも，しかしそれを書いてくれとは言わないでよ」)
☞ 書くと証拠が残る．

"My daughter's music lessons are a fortune to me."
"How is it?"
"They **enable** *me* **to** *buy* the neighbors' houses at half price."
(「娘の音楽のレッスンは私には一つの財産だよ」「またどうして」「おかげで近所の家がいくつも半額で買えるからさ」)

Warning: The consumption of alcohol may **cause** *you* **to** *think* you can sing.
（警告：アルコールの消費は自分は歌えると思い込ませることがあります．）

A husband is a person who **expects** *his wife* **to** *be* perfect and *to understand* why he isn't.
（夫とは妻に完璧であることを望み，なぜ自分は完璧でないかを理解してもらいたいと思っている人である．）

Doctor: Deep breathing, you understand, destroys microbes.
Patient: But, doctor, how can I **force** *them* **to** *breathe* deeply?
（医師「深呼吸は細菌を殺すことはお分かりですね」患者「しかし先生，どうやって深呼吸させればいいんですか」）
★ **Irish bull** → p. 39

You cannot **teach** *a crab* **to** *walk* straight.　(Aristophanes)
（蟹に真っ直ぐ歩くことを教えることはできない．）
☞ Aristophanes [æristάfni:z]：古代ギリシャ，アテネの喜劇作家．

I went fishing but it was hopeless. Still, the day wasn't a total loss. I **taught** *the worm* **to** *swim*.
（釣りに行ったがどうしようもなかった．それでもその日がまったく無駄だったわけではない．ミミズに泳ぎを教えてやったのだ．）

Jane has a baby each year because she doesn't **want** *the youngest one* **to** *get* spoiled.
（ジェーンが毎年子供を産んでいるのは一番下の子が甘やかされてほしくないからだ．）
★ **Irish bull** → p. 39

cf. get＋O＋to *do*：「（してほしいことを）Oに＿するようにしむける」（→ B. 原形不定詞 (1)）
　"I finally **got** *my boss* **to** *laugh* out loud."
　"Did you tell him a joke?"
　"No, I asked for a raise."

(「とうとうボスを大声で笑わせたよ」「冗談でも言ったのか」「いいや,給料を上げてくれと頼んだんだ」)

Q: How many mothers-in-law does it take to screw in a light bulb?
A: None ... she always **gets** the son-in-law **to** do it.
(問「電球を回して(ソケットに)入れるには何人の義理の母が必要か」答「1人もいらない,義理の息子にさせるから」)
★ **Mother-in-law** → p. 305

(b) 不定詞の意味上の主語を特に示す場合:for+(代)名詞

"How many Harvard grads does it take to change a light bulb?"
"One. He grabs the bulb and wait **for** *the world* to *revolve* around him."
(「電球を取り替えるのにハーバードの卒業生が何人必要か」「1人.彼は電球を掴み,世間の人が彼の周りを回るのを待つ」)

★ **Light-bulb joke** → p. 139

For Christmas I bought my son a set of electric trains **for** *me* to *play* with.
(クリスマスには息子に私が遊ぶための電車のセットを買ってやった.)

The green light is the signal **for** *the man behind you* to *blow* his horn.
(青信号は君の後ろの男が警笛を鳴らす合図だ.)

My parents' dream was **for** *me* to *have* everything they didn't. And thanks to ozone holes, fear of AIDS and no health insurance, their dream has come true.   (Brad Slaight)
(両親の夢は私が彼らが持たなかったものすべてを手に入れることだった.そしてオゾンホール,エイズの恐怖,健康保険を掛けていないおかげで,彼らの夢は実現した.)
☞ Brad Slaight (1964-): アメリカの俳優・コメディアン.

(5) **seem [appear] to** *do*:「＿するように思われる」; **happen to** *do*:「偶然＿する」

The government **seems** *to believe* there is a taxpayer born every minute.
(政府は毎分１人の納税者が生まれるとでも思っているらしい.)
☞ ＝ **It seems that** the government *believes* ...

Luck always **seems** *to favor* the guy who doesn't need it!
(幸運はそれを必要としない奴をいつも贔屓しているように思える.)
☞ ＝**It seems that** luck always *favors* ...

The counselor called and told us that our son was sleeping with a stray dog. "What about the smell?" we asked.
The counselor answered, "The dog **seems** *to be* getting used to it."
(カウンセラーが電話で家の息子が野良犬と寝ていると言ってきた.「臭いはどうですか」と私たちは尋ねた. カウンセラーは答えて「犬は慣れ始めているようです」)
☞ 臭うのは息子の方.
☞ **It seems that** the dog *is getting* used to it.

God **seems** *to have left* the receiver off the hook, and time is running out. (Arthur Koestler)
(神は受話器をはずしたままになされたようだ，そして時間切れになろうとしている.)
☞ ＝**It seems that** God *has left* the receiver off the hook, ...
☞ Arthur Koestler (1905-1983): ハンガリー出身のユダヤ人ジャーナリスト・小説家・哲学者.

"There **appear** *to be* a lot of birds around today," grunted the heavy-handed golfer.
"Probably following us for the worms, sir," observed the caddie.
(「今日はどうもあたりに鳥が多いようだ」と下手なゴルファーがぼやいた. キャディーは言った.「きっと虫を探して私たちの後をついて来ているんです，お客さん」)
☞ **It appears that** *there are* a lot of birds ...

My son was a smart youngster. One time he brought home his report card and said, "Dad, here is my report card and here's one of yours I **happened** *to find* in the attic!"
(息子は抜け目のない子供だった．ある時，通知表を持って帰って来て言った「お父さん，これがぼくの通知表，これが偶然屋根裏部屋で見つけたお父さんのだよ」)

(6) 慣用表現

> By the time a man is rich **enough** *to sleep* late, he is **too** old *to enjoy* it.
> (人は遅くまで寝ていられるほど金持ちになるまでには年を取りすぎてそれを楽しめなくなっている．)

- (a) **too** ～ **to** *do*
- (b) ～ **enough to** *do*
- (c) **in order to** *do* / **so as to** *do*
- (d) **so** ～ **as to** *do*
- (e) **be to** *do*
- (f) **be about to** *do*
- (g) **be supposed to** *do*

(a) **too** ～ **to** *do*:「～すぎて＿できない，＿するには～すぎる」

> *Traffic policeman:* Did you not see the speed limit sign?
> *Motorist:* No, officer. I was driving **too** fast **to** *see* it.
> (交通警官「速度制限の標識を見なかったのかい」運転者「見ませんでした，お巡りさん．速く運転しすぎて見えませんでした」)

My ambition is to marry a rich girl who is **too** proud **to** *let* her husband work.
(私の野心は金持ちで夫を働かせるには自尊心の強すぎる女性と結婚することだ．)

Summer is the time when it's **too** hot **to** *do* the job it was **too** cold **to** *do* in the winter.
（夏は冬には寒すぎてできない仕事を暑すぎてできない季節である．）

(b) ～ **enough to** *do*:「＿するのに十分に～，＿するのに必要なだけの～」(cf.「有り余る」の意味はない．)

One gold digger told another, "He's old **enough to** *be* my father, but he's rich **enough to** *be* my husband!"
（金目当ての女がもう１人に言った「彼は私の父だと言えるほどの年だけど夫になるに十分なお金持ちよ」）

"Dad, can I ask you a question?"
"Sure, son."
"When am I going to be old **enough** not **to** *have* to go to church either?"
（父と息子の対話：「お父さん，聞いてもいい」「いいよ，お前」「いくつになったら僕も教会へ行かなくてもよくなるの」）

(c) in order to *do* / **so as to** *do*:「（目的を表して）＿するために」

In order to *get* a loan, you must prove you don't need it.
（貸し付けを受けるためにはその必要がないことを証明しなければならない．）

Taxpayers: People who don't have to pass civil service examinations **in order to** *work* for the government.
（納税者：政府の仕事をするために公務員試験に合格しなくてもよい人々．）

Most movies end just as the couples are about to get married, **in order** *not* **to** *show* anything brutal.
（ほとんどの映画は２人がまさに結婚しようとする時に終わるが，これは残酷なことを何も見せないためである．）

Memo: A generally pointless or self-evident message penned by management-level employees **so as to** *avoid* the unpleasantness of actual work.
(メモとは実際の仕事の不快さを避けるために経営レベルの従業員によって書かれた概して的外れで分かり切ったメッセージ．)

Amy: Dad bought Mum a bone-china tea set for her birthday.
Zoe: How lovely!
Amy: Yes, but he only did it **so as** *not* **to** *have* to do the washing-up. Mum's too frightened he'll break it!
(エイミーとゾーイの対話：「お父さんはお母さんの誕生日にボーンチャイナの紅茶セットを買ったの」「まあ素敵」「そうなの，でもそうしたのは皿洗いをしないですむようにするためだけだったの．お母さんはお父さんが割りはしないか心配でしょうがないのよ」)

(d) so 〜 as to *do*：「とても〜なので＿する，＿するほど〜」

"Hey, can't you read? That notice says 'Private—No fishing.'"
"But I wouldn't be **so** rude **as to** *read* a private notice."
(「君は字が読めないのか．掲示に「私有地につき釣りを禁ず」とあるだろう」「しかし個人的な通知を読むほど礼儀知らずではありません」)

☞ private:「私有の」⇔「個人的な」　　★ **Pun** → p. 26

Moving along a dimly lighted street, a man was suddenly approached by a stranger who had slipped from the shadows nearby. "Please, sir," asked the stranger, "would you be **so** kind **as to** *help* a poor unfortunate fellow who is hungry and out of work? All I have in the world is this gun."
(男が照明の薄暗い通りを歩いていると，突然近くの暗がりから見知らぬ男がこっそり近づいて来た．「お願いです，旦那」と見知らぬ男は言った「腹を空かした失業中の哀れなついてない男をどうかお助けください．持っているものといったらこのピストルだけなんで」)

(e) **be to** *do*:「＿することになっている（命令・義務・予定などを表す）」

If fame **is to** *come* only after death, I am in no hurry for it.
(Martial)
(もし名声が死後にのみ得られることになっているのなら，私はそれを急いで求めはしない．)

☞ Martial (40 A.D.–104 A.D.): スペイン生まれのローマの風刺詩人．

Two small girls were playing together one afternoon in the park.
"I wonder what time it is," said one of them.
"Well, it can't be four o'clock yet," replied the other, "because my mother said I **was to** *be* home at four, and I'm not."
(2人の少女がある午後公園で遊んでいた．「何時かしら」と1人が言った．「そうね，まだ4時のはずないわ」ともう1人が答えた．「だってお母さんは4時には家にいなさいと言ったけど，わたしいないもん」)
★ **Irish bull** → p. 39

Where else but in the government could you find the following: A clerk is told to destroy a whole series of documents because there isn't enough space to store them.
But the order goes on: he **is to** *make* a copy first!
(政府機関以外のどこに次のようなことがありうるだろうか：事務官は保存するスペースがないという理由で一連の文書を破棄することを命じられる．しかし，命令はさらに続く：まずコピーは取っておくこと．)

It is the weak who are cruel, and gentleness **is to** *be expected* only from the strong.　(Leo Rosten)
(残酷なのは弱い人々であり，優しさは強い人々からのみ期待できる．)
☞ is to be expected＝can be expected
☞ Leo Rosten (1908–1997): ポーランド出身のアメリカのユダヤ系（ユーモア）作家．

(f) **be about to** *do*:「＿しようとしている」
Son, if you really want something in this life, you have to work for it.

Now, quiet, they**'re about to** *announce* the lottery numbers.

(Homer Simpson)

(息子よ，この世で何か欲しかったら，そのために働かなくてはいかんぞ．こら，ちょっと静かにしろ．宝くじの当選番号を発表するぞ．)
☞ Homer Simpson: テレビアニメシリーズの主人公．

(g) be supposed to *do*:「＿することになっている」（予定・義務）

"Football **is supposed to** *build* bodies."
"Baloney! I watched four games this weekend, and look at my flab!"
(「フットボールは身体を作ると思われている」「バカな．この週末4試合見たぜ，それなのにオレのぜい肉を見てみろ」)

"What do you mean by telling everyone I'm an idiot?"
"I'm sorry. I didn't know it **was supposed to** *be* a secret."
(「みんなにオレがバカだと言うとはどういうつもりなんだ」「ごめん．秘密にしておくべきだとは知らなかったんだ」)

(7) 代不定詞：to 不定詞の代わりに **to** だけが用いられるもの

> When a man breaks a date, he has **to**. When a girl does, she has two.
> (男がデートの約束を破るのはやむをえず．女が破るのは二股．)

☞ has to = has to break; to [tu] ⇔ two [tuː]　★ **Pun** → p. 26

Man is the only animal that blushes—or ought **to**.　(Mark Twain)
(人間は赤面する唯一の動物である―あるいはすべき．)
☞ ought to = ought to blush
☞ Mark Twain (1835-1910): アメリカの（ユーモア）小説家．
★ **One-liner** → p. 395

(8) 分離不定詞：to と動詞の原形の間に副詞が入ったもの．一般に避けるべきであると考えられているが，実際にはかなり用いられている．

Be sure **to** *never* **split** an infinitive.
（不定詞を分離しないように気をつけなさい．）

☞ この文自体に分離不定詞が用いられている．

The best way to diet is **to** *always* **keep** your mouth closed as well as your refrigerator.
（ダイエットの最もいいやり方は冷蔵庫だけでなく口もいつも閉じたままにしておくことです．）

Unfortunately, the song is sung in such high octaves that it makes it difficult **to** *accurately* **guess** what is being sung. (A native speaker's comment on Utada Hikaru's singing)
（不幸なことに，その歌はあまりにも高オクターブで歌われるので何が歌われているか正確に推測するのは難しい．（宇多田ヒカルの歌い方についてのネイティブのコメント））

(9) 完了不定詞：to have＋過去分詞

"I'm glad **to have been** of some assistance. Can't we meet again somewhere?"
"Yes. Save my life tomorrow about the same time."
（「お役に立ててうれしいです．またどこかでお会いできませんか」「いいですわ．明日またこの時間に私の命を救ってください」）

☞ ＝ I'm glad that I ***was*** [***have been***] of some assistance.

"Waiter, the portions seem **to have got** a lot smaller lately."
"Just an optical illusion, sir. Now that the restaurant has been enlarged, they look smaller ... that's all."
（「君，どうも最近一皿の分量がだいぶ少なくなったような気がするんだが」「ただの目の錯覚ですよ，お客さん．レストランを広げたので，分量が少なく見える．それだけのことです」）

☞ ＝ it seems that the portions ***have got*** a lot smaller lately

★ **Waiter** → p. 266

What do you do when your opponent claims **to have found** his ball in the rough and you know he's a liar because his ball is in your pocket?
(君はどうする，ゴルフの相手がボールをラフで見つけたと主張するのに君は相手のボールが自分のポケットに入っているから相手は嘘をついていることが分かっているとき.)
☞ ... your opponent claims that he *(has) found* his ball in the rough ...

(10) 受動態の不定詞：to be＋過去分詞

> *Lady:* You should be ashamed **to be seen** begging at my house.
> *Tramp:* Don't feel like that, lady. I've seen a lot worse house than this one.
> (婦人「私の家で物乞いをしているところを見られて恥ずかしいと思うべきです」浮浪者「奥さん，そんなふうに考えなくてもいいですよ．お宅よりもっとひどい家を何度も見てきましたから」)

☞ ＝ You should be ashamed that you *are seen* begging ...
★ **Insulting joke** → p. 97

She's vicious. When she dies, she wants **to be cremated and thrown** in somebody's face!
(彼女は根性が曲がっている．自分が死んだら火葬にしてもらって誰かの顔に投げつけてもらいたいと思っているのだ.)

The service here is so slow, you have to come at lunchtime **to be served** supper.
(ここのサービスは非常にのろいので夕食を出してもらうには昼食時に来なければならない.)
★ **Tall tale** → p. 412

This is not a novel **to be tossed** aside lightly. It should be thrown with great force.　(Dorothy Parker, in a book review)
((書評の中で) この作品は軽々しく脇へほうり投げられるべき小説ではない．力一杯投げられるべきものだ.)

☞ Dorothy Parker (1893-1967): アメリカの詩人・短編作家・風刺作家.
★ **Insulting joke** → p. 97

B. 原形不定詞:「**to** なし不定詞」ともいう.

(1) 使役動詞: **make [let / have]**＋O＋原形不定詞

"How did you **make** your neighbor *keep* his hens in his own yard?"
"One night I hid half dozen eggs under a bush in my garden, and next day I **let** him *see* me gather them. I wasn't bothered after that."
(「どうやって隣りの雌鶏(めんどり)を隣りの家の囲いの中で飼うようにさせたんだい」「ある晩,半ダースの卵を家の庭の茂みの下に隠して,翌朝僕がそれを集めるのを彼に見せて(う)やったのさ.その後は迷惑しなかったよ」)

(a) make＋O＋*do*: 基本的意味「無理に O に＿させる」

I can **make** my wife *do* anything she wants to do.
(私は妻がしたいと望むことを何でもさせることができる.)

Rain **makes** flowers *grow*. It also **makes** cabs *disappear*.
(雨は花を成長させる.雨はまたタクシーを見えなくさせる.)

A small boy's definition of conscience: Something that **makes** you *tell* your mother before your sister does.
(小さな男の子にとっての良心:妹が告げ口する前に自分から母親に打ち明けなければいけないと思わせるもの.)

Imagination is what **makes** a politician *think* he's a statesman.
(想像力とは政治屋に自分は立派な政治家だと思わせるもの.)

He likes to take a drink because it **makes** him *see* double and *feel* single.

（彼が酒好きなのは，酒を飲むと物が2つに見え，独身気分にしてくれるからである．）
☞ double ⇔ single

(b) let＋O＋*do*: 基本的意味「許してOに__させる」

> *Patient:* Am I getting better?
> *Doctor:* I don't know. **Let** me *feel* your purse.
> （患者「私は良くなっていますか」医師「分かりません．財布に触らせてください」）

☞ purse [pəːrs]（財布）⇔ pulse [pʌls]（脈）　　★ **Pun** → p. 26
☞ うっかり本音が出た．　　★ **Doctor** → p. 329

"**Let** me *tell* you we have a wonderful family tree."
"The tree is all right, but the crop is a failure."
（「我が家にはすばらしい家系図［樹］があるんだ」「樹はすばらしいが，収穫は不作だね」）
★ **Insulting joke** → p. 97

"Well, miss," said the traffic cop to the perfectly sweet motorist, "I suppose you know why I stopped you."
"Don't tell me," she replied, "**let** me *guess*. Yes, I know! You're lonely."
（「お嬢さん」と交通警官がとてもかわいい運転者に言った「なぜあなたの車を止めたかお分かりでしょう」「言わないで」と彼女は答えた．「当てさせて，そうだ，わかったわ．あなたさびしいんでしょ」）

Teacher: Ted, your math homework was totally wrong.
Ted: **Don't let** my father *hear* what you said! He says his best subject in school was math.
（先生「テッド，あなたの数学の宿題は全部間違っていましたよ」テッド「今言ったことをお父さんに聞かせないでください．学校のとき一番よかった科目は数学だと言ってますから」）

(c) **have**＋O＋*do*: 基本的意味「頼んで O に＿させる［してもらう］」

"What's the best way to catch a fish?"
"**Have** someone *throw* it at you."
(「魚を捕る最もいい方法は何か」「誰かにそれを投げつけてもらえばいい」)

☞ catch:「捕まえる」⇔「(手で) つかむ」

Old Doc Foster has a unique and effective way for patients to get the most out of a diet. He **has** them *place* their bathroom scale in front of the refrigerator.
(老フォスター医師は患者が最も効果的なダイエットをする独特の方法を持っている．彼らに風呂場の体重計を冷蔵庫の前に置かせるのだ．)

The news broke that the ditchdigger had been willed one million dollars. The press services descended upon the excavation where he was working. "Will one million dollars make any drastic changes in your life?" asked one reporter. "Certainly," said the laborer. "Now I can **have** a chauffeur *drive* me to work."
(溝堀り人夫が遺言によって 100 万ドル贈られたというニュースが発表された．新聞記者たちが彼が働いている切り通しへ突然押しかけた．「100 万ドルあるとあなたの生活に大変な変化をもたらしますか」1 人の記者が尋ねた．「もちろんさ」と人夫は言った．「こうなりゃ，運転手つきで仕事に行けるよ」)

A lady decided to **have** the little neighbor boy *stay* for lunch one day. As he began eating she watched him struggling to manipulate his knife and fork. Hoping to be helpful, she said, "Are you sure you can cut your steak?" "Oh, yes," he replied. "We often have it this tough at home."
(ある婦人が近所の男の子にゆっくりして昼食を食べていかせようとした．彼が食べ始めると，婦人は男の子がナイフとフォークをなんとかうまく扱おうと苦心しているのを見た．彼女は助け舟を出すつもりで「君，ビフテキ切るの大丈夫かな」と言った．すると男の子はこう答えた．「大丈夫さ．これくらい硬いのなら家でよく食べてるよ」)

(d) help＋O＋*do*:「O が＿するのを助ける」

> A diet is what **helps** a person *gain* weight more slowly.
> (ダイエットは人がよりゆっくり体重が増えるのを助けるものである.)

"Papa's buying a dog to **help** him *hitch* hike."
"What kind of a dog could **help** him *hitch* hike?"
"He's buying a pointer."
(「パパはヒッチハイクに役立つ犬を買うよ」「どんな犬がヒッチハイクに役立つんだい」「パパはポインターを買うのさ」)
☞ pointer:「ポインター(猟犬)」⇔「指し示す人〔物〕」　★ **Pun** → p. 26

An old gentleman asked the pretty girl if she wanted to come up to his room to **help** him *write* his will.
(老紳士はそのかわいい女の子に自分の部屋へ上がって来て遺書を書くのを手伝ってくれる気はないかと尋ねた.)

cf. help＋O＋to *do*:「(間接的に手を貸して) O が＿するのを助ける」

"Why are you so late?" the teacher asked Timmy. "Well, there was a man who had lost a dollar bill." "I see. And you were **helping** him *to look* for it?" "No, I was standing on it."
(「なぜこんなに遅れたんだね」先生がティミーに尋ねた.「あのう, 1ドル札をなくした人がいたんです」「なるほど. それで捜すのを手伝ってあげていたんだね」「ちがいます. その上に立っていたんです」)

(2) 知覚動詞: see [hear / watch / listen to]＋O＋原形不定詞

> I can **hear** people *smile*. (David Blunkett)
> (人々が微笑んでいるのが聞こえる.)

☞ David Blunkett (1947-): イギリス労働党の政治家.

(a) see＋O＋*do*:「O が＿するのを見る」

I never **saw** a saw *saw* a saw.

(鋸が鋸を鋸で切るのをのこでも見たことがない．)
☞ saw:「見た (see の過去形)」⇔「鋸 (で切る)」　★ **Pun** → p. 26

Dentist: Have you **seen** any small boys *ring* my bell and *run* away?
Policeman: They weren't small boys—they were grownups.
(歯医者「小さな男の子たちが家のベルを鳴らして逃げて行くのを見ましたか」警官「彼らは小さな男の子じゃなかったですよ—大きな大人たちでした」)

Little Boy: Dad, have you ever **seen** a catfish?
Dad: Yes, I have.
Little Boy: How did it hold its pole?
(少年と父親の対話：「お父さん，ナマズ見たことあるの」「あるとも」「どうやって竿を持ったのかなあ」)
☞ catfish (ナマズ) ⇔ cat fish (ネコが釣りをする)　★ 異分析 → p. 375

(b) hear＋O＋*do*:「O が＿するのを聞く」

Policeman: Didn't you **hear** me *call* you to stop?
Driver: I didn't know it was you. I thought it was someone I'd run over.
(警官「君に止まれと言うのが聞こえなかったのか」運転者「お巡りさんとは分かりませんでした．私が轢いた奴だと思ったんです」)

"Why don't you answer?"
"I did."
"You didn't."
"I did,—I shook my head."
"Well, I didn't **hear** it *rattle*."
(「なぜ返事をしないんだ」「したさ」「しなかったぞ」「本当にしたさ—首を振ったよ」「ふうん．首の鳴る音は聞こえなかったぞ」)
☞ rattlebrain「頭がからっぽの人」　★ **Insulting joke** → p. 97

Pete: My wife doesn't understand me, does yours?
John: I don't know, I have never **heard** her even *mention* your name.

(「家内は僕の言うことを理解しないんだ．君の奥さんは」「分からないよ．家内が君の名前を出すのを聞いたことがないんでね」)

(c) **watch＋O＋*do***:「O が＿するのをじっと見る」

A little boy went to the ballet for the first time with his father and **watched** the girls *dance* around on their toes for a while. Then he asked, "Why don't they just get taller girls?"
(男の子が初めて父親とバレエを見に行き，女の子たちがつま先立って踊り回るのをしばらくじっと見ていた．やがて彼はこう尋ねた．「なぜもっと背の高い女の子にしないの」)

Mrs Able: Our new house is wonderful! I can lie in bed and **watch** the sun **rise**.
Mrs Cable: That's nothing. I've always been able to sit at my breakfast table and **watch** the kitchen **sink**.
(「私たちの新居は素敵よ．ベッドに横になって太陽が昇るのを見られるのよ」「そんなの何でもないわ．私はいつも朝食のテーブルに座って台所が沈むのを見られてるわ」)
☞ the kitchen sink:「台所が沈む」⇔「台所の流し台」　★ 異分析 → p.375

(d) **listen to＋O＋*do***:「O が＿するのを（注意して）聞く」

Listen to her *eat*! She's souprano.
(彼女が食べる音を聞いてごらん．彼女はスープラノだ．)
☞ 音を立てるのはマナー違反．

Do you want to be shaky about history? Just **listen to** two men *describe* what happened at the accident they both saw!
(歴史についてあやふやな態度でいたいのか．それなら2人の男が共に見た事故で何が起こったかを説明するのを聞きさえすればいい．)
☞ 2人とも言うことがまったく違う．

(3) **demand [insist / suggest / propose / recommend] (that) S＋(should)＋原形**

cf. ((米))ではふつう should を省略する．

(a) demand that S+*do*:「Sが__することを要求する」

He's a born wino. When he goes into surgery, he **demands** that they *operate* at room temperature.
（あいつは生まれつきのワイン中毒だ．手術されるとき，室温で手術しろと要求している．）
☞ wino:「アル中；ワイン」

(b) insist that S+*do*:「Sが__することを主張する」

He wanted to paint her in the nude, but she **insisted** he *keep* his clothes on.
（彼は彼女をヌードで描きたかった，しかし彼女は彼に服は着ていてくれと主張した．）

(c) suggest that S+*do*:「Sに__してはどうかと言う」

The director decided to award an annual prize of £50 for the best idea of saving the Company money. It was won by a young executive who **suggested** that in future the prize money *be* reduced to £10.
（社長は会社の金を節約する最もいい考えに毎年 50 ポンドの賞金を出すことにした．賞金は今後賞金を 10 ポンドに減額することを提案した若い役員がもらった．）

A woman is in a gambling casino. At the roulette table, a man **suggests** that she *should play* her age. She puts her money on twenty-eight. Number thirty-six comes up, and she faints.
（女性が賭博場にいる．ルーレットのテーブルで男が自分の歳に賭けてはどうかと言う．彼女は金を 28 のところに置く．36 が当たり彼女は気絶する．）

(d) propose that S+*do*:「Sが__することを提案する」

I **propose** a limitation *be* put on how many squares of toilet paper can be used in any one sitting.　(Sheryl Crow)
（一度座ったらトイレットペーパーを何枚使ってよいかの制限を設けるべきだと提案します．）
☞ Sheryl Crow (1962–)：アメリカのシンガーソングライター，レコード・プロデューサー，女優．

(e) **recommend** that S+*do*:「Sが＿することを勧める」
　Customer: I'm in the mood for a tasty meal. What would you recommend?
　Waiter: I **recommend** you *try* another restaurant.
（客とウエイターの対話：「おいしい食事をしたい気分だ．お勧めは何だい」「他のレストランをお勧めします」）
★ **Waiter** → p. 266

ジョークの常識⑭

★ **Tom Swifties:**「言った言葉とそれを言った態度の副詞を結びつける言葉遊び」Pun の一種．

"I love to eat hot dogs," admitted the boy **frankly**.
（「ホットドッグを食べるのが好きだ」と少年は率直に言った．）
☞ ホットドッグには *frank*furter（フランクフルトソーセージ）がつきもの．

"I don't want ice in my drink," replied the Eskimo **coldly**.
（「酒に氷はいらない」とエスキモーが冷たく答えた．）
☞ ice と cold(ly)は縁語．

"Give me chili peppers," roared the angry Mexican **hotly**.
（「チリペッパーをよこせ」と腹を立てたメキシコ人がかっとなってわめいた．）
☞ hot:「ぴりりと辛い」⇔「（行動などが）激しい」

第15章　分　詞

"What have you got there?"
"A **sleeping** pill."
"Well, don't wake it!"
(「そこに何を持ってるの」「睡眠薬さ」「じゃあ，起こしちゃだめよ」)

☞ sleeping：「眠っている（現在分詞）」⇔「眠るための（動名詞）」

> 分詞には**現在分詞**と**過去分詞**があり，動詞の性質をもちながら，形容詞や副詞の働きをする．

A. 現在分詞：*do*ing

現在分詞には次の用法がある：
  (1) 名詞の前[後]につく形容詞として
  (2) S＋V＋現在分詞
  (3) S＋V＋O＋現在分詞
  (4) 分詞構文に用いられる（→ C）
  (5) be＋*do*ing で進行形をつくる．（→ 第1章 現在(進行)形・過去(進行)形・未来(進行)形）

(1) 名詞の前[後]につく形容詞として
a) 現在分詞が単独で使われる場合：名詞の前

He must be rich. He's got a **walking** wallet.
(あいつは金持ちにちがいない．歩く財布を持っている．)
☞ a walking dictionary：「生き字引（＜歩いている辞書）」のもじり．
  ★ **Parody** → p. 199

(Dog barks)

"Don't be afraid—a **barking** dog never bites."

"You mean, he never barks while he's biting."

((犬がほえる)「こわがることはない．ほえる犬は咬みつかないんだ」「きみが言いたいのは，犬は咬みついている間はほえないってことなんだろう」)

☞ Barking dogs seldom bite.（ほえる犬はめったに咬まない）はことわざ．

Church: a place where you encounter **nodding** acquaintances.

(教会：頷いている知人たちと出会う場所．)

☞ nod:「うなずく」⇔「（居眠りして）こっくりする」　★ **Pun** → p. 26
★ 教会 → p. 345

b) 現在分詞が他の語句を伴う場合：名詞の後

> "Who is that homely woman **standing** *over there*?"
>
> "That's my wife."
>
> "Pardon me—my mistake."
>
> "No—my mistake."
>
> (「あそこに立っている器量の悪い女は誰だい」「私の家内です」「ごめんごめん．私の勘違いだ」「とんでもない．私の勘違いです」)

The longest word in the English language is the one **following** *the phrase*: And now a word from our sponsor!

(英語で一番長い語は次の句に続く語だ：それではスポンサーから一言．)

No Exit: A sign **indicating** *the most convenient way out of a building*.
(Beachcomber)

(「出口ではありません」：建物から出る最も便利な道を示す掲示．)

☞ Beachcomber (J. B. Morton) (1893-1979)：イギリスのユーモア作家．

Q: A lawyer **charging** *a high fee*, a lawyer **charging** *a low fee*, Santa Claus, and Easter Bunny are all seated around a table. In the center of the table is a bag **containing** *$50,000*. The lights go off.

When the lights come back on, the money is missing. Who took it?
A: The lawyer **charging** *a high fee*, because the other three are fictional characters.

(問「高額の報酬を請求する弁護士，低額を請求する弁護士，サンタクロース，復活祭のウサギちゃんがみんなテーブルの周りに座っている．テーブルの中央には 5 万ドル入ったカバンが置いてある．電気が消える．電気がまた点いたとき，金はなくなっている．誰が取ったか」答「高額の報酬を請求する弁護士．他の 3 者は実在しない人物」)

★ **Lawyer** → p. 329

(2) S＋V＋現在分詞：go [come] *do***ing; keep** *do***ing**

"Doctor, Doctor, I feel like a pound note."
"**Go** ***shopping***, the change will do you good."
(「先生，先生，わたくし 1 ポンド札のような気分ですの」「買い物にお出でなさい．気分転換はあなたのためになります」)

☞ change:「気分転換」⇔「小銭・釣銭」　★ **Pun** → p. 26

(a) come [go] *do***ing**：「＿しながら来る［行く］」

The boy **came** *running* into the basement. "Father," he called, "you can take your finger off the leak in the pipe."
"Thank heavens," muttered father. "Is the plumber here at last?"
"No," said Junior. "The house is on fire."
(少年が地下室へ走ってやってきて呼ぶ．「お父さん，水道管のもれ口から指を抜いてもいいよ」「ありがたい」と父親はつぶやいた．「やっと配管工が来てくれたのか」「ちがうよ」と息子．「家が火事なんだ」)

A little fledgling fell out of its nest and **went** *crashing* through the branches of the elm tree towards the ground.
"Are you all right?" called out an owl as the chick **went** *hurtling* past his perch.
"So far," said the little bird.
(幼いひな鳥が巣から落ち，楡の木の枝を通り抜けて地面に向かって墜落して行くところだった．「大丈夫か」とフクロウはひな鳥が止まり木の前を通って落ちていくとき叫んだ．

「今のところはね」とひな鳥は言った.）

(b) go *do*ing:「＿しに行く，＿する」(cf.「行く」より「＿する」に重点がある.）
When she **went** *camping*, the bears built a fire to keep her away!
（彼女がキャンプへ行くと，熊たちは彼女を近づけないために火を起こした.）
★ Tall tale → p. 412

I used to have a swimsuit made entirely of sponges. I **went** *swimming* in a pool and when I got out, nobody could **go** *swimming* until I got back in.
（私は全体がスポンジ製の水着を着ていたものだった．プールで泳いで出ると，私がプールに戻るまで誰も泳げなかった.）
★ Tall tale → p. 412

My wife and I always hold hands. If I let go, she **goes** *shopping*.
（妻と私はいつも手を取り合っている．離すと妻は買い物に行くのだ.）

When he **goes** *hitchhiking* he leaves early to avoid the traffic.
（彼はヒッチハイクに出かけるとき早く出て車の往来を避ける.）
☞ それではヒッチハイクはできない.

(c) keep *do*ing:「＿し続ける」
Patient: Doctor, doctor! People **keep** *ignoring* me.
Doctor: Next!
（患者「先生，先生，みんなが私を無視しし続けるんです」医師「次の方」）

(3) S＋V＋O＋現在分詞：see [hear / catch]＋O＋*do*ing；keep [leave]＋O＋*do*ing など

"Who was that man I **saw** you *kissing* last night, daughter?"
"What time was it?"
（「娘や，私が夕べお前がキスをしているのを見た男の人はだれだい」「何時だったの」）

(a) see＋O＋*do*ing:「O が＿しているのが見える」

"You drink too much."

"I don't drink."

"Why, I **saw** you *drink**ing*** Scotch the other night."

"Oh, I didn't mean to drink it. I was gargling with it and it slipped."

(「あなた飲み過ぎよ」「飲んでるもんか」「まあ，この間の晩ウイスキーを飲んでいるのを見たわ」「ああ，あれは飲むつもりはなかったんだ．うがいをしていたら滑り込んだだけさ」)

  Boss: I thought you wanted the afternoon off to see your dentist.
Mr. Brown: That's right.
  Boss: Then how come I **saw** you *leav**ing*** the football ground with a friend?
Mr. Brown: That was my dentist.

(ボスと社員の対話:「歯医者に診てもらうために午後休みたいのかと思ったよ」「その通りです」「じゃあどうして君が友だちとフットボール場から出るのを私が見たことになるんだ」「あれが歯医者です」)

☞ see:「(医師に) 診てもらう」⇔「会う」　★ **Pun** → p. 26

(b) hear＋O＋*do*ing:「O が＿しているのが聞こえる」

"Can you **hear** her *sing**ing***?"

"No, there are good seats."

(「彼女が歌っているのが聞こえますか」「いえ，いい席があります」)

☞ 聞こえない席があります．

I **heard** two rabbits *talk**ing***. One rabbit said to the other: "Well, goodbye. Winter is here—and you'll soon be an ermine and I'll be a seal."

(2羽のウサギがしゃべっているのが聞こえた．一方がもう一方に言った．「じゃあ，さようなら．冬が来たね．そして君はやがて白テンになり、僕はアザラシになるんだね」)

☞ 偽物の毛皮にされる．

第 15 章　分　詞　　　　　　　　　　　　　　235

(c) catch＋O＋*do*ing:「O が＿しているのを見つける［捕まえる］」

"Is your daddy home?"

"No, sir. He hasn't been home since mother **caught** Santa Claus *kissing* the maid."

(「お父さんは家にいるかい」「いません. お母さんがサンタクロースがお手伝いさんにキスしているのを見つけてから家にいないんです」)

　　　Boss: If Mr Simmons comes to see me today, tell him I'm out.
Receptionist: Yes, sir.
　　　Boss: And don't let him **catch** you *doing* any work, or he won't believe you.

(ボスと受付係の対話:「今日シモンズ氏が会いに来たら, 外出中だと言ってくれたまえ」「承知しました」「それから, きみが何か仕事をしているところを見られないように. さもないときみの言うことを信じないよ」)

☞ きみは私がいる時だけは仕事をするのだから.

(d) feel＋O＋*do*ing:「O が＿しているのを感じる」

I **feel** the end *approaching*. Quick, bring me my dessert, coffee, and liqueur.　(Pierette Brillat-Savarin)

(終りが近づいて来る感じよ. 急いで, デザートとコーヒーとリキュールを持ってきてちょうだい.)

☞ Pierette Brillat-Savarin: 100 歳まで生きたフランスの美食家.

(e) find＋O＋*do*ing:「O が＿しているのを見つける」

When I was three, my parents told me that carrots help you see in the dark. That night they **found** me *trying* to use a carrot as a flashlight.

(3 歳のころ, 両親は私にニンジンは暗闇で見るのに役立つと言った. その晩, 両親は私がニンジンを懐中電灯として使おうとしているのに気づいた.)

(f) watch＋O＋*do*ing:「O が＿しているのを見守る」

A visiting aunt **watched** little Carol *learning* to write. The aunt asked, "Where's the dot over the *i*?"

Carol answered, "It's still in the pen!"

（家にやって来た叔母は可愛いキャロルが字を書くことを覚えているのを見ていた．叔母は尋ねた．「i の上の点はどこにあるの」キャロルは答えた．「まだペンの中よ」）
- ☞ いちいちうるさいわね．
- ☞ dot *one*'s [the] i's and cross *one*'s [the] t's:「i に点を打ち，t に横線を引く」（「細心の注意を払う」の意．

(g) keep＋O＋*do*ing:「O が__しているようにしておく」

Vanity may be bad, but it **keeps** the looking-glass industry *go***ing**.
（虚栄心は良くないかもしれない，しかし鏡産業を動かし続けている．）

"Just what good have you done to humanity?" asked the judge before passing sentence on the pickpocket.

"Well," replied the criminal, "I've **kept** three or four detectives *work***ing** regularly."
（「一体あなたは人類にどんないいことをしましたか」と裁判長はスリに判決を言い渡す前に尋ねた．「ええと」と犯人は答えた．「3，4 人の刑事をきちんと働かせてきました」）
- ☞ 尾行，現行犯逮捕などのために．

(h) leave＋O＋*do*ing:「O が__するままにしておく」

A man and his wife are on holiday, when the wife suddenly gasps in alarm. "I just remembered I left the oven on! The house will catch fire." "Don't worry," replies her husband. "I just remembered I **left** the tap *run***ning**."
（夫婦が休暇中，妻は突然はっと息をのみ不安になって言う「オーブンを点けっぱなしにしたのをちょうど思い出したわ．家が燃えてしまうわ」「心配しなくていいよ」と夫は答える．「ぼくも蛇口を流しっぱなしにしたのをちょうど思い出したよ」）
- ★ **Irish bull** → p. 39

(i) listen to＋O＋*do*ing:「O が__しているのを（注意して）聞く」

Jack and Jill wanted to get married but couldn't find anywhere to live. One of Jack's friends **was listening to** them *talk***ing** over their problem one evening and he thought he had the solution.

"Why don't you live with Jill's parents?"

"We can't do that," said Jack and Jill in horror. "They're still living with *their* parents!"

(ジャックとジルは結婚したかったが住むところがどこにも見つからなかった．ジャックの友達のひとりがある晩，彼らがその問題について話し合っているのを聞いていた，そして解決策があると思った．「ジルの両親の家に住めばいいじゃないか」「それはできないよ」とふたりはぞっとして言った．「両親はまだ彼らの両親の家に住んでいるんだ」)

(j) smell＋O＋*doing*:「O が＿＿しているにおいを感じる」

Wife: How did you know we were having salad tonight?
Husband: I didn't **smell** anything *burn**ing***.

(夫婦の対話：「今夜はサラダを食べるってどうして分かったの」「何も焦げているにおいがしなかったよ」)

(k) spend＋O＋*doing*:「O を＿＿して過ごす」

Some folks **spend** their youth *think**ing*** how to spend their youth.

(青春をいかに過ごすかを考えて青春を過ごす人もいる．)

B. 過去分詞：*done*

過去分詞には次の用法がある：
- **(1)** 名詞の前［後］につく形容詞として
- **(2)** S＋V＋O＋過去分詞
- **(3) have [get]＋O＋過去分詞 [*doing*]**
- **(4)** 分詞構文に用いられる．（→ C）
- **(5)** 「have [has, had]＋過去分詞」で完了形を作る（→ 第5章 完了形）
- **(6)** 「be 動詞＋過去分詞」で受動態（受け身）をつくる（→ 第6章 受動態）

(1) 名詞の前［後］につく形容詞として
(a) 過去分詞が単独で使われる場合：修飾する名詞の前に置かれる．

Teacher: I asked for a two-page composition about milk. Your paper is only half a page long.

Pupil: That's right—I wrote about **condensed** milk.

(先生「先生は牛乳について2ページ分の作文を書きなさいと言ったのよ．あなたのは半ページしかないじゃないの」生徒「そうなんです．ぼくはコンデス・ミルクについて書いたんです」)

1) 他動詞の過去分詞:「＿された［されている］」

My mother-in-law is a real treasure. I wish she was a **buried** treasure.

(義理の母は本当の宝物だ．埋められている宝であればいいのに．)

★ **Mother-in-law** → p. 305

You can save some money on a funeral if the mortician has a **used** box!

(もし葬儀屋が中古の棺を持っていれば葬式でいくらか節約できる．)

Father's Day is the day to remember the **forgotten** man.

(父の日は忘れられている男を思い出す日である．)

2) 自動詞の過去分詞:「＿した（完了）」

Q: Why do elephants have **wrinkled** knees?

A: Because they play marbles so often.

(問「なぜ象は膝がしわくちゃなのか」答「よくビー玉をするから」)

☞ 象は膝をつかなくてはビー玉遊びはできない．　　★ **Elephant joke** → p. 72

Q: Why did the **escaped** convict saw the legs off his bed?

A: He wanted to lie low.

(「逃亡した罪人はなぜベッドの脚を鋸(のこぎり)で切り取ったか」「目立たないようにしたかったから」)

☞ lie low:「うずくまる；身を潜める」

"I want to speak to my **departed** husband."
"Why?"
"He died before I finished telling him what I thought of him."
(「亡くなった夫と話がしたいわ」「なぜ」「夫をどう思っているか言い終わらないうちに亡くなったからよ」)

(b) 過去分詞が他の語句を伴う場合：修飾する名詞の後に置かれる．

A sweater is a garment **worn** *by a child* when his mother feels chilly.
(セーターは母親が寒いと感じたとき子供が着る衣服．)

★ **One-liner** → p. 395

First the doctor told me the good news—I was going to have a disease **named** *after me*．　(Steve Martin)
(まず医師は私に良い知らせを告げた―私は私の名前に因んだ病気に罹ろうとしているということだった．)
☞ Steve Martin (1945-)：アメリカのコメディアン・俳優・脚本家．

A conference is a meeting **held** *to decide when the next meeting will take place*．
(会議とは次の会議をいつ行うかを決めるために開かれる会である．)

Divorce is a game **played** *by lawyers*．　(Cary Grant)
(離婚は弁護士によって演じられるゲームである．)
☞ Cary Grant (1904-1986)：イギリス生まれのアメリカの映画俳優．

(2) S＋V＋O＋過去分詞：see [hear / catch]＋O＋*done*; keep [leave]＋O＋*done* など

At Christmas time, every girl **wants** her past *forgotten* and her present *remembered*.
(クリスマスの時期になると，すべての女の子は自分の過去が忘れられ，現在が思い出されることを望むものだ．)

☞ present:「現在」↔「贈り物」　★ **Pun** → p. 26

(a) see＋O＋*done*:「O が＿されるのを見る」

The greatest happiness is to scatter your enemy, to drive him before you, to **see** his cities *reduced* to ashes, to **see** those who love him *shrouded* in tears, and to gather into your bosom his wives and daughters.　(Genghis Khan)
（最大の幸せは敵を蹴散らし，目の前で追い立て，町が灰塵(かいじん)と化すのを見，彼を愛する人々が涙にくれるのを見，彼の妻たち娘たちを自分の胸の中に集めることだ．）（ジンギス・カン）

☞ Genghis Khan (1162?-1227): アジアからヨーロッパ東部を征服したモンゴルの英雄．

(b) hear＋O＋*done*:「O が＿されるのを聞く」

A teenager is someone who can **hear** a rock song *played* three blocks away but not his mother calling from the next room.
（10 代の人とはロックの歌が 3 ブロック離れているところで演奏されるのは聞こえるが，母親が隣部屋から大声で呼ぶのは聞こえない人．）

(c) find＋O＋*done*:「O が＿されるのを見つける」

A camper **found** himself *bothered* by mosquitoes during the first day at camp. At night he saw some fireflies and said, "Now they're coming after me with flashlights!"
（キャンプする人がキャンプの初日蚊(か)に悩まされた．夜，ホタルを見て言った「こんどは懐中電灯をもって追いかけて来やがる」）

★ **Irish bull** → p. 39

(d) keep＋O＋*done*:「O が＿されるようにしておく」

"Doc, there's something wrong with my stomach."
"**Keep** your coat *buttoned* and no one will notice it."
（「先生，お腹の具合が悪いのです」「上着のボタンをしたままにしておきなさい，そうすれば誰も気がつきません」）

☞ その太鼓腹には．

第 15 章　分　詞

(e) make＋O＋*done*:「O が＿されるようにする」

A guest speaker is trying to **make** himself *heard* over the racket of a boisterous rugby club dinner. He complains to the president sitting next to him, "It's so noisy I can't hear myself speak." "I wouldn't worry about it," replies the president. "You're not missing any."

（招かれた講演者は騒々しいラグビー・クラブのディナーの喧騒の中で自分の話を聞いてもらおうとしている．彼は隣に座っている会長に不満を言う「喧しくて自分の話すのが聞こえません」「私ならそんなことは気にしませんな」と会長は答えた．「あなたは何も聞き逃していませんよ」）

☞ miss:「聞き逃す」⇔「（い）なくて困る」　　★ **Pun** → p. 26

(f) need＋O＋*done*:「O が＿される必要がある」

Passenger: Can you telephone from a plane?
Stewardess: If I couldn't do that, I'd **need** my eyes *tested*.

（乗客「飛行機から電話できますか」スチュワーデス「できなければわたくし眼の検査をしてもらう必要がありそうですわ」）

☞ telephone ⇔ tell phone　　tell A from B:「A と B を区別する」
★ 異分析 → p. 375

(g) want＋O＋*done*:「O が＿されるのを望む」

In politics, if you **want** anything *said*, ask a man—if you **want** anything *done*, ask a woman.　(Margaret Thatcher)

（政治では，何か言ってほしければ男性に頼みなさい—何かしてほしければ女性に頼みなさい．）

☞ Margaret Thatcher (1925-2013): イギリスの政治家．保守党初の女性党首．首相 (1979-1990)．

3) have [get]＋O＋過去分詞 [*do*ing]

> *Fortune teller:* You have very peculiar lines.
> 　*Woman:* I came here to **have** my fortune *told*, not to **have** my lines *criticized*.
>
> （占い師「あなたなかなか風変わりな手相ですな」婦人「わたくし運勢を見てもらいに来ましたの，手相をとやかく言っていただくためではございませんのよ」）

(a) have＋O＋*done*

1)「＿してもらう［させる］」

Now, have you ever **had** this tooth *pulled* before?　(W. C. Fields)
(ところで，この歯を以前抜いてもらったことがありますか．)
　★ **Irish bull** → p. 39
　☞ W. C. Fields (1880–1946): アメリカのコメディアン．

Brian:　I took my dog to the vet today because it bit my professor.
Carol:　Did you **have** it *put* to death?
Brian:　No, of course not―I **had** its teeth *sharpened*.
(「家の犬を今日獣医に連れて行ったのは教授に咬みついたからなんだ」「殺してもらったの」「もちろん違うさ．歯を研いでもらったんだ」)

2)「＿される」(一種の受動態 →「第6章　受動態」C)

I was a beautiful child. My parents used to **have** me *kidnapped* just to see my picture in the papers.
(わたしはきれいな子供だった．両親がわたしを誘拐されるようにしたのはわたしの写真が新聞に載るのを見たいからだけだった．)

(b) get＋O＋過去分詞

1) get＋O＋*done*:「O を＿してもらう［させる］」
Q:　How do most men define marriage?
A:　A very expensive way to **get** your laundry *done* free.
(問「ほとんどの男は結婚をどう定義するか」答「洗濯を無料でしてもらう極めて高価な方法」)

2) get＋O＋*done*:「O を＿される」

You have to be careful with your fax machine. I **got** my tie *caught* in one, and four minutes later I was in Chicago.
(ファックスの機械の扱いには気をつけなければいけない．ネクタイを挟まれたら4分後にはシカゴにいた．)
　★ **Tall tale** → p. 412

(c) **have**+O+*do*ing:「O を＿している状態にする」

I went to my doctor with a sore foot. He said, "I'll **have** you *walk***ing** in an hour." He did. He stole my car.　(Henny Youngman)
（足が痛くて掛かりつけの医者へ行くと，「1時間で歩けるようにしてあげます」と言った．確かにそうしてくれた．私の車を盗んだのだ．）
☞ Henny Youngman (1906–1998): アメリカのコメディアン．

Did you hear about the scientist who tamed a wild mosquito? Now he **has** it *eat***ing** out of his hand.
（野生の蚊を飼いならした科学者のことを聞いたか．今は手から食べさせているんだ．）
★ Tall tale → p. 412

C. 分詞構文

> (1) 現在分詞, (2) 過去分詞が中心になって副詞節（→ 第22章）のような役目をする．（cf. 主に文章体で用いられる．）
> (a) 時　(b) 理由　(c) 付帯状況などを表す．(c) 以外は「接続詞＋S＋V」で書き換えが可能であるが，多くの場合曖昧さをその特徴とする．

(1) 現在分詞によるもの

> The glass eater from the circus was in the hospital. The nurse, **wanting** to take his temperature, put a thermometer in his mouth. Two minutes later he said: "That was delicious. I'd like some more of that."
> （サーカスのガラス食い芸人が入院していた．看護師が彼の熱を計りたいと思い体温計を彼の口の中へ入れた．2分後彼はこう言った．「おいしかったよ．もう少し食べたいんだけど」）

(a) 時

Concluding a powerful and impassioned speech enumerating his many splendid qualities, the candidate finally asked if anyone had any questions. "Yes, Sir," called out a voice from the crowd. "Who else is running?"

（候補者は自分の多くのすばらしい長所を列挙する力強い熱のこもった演説を締めくくって最後に誰か何か質問はないかと尋ねた.「ありますよ，先生」と群衆の中から叫ぶ声が聞こえた.「他に誰が出るんですか」）

☞ Concluding ＝ When [As] he concluded ...（...を締めくくるとき［締めくくりながら］）

Considering what's taking place outside, you wonder why these prisoners keep breaking out of prisons.

（外で起きていることを考えると，なぜこの囚人たちが脱獄し続けるのか不思議に思うでしょう.）

☞ Considering ... ＝ When you consider ...

(b) 理由

The graduation banquet was about to begin when the master of ceremonies was informed that the invited clergyman would not be able to attend. He quickly asked the main speaker to give the blessing. The speaker nodded, rose, bowed his head, and, in all sincerity, said, "There **being** no clergyman present, let us thank God."

（卒業の正式な宴会がまさに始まろうとしていた．すると司会者は招いていた牧師が出席できないと知らされた．司会者は急いで主賓の講演者に祝福の言葉を頼んだ．話し手は頷き，立ち上がり，頭を下げると，大真面目に言った．「牧師様が出席されていないので，神に感謝いたしましょう」）

☞ 牧師が出席していないことを． ★ **Irish bull** → p. 39
☞ There being ＝ Because there is

A newsboy was standing on the corner with a stack of papers calling out, "Read all about it! Fifty people swindled! Fifty people swindled!" **Curious**, a man walked over, bought a paper, and checked the front page.
Finding nothing, the man said, "There's nothing in here about fifty people being swindled." The newsboy ignored him and went on calling out, "Read all about it! Fifty-one people swindled!"

（新聞売りの少年が新聞を積み上げて街角に立ち大声で叫んでいた．「全部読んで．50人

が詐欺にあったよ．50 人が詐欺にあったよ」好奇心を感じて，男は歩いて行き，新聞を買うと第 1 面を読んでみた．特に何も見つからないので，男は言った「ここには 50 人が詐欺にあったこと何も書いてないじゃないか」少年は彼を無視して叫び続けた．「全部読んで．51 人が詐欺にあったよ」）

☞ Curious = Being Curious = Because he was [felt] curious; Finding nothing = Because [As] he found nothing

A kind lady, **being** duly **impressed** by a tramp calling at her back door, gave him a whole cake. The tramp said: "That's very nice, lady; would you mind sticking forty candles in it? Today's my birthday."
（親切な女性が，裏口にやって来た浮浪者に本当に感銘を受けて，ケーキを丸ごと与えた．浮浪者は言った．「ほんとにありがとう，奥さん．ローソクを 40 本さしてもらえませんか．今日が誕生日なんで」）

☞ being duly impressed = because she was duly impressed

(c) 付帯状況：「＿しながら」の意味になることが多い．

I went round **replacing** every window in the house, then discovered I'd got a crack in my glasses.
（家の窓という窓のガラスを入れ替えて回って，ふと自分のメガネにひびが入っていることに気づいた．）
★ Irish bull → p. 39

A scientist, **showing** slides of the Grand Canyon, explained, "It took two hundred million years to make this."
A man in the audience said, "Was it a government project?"
（科学者がグランドキャニオンンのスライドを見せながら説明して「これができるには 2 億年かかったのです」と言った．聴衆の 1 人の男が言った．「それは政府の開発事業だったんですか」）
☞ だからそんなに時間が掛かったのですか．

I want to die like my father, peacefully in his sleep, **not screaming and terrified**, like his passengers.　(Bob Monkhouse)
（私は父のように死にたい，穏やかに眠りながら，父の乗客のように悲鳴を上げたり恐怖を感じたりせずに．）
☞ Bob Monkhouse (1928-2003)：イギリスのコメディー作家・コメディアン・俳優．

A blonde asked a brunette: "What does inexplicable mean?"
The brunette said, "I can't explain."
The blonde stormed off in a huff, **complaining**: "Well, I'm so sorry I asked!"
(ブロンドがブルーネットに聞いた.「inexplicable ってどういう意味なの」ブルーネットは言った「説明できないわ」ブロンドはむっとして怒って言った.「まあ,聞かなければよかったわ」)
☞ complaining = and complained
★ **Blonde** → p. 249

cf. 場合によって接続詞を加えて意味をはっきりさせる.

On instructions for a hairdryer: "Do not use *while* **sleeping**."
(ヘアードライヤーの使用説明書:「睡眠中は使用しないこと」)
☞ while sleeping = while you are sleeping

A scandalous movie actress died in an accident *when* **shooting** her last film. Her tombstone reads, "At last she sleeps alone."
(スキャンダルの多い映画女優が最後の映画の撮影中に事故で亡くなった.墓石にはこう刻まれている「やっと1人で眠る」)
☞ when shooting = when they are shooting

(2) 過去分詞によるもの:受動態の意味になる.

Golf is a lot of walking, **broken** up by disappointment and bad arithmetic.
(ゴルフとは大いに歩いて,失望と計算間違いによって破たんさせられるもの.)
☞ broken = which *is broken*
☞ 自分のスコアー(の合計)を不正に記入して,信用を失う.

Husbands: Small bands of men, **armed** only with wallets, **besieged** by hordes of wives and children. (*National Lampoon*, 1979)
(夫族:財布だけを装備し妻子の群れに包囲されている男の小集団.)
☞ armed = who are armed ...; besieged = who are besieged
☞ *National Lampoon*: 1970-1998 年に刊行されたアメリカのユーモア雑誌.

Asked to write an essay on water, little Willie thought for a moment and then wrote:

"Water is a colorless liquid that turns dark when you wash in it."
（水に関する作文を書きなさいと言われて，ウィリーはちょっと考えてからこう書いた.「水は無色の液体でその中で（手を）洗うと黒くなる」）
☞ Asked = When he *was asked*

A man's wife phoned him while she was out in the car to tell him she'd broken down.

"There's water in the carburetor," she said confidently. The man, not a little **impressed**, asked, "Where's the car?"

"In the river."
（ある男の細君が車で外出中に彼に電話してきて車が故障したと言った.「キャブレターに水が入ったの」と彼女は自信満々に言った. 男は大いに感心して尋ねた.「車はどこだい」「川の中よ」）
☞ The man, not a little impressed = Because the man *was* not a little *impressed*

(3) 完了形の分詞構文：having＋過去分詞

A man went into a restaurant and called for a glass of whisky and water. **Having *tasted*** it, he exclaimed: "Which did you put in first, the whisky or the water?"

"The whisky, of course," the waiter replied.

"Ah, well," said the man, "perhaps I'll come to it by and by."
（ある男がレストランでウイスキーの水割りをたのんだ. それを味わってから彼は叫んだ.「最初に入れたのはウイスキーかね水かね」「もちろんウイスキーです」とウエイター. 男は言った.「ああ, それならひょっとするとそのうちにウイスキーに出会うな」）

☞ Having tasted = After he *had tasted*

A young man, **having** just ***received*** his degree from the university, rushed out saying, "Here I am, world; I have a B.A."

The world replied: "Sit down, son, and I'll teach you the rest of the alphabet."

(若い男が，大学から学位をもらったばかりで，飛び出して来て言った．「さあ来たぞ，世間のやつら．オレは学位を持っているんだ」世間が答えた．「君，座りたまえ，そしたらアルファベットの残りを教えてあげるよ」)
☞ B.A. = *Bachelor of Arts*（文学士）

"Doctor, will you operate on me?"
"What for?"
"Oh, anything you like. You see, I attend a lot of women's bridge parties, and **never having** *had* an operation, I simply can't take part in the conversation."
(「先生，わたしに手術していただけませんか」「また何のために」「何でもいいんです．先生ご存知のとおり，わたしたくさんの女性ブリッジ・パーティーへ行きますの．でも一度も手術を受けたことがないので，どうしても会話に加われないんです」)
☞ never having had an operation = Because I *had* never *had* an operation

(4) 慣用表現

> **Frankly [Generally / Strictly / Roughly] speaking**（率直に［一般的に／厳密に／おおざっぱに］言えば），**Judging from [by]** 〜（〜から判断すると），**Speaking of** 〜（〜と言えば）など．

Woman, **generally speaking**, is generally speaking.
(女性は，概して言うと，概してしゃべっている．)

Alphabetically speaking, it's the I's of a woman that disturb the E's of a man.
(アルファベットで言えば，男性のEを乱すのは女性のIである．)
☞ I's ⇔ eyes　　E's ⇔ ease（安らぎ）　　★ **Pun** → p. 26

Biologically speaking, if something bites you, it is more likely to be female.　(Desmond Morris)
(生物学的に言うと，何かが刺したら，メスである可能性の方が高い．)
☞ Desmond Morris (1928-): イギリスの動物学者．

"**Speaking of** milk," said the milk bottle, "have you heard of the strange case of the Boston baby brought up on elephant's milk?"
"No."
"It was the elephant's baby."
(「ミルクと言えば,象のミルクで育てられたボストンの赤ん坊の噂を聞いたかい」と牛乳ビンが尋ねた.「いや」「象の赤ん坊だったんだ」)

"What kind of bridge does your wife play?"
"**Judging by** the cost, I'd say it was a toll bridge."
(「奥様はどんなブリッジをなさるのですか」「費用から判断すると料金徴収橋だと言いたいです」)
☞ bridge:「(トランプの)ブリッジ」⇔「橋」　　★ **Pun** → p. 26
☞ toll bridge:「通行料を取る橋」

There will be a rain dancing on Friday, **weather permitting**.

(George Carlin)

(金曜日に雨乞いの踊りが行われます,天候が許せば.)
☞ George Carlin (1937–2008): アメリカのコメディアン.

ジョークの常識⑮

★ **Blonde:** ジョークの世界ではブロンド(金髪・色白・青い目)の女性は頭が空っぽの女性として登場する.

Q: Why does it take longer to build a blonde snowman than a regular one?
A: Because you have to hollow out the head.

(「ブロンドの雪だるまを作るのに普通の雪だるまより時間が掛かるのはなぜか」「頭の中をくり抜かなければならないから」)

第16章　動 名 詞

Giving money and power to the government is like **giving** whiskey and car keys to teenage boys.　(P. J. O'Rouke)
(政府に金と権力を与えるのは10代の少年にウイスキーと車のカギを与えるようなものだ.)

☞ 文頭の Giving は主語, 2 番目は前置詞 (like) の目的語.
☞ P. J. O'Rouke (1947-): アメリカの政治風刺作家・ジャーナリスト.
★ **One-liner** → p. 395

> 動名詞は「動詞の原形＋**ing**」で動詞の性質をもちながら, 文中で「＿すること」の意味で名詞の働きをする.

◆ 動名詞の形

形　＼　Voice	能　動	受　動
単純形	*doing*	being *done*
完了形	having *done*	having been *done*

A. 文の主語, 他動詞・前置詞の目的語, 補語として

"**Going** to school is a waste of time," says Little Johnny. "I can't read, I can't write, and they won't let me talk."
(「学校へ行くのは時間の無駄だよ」と幼いジョニーが言った.「ぼくは読めないし, 書けないし, それにしゃべらせてくれないんだもん」)

(1) 主語として

> **Being** busy is the best excuse for not working.　(Kenneth Tynan)
> (忙しいことは働かないための最良の言いわけである.)

☞ Kenneth Tynan (1927-1980): イギリスの劇評家・作家.

Not **having** to worry about money is almost like not having to worry about dying.　(Mario Puzo)
(金の心配をしなくてよいことは死ぬ心配をしなくてよいこととほとんど同じだ.)
☞ Mario Puzo (1920-1999): アメリカの小説家・映画脚本家.

　　Mother:　Suzie, have you finished putting the salt into the salt shaker?
Little Suzie:　Not yet. **It**'s hard work **pushing** the salt through all those little holes.
(「スージー, お塩を塩入れに入れ終わったの」「まだよ. お塩をあの小さな穴から押し込むのは大変な仕事よ」)
★ **Irish bull** → p. 39

It isn't easy **being** a mother. If it were, father would do it.
(母親であるのは簡単ではない. 簡単なら父親がそうするだろう.)

(2) 他動詞・前置詞の目的語として

> "Do you want the porter to call you?"
> "No, thanks. I awaken every morning at seven."
> "Then, would you mind **calling** the porter?"
> (「ボーイにモーニング・コールさせましょうか」「いや, けっこう. 私は毎朝7時に目を覚ますから」「では, ボーイを起こしていただけませんでしょうか」)

(a) 他動詞の目的語として: **avoid** / **consider** / **enjoy** / **escape** / **finish** / **give up** / **mind** / **miss** / **postpone** / **practice** / **put off** / **resist** / **stop** / **suggest** など+*do***ing**

> It took a lot of willpower, but finally I've **given up** *trying* to **give up** *smoking*.
> (それには大いに意志力が必要でしたが，タバコをやめようとすることをやめました．)

1) avoid *do*ing:「＿することを避ける」

"How can I **avoid** *falling* hair?"

"Jump out of its way."

(「どうしたら髪が抜けるのを避けられますか」「そこから飛び退きなさい」)

☞ falling:「(髪が) 抜ける」⇔「落ちて来る」

2) consider *do*ing:「＿しようかと考える」

"My dog digs holes in my garden all the time. What can I do about it?"

"Have you **considered** *hiding* the spade?"

(「私の犬はいつも庭に穴を掘るんです．どうしたらいいですか」「鍬を隠すことを考えましたか」)

★ Irish bull → p. 39

3) enjoy *do*ing:「＿して楽しむ」

"Did you know that the people of Prague **enjoy** *reading* books about money?"

"Really? What kind of books are they?"

"Czech books!"

(「プラハの人たちはお金についての本を読んで楽しむのを知ってたか」「本当か．どんな種類の本だい」「チェック・ブックさ」)

☞ Czech [tʃek]（チェコ人）⇔ check [tʃek]（小切手）　★ Pun → p. 26

4) escape *do*ing:「＿することを免れる」

What a sense of superiority it gives one to **escape** *reading* some book which everyone else is reading.　(Alice James)

(他の誰もが読んでいる何かの本を読まずに済ませることは何という優越感を与えてくれることだろう．)

☞ Alice James (1848–1892): アメリカの日記作家．

5) **finish** *do*ing:「__し終える」

"What did the duck say when it **finished** *shopping*?"

"Just put it on my bill."

(「買い物を終えたアヒルはなんと言ったか」「付けにしておいてくれ」)
☞ bill:「請求書」⇔「くちばし」　　★ **Pun** → p. 26

6) **mind** *do*ing:「__するのをいやと［迷惑に］思う」

Talkative Barber (about to lather)*:* Do you **mind** *shutting* your mouth, sir?

Tired Customer: No—do you?

(おしゃべりな床屋（石けんの泡を塗ろうとしながら）「口を閉じてください，お客さん」うんざりしていた客「いいとも．君もね」)

7) **miss** *do*ing:「__しそこなう」

A young boy said to his mother, "How old were you when I was born?" His mother replied, "Twenty-three."

"Wow, that's a lot of time we **missed** *spending* together."

(幼い男の子が母親に「ぼくが生まれたときお母さんいくつだったの」「23 よ」と母親．「わあ，ずいぶん長い間一緒に過ごせなかったんだね」)

★ **Irish bull** → p. 39

8) **practice** *do*ing:「__することを練習する」

Watching Sam Snead **practise** *hitting* a golf ball is like watching a fish **practise** *swimming*.　　(John Schlee)

(サム・スニードがゴルフボールを打つ練習を見るのは魚が泳ぐ練習を見るようなもの．)
☞ Sam Snead (1912-2002): アメリカの往年の名プロゴルファー．
☞ John Schlee (1939-2000): アメリカのプロゴルファー．

9) **put off** *do*ing:「__するのを延ばす」

And there's the Scotchman who is **putting off** *buying* an atlas until world affairs look a little more settled.

(そして世界情勢がもう少し安定するまで地図帳を買うのを延ばし続けているスコットランド人がいる．)

☞ Scotchman: ジョークの世界では「ケチ」ということになっている．スコットランド人はこの言い方を嫌い，Scot, Scotsman[woman]を用いる．

10) **resist** *do***ing**:「＿することに抵抗する」
　　Sally:　Whenever I see a mirror I can never **resist** *looking* into it for at least a few minutes to admire my flawless complexion. Do you think that's vanity?
　　Samantha:　No. More like imagination.
（2人の女性の対話:「鏡を見るたびに少なくとも数分鏡をのぞき込んで私の欠点のない顔を見ないではいられないの．うぬぼれかしら」「いいえ．それより想像力よ」）

11) **stop** *do***ing**:「＿するのをやめる」
"What's an adult?"
"Someone who has **stopped** *growing* except in the middle."
（「大人って何だ」「真ん中以外は成長が止まってしまった人さ」）
☞ 胴回りは成長を続ける．

When you retire, they give you a gold watch. Just when time **stops** *being* important.
（退職するとき金時計をくれる．ちょうど時間が重要でなくなる時に．）

cf. You might be a computer nerd if you wake up at 3 a.m. to go to the bathroom and, on your way back to bed, you **stop** *to check* your e-mail.
（午前3時に目が覚めてトイレに行き，ベッドへ戻る途中で立ち止まってEメールをチェックするようなら，立派なコンピューター・オタクだろう．）

cf. stop to *do* ＝ stop (doing something) to *do*:「＿するために（今までしていたことを）やめる」stop は「立ち止まる」とは限らない．次例参照．
Why is doing nothing so tiring?
Because you don't **stop** *to rest*.
（「なぜ何もしないとこんなに疲れるのか」「休憩するために中断しないから」）

12) suggest *do*ing:「＿することを提案する」

(*On a bus.*) "Please have your tickets ready for inspection."
"I'm sorry, Inspector, but my son has eaten his bus ticket."
"Well, madam, may I **suggest** *buying* him a second helping?"
((バスで)「切符を拝見いたしますのでご用意ください」「すみませんが,検札の方,息子はバスの切符を食べちゃったんです」「じゃあ,奥さん,おかわりをお買いになったらいかがでしょうか」)

(b) 自動詞＋前置詞の目的語として

> *Daughter:* He says he thinks I'm the nicest girl in town. Shall I ask him to call?
> *Mother:* No, dear, let him **keep on** *thinking* so.
> (「彼ったら私が町中で一番すばらしい女性だと思うって言うの.招待しようかしら」「やめておおき.その方にいつまでもそう思い続けさせておやり」)

My wife takes three hours to eat a plate of alphabet soup—she **insists on** *eating* it alphabetically.
(妻はアルファベット・スープを飲むのに3時間かけるのです.アルファベット順に食べると言ってきかないんです.)

A dentist said to a gorgeous patient, "We can't **go on** *meeting* like this. You have no more teeth left."
(歯科医はこの上なく美人の患者に言った.「こんなふうにお会いし続けることはできません.あなたはもう歯が残っていないのです」)

Good breeding **consists in** *concealing* how much we think of ourselves and how little we think of the other person.　(Mark Twain)
(育ちの良さは自分をどれほど高く評価し,他人をどれほど何とも思っていないかを隠すことにある.)
☞ Mark Twain (1835-1910): アメリカの(ユーモア)小説家.

"The art in telling a story **consists of** *knowing* what to leave unsaid."

"It doesn't make any difference, my boy. My experience is that she finds out anyway."
(「話のこつは何を言わないでおくかから成り立っている」「君,そんなことでは大した違いはないよ.僕の経験じゃ,彼女はとにかくすべてかぎ出してしまうんだから」)

(c) 前置詞の目的語として

> "Could I see the man who was arrested **for** *robbing* our house last night?"
> "Why do you want to see him?"
> "I want to ask him how he got in the house **without** *awakening* my wife."
> (「夕べ家に強盗に入って逮捕された男に会えませんか」「なぜ会いたいんですか」「彼に聞きたいんです,どうやって妻を起こさずに家に入れたのか」)

"What person makes a living **by** *talking* to himself?"
"A ventriloquist."
(「ひとりごとを言って生活しているのはどんな人物か」「腹話術師」)

Mike: What did you get the little medal for?
Mack: **For** *singing*.
Mike: What did you get the big medal for?
Mack: **For** *stopping*.
(「その小さいメダルはなぜもらったんだい」「歌を歌ったからさ」「その大きなメダルはなぜもらったんだい」「やめたからさ」)

There is no pleasure **in** *having* nothing to do; the fun is **in** *having* lots to do and not *doing* it.   (Mary Wilson Little)
(何もすることがないことに喜びはありません.楽しいのはするべきことがたくさんあるのに何もしないことです.)
☞ Mary Wilson Little (1944–): アメリカのボーカリスト.

Rick: Can you name five days of the week **without** *saying* Monday, Tuesday, Wednesday, Thursday or Friday?

Nick: Oh, yes. The day before yesterday, yesterday, today, tomorrow and the day after tomorrow.

(リック「1 週の 5 日を月, 火, 水, 木, 金と言わずに言えるか」ニック「言えるさ. 一昨日, 昨日, 今日, 明日, 明後日さ」)

(3) 補語として

> The hardest job of all is **trying** to look busy when you're not.
> (William Feather)
>
> (何より難しい仕事は忙しくないときに忙しそうに見えるようにすることだ.)

☞ William Feather (1889–1981): アメリカの出版業者・作家.

The most difficult part of a diet isn't **watching** what you eat. It's **watching** what other people eat.
(ダイエットで最もむずかしいことは自分の食べるものに気をつけることではない. 他人が食べているものをじっと見ていることだ.)
☞ difficult:「むずかしい」⇔「つらい」; watch:「気をつける」⇔「じっと見る」
★ **Pun** → p. 26

The worst thing about retirement is **having** to drink coffee on your own time.
(退職に関して最悪のことは自分の時間にコーヒーを飲まねばならないことだ.)

Middle age is **having** the choice of two temptations and **choosing** the one that will get you home earlier.
(中年とは 2 つの誘惑の選択肢のうち家に早く帰れる方を選ぶことだ.)

The hardest thing is **writing** a recommendation for someone we know. (McKinney Hubbard)
(もっともむずかしいことは知っている人の推薦状を書くことである.)
☞ hard:「むずかしい」⇔「つらい」　★ **Pun** → p. 26
☞ McKinney Hubbard (1868–1930): アメリカの劇作家・映画脚本家.

(4) need [forget / remember / try] *do*ing

> An accountant was having difficulty sleeping at night. He went to the doctor.
> "Have you **tried** *counting* sheep?" inquired the doctor.
> "That's the problem," said the accountant. "I make a mistake and spend the next six hours **trying** *to find* it."
> (会計士が夜眠れず困っていた．彼は医者へ行った．「羊を数えてみましたか」と医者は尋ねた．「それが問題なんです」と会計士は言った．「間違うと，その間違いを見つけようとしてあと6時間過ごしてしまうんです」)

☞ try counting（数えてみる）；try to find（見つけようとする）

(a) need *do*ing:「＿される必要がある」（= need to be *done*）

> "Your hair **needs** *cutting* badly, sir."
> "No, it doesn't. It **needs** *to be cut* nicely. You cut it badly last time."
> (「髪を刈る必要がひどくありますね，お客さん」「それはだめだ．上手く切ってもらいたいよ．この前はひどかったぞ」)

☞ badly:「(need, want などに付けて) ひどく，大いに」⇔「悪く，下手に」
★ **Pun** → p. 26

(b) remember *do*ing:「＿したのを覚えている」

> You know you're getting old when you begin to realize that history textbooks include events you **remember** *reading* about in newspapers.
> (年を取りつつあるなと分かるのは歴史の教科書に新聞で読んだ事件が載っていることに気づき始めるときだ．)

★ **One-liner** → p. 395

cf. remember *to* do:「＿するのを覚えている；忘れずに＿する」

> A teenager is a person who can't **remember** *to walk* the dog but never forgets a phone number.
> (10代とは犬の散歩は忘れても電話番号は忘れない人だ．)

(c) try *do***ing**:「__してみる」

Maurice: Doc, I'm a nervous wreck. What should I do?

Doctor: You need to relax. Give up golf and **try** *spending* more time at the office.

(モーリス「先生，私は精神的に参っています．どうしたらいいでしょうか」医者「リラックスする必要がありますね．ゴルフをやめて，会社でもっと時間を使ってみてはどうですか」)

If you think nobody cares if you're alive or dead, **try** *missing* a couple of car payments.　(Flip Wilson)

(生きていようが死んでいようが誰も気にしないと思うなら，車の月賦の支払いを 2, 3 回抜かしてみればいい．)

☞ すぐに督促状がくる．

☞ Flip Wilson (1933–1998): アメリカのコメディアン・俳優．

cf. try *to* **do**:「__しようとする」

"Are you ever troubled by diphtheria?"

"Only when I **try** *to spell* it."

(「ジフテリアに悩まされることがあるかい」「綴りを正しく書こうとするときだけはね」)

(d) forget *do***ing**:「__したのを忘れる」

Forget *exercising* and *dieting*—let somebody come up with younger mirrors!

(運動したこと，ダイエットしたことなど忘れなさい．誰かにより若く見える鏡でも作ってもらいなさい．)

cf. forget *to* **do**:「__するのを忘れる」

Terry: How did Mama find out you didn't really take a bath?

Jerry: I **forgot** *to wet* the soap.

(テリー「どうしてママはほんとはお風呂に入らなかったことが分かったの」ジェリー「石鹸を濡らすのを忘れたの」)

(5) 動名詞＋名詞:「＿するための〜（名詞）」

> I think I was an unloved child. They gave me **drowning** lessons!
> （私は愛されていない子供だったと思う．両親は溺れるためのレッスンをさせたのだ．）

"Darling, do you have a good memory for faces?"
"Yes, I think so. Why do you ask?"
"Because I've just broken your **shaving** mirror."
（「あなた，人の顔をよく覚えてるの」「そう思うよ．なぜ聞くんだい」「あなたのひげそり用の鏡をたった今割ってしまったの」）

"Your husband must be absolutely quiet. Here is a **sleeping** pill."
"When do I give it to him?"
"You don't, you take it yourself."
（「あなたのご主人は絶対安静です．これが睡眠薬です」「いつ夫に飲ませるのですか」「いえいえ，お飲みになるのはあなたご自身です」）

B. 動名詞の意味上の主語：名詞・代名詞の所有格・目的格

> "How do you stop *your husband* **reading** your e-mail?"
> "Rename the folder 'Instruction Manual.'"
> （ご主人があなたのＥメールを読むのをどうやってやめさせるの」「フォルダーを「使用説明書」と新しい名前にするの」）

"Does your wife object to *your* **smoking** in the house?"
"Oh, she objects to *my* **smoking** anywhere; she says it's too expensive having both of us do it."
（「奥さんは君が家の中で煙草を吸うのに反対するかい」「どこで吸うのにも反対さ．2人とも吸うのは費用がかかり過ぎるって言うんだ」）

I don't mind *my wife* **finding** the letters I forgot to mail. I just don't want her to find letters I forgot to burn.

（妻が私が出し忘れた手紙を見つけることは気にはしない．焼くのを忘れた手紙を見つけてほしくないだけだ．）

No one has ever complained of *a parachute* not **opening**.
（いまだかつてパラシュートが開かないことについて文句を言った人はいない．）

I won't mind *you* **talking** as long as you won't mind *me* not **listening**.
（君が話すのを気にしないよ，私が聴いていないのを君が気にしない限りはね．）

We apologise for the late running of the train. This is due to *us* **following** a train that is in front of us. (British Railway announcement)
（列車が遅れておりますことをお詫びいたします．これは前におります列車の後を走っているからでございます．）（英国鉄道のアナウンス）

C. 動名詞の慣用表現

(1) keep [prevent]＋O＋from *do*ing：「O に＿させない；O が＿するのを妨げる」

> "How do you **keep** fish **from** *smelling*?"
> "Cut off their noses."
> （「魚がにおわないようにするにはどうしたらいい」「魚の鼻を切り落とせばいい」）

☞ smell:「においがする」⇔「においをかぐ」　　★ **Pun** → p. 26

Before they are married, a man holds an umbrella over a woman's head to **keep** her from *getting* wet, afterward, to **keep** her hat from *getting* wet.
（結婚前に男が傘を女の頭上にさすのは彼女が濡れないようにしておくため，その後は，帽子が濡れないようにしておくため．）

The best way to **prevent** milk **from** *going* sour is to keep it in the

cow.
（牛乳がすっぱくなるのを防ぐ最良の方法はそれを牛の中に入れておくことだ．）
★ **Irish bull** → p. 39

A lawyer is a man who **prevents** somebody else **from** *getting* your money.
（弁護士とは誰か他の人があなたの金を取るのを邪魔する人だ．）
★ **Lawyer** → p. 329

(2) **(up)on** *do***ing**:「＿するとすぐ」「＿したとき」

A boy, **on receiving** a poor school report card, asked his father: "What do you think the trouble with me is—heredity or the home environment?"
（少年はお粗末な学校の成績表を受け取って，父に尋ねた．「ぼくの問題は何だと思う，遺伝かな家庭環境かな」）

An absent-minded professor went into a barber shop, and **on being told** to take off his hat, replied, "Certainly—I didn't know there were ladies present."
（ぼんやり教授が理髪店に入って行き，帽子を脱ぐように言われたとき，こう答えた．「もちろんだとも，ご婦人が居られるとは気がつかなかった」）
★ **Absent-minded professor** → p. 320

(3) **in** *do***ing**:「＿するとき」

A judge, **in sentencing** an old offender, concluded by saying: "And I hope that this is the last that you'll appear before me."
"Why, Judge," said the prisoner, "Are you retiring?"
（裁判官は常習犯に判決を言い渡すときこう締めくくった．「そしてこれが私の前に君が現れる最後にしてもらいたい」「おや，裁判長さん」と犯人は言った．「引退するんですか」）

A young man purchased a large grandfather clock from an antique shop in Brighton.

He put the unwrapped clock over his shoulder and began to look for a taxi. He hailed one approaching from the right, but it ignored him, so, swinging around, he tried to flag one down approaching from the left. Unfortunately, **in turning** around, the clock over his shoulder struck an old lady on the head and she fell into the gutter.

"Idiot!" she shrieked. "Why can't you wear a normal wrist-watch like the rest of us?"

（ある若者がブライトンの骨董店から大時計を買った．彼は包装していない時計を肩にのせ，タクシーを探し始めた．彼は右から来たタクシーを大声で呼んだが，無視されたので，ぐるっと回って，左から来るタクシーを手で合図して止めようとした．不幸なことに，向きを変えるときに，肩の時計が老婦人の頭を一撃し，彼女は溝に倒れた．「バカ！」と彼女は金切り声で言った．「なぜあなたは私たちのように普通の腕時計をはめないの」）

☞ Brighton: イングランド南部 East Essex 州にある都市；海浜保養地．

★ Tall tale → p. 412

(4) worth *do*ing:「＿するに値する」

The chief knowledge that a man gets from reading books is the knowledge that very few of them are **worth reading**.

(H. L. Mencken (Attrib.))

（人が読書から得る最も重要な知識は読むに値する本はほとんど無いという知識である．）

☞ H. L. Mencken (1880–1956): アメリカの批評家・ジャーナリスト．

(5) feel like *do*ing:「＿したい気がする」

"I **feel like** *whipping* you, son."

"Don't give in to your feelings, dad."

（「お前をむちでひっぱたきたい気分だ」「感情に負けちゃだめだよ，お父さん」）

"Before sending you to the chair, is there any request you would like to make?"

"Yes, Judge. I would like my wife to cook my last meal, then I'll **feel** more **like** *dying*."

（「君を電気椅子へ送る前に，最後に何か要求することはあるか」「あります，裁判長，女

房に最後の食事を作ってもらいたいんで，そうすりゃあもっと死にたい気分になりまさあ」）

(6) cannot help *do*ing:「＿せざるをえない」

"What a lovely coat you have, Mrs. Astor. But I **can't help** *thinking* of the poor animal that had to suffer in order that you might have that coat." "How *dare* you call my husband an animal!"

（「アスターさん，なんて素敵なコートを着てらっしゃるんでしょう．でもわたくし，あなたがそのコートを着るために苦しまなければならなかった可哀相な動物のことを考えてしまいますわ」「まあ，何ということを．わたくしの夫を動物呼ばわりなさるなんて」）

☞ in order that S may *do*:「S が＿するために」

cf. cannot help but *do*:「＿せざるをえない」

The visitor **couldn't help but** *notice* the pigs dozing in the farmer's living room. He couldn't contain himself.

"It's not healthy to let pigs sleep in your house," he said.

"Phooey," was the farmer's reply. "We ain't lost a pig in years."

（客はブタたちが農場主の居間で居眠りをしているのに気づかないわけにはいかなかった．彼は激しい気持ちを抑えられなかった．「家の中でブタを寝させるのは不健康です」と彼は言った．「ヘー」と農場主は答えた．「ここ何年も1匹も死んじゃいませんよ」）

☞ ain't ＝ haven't

(7) it is no good [use] *do*ing:「＿するのは無駄である」

If you board the wrong train, **it is no use** *running* along the corridor in the other direction. (Dietrich Bonhoeffer)

（行き先の違う列車に乗ったら，通路を反対方向へ走っても無駄である．）

☞ Dietrich Bonhoeffer (1906-1945)：ドイツルター派の牧師・キリスト教神学者．

An old man and a young boy were sitting on opposite benches in the park. Suddenly the old man leaned across and shouted, "**It's no good** your *talking* to me from over there. I'm deaf."

"I'm not talking to you," the boy shouted back. "I'm chewing bubble-gum."

(老人と若者が公園のベンチに向かい合って座っていた．突然老人は身を乗り出して叫んだ「そこから私に話しかけてもむだだよ．私は耳が聞こえないんだ」「あなたに話しかけてなんかいません」と若者は叫び返した．「風船ガムをかんでるんです」)

(8) there is no *do*ing:「＿することはできない」

"Golf, golf, golf. I believe that if you spent a Sunday home I would die."

"But, honey, **there's no** *talking* like that. You can't bribe me."

(「ゴルフ，ゴルフ，ゴルフ．あなたが日曜日に家で過ごしてくれたら，わたし死んでもいいと思うわ」「でも，おまえ，そんな言い方はだめだよ．買収はされないよ」)

cf. No *Do*ing（＜ there is no *do*ing（＿することはできない））:「＿するな」

A mother kangaroo leaps in the air with a yelp. She looks into her pouch and says, "How many times do I have to tell you? **No smoking in bed!**"

(母親カンガルーは悲鳴を上げて空中に跳び上がる．彼女は袋の中を覗き込んで言う．「何度言わなきゃならないの．ベッドでは禁煙よ」)

(9) It goes without saying that ＿＿＿:「＿＿＿は言うまでもない」

I don't have to tell you **it goes without saying** there are some things better left unsaid. I think that speaks for itself. The less said about it the better. (George Carlin)

(言う必要はないと思うが，言わずにいたほうが良いことがあることは言うまでもない．それは説明を要しないと思う．それは言わなければ言わないほど良いのだ．)

☞ speak for *one*self:「(事実・記録などが) はっきり証明している」
☞ George Carlin (1937–2008): アメリカのコメディアン．

(10) When it comes to *do*ing:「＿することになると」

When it comes to *pay*ing, he is the first to put his hand in his pocket. And leave it there.

(支払いとなると，彼は最初にポケットに手を突っ込む．そして手はそのままにしておく．)

(11) ***be* used to *do*ing**:「＿するのに慣れている」（cf. **used to** *do* →「第 7 章 助動詞」G）

Married men make the best salesmen because they **are used to** *taking* orders.
（既婚の男性が最良のセールスマンになるのは命令されることに慣れているからである．）

(12) ***be [get]* busy *do*ing**:「＿するのに忙しい［忙しくなる］」

I never read much because I **was** too **busy** *living*. （Mae West）
（あまり多くの本を読まなかったのは生きるのに忙しすぎたからよ．）
☞ Mae West (1893–1980): アメリカの女優・劇作家・映画脚本家．

Sometimes a person **gets** so **busy** *hunting* for advantages that he forgets there is work to do.
（ときどき人は有利な地位を探し求めるのにあまりにも忙しくなり，やるべき仕事があるのを忘れてしまう．）

(13) look forward to *do*ing:「＿するのを楽しみにして待つ」

I **look forward to** *running* into you again—some day when you're walking and I'm driving.
（また君に偶然出会うのを楽しみにしているよ．いつか君は歩いていて私は車に乗っているときに．）
☞ 君には二度と会いたくない．

ジョークの常識⑯

★ **Waiter**（レストランのウエイター）：現実とは異なり，客の不平・不満に対してはぐらかすような発言をする．スープにハエが入っているジョークは定番になっている．普通はウエイターが客をやりこめる．

第17章　前置詞

'A preposition is a word you mustn't end a sentence **with**!'

(Berton Braley)

(前置詞はそれで文を終わらせてはならない語なのだ．)

☞ Berton Braley (1882-1966): アメリカの詩人．

> 前置詞は「名詞の前に置く詞」のことで，ふつう名詞や代名詞の前に置かれ，全体として，(動詞・形容詞を修飾する)副詞句または(名詞を修飾する)形容詞句を作る．そのいずれになるかは文中での働きによって決まる．
> 　次の9個の前置詞の使用頻度が前置詞全体の93％を占めると言われる．
> 　　**at, by, for, from, in, of, on, to, with**

A Scotsman was fined **for** indecent conduct **at** Edinburgh **on** Friday. **According to** witnesses the man had continually wiped the perspiration **off** his forehead **with** his kilt.

(スコットランドの男が金曜日にエジンバラで下品な行為のために罰金を課せられた．目撃者によると，男は絶えず額の汗をキルトで拭ったという．)

☞ キルトの下には何もはいていない．

A. at: 〈基本的意味〉「場所の一点」

Father: Why are you always **at** the bottom of your class?
Dennis: It doesn't make any difference. They teach the same thing **at** both ends.

(父親「おまえはどうしていつもクラスのびりなんだ」デニス「どうでもいいじゃん．だって，先生は同じことをどっちの端にも教えるもん」)

☞ bottom:「最下位」⇔「いちばん奥」　　★ **Pun** → p. 26

(1) 場所の一点

"I know a guy who makes his living **at** baseball and football games."
"Is he a professional athlete?"
"No. He is a hot dog vendor **at** the stadium."
(「野球とフットボールの試合で生活している奴を知ってるよ」「プロの選手かい」「いいや．スタジアムでホットドッグを売っているんだ」)

(2) 時の一点

"I have to be in London **at** 6.30 a.m. How long does it take to fly there?"
"Just a minute."
"Thanks very much."
(「午前 6 時にロンドンにいなければなりません．ロンドンまで飛行機でどのくらいかかりますか」「ちょっとお待ちください」「どうもありがとう」)
☞ Just a minute.:「ちょっと待ってください」⇔「ほんの 1 分」

Teacher: **At** your age I could name all the Presidents―and in the proper order.
Wesley: Yes, but then there were only three or four of them.
(先生と生徒の対話:「あなたの年には全部の大統領の名前が言えたわ，しかも正しい順に」「そうだと思います，でもその頃は 3 人か 4 人しかいませんでした」)

(3) 方向・目標:「〜をめがけて」

"Who broke the window?"
"It was Andrew, Dad. He ducked when I threw a stone **at** him."
(「誰が窓を割ったんだ」「アンドルーだよ，お父さん．石を投げつけたらひょっと頭を下げたんだ」)

Old Lady: Little boy, don't make faces **at** that poor bulldog.
Little Boy: Well, he started it!"
(老婦人と少年の対話:「きみ，かわいそうなブルドッグにしかめっ面をしてはだめよ」「でも，最初にしたのはあっちだよ」)

(4) 従事・状態

Club: Place where you feel more **at** home than **at** home.
(クラブ：家にいるよりもっと寛(くつろ)げる場所．)
☞ at home:「在宅して」⇔「寛いで」　　★ **Pun** → p. 26

"Did you enjoy your first day **at** school, son?"
"What! Do you mean I have to go back tomorrow?"
(「おまえ，学校の初日は楽しかったかい」「何だって．明日また学校へ行かなきゃならないの」)

This restaurant is consistent. It serves steak, coffee, and ice cream—all **at** the same temperature!
(このレストランは首尾一貫している．ステーキもコーヒーもアイスクリームも出してくれて全部同じ温度だ．)

(5) 代価・割合

Smart Stan: Light travels from the sun **at** the rate of 186,000 miles a second.
Wise Willie: So what? It's downhill all the way.
(賢いスタン「光は太陽から秒速18万6千マイルの速度で進むんだ」利口なウィリー「だから何なんだ．ずーっと下り坂じゃないか」)
★ **Irish bull** → p. 39

(6) 感情の原因：「～を見て［聞いて／知って］」

The boy of sixteen thinks his father is pretty dumb. When the boy becomes a man of twenty-one, he's surprised **at** how smart the old man became in five years.
(16歳の少年は父親がひどいバカだと思っている．21歳の男になったとき，彼は老いた父親が5年で何と利口になったかに驚く．)
☞ 自分がバカになったことに気づかない．

B. by:〈基本的意味〉近接「～のそばに；そばを通って」

> Landlord: I have a very lovely apartment for you.
> Tenant: **By** the week or **by** the month?
> Landlord: **By** the incinerator.
> (アパートの主人と入居希望者の対話:「あなたにぴったりのいい部屋があります」「週ぎめですか月ぎめですか」「焼却炉の脇です」)
> ☞ by ～:「～単位で」⇔「～のそばに」　　★ **Pun** → p. 26

(1) 近接:「～のそばに；そばを通って」

"Do you play the piano by ear?"
"No, I play it **by** the window to annoy the neighbors."
(「暗譜でピアノを弾きますか」「いいえ，窓際で弾いて近所の人を悩ませています」)
☞ play ～ by ear:「～を暗譜で演奏する」

(2) 手段:「～によって」

An elderly lady walked into a Toronto ticket office and asked for a ticket to New York.
"Do you want to go **by** Buffalo?" inquired the ticket agent.
"Certainly not!" she answered indignantly. "I want to go **by** train!"
(年配の婦人がトロントの切符売り場に行きニューヨーク行きの切符を求めた．「バッファロー経由で行きたいですか」と切符係は尋ねた．「とんでもありません」と彼女は憤然として言った「列車で行きたいんです」)
☞ by Buffalo:「バッファロー経由で（= by way of Buffalo)」⇔「バッファローに乗って」
☞ Buffalo: アメリカ，ニューヨーク州の都市．

He's the kind of guy who can brighten a room **by** leaving it.
(彼は部屋を出て行くことによって部屋を明るくするタイプだ．)
☞ いなくなると喜ばれる．　　★ **Insulting joke** → p. 97

(3) 基準:「～に基づいて」

You can tell German wine from vinegar **by** the label.　(Mark Twain)

（ドイツワインと酢の違いはラベルで分かる.）
☞ ラベルを見ないと区別がつかない.　★ **Insulting joke** → p. 97
☞ Mark Twain (1835-1910): アメリカの（ユーモア）小説家.

Judge not a man **by** his clothes, but **by** his wife's clothes.
(Thomas R. Dewar)

（男を彼の衣服で判断せず，妻の衣服で判断せよ.）
☞ Thomas R. Dewar (1864-1930): スコッチウイスキー製造業者.

(4) 単位・差：「～単位で；～の差で」

This morning I missed a hole in one **by** only eight strokes.
（今朝たった8ストローク差でホールインワンを逸した.）

My secretary is so fat, I don't know whether to pay her **by** the week or **by** the pound.
（私の秘書はとても太っているので週給で払うべきかポンドで払うべきか分からずにいる.）
☞ pound:「（イギリスの通貨単位の）ポンド」⇔「（重量の単位の）ポンド」
★ **Pun** → p. 26

"What is bought **by** the meter and worn **by** the foot?"
"A carpet."
（メートル単位で買われてフィート単位ですり減らされる物は何か）「カーペット」）
☞ foot:「（長さの単位）フィート」⇔「足」　★ **Pun** → p. 26

(5) 時の期限：「～までに」

A woman ran excitedly into her house one morning and yelled to her husband: "John, pack up your stuff. I just won the lottery!"
"Shall I pack for warm weather or cold?" he said.
"Whatever. Just so long as you're out of the house **by** noon."
（女性がある朝興奮して家に駆け込み夫に叫んだ.「ジョン，あなたの持ち物を荷造りしてちょうだい．宝くじに当たったのよ」「暖かい天候用かい寒い天候用かい」と彼は言った.「何でもいいわよ．お昼までにここを出て行ってくれさえすれば」）
☞ so long as ＿＿＿:「＿＿＿でありさえすれば」（→ 第22章　副詞節 (6)）

"It was my grandmother's birthday yesterday."
"Is she old?"
"Well, **by** the time we lit the last candle on her birthday cake, the first one had gone out!"
(「昨日は祖母の誕生日だったんだ」「年とってるのか」「バースデーケーキの最後のローソクに火をつけるまでに最初のは消えてしまってたよ」)

(6) 動作主:「〜によって」

Teacher: Tommy, this letter from your father looks like it was written **by** you.
Tommy: That's because he borrowed my pen to write it.
(先生と生徒の対話:「トミー,あなたのお父さんからのこの手紙あなたが書いたみたいに見えるわね」「お父さんは書くのにぼくのペンを借りたからです」)
★ **Irish bull** → p. 39

A young writer brought a manuscript into a publisher. The publisher said, "We only publish books **by** authors with well-known names." The writer said, "Terrific! My name's Jones."
(若い作家が原稿を出版業者に持ち込んだ.業者は言った「よく知られた名前の作家の本しか出版しません」作家は言った.「すばらしい.私の名前はジョーンズです」)
☞ Jones はよくある姓.　★ **Irish bull** → p. 39

C. for: 〈基本的意味〉方向「〜に向かって」

"Where's old Bill been lately? I haven't seen him **for** months."
"What? Haven't you heard? He's got three years **for** stealin' a car."
"What did he want to steal a car **for**? Why didn't he buy one an' not pay **for** it, like a gentleman!"
(「ビルのやつ近ごろどこにいるんだ.何か月も会っていないが」「何だって,聞かなかったか.車を盗んで3年喰らい込むことになったんだ」「なぜ車なんか盗みたくなったんだろう.紳士らしくなぜ買うだけは買っておいて払いはしないことにしなかったんだ」)

☞ an' = and

(1) 方向:「〜に向かって；〜行きの」

　　Woman: Can I get a ticket **for** Remington?

　Ticket agent: Where is Remington?

　　Woman: Right over there—he's my little boy.

（女性と切符係の対話:「レミントン行きの切符をちょうだい」「レミントンってどこですか」「ほらあそこにいるでしょう．わたしの坊やよ」）

☞ for:「〜行きの」⇔「〜のための」　　★ **Pun** → p. 26

(2) 目的:「〜のために；〜を求めて」

I jog everywhere **for** my health, but I never find it!

（健康のためにあらゆる所でジョギングをしているが，どうしても見つからない．）

☞ for my health:「私の健康のために」⇔「私の健康を捜して」

"I asked her **for** her hand."

"What happened?"

"I got it—on the ear."

（「彼女に結婚申し込んだんだ」「どうなった」「耳に平手打ちを食らった」）

☞ ask for A's hand「Aに結婚の承諾を求める」⇔「Aに手を求める」

I played my trumpet until 3 A.M., and the fella next door kept knocking on the wall **for** encores.

（午前3時までトランペットを吹いていたら隣の奴がアンコールを求めて壁を叩き続けやがった．）

☞ fella = fellow

　Son: Dad, can I borrow your car?

　Dad: What are your feet **for**?

　Son: One **for** the brake and the other **for** the gas!

（「お父さん，車を借してくれない」「足は何のためについているんだ」「片方はブレーキ，もう片方はアクセルを踏むためさ」）

(3) 交換・代価:「〜と交換に」

"Why did you buy that hat?"

"Because I couldn't get it **for** nothing."
(「なぜあの帽子を買ったの」「ただでは手に入らなかったからさ」)

One day my father came running into the room waving a five-pound note, saying, "Look what I got **for** you, son!" He'd sold me.

(Ken Dodd)

(ある日父が 5 ポンド札を振りながら部屋へ駆け込んで来て言った.「お前のために手に入れたものを見てみろ」父は私を売ったのだった.)

☞ for 〜:「〜のために」↔「〜と交換に」　　★ **Pun** → p. 26; **Tall tale** → p. 412
☞ Ken Dodd (1927-): イギリスのコメディアン・シンガーソングライター.

(4) 原因・理由:「〜のための［に］」

First man:　I got married because I got tired of eating restaurant food, washing my own laundry, and wearing clothes with holes in them.
Second man:　That's funny! I got divorced **for** the same reasons.

(「ぼくが結婚したのはレストランの食事,自分でする洗濯,穴のあいた服を着ていることがいやになったからさ」「それはおかしい.ぼくは同じ理由で離婚したんだ」)

Golf is a wonderful excuse **for** taking a walk and not having to take your wife or your children with you.
(ゴルフは散歩をしてしかも妻や子供たちを連れて行く必要のないすばらしい言いわけである.)

(5) 期間:「〜の間」

"What do you know about love?"
"Plenty. I drove a taxi **for** five years."
(「愛についてどんなことを知ってる」「たくさん知ってるさ.5 年タクシーを運転してたんだ」)

(6) 対比・割合:「〜に対して」

For every person who dreams of making fifty thousand dollars, a hundred people dream of being left fifty thousand dollars.

"My parrot is over a hundred years old."

"He looks very green **for** his age."

(「ぼくのオウムは100歳以上だ」「年の割に青いね」)
☞ green:「緑色の」⇔「未熟な」　★ **Pun** → p. 26

(7) 不定詞の意味上の主語の前

"I didn't come here **for** you *to insult* me."

"Really! Where do you usually go?"

(「君に侮辱してもらいにここへ来たんじゃないぞ」「本当か．普段はどこへ行くんだ」)
(→「第14章　不定詞」A. (4) (b))

D. from:〈基本的意味〉起点「〜から」

> *John:* Are you tan **from** the sun?
>
> *Joe:* No, I'm Smith **from** the earth.
>
> (ジョン「太陽で焼いたのか」ジョー「いいや，地球出身のスミスだ」)

☞ from:「〜が原因で」⇔「〜出身の」；tan（日焼け）⇔ Tan（人名）
★ **Pun** → p. 26

(1) 起点・出所:「〜から(の)」

How to Lose Weight: Try the garlic and limburger cheese diet. You don't lose weight but you'll look thinner **from** a distance.

(体重の減らし方：ニンニクとリンバーガー・チーズを試しなさい．体重は減りませんが離れるとやせて見えます．)
☞ 臭いが強いので他人は近づかないから．
☞ limburger cheese: ベルギー産のチーズ．香りと味が強い．

Business is so bad, some hotels are stealing towels **from** the guests.

(景気が非常に悪いのでタオルを客から盗んでいるホテルもあるほどだ．)
☞ 普通は客が盗むのに．　★ **Tall tale** → p. 412

"Name nine animals **from** Africa."
"Eight elephants and a giraffe."
(「アフリカ産の動物の名前を9つ言いなさい」「8頭の象と1頭のキリン」)

From the dog's point of view, his master is an elongated and abnormally cunning dog.　(Mabel Louise Robinson)
(犬の見地から見ると，主人は縦長の異常なほど狡猾な犬である.)
☞ Mabel Louise Robinson (1874-1962): アメリカの児童文学作家.

cf. from ～ to ...:「～から...まで」
Insomnia: a contagious disease often transmitted **from** babies **to** parents.　(Shannon Fife)
(不眠症：しばしば赤ん坊から両親にうつる感染症.)
☞ Shannon Fife (1888-1972): アメリカのジャーナリスト・ユーモア作家・映画シナリオライター.

From birth **to** age 18, a girl needs good parents. **From** 18 **to** 35, she needs good looks. **From** 35 **to** 55, she needs a good personality. And **from** 55 **on,** she needs cash.　(Sophie Tucker)
(誕生から18歳まで，女の子には良い両親が必要です. 18から35までは美貌が必要です. 35から55までは立派な人格が必要です. そして55以降は現金が必要です.)
☞ Sophie Tucker (1886-1966): ロシア生まれのアメリカの歌手・コメディアン・俳優.

(2) 分離:「～から(の)」
I thought that birds had special boots to protect them **from** the electricity when they stood on high wires.
(鳥は高い電線に止まっているとき電気から身を守るために特別のブーツを履いているのだと思っていた.)

(3) 相違・区別:「～から」
"What's in this soup?"
"I dunno, sir. I can't tell one bug **from** another."
(「このスープには何が入っているんだ」「分かんないす，お客さん. 虫の区別はつかない

んで」)
☞ dunno = don't know ; tell A from B「A と B を区別する」

(4) 原因:「～が原因で」

You know you're getting older when birthday cake collapses **from** the weight of candles.
(自分が年取って来たなと分かるのはバースデーケーキがローソクの重みで崩れてしまうときだ.)

I don't believe in jogging. When I die, I want it to be **from** an illness!
(ジョギングが良いとは思わない. 死ぬときは病気が原因であってほしい.)

E. in:〈基本的意味〉「～の中に」

> *Customer:* I would like to try on that suit **in** the window, please.
> *Assistant:* I'm sorry, sir, you'll have to try it on **in** the changing-rooms like everybody else.
> (客「ウインドーの中のあのスーツを着てみたいんだが」店員「申し訳ありません, お客様, 他のみなさんと同じように試着室で着てみていただかなくてはなりません」)

☞ in ～:「～の中の」(形容詞句) ⇔「～の中で」(副詞句)
(→「形容詞句」「副詞句」については「第 18 章 句と節」参照.)

(1)「～の中に [で]」

"How did the accident happen?"
"My wife fell asleep **in** the back seat."
(「どうして事故が起きたのですか」「妻が後ろの席で眠ってしまったんです」)
☞ 妻が運転の指示をしてくれなかった.
☞ back-seat driver:「(後ろの座席から) 運転の指図をする人」

The people of Japan ride about **in** jigsaws.
(日本人はジグソーを乗り回す.)
☞ jigsaw [dʒígsɔː]（糸のこぎり）⇔ rickshaw [ríkʃɑː / ríkʃɔː]（＝rikisha）（人力車）
★ **Boner** → p. 46

Stranger: How many students are there **in** this school?
Principal: About one **in** every five.
(訪問者「この学校には学生が何人いるのですか」校長「約 5 人に 1 人です」)
☞ 残りは欠席しています．

"Mom, can I go out and play?"
"What, **in** those clothes?"
"No, **in** the park."
(「お母さん，外へ行って遊んでいい」「何ですって，そんな服で」「違うよ，公園で」)
☞ in 〜:「〜を着て」⇔「〜の中で」　　★ **Pun** → p. 26

(2) 状態:「〜の（状態の）中で」
Jeff came in the house, groaning and holding his stomach.
"Are you **in** pain?" his mom asked anxiously.
"No, the pain's **in** me!" replied Jeff.
(ジェフがうめきながらお腹をおさえて家に入って来た．「痛いの」とお母さんが心配そうに尋ねた．「違うよ，痛いのは僕の中だよ」とジェフは答えた．)
☞ in pain（痛みの中に）⇔ in me（自分の中に）

He's worn that suit so long it's been **in** style six times!
(彼はあの服をあまりにも長く着ているので 6 回も流行してきた．)

Wise words are sometimes spoken **in** jest, but many more foolish ones are spoken **in** earnest.
(思慮に富む言葉はときどき冗談めかして語られるが，もっと多くの愚かな言葉が大真面目に語られる．)
★ **One-liner** → p. 395

(3) 形状・材料:「〜の形で；〜を使って」
"Why are fish so smart?"
"Because they go round **in** schools."
(「魚はなぜ頭がいいか」「学校の中を動き回っているから」)
☞ in schools:「学校の中を」⇔「群れをなして」　　★ **Pun** → p. 26

One woman wanted to see something **in** a fur, so her husband took her to the zoo!
(ある女性が毛皮を見たがった，そこで夫は彼女を動物園へ連れて行った．)
☞ something in a fur:「毛皮の形のもの」⇔「毛皮に入ったもの」
★ **Pun** → p. 26

An optimist is someone who start filling in his crossword puzzle **in** ink.
(楽天家とはクロスワード・パズルをインクで埋め始める人である．)
★ **One-liner** → p. 395

"I've only got one piece of meat!"
"All right, I'll cut it **in** two for you."
(「肉が1切れしかないじゃないか」「いいわ，2切れに切ってあげるわ」)

(4) 時の経過:「～たてば，～後に；～のうちに」
"What did the big hand say to the little hand?"
"I'll be back **in** an hour."
(「(時計の) 長針は短針に何と言ったか」「1時間後に戻って来るよ」)

Employer: We can pay you 80 dollars a week now and 100 dollars a week **in** eight months.
Applicant: Thank you. I'll drop back **in** eight months.
(雇い主と応募者の対話:「今は週給80ドルだが，8か月後には週給100ドルにしてあげるつもりだ」「ありがとうございます．では8か月後に戻って来ます」)

F. of:〈基本的意味〉「分離」

> The government just put a wonderful machine in all **of** its buildings. It does the work **of** six people. **Of** course, it takes twelve to operate it.
> (政府はそのすべての建物にすばらしい機械を入れたところだ．この機械は6人分の仕事をする．もちろん，動かすには12人必要である．)

(1) 部分関係・所属:「〜の，〜に属する」

"What's the name **of** your parents?"
"Mama and papa."
(「両親のお名前は」「ママとパパ」)

"What do you see when you look into a dumb blonde's eyes?"
"The back **of** her head."
(「ばかなブロンド女性の目の中をのぞくと何が見えるか」「頭の後ろ側」)
☞ 頭が空っぽだから．　　★ **Blonde** → p. 249

"Have you read any of Shakespeare's plays?"
"Only two **of** them."
"Which ones?"
"Romeo and Juliet."
(「シェイクスピアの作品を何か読んだかい」「2 つだけだけど」「どれとどれだい」「ロメオとジュリエット」)

(2) 修飾関係

(a) A **of** B: B の性質を持つ A

He's got a great way **of** starting a day. He goes back to bed!
(彼には一日を始めるすばらしいやり方がある．また寝ることだ．)

Teacher: Who can tell me something **of** importance that didn't exist one hundred years ago?
Smallest Girl in the Class: Me!
(先生「誰か 100 年前には存在していなかった重要なものが言えますか」クラスで一番小さい女の子「わたしです」)
☞ something of importance = something important

(b) 主格関係：A **of** B「B が A すること」

Newspapers are unable ... to discriminate between a bicycle accident and the collapse **of** civilization.　(George Bernard Shaw)

(新聞は自転車事故と文明の崩壊の区別ができないのだ.)
☞ 両者を同等に扱う. civilization collapses (文明が崩壊する) (S+V)
☞ George Bernard Shaw (1856-1950): アイルランド出身のイギリスの劇作家.

The principal export **of** the United States is money.
(合衆国の主要な輸出品は金である.)
☞ the United States exports (合衆国は輸出する) (S+V)

(c) 目的関係: A **of** B「B を A すること」

Some people say that a discussion is the exchange **of** knowledge, but an argument is the exchange **of** ignorance.
(話し合いは知識を交換することだと言う人もいるが, 言い争いは無知を交換することである.)
☞ exchange knowledge [ignorance] (知識［無知］を交換する) (V+O)

My grandfather was the unluckiest criminal in the country. He made a deathbed confession **of** all his crimes—then got better.
(祖父は国で最もついていない犯人だった. 臨終の床で今までの犯罪をすべて自白した. すると良くなってしまったのだ.)
☞ confess all his crimes (すべての罪を告白する) (V+O)

cf. 次の例は (b)(c) 両者を含む:

Fear **of** the policeman is the beginning **of** wisdom.　(Charles Pasqua)
(警官を恐れることが知恵の始まりである.)
☞ fear of the policeman ＜ fear the policeman (V+O) (警官を恐れる): 目的関係
　 the beginning of wisdom ＜ wisdom begins (S+V) (知恵がはじまる): 主格関係
☞ Charles Pasqua (1927-　): フランスの政治家・実業家.

(d) 同格関係: A **of** B「B という A」

The highest tuition in the world is for the school **of** experience.
(この世で最も高い授業料は経験という学校へ納めるものである.)

Originality is the fine art **of** remembering what you hear but forgetting where you heard it.　(Laurence J. Peter)

（独創力とは聞いたことを覚えているがどこで聞いたか忘れる素晴らしい技能である．）

☞ Laurence J. Peter (1919-1990): アメリカの教育学者・社会学者．

(3) 原因：「～（が原因）で」

Be careful about reading health books. You may die **of** a misprint.

(Mark Twain)

（健康に関する本を読むのに気をつけなさい．誤植が原因で死ぬかもしれない．）

☞ Mark Twain (1835-1910): アメリカの（ユーモア）小説家．

"I'm really worried," says a nervous patient to his nurse. "Last week, I read about a man who was in hospital because of heart trouble and he died **of** malaria." "Relax," replied the nurse. 'This is a first-rate hospital. When we treat you for heart trouble, you die **of** heart trouble."

（「ほんとに心配です」と不安そうな患者が看護師に言う．「先週心臓病のために入院していた男の人のことを読んだんです，そしてその人マラリアで死んだんですって」「落ち着いてください」と看護師は答えた．「ここは一流の病院ですよ．心臓病で治療したら，心臓病で死ぬんです」）

(4) 分離：「～から」

"Doctor, how can I cure myself **of** sleepwalking?"

"Sprinkle thumbtacks on your bedroom floor."

（「先生，どうしたら夢遊病を治せますか」「寝室の床に画びょうを撒きなさい」）

We call my father-in-law the exorcist. Every time he visits he rids the house **of** spirits.

（私たちは義理の父をエクソシストと呼んでいる．彼は来るたびに家の悪霊を追い払ってくれるのだ．）

☞ rid 〜 of ...:「〜から...を取り除く」

☞ spirits:「霊」⇔「蒸留酒（ウイスキー・ブランデーなど）」　　★ **Pun** → p. 26

(5)「〜について」

Fay: What did you think **of** the Grand Canyon?
Ray: It was just gorges.
(「グランドキャニオンをどう思いましたか」「ただの峡谷でした」)
☞ gorges [gɔːrdʒz]（渓谷）⇔ gorgeous [gɔ́ːrdʒəs]（すばらしい）
★ **Pun** → p. 26

G. on:〈基本的意味〉「接触」

At school, our teacher told us to write an essay **on** anything we wanted. So I wrote it **on** the side of a train.
(学校で先生はぼくたちになんでも欲しいものの上に作文を書きなさいと言った。だから，ぼくは電車の側面に書いた．)

☞ an essay on 〜（〜についての作文）⇔ write an essay on 〜（〜の上に作文を書く）

(1) 場所：「〜の上に；〜に接触して」

"Our dog's been chasing a man **on** a bicycle."
"Don't be silly. My dog can't ride a bike."
(「家の犬は自転車の男を追いかけているんだ」「バカ言うな．僕の犬は自転車に乗れないぞ」)
☞ a man on a bicycle（自転車に乗った男）⇔ chaise ... on a bicycle（自転車に乗って... を追う）(→「第18章 句と節」B. 形容詞句；C. 副詞句)

Customer: I see you have gravy **on** your menu today.
 Waiter: Yes, sir. What would you like to have?
Customer: A clean menu!
(客とウエイターの対話：「今日のメニューに肉汁ソースがのっているねえ」「はい，お客様．何をお持ちいたしましょうか」「きれいなメニューをたのむ」)

Landlady (to New Roomer): An inventor once had this room. He invented an explosive.
New Roomer: Oh, I suppose those spots **on** the ceiling are the

explosive.

Landlady: No, that's the inventor.

（アパート所有の女性と新しい間借り人の対話：「発明家が昔この部屋にいたのよ．爆薬を発明したの」「ああ，あの天井のしみはその爆薬ですね」「違うのよ．発明家なの」）

I love her so much, I worship the ground her father found oil **on**.
（私は彼女をとても愛しているので，彼女のお父さんが石油を見つけた土地を崇拝している．）

(2) 時：「（特定の）日［朝／昼／晩など］に」

"If a cowboy rides into town **on** Friday and three days later leaves **on** Friday, how does he do it?"

"The horse's name is Friday!"

（「もしカウボーイが馬に乗って金曜日に町へ入って来て 3 日後の金曜日に出て行くとすると，どうやってそれをするか」「馬の名前がフライデー」）

☞ on Friday:「金曜日に」⇔「フライデーに乗って」

★ **Pun** → p. 26

"Why are soldiers always tired **on** the first of April?"

"Because they have just finished a march of 31 days!"

（「なぜ兵士は 4 月 1 日にいつも疲れているか」「31 日の行進を終わったばかりだから」）

☞ march（行進）⇔ March（3 月）　　★ **Pun** → p. 26

Most people don't mind setting their clocks ahead **on** a Saturday night. They make up the hour's sleep in church!

（たいていの人は土曜の夜前もって目覚まし時計をセットすることなど気にしない．教会でその時間の睡眠を取り戻す．）

★ 教会 → p. 345

(3) 支え・根拠：「〜に基づいて」

They lived **on** money borrowed from each other.　　(George Moore)

（彼らはお互いから借りた金で生活した．）

☞ George Moore (1852-1933): アイルランドの小説家．

★ **Irish bull** → p. 39

He's really tough. He went to a reform school **on** a dean's scholarship!
(あいつはほんとに大した奴だ．学部長の奨学金で更生保護施設に行ったんだ．)

(4) 従事・状態：「～して，～中で」

"Dad, do you like baked apples?"

"Yes. Why do you ask?"

"Because your apple tree is **on** fire."
(「お父さん，焼きリンゴ好き」「好きだよ．なぜ聞くんだい」「リンゴの木が燃えてるんだ」)

A speeding motorist was stopped by a police officer.

"I'm a good friend of the mayor," pleaded the speeder.

"That's fine," said the officer as he wrote out the ticket. "Now he'll know I'm **on** the job."
(スピード違反のドライバーが警官に止められた．「おれは市長の親友だ」と違反者は言い張った．「それはすばらしい」警官は違反切符に書き込みながら言った．「これで市長は私が働いているのが分かるはずだ」)

(5) 主題：「～について(の)」

Tom: I have to write an essay **on** an elephant.

Jim: You'll need a ladder.
(トム「象についての作文を書かなければならないんだ」ジム「梯子(はしご)がいるね」)
☞ on ～:「～について」⇔「～の上で」　　★ **Pun** → p. 26

A man went into a library and asked to borrow a book **on** suicide.

"No way," said the librarian. "You won't bring it back."
(男が図書館に入って行き自殺の本を借りたいと頼んだ．「だめです」と司書が言った．「返しに来ないでしょう」)

(6) 時間的接触：「＿したとき，＿するとすぐに」

An idealist is one who, **on** noticing that a rose smells better than a cabbage, concludes that it will also make better soup.　　(H. L. Menken)

(理想主義者とはバラがキャベツより良い匂いがするのに気づくと，バラはスープとしてもキャベツより良いと結論を下す人である．)(→「第 16 章　動名詞」C. (2))
☞ H. L. Menken (1880–1956): アメリカの批評家・ジャーナリスト．
★ **One-liner** → p. 395

H. to:〈基本的意味〉「(到着を前提とする) 方向」

> "What is the most common answer **to** a teacher's questions in school?"
> "I don't know, sir."
> "Correct."
> (「授業中に先生の質問に対する最も普通の答えは何ですか」「分かりません，先生」「その通り」)

(1) 方向・到達点:「〜へ［に］，〜まで」

"Excuse me, do you know the quickest way **to** the station?
"Yes. Run!"
(「すみませんが駅へ行く一番速い方法をご存知ですか」「知ってるさ．走れ」)

"What's your name, boy?"
"Harold."
"Say, 'sir' when you speak **to** me. Now boy, what's your name?"
"Sir Harold."
(「君，名前は」「ハロルド」「私に話すときは「先生」と言いなさい．じゃあ君，名前は」「ハロルド先生」)

My dad was in the navy when I was young and was away quite a lot. My sister and I wrote letters **to** him, and my mum would take us **to** the mailbox. My sister thought he lived inside it and shouted things **to** him through the slot.
(幼い頃父は海軍にいてしょっちゅう家にいなかった．妹と私は父に手紙を書き，母は私たちを郵便ポストへ連れて行ってくれたものだった．妹は父はポストの中に住んでいる

と思い手紙の投入口から父にいろいろ叫んでいた．）

(2) 結果：「〜になるまで」

Born free. Taxed **to** death.
（自由に生まれ，税金を払わされて死ぬ．）

I was almost frightened **to** death recently. I saw this surgeon who was going to operate on me reading a magazine with large type!
（最近恐ろしくて死にそうになった．私の手術をすることになっていたこの外科医が大きな活字の雑誌を読んでいるのを見てしまったのだ．）

I find **to** my astonishment that an unhappy marriage goes on being unhappy when it is over.　(Rebecca West)
（不幸な結婚は終わったあとも不幸であり続けることを知って本当にびっくりする．）
☞ 終わったら結婚とは言わない．
☞ Rebecca West (1892-1938)：イギリスの作家・ジャーナリスト・評論家．
★ **Irish bull** → p. 39

(3) 程度：「〜まで（も）」

His problem is he doesn't just drink **to** excess; he drinks **to** anything.
（彼の問題はただ飲み過ぎるだけではない．何のためにでも飲むことだ．）
☞ drink to 〜：「〜（人・人の成功・健康など）を祈って［祝って］乾杯する」
☞ to excess = excessively（極度に（まで））

(4) 比較：「〜に比べて，〜に対して」

The odds of going to the store for a loaf of bread and coming out with only a loaf of bread are three billion **to** one.　(Erma Bombeck)
（パンを1つ買いに店に行ってパン1つだけで帰ってくる可能性は30億分の1．）
☞ Erma Bombeck (1927-1996)：アメリカのユーモア作家．

The other day I was driving under the influence of my wife. She talks and talks and talks. She gets two thousand words **to** the gallon.
（先日妻の影響下で運転していた．彼女はしゃべりにしゃべる人だ．1ガロンにつき2000

語しゃべるのだ.）
☞ under the influence (of alcohol)「酔って」; 1 gallon = 3.785 litters

I. **with**:〈基本的意味〉プラスの関係:「～といっしょに」

Fred: Mom, may I go out and play?
Mom: What? **With** those torn trousers?
Fred: No, **with** the kids across the street.
（フレッドと母親の対話:「お母さん，外へ遊びに行ってもいい」「何ですって．その破れたズボンでかい」「違うよ，通りの向こうの子供たちとだよ」）

Customer: Give me a hot dog.
Waiter: **With** pleasure.
Customer: No, **with** mustard.
（客とウエイターの対話:「ホットドッグ1つ」「喜んで」「いや，マスタードで」）

(1) 同伴:「～といっしょに」

"I had an awful headache last night." "Yes, I saw you **with** her."
（「ゆうべはひどく頭が痛かったよ」「そうだろうとも．彼女と一緒だったのを見たよ」）
☞ headache:「頭痛」⇔「頭痛の種」　　★ **Pun** → p. 26

For Sale: Piano by lady **with** elegant carved legs.
（売り物：上品な彫刻を施した脚のご婦人によるピアノ.）
☞ piano *with elegant carved legs*（上品な彫刻を施した脚のついたピアノ）⇔ lady *with elegant carved legs*（上品な彫刻を施した脚の婦人）（→ 第18章　句と節）

A husband asked his wife what she wanted for her birthday. "Oh, just give me something **with** diamonds," she replied. So he bought her a pack of playing cards.
（夫が妻に誕生日に何が欲しいか尋ねた．「まあ，それじゃダイアの付いている物をちょうだい」と妻は答えた．そこで彼はトランプ1組を買ってやった.）

"I see the police in Manchester are looking for a man **with** a hearing aid."

"Why don't they use glasses?"

(「マンチェスターの警察は補聴器をつけた男を捜しているらしい」「なぜメガネを使わないんだ」)

☞ with a hearing aid:「補聴器を付けた（男）」⇔「補聴器を付けて」（→ 第18章　句と節）

(2) 道具・手段:「〜で，〜を用いて」

"You should pay your taxes **with** a smile."

"I tried that but they wanted cash."

(「税金は笑顔で払った方がいいぞ」「やってみたけど，現金で欲しがったぞ」)

★ Irish bull → p. 39

"Tommy, the canary has disappeared."

"That's funny. It was there just now when I tried to clean it **with** the vacuum cleaner."

(「トミー，カナリアがいなくなったわよ」「おかしいな．たった今掃除機できれいにしてしてやろうとしたときはそこにいたのになあ」)

Say it **with** flowers,
Say it **with** sweets,
Say it **with** kisses,
Say it **with** eats,
Say it **with** jewelry,
Say it **with** drink,
But always be careful
Not to say it **with** ink.

(「花でそれを語れ，お菓子でそれを語れ，キスでそれを語れ，食べものでそれを語れ，宝石でそれを語れ，飲みものでそれを語れ，しかしインクでそれを語らぬように常に注意せよ」)

☞ インクで語ると証拠が残る．

(3) 付帯状況：**with**＋名詞＋〜「名詞が〜の状態を伴って」
(a) **with**＋名詞＋形容詞

It's not bad manners to speak **with** your mouth *full* when you're praising your wife's cooking.
（奥方の料理を褒めているときは口を一杯にして話すことはマナー違反ではない．）

A yawn is silence **with** the mouth wide *open*.
（あくびは口を大きく開けた沈黙である．）
★ **One-liner** → p. 395

(b) **with**＋名詞＋前置詞句［副詞］

"Dad, I hate cheese **with** holes *in it*."
"Well, just eat the cheese and leave the holes on your plate!"
（「お父さん，穴が開いてるチーズは嫌いだ」「じゃあ，チーズを食べて穴はお皿に残しなさい」）

You can recognize him in any restaurant. He's always sitting **with** his back *to the check*.
（どんなレストランでも彼だとすぐ分かる．いつでも支払い伝票に背を向けて座っている．）

"How would you define a best seller?"
"That's a book **with** a heroine *on the jacket* and no jacket *on the heroine*."
（「君ならベストセラーをどう定義する」「ヒロインがジャケットに載っていて，ヒロインにはジャケットがない本さ」）
☞ jacket:「上着」⇔「（本の）カバー」　★ **Pun** → p. 26

Said Mrs. Thomas A. Edison: "I don't know what you're doing, Tom, but I can't sleep **with** that light *on*.
（トマス・エジソン夫人が言った．「あなたが何しているか知らないけど，その電気点けっぱなしでは眠れないわ」）

Ron: Are Ted's feet big?
Don: I don't know. I've never seen him **with** his shoes *off*.
(ロン「テッドの足は大きいかい」ダン「知らないよ．靴を脱いでいるところを見たことはないもん」)
★ **Irish bull** → p. 39

(c) with＋名詞＋現在分詞［過去分詞］

"My father fell asleep in the bathtub **with** the water *running*."
"Did the bathtub overflow?"
"Nope. Pop sleeps **with** his mouth open."
(「父は浴槽でお湯を出しっぱなしにして眠ってしまったんです」「浴槽はあふれませんでしたか」「いいえ．父は口を開けて眠るんです」)
☞ だから飲んでしまうのであふれません． ★ **Tall tale** → p. 412

I found it impossible to work **with** security *staring* me in the face.
(Sherwood Anderson)
(警備員がおれの顔をじろじろ見ている状態で仕事をするのは不可能だと分かった．)
☞ Sherwood Anderson (1876–1941): アメリカの小説家．

With airline fares *plummeting*, it now costs as much to get to the airport as it does to fly somewhere!
(航空運賃が急落しているから，今では空港へ行くのにどこかへ飛行機で行くのと同じ費用が掛かる．)

"Give an example of nonsense."
"An elephant hanging over a cliff **with** his tail *wrapped* around a daisy."
(「ナンセンスの例をあげなさい」「尾がヒナギクに包まれて崖からぶら下がっている象」)
★ **Elephant joke** → p. 72

Etiquette: learning to yawn **with** your mouth *closed*.
(エチケット：口を閉じたままあくびができるようになること．)

Those bell hops are tip-happy. They walk around **with** their hands *outstretched*. I was in my room, I ordered a deck of playing cards, and the man made fifty-two trips.
（ホテルのあのボーイたちはチップさえもらえば幸せなのだ．両手を伸ばして歩き回る．私は部屋にいて，トランプ1組注文すると，そのボーイは52回往復した．）
☞　トランプは（ジョーカーを除くと）52枚．
★ **Tall tale** → p. 412

(4) 関係：「～に関して」

　　First Student:　How were your exam questions?
　Second Student:　They were easy, but I had trouble **with** the answers.
（2人の学生の対話：「試験の問題はどうだった」「易しかったけど答えには苦労した」）

"This match won't light."
"Why? What's wrong **with** it?"
"I don't know. It was all right a few minutes ago."
（「このマッチどうしても火がつかないよ」「なぜだ．どうしたんだ」「さあ，ちょっと前は大丈夫だったんだけど」）
★ **Irish bull** → p. 39

(5) 原因：「～のために」

"Who spilled that ink on the floor? Come on, own up ... Was it you, Faulkner?"
"I can't tell a lie, sir. Yes, I done it."
"Where's your grammar?"
"In bed **with** flu."
（「誰が床にインクをこぼした．さあ，白状しなさい．君だろう，フォークナー」「ぼくは嘘がつけません，先生．はい，やっちゃいました」「文法はどこへ行ったんだ」「インフルエンザで寝てます」）
☞　grammar [grǽmər]（文法）↔ grandma [grǽndmà:]（おばあさん）
★ **Pun** → p. 26
☞　I done it. は正しくは I have done it. または I did it.

J. その他の前置詞

(1) about:「～について」「およそ～」

I took a speed reading course and read *War and Peace* in twenty minutes. It's **about** Russia.　(Woody Allen)
（速読のコースを取って『戦争と平和』を20分で読んだ．ロシアについての話だ．）
☞ Woody Allen (1935-　)：アメリカの映画監督・脚本家・俳優・作家．

I speak **about** six or seven languages—Spanish, Argentinian, Cuban, Mexican ...　(Seve Ballesteros)
（私は約 6，7 ヶ国語話すースペイン語，アルゼンチン語，キューバ語，メキシコ語などなどだ．）
☞ Seve Ballesteros (1957-2011)：スペイン出身のプロゴルファー．

(2) above:「～の上方に」「～を越えて」

Dumb Dan:　My uncle shot himself two feet **above** his head.
Smart Sam:　How could he shoot himself two feet **above** his head?
Dumb Dan:　He jumped.
（バカなダンとお利口サムの対話：「伯父さんは頭上 2 フィートのところでピストル自殺したんだ」「頭上 2 フィートでどうやって自殺できたんだ」「飛び上がったのさ」）
★ Irish bull → p. 39

　Wife:　Scientists claim that the average person speaks 10,000 words a day.
Husband:　Yes, dear, but remember, you are far **above** average.
（妻「普通の人は 1 日に 1 万語話すと科学者たちは主張しているわ」夫「そうだよ，きみ，しかし，いいかい，きみははるかに平均以上なんだよ」）

(3) after:「～の後に」「～を求めて」「～の名にちなんで」

"Is the doctor in?"
"No, he stepped out for lunch."
"Will he be in **after** lunch?"
"Why no, that's what he went out **after** ..."
（「お医者様はいらっしゃいますか」「いいえ，昼食に出ています」「昼食後はいらっしゃ

いますか」「いいえ，昼食を食べに外へ出ているんです」）
☞ after 〜:「〜のあとで」⇔「〜を求めて」　　★ **Pun** → p. 26

The developer who put up the houses in our neighborhood was a genius. He bulldozed all the trees, then named the street **after** them!
（家の近所に家を建てた開発業者は天才だった．すべての樹木をブルドーザーでなぎ倒して，その後通りにその樹木の名前を付けたのだ．）

(4) **against:**「〜に逆らって［反対して］」「〜に寄りかかって」

A patient, his ear **against** the wall, listened for hours. Seeing him, an orderly put his ear **against** the wall and also listened. After a moment the orderly said, "I don't hear anything." The patient said, "It's been that way for two days."
（患者が耳を壁に押し当てて何時間も聞き耳を立てていた．彼を見て，用務員も耳を壁に当てて耳を澄ました．すぐ後，用務員は言った．「何も聞こえないよ」患者は言った．「2日間ずっとこんな具合です」）

I met a girl I want to marry, but his family is **against** it. Particularly her husband.
（結婚したいと思う女性に会ったが，彼女の家族は反対している．特に，彼女の夫が．）

(5) **around:**「〜のまわりに［近くに］」

If you want to remember, tie a short string **around** your finger. If you want to forget, tie a long rope **around** your neck.
（覚えていたければ指に短いひもを結びなさい．忘れたければ首にロープを結びなさい．）
☞ 死ねば忘れられます．　　★ **Black humor** → p. 118

The only chance I get to open my mouth **around** my wife is when I yawn.
（妻のそばで私が口を開く唯一の機会はあくびをするときだけだ．）

(6) **before:**「〜の前に」

Before marriage a man yearns for a woman. After marriage the "y" is silent.

(結婚前は男は女にあこがれる．結婚後は"y"は発音されなくなる．)
☞ yearn（あこがれる）−y＝earn（稼ぐ）　　★ Pun → p. 26

"Say, Doctor, about those eyedrops, do I take them **before** or after meals?"

(「ねえ，先生，目薬のことですけど，食前につけるのですか食後ですか」)
★ Irish bull → p. 39

(7) behind:「〜の後ろに」

In New York's zoos, animals are kept **behind** bars—for their own safety!

(ニューヨークの動物園では動物は鉄格子の後ろに入れられている―動物自身の安全のために．)
☞ behind bars には「刑務所に入って」の意味もある．

Behind every beautiful woman there is a beautiful **behind**.

(すべての美しい女性の後ろには美しい後ろがある．)
☞ behind:「〜のうしろに」⇔「おしり」　　★ Pun → p. 26

(8) below:「〜の下方に」

Son (to father): About my allowance, Pop. It's fallen **below** the national average for teenagers.

(息子が父親に「お父さん，小遣いのことだけど，10代の国内平均を下まわってしまったよ」)

When an application asks him for "marital status," he writes, "**Below** wife!"

(応募用紙で「婚姻状況」を尋ねると，彼は「妻の下」と書く．)
☞ marital status: married（既婚），single（独身），divorced（離婚）などの区別．

(9) between:「〜の間に［で］」

　　Judge: Where were you **between** five **and** six?

Defendant: In kindergarten!
（裁判官「5 時から 6 時の間どこにいましたか」被告「幼稚園にいました」）
☞ five [six]:「5 [6] 時」⇔「5 [6] 歳」　　★ **Pun** → p. 26

"How can you divide seven potatoes equally **between** four people?"
"Mash them."
（「どうやったら 4 人で 7 個のじゃがいもを平等に分けられるか」「マッシュポテトにすればいい」）

(10) during:「（時間的に）〜の間に」

And now for the news that happened **during** the commercials.
（ではコマーシャルの間に起こったニュースです．）

(11) into:「〜の中へ」「（変わって）〜に」

In youth we run **into** difficulties; in old age difficulties run **into** us.
（若い時には困難に飛び込んでいく．年を取ると困難が飛び込んでくる．）
　★ **One-liner** → p. 395

"Why is the letter 'G' scary?" "It turns a host **into** a ghost."
（「なぜ G という文字は恐ろしいか」「主人を幽霊に変えるから」）
☞ G＋host＝Ghost　　★ **Riddle** → p. 64

(12) out of:「〜から（外へ）」

"How many people work here?"
"Oh, about one **out of** every ten."
（「ここでは何人の人が働いていますか」「まあ 10 人に 1 人というところでしょう」）

In America we drink our coffee **out of** cups—in China they drink their tea **out of** doors.
（アメリカではコーヒーをカップで飲む―中国ではお茶を屋外で飲む．）
☞ *out of* cups（カップから）⇔ *out of* doors（屋外で）

(13) **over**:「〜の(真)上に」「〜の上位に」「〜について」「(電話など) によって」

Rick:　I spent eight hours **over** my chemistry books last night.
Nick:　That's a lot of studying!
Rick:　I never said anything about studying. The books were under my bed.
(リックとニックの対話：「昨日の夜は化学書の上で8時間過ごした」「すごい勉強だね」「勉強のことなんか言ってないよ．本はベッドの下にあったんだ」)

"What did you two argue **over**?"
"**Over** the telephone."
(「何で君たち2人は言い争ったんだ」「電話で」)
☞ over:「〜について」⇔「(電話など) によって」　　★ **Pun** → p. 26

Diet: The temporary triumph of will **over** metabolism.
(ダイエット：新陳代謝に対する意志の一時的勝利．)

(14) **through**:「〜を貫いて」「〜を通して」「〜が原因で」

He had a bad accident. He tried to fly his plane **through** a tunnel without checking the train schedules.
(彼はひどい事故に遭った．飛行機でトンネルを抜けようとしたが，列車の時刻表を調べていなかったのだ．)
★ **Tall tale** → p. 412

When a man tells you that he got rich **through** hard work, ask him: "Whose?"
(誰かが自分は勤勉によって金持ちになったと言ったら，「誰の」と聞くがいい．)
☞ Whose = Whose hard work　親の勤勉のおかげかもしれない．

(15) **till / until**:「〜まで（ずっと）」

A woman, **till** five and thirty, is only looked upon as a raw girl, and can possibly make no noise in the world **till** about 40.
　　　　　　　　　　　　　　　　　　　　(Lady Mary Wortley Montagu)
(女性は5歳から30歳までは生娘とみなされるだけで，40歳ころまで世の中で全く騒げ

☞ make noises:「不平を言う」; make a noise in the world:「世間の評判になる」
☞ Lady Mary Wortley Montagu (1689–1762): イギリスの貴族・作家.

"I have a problem. I have to go to the toilet at six o'clock in the morning."
"Why is that a problem?"
"I don't wake up **until** seven o'clock."
(「問題があるんです．朝6時にトイレに行かなければならないんです」「なぜそれが問題なんですか」「7時まで目が覚めないんです」)

(16) **under:**「～の下に」

"I tell you what I like about Christmas. Kissing girls **under** the mistletoe."
"I prefer kissing them **under** the nose."
(「クリスマスのどこが好きか教えてあげる．ヤドリ木の下で女の子にキスをすることだよ」「僕は女の子の鼻の下にキスするほうがいいな」)
☞ この木の下にいる異性にキスしてもよいことになっている．

Where he worked, he had four hundred people **under** him. He was a guard in a cemetery.
(仕事場には彼の下に400人いた．共同墓地の警備員だった．)

(17) **within:**「～の内側に」

Did you hear about the man who was told that most car accidents happen **within** two miles of home? He moved.
(ほとんどの自動車事故が自宅から2マイル以内の所で起こると言われた男について聞いたか．彼は引っ越した．)

"Do you live **within** your income?"
"Good heavens, no! It's all I can do to live **within** my credit."
(「収入の範囲内で生活していますか」「とんでもありません．借金の範囲内で生活するので精一杯です」)

★ **Irish bull** → p. 39

(18) without:「～なしで［の］」「～がなければ」(→「第 23 章　条件・仮定表現」D. (4))

> *Little boy, crying* (to floor walker): Have you seen a lady **without** a boy that looks like me?
> (幼い男の子，泣きながら（売り場監督に）「ぼくに似ている男の子を連れていなかった女の人を見ましたか」)

★ **Irish bull** → p. 39

A little boy was in the garden and he saw a snake for the first time. He ran to his mother and said, "Come quick, mom. There's a tail **without** a body in the garden."
(幼い男の子が庭にいて初めてヘビを見た．母のところへ走って行って言った．「急いで来て，ママ．庭に胴体のないしっぽがいるよ」)

Man (describing speaker): He could speak for an hour **without** a note and **without** a point.
(男が講演者の特徴を述べて「あいつはメモなしで要領を得ないで 1 時間しゃべれる」)
★ **Insulting joke** → p. 97

"Would you like to work on a submarine?"
"No, I can't sleep **without** the windows open."
(「潜水艦で働きたくないか」「いやだ．窓を開けないで眠れないんだ」)

Stupid? He can't count to twenty **without** taking his shoes off.
(バカだって．あいつは靴を脱がずに 20 まで数えられないんだぞ．)

The telephone is a good way to talk to people **without** having to offer them a drink.　(Fran Lebowitz)
(電話は人に飲み物を出す必要なしに人と話をする良い方法だ．)
☞ Fran Lebowitz (1950-)：アメリカの作家・ジャーナリスト．

(19) **as:**「〜として」, **but / except (for):**「〜を除いて」, **like:**「〜のような［に］」

Economics is extremely useful **as** a form of employment for economists.　(J. K. Galbraith)
（経済学は経済学者の雇用形態として極めて有用である．）
☞ J. K. Galbraith (1908-2006): アメリカの経済学者．

Some adults are willing to blame juvenile delinquency on everything **but** heredity.
（青少年犯罪を遺伝以外のあらゆることのせいにして何とも思わない大人たちもいる．）

It's true that nothing is certain **but** death and taxes. Sometimes I wish they came in that order.　(Sam Levenson)
（死と税金以外に確実なものはない．ときどきこの順で来てくれればいいのにと思う．）
☞ Sam Levenson (1911-1980): アメリカのユーモア作家・ジャーナリスト．

Love conquers all things **except** poverty and toothache.　(Mae West)
（愛はすべてを征服する，貧乏と歯痛以外は．）
☞ Mae West (1893-1980): アメリカの女優・歌手・映画脚本家．

Everything you read in the newspapers is absolutely true **except for** the rare story of which you happen to have first-hand knowledge.
　　　　　　　　　　　　　　　　　　　　　　　　　　　(Erwin Knoll)
（新聞で読むものすべてまったく本当だ，たまたま直接知っている稀な話を除けば．）
☞ 直接知っていることについては新聞は常に間違っている．
☞ Erwin Knoll (1931-1994): アメリカのジャーナリスト・編集者．この文は "Knoll's Law of Media Accuracy"（メディアの正確さに関する Knoll の法則）と言われる．

I just broke up with someone and the last thing she said to me was, "You'll never find anyone **like** me again."
I'm thinking: "I should hope not! If I don't want you, why would I want someone **like** you."　(Larry Miller)
（私はある人と別れたばかりだ，そして彼女が最後に言ったのは「わたしのような人は2度と見つからないわよ」だった．私はこう考えている「見つけるもんか．僕が君を望ま

ないのに，なぜ君みたいな人を望むというんだ」）
☞ Larry Miller (1944-2009): アメリカの実業家．プロバスケットボール Utah Jazz のオーナー．

Analyzing humor is **like** dissecting a frog. Few people are interested and the frog dies.　(E. B. White)
（ユーモアを分析するのはカエルを解剖するようなものだ．ほとんど誰も興味を持たないしカエルも死んでしまう．）
☞ E. B. White (1899-1985): アメリカの評論家・詩人・小説家．

K. 二重前置詞：前置詞が2つ重なるもの．前の前置詞に後ろの前置詞句が付いたと考えればよい．

(Is he henpecked?)
Every once in a while she comes to him on her bent knees. She dares him to come out **from under** the bed.
（（尻に敷かれているか．）：ときどき彼女は膝をついて彼に近寄る，そして彼にベッドの下から出て来られるものなら出て来てなさいと言う．）

I saw the mother-in-law walking down the path so I jumped **from behind** the garage and shouted "BOO!"
She said, "You nearly frightened me to death," so I shouted, "BOO! BOO! BOO!"
（義理の母が道をやって来るのを見たのでガレージの後ろから飛び出して「ブー！」と叫んだ．彼女が「びっくりして死にそうになったわ」と言ったので，私は「ブー！ブー！ブー！」と叫んだ．）
★ **Mother-in-law** → p. 305

Change is inevitable, **except from** a vending machine.
（変化は避けられない，自動販売機から以外は．）
☞ change:「変化」⇔「釣銭」　★ **Pun** → p. 26
☞ 自販機から釣銭が出ないことがある．

L. 前置詞句：2語以上がまとまって1つの前置詞の役割をするもの．

"**Apart from** that, Mrs. Lincoln, how did you enjoy the play?"
(Tom Lehrer)
(「それはさておき，リンカン夫人，芝居はいかがでしたか」)
☞ Tom Lehrer (1928-): ユダヤ系アメリカ人のシンガーソングライター・ピアニスト・数学者．
☞ Abraham Lincoln は観劇中に暗殺された．　　★ **Black humor** → p. 118

Outside of the killings, Washington has one of the lowest crime rates in the country.　(Marion Barry)
(殺人を除けば，ワシントンはわが国で最低の犯罪率である．)
☞ Marion Barry (1936-2014): アメリカ民主党の政治家．
★ **Irish bull** → p. 39

There may be other cities in England foggier than London, but it's hard to tell which they are, **because of** the fog.
(イングランドにはロンドンより霧の濃い都市が他にあるかもしれない，しかし霧のためにそれがどの都市であるかは分かりにくい．)

The young secretary changed her job **due to** men trouble. There weren't any men in her office.
(若い秘書が仕事を変えたのは男の問題のせいだった．仕事場には1人も男がいなかった．)

The teacher told the class to write a composition on baseball. One minute later, little Johnny turned in his written effort. It read, "Game called **on account of** rain."
(先生は生徒たちに野球についての作文を書きなさいと言った．1分後ジョニー君は努力して書いたものを提出した．それにはこうあった．「試合は雨のために中止」)

Owing to a strike at the Meteorological Office, there will be no weather tomorrow.

(気象庁のストライキのため,明日の天気はありません.)
★ **Irish bull** → p. 39

According to dieticians, there are four basic food groups—fresh, frozen, fast, and junk!
(栄養士によると,4つの基本的な食品群があるという—生鮮,冷凍,ファースト,そしてジャンクである.)

All right, everybody line up alphabetically **according to** your height.
(Casey Stengel)
(よし,みんな背の順にアルファベット順に並びたまえ.)
☞ Casey Stengel (1890-1975): アメリカ,メジャーリーグのニューヨークヤンキース,ニューヨークメッツの監督.
★ **Irish bull** → p. 39

The average family consists of 4.1 persons. You will have to guess **as to** who constitutes the .1.
(平均的な家族は 4.1 人から成る.誰が .1 を構成しているのかについて推測しなければならない.)

Van Gogh painted 72 pictures. **As of** this morning, Americans have 423 of them.
(ゴッホは 72 枚の絵を描いた.今朝現在,アメリカ人はそのうち 423 枚所有している.)

His designs were strictly honourable; that is to rob a lady of her fortune **by way of** marriage.　(Henry Fielding)
(彼のやり口は全く立派だった.それは結婚によってご婦人から財産を奪うのだ.)
☞ Henry Fielding (1707-1754): イギリスの小説家・劇作家.

Miniskirts give men manners. I never saw a man get on a bus **in front of** one!
(ミニスカートは男たちに礼儀作法を教えている.男が先にバスに乗るのを見たことがない.)

Children are natural mimics; they act like their parents **in spite of** every attempt to teach them good manners.
(子供は生来の物まね芸人である．彼らは良いマナーを教えようとするあらゆる試みにもかかわらず両親そっくりの行動をする．)
★ **One-liner** → p. 395

I heard of a well-known actor who used to carry a note in his wallet which read, "I'm a famous celebrity. **In case of** an accident, please call a reporter."
(財布に次のメモを入れていた有名な俳優のことを聞いたことがある：「私は有名なセレブです．事故の場合は記者に電話願います」)

"You see that old boy over there? He thinks **in terms of** millions."
"He doesn't look like a financier."
"He isn't. He's a bacteriologist."
(「あの元気な老人が見えるだろう．彼は100万単位で物を考えるんだ」「金融業者には見えないなあ」「違うよ．細菌学者だよ」)

An opera is a place where a guy gets stabbed in the back and, **instead of** bleeding, he sings.
(オペラは男が背中を刺され，血を流す代わりに，歌いだす場である．)

The business man—the man to whom age brings golf **instead of** wisdom.　(George Bernard Shaw)
(ビジネスマンとは年齢が知恵ではなくゴルフをもたらす男．)
☞ George Bernard Shaw (1856–1950)：アイルランド出身のイギリスの劇作家．

The violence on the field is nothing **compared to** what happens when a wife catches her husband drooling over the cheerleaders.
(戦場における暴力なんて何でもないことだ．夫がチアリーダーを見てよだれをたらしているところを妻が見つけたときに起こることと比べれば．)

"I love you. **Next to** me I love you best."
(「わたしあなたを愛している．わたしの次にあなたを一番愛してる」)

I don't have any prejudice. I hate everyone **regardless of** race, color or creed.
(私は何らの偏見も持っていない．人種，肌の色，信条に関わりなくすべての人が嫌いだ．)

My parents are certainly great role models for me. **Thanks to** them, I certainly know how not to raise a child.
(両親は私にとって確かに模範的な存在だ．彼らのおかげで，子供をどう育ててはいけないかがはっきり分かる．)

ジョークの常識⑰

★ **Mother-in-law**（義理の母親）：ジョークの中では夫の義理の母，つまり，妻の母親．日本では妻と夫の母親との確執が問題になるが，英語のジョークの世界では夫と妻の母親との確執が頻出する．虐げられた夫の憂さ晴らしであることが多い．

第18章　句と節

"My father can lift a pig **with one hand**. Can your dad do that?"
"I'm not sure. Where do you get a pig **with one hand**?"
(「父さんは片手でブタを持ち上げられるぞ．君の父さんにできるか」「さあどうかな．どこで片手のブタを手に入れるんだい」)

☞ lift ... *with one hand*（片手で上げる）（副詞句）⇔ a pig *with one hand*（片手のブタ）（形容詞句）（→ D. 形容詞句か副詞句か）

句（phrase）は「主語＋動詞」を含まずに，文中で名詞・形容詞・副詞の働きをする語群をいう．それぞれ名詞句・形容詞句・副詞句という．

節（clause）は文の一部になっていて「主語＋動詞」を含み名詞・形容詞・副詞の働きをする語群をいう．

文中に2つ以上の節があるとき，従属節を支配して主位に立つ節を**主節**といい，主節に支配されている節を**従属節**という．

節には，(1) and, but, or などの等位接続詞で結ばれる**等位節**と，(2) that, when, because, though などの従属接続詞，who, which, that, when, where などの関係詞で導かれる**従属節**がある．

(1) |John played soccer| but |I played tennis|.
　　　〈等位節〉　　　　　　〈等位節〉
　　（ジョンはサッカーをしたが私はテニスをした．）

(2) |I didn't go there| |because I was sick.|
　　　〈主節〉　　　　　〈従属節〉
　　（病気だったので，そこへ行かなかった．）

　　|Though it was raining,| |she went out.|
　　　〈従属節〉　　　　　　　〈主節〉
　　（雨が降っていたが，彼女は出かけた．）

☞ 節について詳しくは以下を参照：
名詞節については「第20章 名詞節」，形容詞節については「第21章 形容詞節」，副詞節については「第22章 副詞節」．

A. 名詞句（Noun Phrase）：文中で名詞の働きをする句．ふつう (1) 不定詞，(2) 動名詞で始まる．

(1) 不定詞（→ 詳しくは「第14章 不定詞」A）

It's easy **to recognize** *a modern painting*. It's the one you can't recognize.［主語］

（現代絵画だと分かるのは簡単だ．分からないのがそれだ．）

"Say, listen, I'm not dead."
"No? Well, the doctor says you are."
"But I tell you I'm not."
"Lie down—do you want **to make** *a liar out of a doctor*?"
　　　　　　　　　　　　　　　　　　　　　　　　［他動詞の目的語］

（「ねえ，聞いてくれ，おれは死んではいないんだ」「死んでないだと．医者はお前は死んでいると言っているぞ」「しかし本当に死んでいないんだ」「横になって死んでいろ．お前は医者を嘘つき呼ばわりするつもりか」）

A great man's greatest good luck is **to die** *at the right time*.［補語］
　　　　　　　　　　　　　　　　　　　　　　　　　　　　(Eric Hoffer)

（偉人の最大の幸運は最も相応しい時に死ぬことだ．）
☞ Eric Hoffer (1902–1983): アメリカの社会哲学者．

(2) 動名詞（→ 詳しくは「第16章 動名詞」）

Marrying *a woman for her beauty* is like **buying** *a house for its paint*.
　　　　　　　　　　　　　　　　　　　　　　［主語・前置詞の目的語］

（女性ときれいだからと結婚するのはペンキの塗り具合で家を買うようなものだ．）
　★ **One-liner** → p. 395

I do wish I could tell you my age but it's impossible. It **keeps** *changing all the time.* ［動詞の目的語］(Greer Garson)

（ぜひわたしの年をお教えしたいのですができないのです．いつも変わり続けていますもの．）

☞ Greer Garson (1904–1996): イギリスの女優．

The secret of creativity is **knowing** *how to hide your sources.* ［補語］

(Albert Einstein)

（独創性の秘訣は情報源の隠し方を知っていることだ．）

☞ Albert Einstein (1879–1955): ドイツ生まれの理論物理学者．

★ **One-liner** → p. 395

B. 形容詞句（Adjective Phrase）：文中で形容詞の働きをする句．(1) 名詞・代名詞の後ろに置かれてそれらを修飾する．(2) 文中で補語になる．

(1) 名詞・代名詞の後ろ（→「第 14 章 不定詞」A (2); 「第 15 章 分詞」A (1), B (1)）

"What is the best way **to double** *a dollar bill*?"

"Fold it."

（「1 ドル札を 2 倍にする最もいい方法は何ですか」「2 つに折りたたむことです」）

You can always tell who the host is at a party. He's the one **watching** *the clock.*

（パーティーでだれが主人かはいつでも分かる．時計をじっと見ている人だ．）

'Poor but happy' is not a phrase **invented** *by a poor person.*

(Mason Cooley)

（「貧しいが幸せ」は貧しい人が発明した文句ではない．）

☞ Mason Cooley (1927–2002): アメリカの金言・警句家．

Q: What is a computer's sign **of old age**?

A: Loss **of memory**.

（問「コンピューターが年取った兆候は何か」答「記憶喪失」）

☞ memory:「記憶」⇔「（コンピューターの）メモリー」　★ **Pun** → p. 26

(2) 補語

"Nice to see you again. You haven't changed at all."
"I know. The laundry has been **on strike** for six months."
(「また会えてよかった．ちっとも変わらないね」「分かってる．クリーニング屋が半年ストライキをしているんだ」)

There are few sorrows, however poignant, in which a good income is **of no avail**.　(L. P. Smith)
(どんなに痛切でも十分な収入が何の役にも立たないような悲しみはほとんどない．)
☞ L. P. Smith (1915-2001): スコットランドの経済学者．

C. 副詞句（Adverb Phrase）：文中で副詞の働きをする句．(1) 前置詞，(2) 不定詞，(3) 一般語句によるもの，がある．

(1) 前置詞句

"Did you eat much **at** *that French restaurant*?"
"No. It was so expensive that I took one look **at** *the menu* and lost my appetite."
(「あのフランス料理屋でたくさん食べたか」「いいや．あまり高いんでメニューを一目見て食欲をなくしたよ」)

　First man:　I tried to kill myself yesterday **by** *taking 1,000 aspirins*.
　Second man:　What happened?
　First man:　Oh, **after** *the first two* I felt better.
(「きのうアスピリンを1000錠飲んで自殺しようとしたんだ」「どうなった」「最初の2錠で気分が良くなった」)

(2) 不定詞（→「第14章 不定詞」A (3)）

"Weren't you in the hospital last week?"
"Yeah, I had a terrible high fever."
"What did they give you **to slow** *down your heart action*?"
"An elderly nurse."

(「先週入院していなかったか」「していたよ．ひどい高熱だったんだ」「君の心臓の動きをゆるめるために何をくれた」「年配の看護師さ」)
☞ 若い美人の看護師ではますます心臓の具合が悪くなる．

(3) 一般語句

Judge: Have you ever stolen before?
Prisoner: **Now and then**, sir.
Judge: Where have you stolen from?
Prisoner: Oh, **here and there**.
Judge: Lock him up!
Prisoner: But when do I get out?
Judge: Oh, **sooner or later**.

(裁判官と被告の対話:「前に盗みを働いたことがあるかね」「はい，ときどき」「どこから盗んだんだ」「あちこちから」「収監しなさい」「でもいつ出られるんです」「遅かれ早かれ」)

On the Continent people use a fork as though a fork were a shovel; in England they turn it **upside down** and push everything—including peas—on top of it.　(George Mikes)

(ヨーロッパ大陸ではフォークをまるでシャベルのように使う．イギリスではフォークをひっくり返して，(豆も含めて)何でもその上に押しつける．)
☞ フォークの背にナイフで物をのせて食べる．
☞ George Mikes (1912–1987): ハンガリー生まれのイギリスの作家．

Don't knock the weather; nine tenths of the people couldn't start a conversation if it didn't change **once in a while**.　(Kin Hubbard)

(天気に文句を言ってはいけない．人の9割は，ときどき天気が変わらないと，会話を始めることができないだろう．)
☞ Kin Hubbard (1868–1930): アメリカのユーモア作家．

D. 形容詞句か副詞句か

> "I'd like to buy that hat **in the window**."
> "That's not necessary. They sell it to you over the counter."
> (「ウインドーの中のあの帽子が買いたいんだが」「その必要はないよ.あそこのカウンターで売ってくれるよ」)

☞ that hat *in the window*（ウインドーの中のあの帽子）（形容詞句）⇔ buy *in the window*（ウインドーの中で買う）（副詞句）

"The best *reason* **for going swimming** is that swimming is *good* **for the figure**."
"Did you ever see a duck?"
(「泳ぎに行く一番の理由は水泳は体型にいいからだ」「今までにアヒルを見たことがあるか」)

☞ 前者は The best *reason* を修飾する形容詞句, 後者は *good*（形容詞）を修飾する副詞句.

Dog owner: My dog chases anyone **on a skateboard**. What should I do?
  Vet: Take away its skateboard.
(犬の持ち主「私の犬はスケボーに乗っている人を誰でも追いかけるんです.どうしたらいいでしょうか」獣医「スケボーを取り上げなさい」)

☞ anyone *on a skateboard*（スケボーに乗っている人誰でも）（形容詞句）⇔ chase *on a skateboard*（スケボーに乗って追いかける）（副詞句）

Eric: I was a pretty handy fighter in my youth. I could lick any man **with one hand** ...
Ernie: Really?
Eric: Yes, unfortunately, I could never find anyone **with one hand** who wanted a fight.　(Eric Morecombe & Ernie Wise)
(エリックとアーニーの対話:「僕は若い頃かなりケンカが強かったんだ.どんな奴でも片手でやっつけることができたんだ」「ほんとなの」「ほんとさ.運悪くケンカしたい片手の奴が全然見つからなかったけど」)

☞ with one hand:「片手で（副詞句）」⇔「片手の（形容詞句）」
☞ Eric Morecombe (1926-1984) & Ernie Wise (1925-1999): イギリスの 2 人組のコメディアン．

ジョークの常識⑱

★ **Jewish mother**（ユダヤ人の母親）:「教育ママ」の意味で用いられる．

"What is the definition of a genius?"
"An average student with a Jewish mother."
(「天才の定義はなにか」「母親がユダヤ人の平均的学生」)
☞ 母親がついているからどんな難問にも正解できる．

第 19 章　等位接続詞

A man hurried into a quick-lunch restaurant **and** said: "Give me a ham sandwich."
"Yes, sir," said the waiter, reaching for the sandwich, "will you eat it **or** take it with you?"
"Both," was the unexpected **but** obvious reply.
(ある男，ファーストフードの店へ急いで入って言った．「ハムサンドをくれ」ウエイター，サンドイッチに手を伸ばしながら，「お食べになりますか，持って行かれますか」「両方だ」は予期せぬしかし明快な返事だった．)

☞ 食べたものは胃袋の中に入れて持って行く．

等位接続詞には **and, but, or** などがあり，語・句・節を対等な関係で結びつける．

(1) and

(a) 普通の用法

Love is one long sweet dream, **and** marriage is the alarm clock.
(恋愛は1つの長い甘美な夢である，そして結婚は目覚まし時計である．)

★ **One-liner** → p. 395

Teacher:　How much is half of 8?
　Suzie:　Up **and** down **or** across?
Teacher:　What do you mean?
　Suzie:　Up **and** down it's 3, **and** across it's 0.
(先生と生徒の対話：「8の半分はいくつですか」「縦にですか横にですか」「どういう意味なの」「縦なら3です，そして横なら0です」)

313

An American tourist was being shown round London's Westminster Abbey. The guide pointed to a splendid monument and declared: "There lies a great and honest man **and** a most distinguished lawyer."

"That's interesting," said the American. "I never knew that in England you buried two men in the same grave."

(アメリカ人の旅行者がロンドンのウエストミンスター寺院を案内されていた．ガイドは見事な記念像を指差して「偉大で誠実な人で非常に有名な弁護士が眠っておられます」と厳かに言った．「それは面白い」とアメリカ人．「イングランドでは2人を同じ墓に埋めるとは知らなかった」)

☞ Westminster Abbey: ロンドンにある大教会堂．

I don't make jokes; I just watch the government **and** report the facts.
(Will Rogers)

(私はジョークを作らない．ただ政治をじっと見て事実を報告するだけだ．)

☞ それがジョークになってしまう．

☞ Will Rogers (1879–1935): アメリカの俳優・新聞コラムニスト．

(b) both A and B:「AもBも両方とも」

"What is one thing we can **both** eat **and** drink?"
"A toast."

(「食べることも飲むこともできるものは何か」「トースト」)

☞ toast:「(パンの) トースト」⇔「乾杯」　★ **Pun** → p. 26; **Riddle** → p. 64

We should learn from the snail: it has devised a home that is **both** exquisite **and** functional.　(Frank Lloyd Wright (attrib.))

(我々はカタツムリから学ぶべきだ．実にみごとでかつ機能的な家を発明したのだ．)

☞ Frank Lloyd Wright (1867–1959): アメリカの建築家．

Music with dinner is an insult **both** to the cook **and** the violinist.
(G. K. Chesterton)

(ディナーつきの音楽は料理人にとってもバイオリニストにとっても侮辱である．)

☞ G. K. Chesterton (1874–1936): イギリスの批評家・小説家．

★ **One-liner** → p. 395

(c) 命令文＋and（→「第3章 命令文・感嘆文」A (2)）

(2) but

> **But** me no **buts**.
> （しかししかしと言うのはやめてくれ.）

(a) 普通の用法

Poverty is not a disgrace, **but** it's terribly inconvenient.
（貧乏は恥ではないがひどく不便である.）

Money is a good servant **but** a bad master.
（金はよい僕だが悪い主人である.）
★ **One-liner** → p. 395

I said to my caddie, "Do you like my game?"
He said, "It's okay, **but** I prefer golf."
（キャディーに「私のゲームは好きかい」と言うと，彼は言った「結構ですが，ゴルフの方が好きです」）
☞ あなたのプレーはゴルフとは呼べません. ★ **Insulting joke** → p. 97

There are beautiful girls in Hollywood. **But** I never see them. I work in a beauty parlor.
（ハリウッドには美しい女性がいます．でもわたしは会うことはないんです．わたし美容院で働いてますから．）
☞ いつも素顔しか見ていません．

(b) not only A but (also) B:「A だけでなく B もまた」（=**B as well as A**）
Playing dead **not only** comes in handy when face to face with a bear, **but also** at important business meetings.　(Jack Handey)
（死んだふりをすることは熊と直面したとき役に立つだけでなく重要な仕事の会議でも役に立つ．）
☞ Jack Handey (1949–): アメリカのユーモア作家．

"Daddy, what is a pessimist?"
"A man who wears a belt **as well as** suspenders, my son."
(「お父さん，悲観主義者ってどんな人なの」「ズボンつりだけでなくベルトもしている人さ」)

The speeches of some politicians are quite interesting because they give so many facts **as well as** dreams you can't find elsewhere.
(政治家の演説に極めて興味深いものがあるのは他では見つからない夢だけではなくあまりにも多くの事実を教えてくれるからだ．)

cf. as well as A は「A と同じようによく」の意味になることがある．
"Now tell me the truth—do you men like the talkative women **as well as** you do the other kind?"
"What other kind?"
(「じゃあ本当のことを言って．あなたたち男の人は話好きの女性も他の女性と同じように好きなの」「他のって何だい」)

cf. as well:「もまた」の意味になることがある．
　Teacher: I hope I didn't see you cheating just then.
　　Pupil: I hope you didn't **as well**.
(先生「ちょうどあのとき君のカンニングを見なかったと思いたいわ」生徒「ぼくも先生は見なかったと思いたいです」)

(c) as A, so B:「ちょうど A であるように B でもある」
Whatever you may look like, marry a man your own age—**as** your beauty fades, **so** will his eyesight.　(Phyllis Diller)
(あなたの姿形（すがたかたち）がどうあれ，同い年の男性と結婚しなさい．あなたの美貌が衰えていくのと同じように彼の視力も衰えていきます．)
☞ Phyllis Diller (1917–2012): アメリカの女優・コメディアン．

(d) not A but B:「A ではなく B である」
Marriage is **not** a word **but** a sentence.　(Anon.)
(結婚は語ではなく文である．)

☞ sentence:「文」⇔「(刑の) 宣告」　★ **Pun** → p. 26

The aim of a joke is **not** to degrade the human being **but** to remind him that he is already degraded.　(George Orwell)
(ジョークの目的は人間の評価を落とすことではなくすでに評価は地に落ちていることを思い出させることだ.)
☞ George Orwell (1903-1951): イギリスの小説家.
★ **One-liner** → p. 395

The real danger is **not that** computers will begin to think like men, **but that** men will begin to think like computers.　(Sydney J. Harris)
(真の危険はコンピューターが人間のように考え始めることではなく, 人間がコンピューターのように考え始めることである.)
☞ Sydney J. Harris (1917-1986): アメリカのジャーナリスト.
★ **One-liner** → p. 395

cf. 前置詞としての **but**（→「第 17 章　前置詞」J (19)）
Some people know how to live everybody's life **but** their own.
(すべての人がどう生きるべきかを知っている人もいる, 自分自身の人生は除いて.)

(3) or

(a) 普通の用法：**A or B**「A または B」

"Have you any brothers **or** sisters?"
"No, my parents were orphans."
(「君には兄弟か姉妹がいますか」「いません. ぼくの両親は孤児だったんです」)

★ **Irish bull** → p. 39

"What are you drinking, tea **or** coffee?"
"They didn't say."
(「何飲んでるの, 紅茶それともコーヒーなの」「店の人は何も言わなかったわ」)
☞ だからどちらだか分からない.

A small boy asked the girl next door, "Are you the opposite sex, **or** am I?"
(幼い男の子が隣の女の子に尋ねた「異性って君なのそれとも僕なの」)
★ **Irish bull** → p. 39

"Is there a way to avoid alimony?"
"Sure, stay single **or** stay married."
(「離婚手当を避ける方法があるか」「あるとも, 独身を通すか結婚を通すかだ」)

(b) either A or B:「A か B か (のどちらか)」

When a man opens the door of his car for his wife, you can be sure of one thing: **either** the car **or** wife is new.
(男が妻のために車のドアを開けるとき, 1つ確実なことは車か妻のどちらかが新しいということだ.)

Men have two reasons for staying at the pub all night. **Either** they've got no wives to go home to **or** they have.
(男が一晩中パブにいる2つの理由がある. 家に帰っても妻がいないか, あるいは, いるかだ.)

(c) 命令文＋or (→ 第3章 A. 命令文 (2))

(4) so, for など
(a) so:「だから」

Professor: Junior, please wake up that student next to you!
  Junior: You put him to sleep, **so** you wake him up!
(教授「君, 隣の学生を起こしてくれたまえ」大学3年生「先生が眠らせたのです, ですから先生が起こすべきです」)

My dog was my only friend. I told my wife that everyone needs at least two friends, **so** she bought me another dog.
(犬が唯一の友達だった. 妻にだれでも少なくとも2人の友達が必要だと言った, だから彼女はもう1匹犬を買ってくれた.)

(b) for:「というのは〜だから」

I love children, especially when they cry, **for** then someone takes them away.　(Nancy Mitford)
（私は子供たちが好き，特に泣くときは，というのはそうすれば誰かが連れて行ってくれるから．）
☞ Nancy Mitford (1904-1973): イギリスの小説家・伝記作家．

Marry not a tennis player. **For** love means nothing to them.
（テニスの選手と結婚するな．というのは愛は彼らには何も意味しないからだ．）
☞ love:「愛」⇔「(テニスの) 0 点」; nothing:「何も〜ない」⇔「0 (ゼロ)」
★ **Pun** → p. 26

(c) only（ただし），yet（けれども），therefore（それゆえに），still（しかしながら）

Many women have always been firm believers in recycling, **only** they call it by a different name—garage sales.
（多くの女性は常にリサイクルが正しいことだと固く信じてきた，ただそれを違う名前で呼んでいる―ガレージセールと．）

'My wife kisses the dog on the lips, **yet** she won't drink from my glass!'　(Rodney Dangerfield)
（妻は犬の唇にキスする，しかし私のグラスからは飲もうともしない．）
☞ Rodney Dangerfield (1921-2004): アメリカのコメディアン・俳優・声優．

I think, **therefore** I'm single.　(Lizz Winstead)
（我思う，故に独身．）
☞ I think, therefore I am. (Descartes)「我思う，故に我在り．(デカルト)」のもじり．
★ **Parody** → p. 199
☞ Lizz Winstead (1961-): アメリカのコメディアン・ラジオテレビタレント．

His hair is getting thin—**still**, who wants fat hair?　(Milton Berle)
（彼の髪は薄くなりかけている，しかし誰が太った髪を望むのか．）
☞ thin:「薄い」⇔「痩せた」　★ **Pun** → p. 26
☞ Milton Berle (1908-2002): アメリカのコメディアン・俳優．

ジョークの常識⑲

★ **Absent-minded professor:**「上の空教授」

　ジョークの世界では professor にほとんど常に absent-minded（心ここにあらず）が付く．象牙の塔にこもり浮世離れしていることが笑いの対象になっている．

第20章　名　詞　節

> My wife admits **that** she's not perfect. She's the first one to say / she'd made mistakes in the past. That's **how** she explains our marriage.
> （妻は自分が完全でないことを認めている．彼女は過去に間違いをしたと言った最初の女性だ．それが我々がどうして結婚したかの彼女の説明になっている．）

☞　/ ＝ (that)

　　名詞節は文中で主語・目的語・補語・名詞の同格になる節をいう．ふつう **that**, **if**, **whether** などの接続詞，**what**, **where**, **why** などの疑問詞，関係代名詞 **what**，関係副詞 **when**, **where**, **how** などが節（S＋V＋...）の先頭にくる．

A. that に導かれるもの

> It is unfortunate **that** providence didn't think to give us our neighbors' children, since these are the only ones we know how to raise.
> （神が我々に近所の子供たちを与えようとお思いにならなかったのは不幸なことである，なぜなら近所の子供たちの育て方しか我々には分からないのだから．）

☞　自分の子供の育て方は分からない．

(1) 主語として（→「第10章　It の用法」C）

That trees should have been cut down to provide paper for this book was an ecological affront.　(Anthony Blond)
（こんな本の用紙を提供するために木が切り倒されるべきだったとは生態学的侮辱であった．）

☞　Anthony Blond (1928-2008): イギリスの出版業者．

★ **Insulting joke** → p. 97

"Is it true **that** married men live longer than single men?"
"No, it only seems longer."
(「結婚している男のほうが独身の男より長生きするというのは本当ですか」「とんでもない. より長く思えるだけです」)

(2) 動詞の目的語・補語として

Every generation believes **that** there was a golden age that ended about forty years ago.　(Anon.)
(どの世代の人も約 40 年前に終わった黄金時代があったと信じている.)

"What makes you think **that** my son Martin is always playing truant?"
"There's no Martin in this school!"
(「なぜ息子のマーチンがいつも無断欠席しているなんて思うのですか」「この学校にはマーチンなんて生徒はいません」)
☞ そもそも初めから学校へ行っていない.

The best thing about animals is **that** they don't talk much.
(Thornton Wilder)
(動物の一番いいところはあまりしゃべらないことだ.)
☞ Thornton Wilder (1897–1975): アメリカの小説家・劇作家.

A woman motorist greets her husband at the door when he gets home. "I've got good news and bad news about the car," she said. "The good news is **that** the air bag works."
(車を運転する女性が夫が帰宅すると玄関で出迎えて「車のことでいい知らせと悪い知らせがあるわ」と言った. 「いい知らせはエアバッグはちゃんと使えるってこと」)

"Well, what was the matter? Didn't the alarm clock go off?"
"Oh, yes, sir, it went off all right, but the trouble was **that** it went off while I was asleep."

(「どうしたの．目覚ましが鳴らなかったの」「いいえ，先生，確かに鳴ったんです．でも困ったことにぼくが眠っている間に鳴ったんです」)

cf. say, think, know などの動詞の後では that は省略されることが多い．

My autobiography is straight from the horse's mouth. Not that I'm **saying** / I'm a horse. (Victoria Beckham)

(私の自伝は馬の口から直接聞いたものです．私が馬だと言っているのではありませんが．)
- ☞ straight from the horse's mouth:「当の本人から直接に」
- ☞ Victoria Beckham (1974-): イギリスの歌手・ファッションデザイナー・女優・実業家．

I don't **think** / anyone should write his autobiography until after he's dead. (Samuel Goldwyn)

(誰も死んだ後まで自伝を書くべきではないと思う．)
- ☞ Samuel Goldwyn (1879–1974): アメリカの映画製作者．
- ★ **Goldwynisms** → p. 56

"You were cheating at cards tonight."
"But how did you **know** / I was cheating?"
"Because you weren't playing with the cards I gave you."

(「君は今夜トランプでインチキしてたぞ」「でもどうしてインチキしてたと分かるんだ」「僕が渡したトランプを使ってなかったからさ」)

(3) **同格の that**: 〜 that ...「...という〜」前の名詞の内容を説明する．

The chief value of money lies in *the fact* **that** one lives in a world in which it is overestimated. (H. L. Mencken)

(金銭の主要な価値は人が金銭が過大評価されている世界に生きているという事実にある．)
- ☞ H. L. Mencken (1880–1956): アメリカの批評家・ジャーナリスト．
- ★ **One-liner** → p. 395

The greatest problem about old age is *the fear* **that** it may go on too long. (A. J. P. Taylor)

（老年の最大の問題はそれが長く続きすぎるかもしれないという恐怖である．）
☞ A. J. P. Taylor (1906-1990): イギリスの歴史学者．

B. if, whether に導かれるもの：「＿＿かどうか」

"How can you tell **if** a teacher is in a good mood?"
"Let me know **if** you ever find out."
（「先生がご機嫌がいいかどうかどうして分かる」「もし分かったら教えてよ」）

☞ 前者は名詞節を導く if（〜かどうか），後者は副詞節を導く if（もし〜なら）

Little Girl: Mummy, teacher was asking me today **if** I had any brothers and sisters.
Mother: That's nice, dear, and what did she say when you told her you were an only child?
Little Girl: Oh, she just said, "Thank goodness."

（母親と娘の対話：「お母さん，今日先生がわたしにきょうだいがいるかって聞いていたわよ」「それはよかったね．それでお前がひとりっ子だと言ったら先生何とおっしゃったの」「『まあよかった』っておっしゃっただけよ」）

☞ Thank goodness!:「やれやれ（助かった）」

"What made you give up singing in the choir?"
"I was absent one Sunday and someone asked **if** the organ had been fixed."
（「なぜ聖歌隊で歌うのをやめる気になったんだい」「日曜日にぼくが休んだら，誰かがオルガンが直ったのかって聞いたんだ」）

I always read the obituary columns every morning to see **if** I'm alive or dead.
（私はいつも毎朝自分が生きているか死んでいるかを知るために死亡欄を読むことにしている．）

★ **Irish bull** → p. 39

"When he asked me how old I was, I couldn't remember **whether** I was twenty-four **or** twenty-five."
"And what did you say?"
"Eighteen."
(「彼がいくつだと聞いたとき24だか25だか思い出せなかったの」「それで何と言ったの」「18って」)

"I have just heard that my sister has a baby. They don't say what sex and so I don't know **whether** I am an uncle **or** aunt."
(「姉に赤ん坊が生まれたと聞いたところなんだ．男か女か言わないから自分が叔父なのか叔母なのか分からないんだよ」)

★ Irish bull → p. 39

"I'm so nearsighted I nearly worked myself to death."
"What's being nearsighted got to do with working yourself to death?"
"I couldn't tell **whether** the boss was watching me **or not**, so I had to work all the time."
(「僕はひどい近眼だから過労死しそうになったよ」「近眼と過労死とどういう関係があるんだい」「ボスが僕を見ているかどうか分からないから，ずっと仕事を続けなくてはならなかったんだ」)

C. 関係代名詞 what / whatever などで導かれるもの

> A holiday is a day a man stops doing **what** his boss wants and starts doing **what** his wife wants.
> (休日とは男がボスが望むことをするのをやめて妻が望むことをし始める日である．)

(1) what = that which ＿＿＿ / thing(s) which ＿＿＿：「＿＿＿すること／＿＿＿するもの」

"Oh, honey, you gave me just **what** I needed to exchange for **what** I wanted."
(「まあ，あなた，ちょうどいい具合に欲しかったものと交換する必要がある物をくださっ

たわ」)

What you don't like or can't afford is precisely **what** the menu offers.
(食べたくないか金銭的に余裕がないものがまさにメニューには載っている.)

Advertising is **what** makes you think you've longed all your life for something you've never heard of before.
(広告は以前聞いたこともなかった物をずっと欲しいと思っていたと思わせるもの.)
★ **One-liner** → p. 395

(2) whatever = anything that ___:「___する物［こと］は何でも」; whoever = anyone who ___:「___する人はだれでも」(→「第22章　副詞節」(5) 譲歩)
Whatever my wife buys today is usually on sale tomorrow.
(妻が今日買うものは何でもたいてい明日は特売品になっている.)

A baby sitter is a young girl you hire to let your children do **whatever** they want.
(ベビーシッターは子供たちにしたい放題させるために雇う若い女の子だ.)

Whoever gossips *to* you will gossip *about* you. (Sir Philip Sidney)
(あなたに誰かのうわさ話をする人は誰でもあなたについてのうわさ話をするものだ.)
☞ Sir Philip Sidney (1554–1586): イギリスの軍人・政治家・詩人・批評家.

Teacher: What does it mean when the barometer is falling?
　Pupil: It means that **whoever** nailed it up didn't do such a good job.
(先生と生徒の対話:「晴雨計が下がっているのはどういう意味ですか」「それを釘づけした誰もあまり良い仕事をしなかったという意味です」)

(3) 慣用表現
(a) **A is to B what C is to D**:「AのBに対する関係はCのDに対する関係と同じである」

What garlic **is to** salad, insanity **is to** art. (Augustus Saint-Gaudens)
(ニンニクとサラダの関係は狂気と芸術の関係に等しい.)
☞ Augustus Saint-Gaudens (1848-1907): アイルランド生まれのアメリカの彫刻家.

There's a sign at the entrance to the Los Angeles General Hospital that reads, "**WHAT** SUNSHINE **IS TO** FLOWERS, SMILES **ARE TO** HUMAN BEINGS."
(ロスアンゼルス総合病院の入口に次のような掲示がある:「日光が花に必要なように微笑が人間に必要です」)

cf.「A is to B as C is to D」も同じ意味になる:
Poetry **is to** prose **as** dancing **is to** walking.　(John Wain)
(詩と散文は踊りと歩行の関係に等しい.)
☞ John Wain (1925-1994): イギリスの小説家・詩人.

D. 疑問詞に導かれるもの

> I can remember **when** I got married. And **where** I got married. What I just can't remember is **why**.
> (私はいつ結婚したかを思い出せる. そしてどこで結婚したかも. どうも思い出せないのはなぜかだ.)

Singer:　Did you notice **how** my voice filled the hall?
Critic:　Oh, yes. And did you notice **how** the people left the hall to make room for it?
(歌手「私の声がどれほどホールを満たしたか気がつきましたか」批評家「もちろんです. そして人々がどんなふうにあなたの声のために場所を空けようとしてホールを出たか気がつきましたか」)
★ **Insulting joke** → p. 97

"I once had a beard like yours, and when I saw **how** terrible I looked, I got it cut off."
"I used to have a face like yours, too, and when I saw **how** terrible it

made me look, I grew a beard."
(「以前は君のようなあごひげを生やしていたけど，何とひどく見えるかが分かって切ってもらったよ」「ぼくも以前は君のような顔だったんだ，そしてそのために何とひどく見えるか分かったとき，あごひげを生やしたんだ」)

★ **Insulting joke** → p. 97

My girlfriend can never understand **why** her brother has five sisters and she only has four.
(僕のガールフレンドはなぜ兄さんには5人姉妹がいるのに自分には4人しかいないのかがまったく理解できない．)

Bob:　Does your uncle carry life insurance?
Paul:　No, he just carries fire insurance. He knows **where** he is going.
(ボブ「伯父さんは生命保険を掛けているか」ポール「いいや，火災保険だけだ．どこへ行くことになるか知っているんだ」)
☞　地獄だということを．

"Jimmie," said the teacher, "why don't you wash your face? I can see **what** you had for breakfast this morning."
"What was it?"
"Eggs."
"Wrong, teacher. That was yesterday."
(「ジミー，なぜ君は顔を洗わないの．今朝朝食に何を食べたか分かるわよ」「何だったでしょう」「卵でしょう」「違います，先生．それは昨日です」)

I sure love golf. It makes me forget **whom** I'm married to, and **whom** I'm working for.
(私はほんとにゴルフが好きだ．ゴルフは自分が誰と結婚しているか，誰のために働いているかを忘れさせてくれる．)

ジョークの常識⑳

★ **Doctor, Lawyer, Politician**:「医師, 弁護士, 政治家」
　ジョークに頻出する人物. 社会的地位・高収入が一般人の羨望の的になり, 皮肉・嫌味を言いたくなる存在になる. 次の言葉もそれを裏付けている.

The secret of much humor lies in an attack on authority.
(Milton Berle)
(多くのユーモアの秘訣は権威に対する攻撃にある.)

Doctor:「医は仁術」ではなく「医は算術」と考える人として登場することが多い.
Lawyer: 依頼人からの相談料［報酬］のためなら黒も白と言いくるめてしまう.
Politician: 実現できない公約をし, 汚職による蓄財に励む人として登場することが多い.

第 21 章　形容詞節

That "that" **that** that English teacher used in that place is wrong.
（あの英語の先生があそこで使ったあの「that」は間違いだ．）

> 形容詞節は関係代名詞（who, that, which など），関係副詞（when, where, why など）に導かれる節で，ふつう直前の名詞・代名詞（先行詞という）を修飾する．関係詞がなく［省略されて］直接，名詞・代名詞を修飾することもある．

◆ 関係代名詞

先行詞 ＼ 格	主格	所有格	目的格
人	who / that	whose	(whom / that)
物・動物	that / which	whose / of which	(that / which)
人・動物・物	that	—	(that)
—	what	—	what

cf. what は名詞節を導く．（→「第 20 章　名詞節」C）

A. 関係代名詞に導かれるもの

Hospitality is that generous spirit **which** leads us to have someone to dinner **who** doesn't need it and **who** will be expected to invite us later.
（親切なもてなしの心とは招待する必要のない人で後で我々を招待してくれそうな人をディナーに招待する気にさせるあの寛大な精神である．）

(1) who / whose / whom に導かれるもの

> Highbrow: a person who can use the word **"whom"** without feeling self-consciousness.
> (インテリぶる人とは自意識を感じないで「whom」を使える人.)

☞ 今では whom はめったに使われない.

> MC: a man **who** introduces people **who** need no introduction.
> (司会者：紹介の必要のない人を紹介する人.)

A book is a success when people **who** haven't read it pretend they have.　(*Los Angeles Times*)
(本はそれを読んだことがない人が読んだふりをするようになれば成功である.)
　　　　　　　　　　　　　　　　　　　(『ロスアンゼルス・タイムズ』紙)

A successful man is one **who** makes more money than his wife can spend. A successful woman is one **who** can find such a man.
　　　　　　　　　　　　　　　　　　　　　　　(Lana Turner)
(成功した男は妻が使える以上の金をかせぐ男である. 成功した女はそんな男を見つけることのできる女である.)
☞ Lana Turner (1921–1995): アメリカの女優.

Never go to a doctor **whose** office plants have died.　(Erma Bombeck)
(診察室の植物が枯れてしまっている医者には決して行ってはいけません.)
☞ Erma Bombeck (1927–1996): アメリカのユーモア作家.
★ **One-liner** → p. 395

Did you hear about the gambler **whose** wife was terrible in the kitchen? He hid his winnings in her cookbooks.
(奥さんが台所仕事が最悪だという賭博師のことを聞いたか. 彼は勝った金を奥さんの料理の本の中に隠したんだ.)
☞ 料理の本を開くことはないから隠した金は見つからない.

I tend to be suspicious of people **whose** love of animals is exaggerated; they are often frustrated in their relationships with humans.

(Camilla Koffler)

(私は動物への愛情表現が大げさな人を疑う傾向がある．彼らはしばしば人間関係で欲求不満なのだ．)

☞ Camilla Koffler (1911-1955): ハンガリーの動物写真家．

★ **One-liner** → p. 395

Acquaintance: A person **whom** we know well enough to borrow from, but not well enough to lend to.

(知人：物を借りる程度にはよく知っているが貸すほどはよく知らない人．)

(2) which に導かれるもの

> *Doctor:* My man, yours is a case **which** will enrich medical science.
> *Patient:* Oh, dear, and I thought I wouldn't have to pay more than five or ten dollars.
>
> (医師と患者の対話：「あなた，あなたのは医学を豊かにする症例です」「何てこと，5ドルか10ドル以上払う必要はないと思ったのに」)

Conscience is the inner voice **which** warns us that someone may be looking. (H. L. Mencken)

(良心とは我々に誰かが見ているかもしれないと警告する内なる声である．)

☞ H. L. Mencken (1880-1956): アメリカの批評家・ジャーナリスト．

★ **One-liner** → p. 395

A best-seller was a book **which** somehow sold well simply because it was selling well. (Daniel J. Boorstin)

(ベストセラーは良く売れているという理由だけでどういうわけか良く売れた本だった．)

☞ Daniel J. Boorstin (1914-2004): アメリカの作家・歴史学者．

cf. that which＝what（→「第20章 名詞節」C (1)）

Never do today **that which** will become someone else's responsibility tomorrow.
（明日になれば誰か他の人の責任になることを今日やるな．）
☞ Never put off till tomorrow what you can do today.（今日できることを明日まで延ばすな．）（ことわざ）のもじり．
★ **Parody** → p. 199

(3) that に導かれるもの

> Teenage Love: A feeling **that** you feel when you feel you're going to feel a feeling **that** you never felt before.
> （10代の恋心：今まで決して感じなかった感情を感じそうだと感じるときに感じる感情．）

There is no secret about success. Did you ever meet a successful man **that** didn't tell you all about it?　(Kin Hubbard)
（成功に秘密などない．成功についてすべてを語らなかった成功者に会ったことがあるか．）
☞ Kin Hubbard (1868-1930): アメリカの漫画家・ユーモア作家．

There is one thing **that** money can't buy—and that's poverty.
（金で買えないものが1つある，それは貧乏である．）

"Look here, don't you know my office hours are from 8 to 12?"
"Yes, Doctor, but the dog **that** bit me didn't."
（「いいですか，診察時間が8時〜12時だということを知らないのですか」「知ってます，先生．僕に咬みついた犬は知らなかったんです」）

Please accept my resignation. I don't care to belong to any club **that** will accept me as a member.　(Groucho Marx)
（私の脱会届を受け取ってください．私を会員として受け入れるようなクラブには属したくありません．）

☞ Groucho Marx (1890–1977): アメリカのコメディアン．Marx Brothers（マルクス兄弟）の中心．

She always presents the truth in such a way **that** nobody ever recognizes it.
（彼女はいつもだれにもそれと分からないようなやり方で真実を語る．）

cf. 先行詞に first, only, 最上級の形容詞などがつくと **that** を用いるのが原則．
"Father, did Edison make the first talking machine?"
"No, my son, God made the first talking machine, but Edison made *the first* one **that** could be cut off."
（「父さん，エジソンが初めて話す機械を作ったの」「そうじゃないんだ．神さまが最初の話す機械をお作りになったんだが，エジソンは途中で切れる最初の機械を作ってくれたのさ」）
☞ 神様は女性をお造りになった．

Man is *the only* animal **that** can remain on friendly terms with the victims he intends to eat until he eats them.　(Samuel Butler)
（人間は自分が食べるつもりの犠牲と食べるまでずっと友好な関係でいられる唯一の動物である．）
☞ Samuel Butler (1835–1902): イギリスの小説家．
★ **One-liner** → p. 395

(4) 関係詞が省略されたと考えられるもの

> All / my wife wanted for Valentine's Day was a little card—American Express!
> （家内がバレンタイン・デーに欲しがったのはちっぽけなカードだけだった―アメリカン・エクスプレスだ．）

Heredity is something / people believe in if they have a bright child.
（遺伝とは頭のいい子供を持った場合にその存在を信じるもの．）
★ **One-liner** → p. 395

"I'm putting everything / I know into my next story."
"I get it—a short story."
(「こんどの小説には知っていることのすべてを入れるつもりだ」「分かった．じゃあ短篇だろう」)
★ **Insulting joke** → p. 97

Doctor: There goes the only woman / I ever loved.
Nurse: Why don't you marry her?
Doctor: I can't afford to. She is my best patient.
(医師と看護師の対話：「あそこを行くのが私が愛したただ1人の女性だ」「結婚なさったらいいじゃありませんか」「その余裕はないんだ．彼女が私の最良の患者なんだ」)

A friend is a guy who's got the same enemies / you do.
(友とは君と敵を共有する男だ．)
★ **One-liner** → p. 395

Experience is the name / people give their mistakes.
(Talmud / Oscar Wilde)
(経験は人々が自分の間違いにつける名前である．)
☞ Talmud: ユダヤ教の律法集．
☞ Oscar Wilde (1854-1900): アイルランド生まれのイギリスの詩人・小説家・劇作家．
★ **One-liner** → p. 395

(5) 二重限定：先行詞が2つの関係代名詞によって限定されることがある．前の関係代名詞は省略されることが多い．

I've never known a person **who** lives to be 110 **who** is remarkable for anything else. (Josh Billings)
(110まで生きる人でそれ以外のことで注目に値する人をいまだかつて知らない．)
☞ Josh Billings (1818-1885): アメリカのユーモア作家．

An alcoholic is anyone / you don't like **who** drinks more than you do.
(Dylan Thomas)
(自分が気に入らないやつで自分よりたくさん飲むやつは誰でもアル中患者だ．)
☞ Dylan Thomas (1914-1953): イギリスの詩人．

"I'm a college graduate and I'd like to know what I should do to make my living in this world."
"Just marry the first girl / you find **that** has a steady job."
(「僕は大卒でこの世の中で生計を立てるには何をすべきか知りたいのですが」「最初に見つけた，安定した仕事を持っている女性と結婚することです」)

My library consists of books / I have **that** nobody wants to borrow.
(私の書庫は持ってはいるが誰も借りたがらない本から成っている．)

An extravagance is anything / you buy **that** is of no use to your spouse.
(贅沢品とはあなたが買う，配偶者には何の価値もないものすべてである．)

★ **One-liner** → p. 395

(6) 前置詞＋関係代名詞

A pun is a joke **at which** everyone groans, because they didn't think of it first.
(駄じゃれは，だれもが最初にそれを思いつかなかったがゆえに，非難がましくうめき声を上げるジョークである．)

cf. a) A pun is a *joke*. + Everyone groans *at it*.

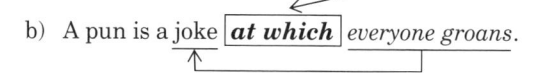

　　b) A pun is a joke *at which* *everyone groans*.

　　c) A pun is a joke *everyone groans at*.

Marriage is the high sea **for which** no compass has yet been invented.
(結婚はそのための羅針盤がまだ発明されていない公海である．)

Youth is a disease **from which** we all recover.　　(Dorothy Fulheim)
（青春は我々すべてが回復する病気である．）
☞ Dorothy Fulheim (1893–1989): アメリカのジャーナリスト・テレビアンカー．

America is the sort of nation **in which** a cigarette testimonial by a famous football player who has never smoked in his life is regarded as persuasive publicity.
（アメリカは，いままでタバコをすったことのない有名なフットボールの選手のタバコの推薦のことばが説得力のある宣伝だと見なされるような国である．）

"I'll lecture today on liars. How many of you have read the twenty-fifth chapter?"
Nearly all raised their hands.
"That's fine. You are the group **to whom** I wish to speak. There is no twenty-fifth chapter."
（「今日はうそつきについて講義をします．あなた方のうちで何人25章を読みましたか」ほとんど全員が手を挙げた．「それは結構．あなた方は私がお話ししたい人たちだ．25章はそもそもないのです」）

A bribe is a gift **with which** the giver says, "Thanks," and the receiver says, "Don't mention it!"
（賄賂とは贈る側が「ありがとう」と言い，受け取る側は「どういたしまして」と言う贈り物である．）
★ **One-liner** → p. 395

Money is like a sixth sense **without which** you cannot make a complete use of the other five.　　(W. Somerset Maugham)
（金は第六感のようなものでそれがないと他の5つを完全に利用することはできない．）
☞ W. Somerset Maugham (1874–1965): イギリスの小説家・劇作家．

cf.　前置詞＋関係代名詞＋**to** 不定詞＝前置詞＋関係代名詞＋**S**＋**V**
"I'll give you three days **in which to pay** your rent."
"All right. I'll pick Fourth of July, Christmas and Easter."

(「部屋代を払うのに 3 日あげよう」「結構です．7 月 4 日，クリスマス，イースターを選びます」)
- ☞ Fourth of July:「(アメリカ合衆国の) 独立記念日」
  in which to pay ＝ in which you pay

The most dangerous position **in which to sleep** is with your feet on your desk.
(眠るのに最も危険な姿勢は両足を机の上にのせた状態である．)
- ☞ in which to sleep ＝ in which you sleep

"When I first came to New York, I had only a dollar in my pocket **with which to make** a start."
"How did you invest that dollar?"
"Used it to pay for a telegram home for more money."
(「最初ニューヨークへ来たとき，スタートを切るのにポケットに 1 ドルしかなかったんだ」「その 1 ドルをどう投資したんだ」「家へもっと金をくれと頼む電報料金に使ったよ」)
- ☞ with which to make ＝ with which I made

(7) 継続用法： 1) 前にコンマ (comma) をつける．2) 目的格も省略しない．3) who, which だけに限られる．関係代名詞以下は先行詞について補足的に説明している．

(a) 文末につける

> With fame I became more and more stupid, **which** of course is a very common phenomenon.　(Albert Einstein)
> (有名になるにつれて，私はますます愚かになった．それはしかしもちろん極めて普通の現象である．)

- ☞ Albert Einstein (1879–1955): ドイツ生まれの理論物理学者．

It is indeed fitting that we gather here today to pay tribute to Abraham Lincoln, **who** was born in a log cabin that he built with his own hands.　(Ronald Reagan)
(今日アブラハム・リンカーンに敬意を表してここに集まっているのは実にふさわしいこ

とです，彼は自分の手で建てた丸太小屋で生まれたのですから．）
☞ Ronald Reagan (1911-2004): アメリカの俳優・政治家．第40代大統領．
★ **Irish bull** → p. 39

With obvious reluctance a small boy handed his report card to his father, **who** studied the card, then sighed. The boy glanced at the signature, then asked, "Why did you sign with an X instead of your name?"
"Because," his father said, "with these grades, I don't think your teacher believe you had a father who could read and write."
（明らかにいやいやの態度で少年が成績表を父に手渡すと，父はそれをよく見てからため息をついた．少年は父のサインをちらと見て尋ねた．「お父さんはなぜ名前ではなくてXとサインしたの」「なぜって」と父は言った．「こんな成績じゃ先生はお前に読み書きできる父親がいるなんて信じないと思うからだよ」）
☞ X:（字の書けない人の）署名代わりの記号．

"Gentlemen," said Jones, raising an empty glass, "I rise to toast absent friends, **among whom** I include the waiter for this table."
（「諸君」とジョーンズは空のグラスを上げながら言った．「起立して欠席の友人たちのために乾杯する，もちろんその中にはこのテーブルのウエイターも含んでいる」）
☞ 乾杯するときになってもまだ飲み物が出されていない．

Marriage is the alliance of two people, **one of whom** never remembers birthdays and the other never forgets them.
(Ogden Nash)
（結婚は2人の同盟で，一方は誕生日を決して覚えていないがもう一方は決して忘れないのだ．）
☞ Ogden Nash (1902-1971): アメリカの詩人．

To get something done a committee should consist of no more than three men, two **of whom** are absent.　(Robert Copeland)
（何かを実行させるには委員会は3人だけで構成すべきで，しかもそのうちの2人は欠席でなければならない．）
☞ Robert Copeland (1945-): アメリカの音楽評論家．

We know a man who thinks marriage is a fifty-fifty proposition, **which** convinces us that he doesn't understand women or percentages.
（結婚は五分五分の問題だと思っている男を知っているが，彼には女性と百分率が分かっていないことが納得できる．）

You pity a man who is lame or blind, but you never pity him for being a fool, **which** is often a much greater misfortune.
(Rev. Sydney Smith)
（あなた方は足の不自由な人や目の不自由な人を気の毒だと思いますが，人が愚かなことを決して気の毒だと思いません，しかしこの方がはるかに大きな不幸なのです．）
☞ Rev. Sydney Smith (1771-1845): イギリス国教会の牧師．

cf. 次のように節全体を先行詞にする場合，関係詞節を独立させる場合がある．
Fortunately, my doctor doesn't believe in unnecessary surgery. **Which** means he won't operate unless he really needs the money.
（幸運にも私の医者は不必要な外科手術は正しくないと信じている．それは本当に金が必要な場合以外は手術をしないという意味である．）

I always felt I was nobody, and the only way for me to be somebody was to be—well, somebody else. **Which** is probably why I wanted to act. (Marilyn Monroe)
（わたしはいつも自分が取るに足らない人間だと感じていました，そしてひとかどの人間になるには誰か他の人になるしかなかったのです．これがきっと演じたかった理由でしょう．）
☞ Marilyn Monroe (1926-1962): アメリカの映画女優．ハリウッド映画最大のセックスシンボル．

(b) 文の途中に挿入する

The president, **who** has been sick for several days, is now in bed with a coed.
（数日病気の学長はいま女子学生と寝ている．）

☞ coed((男女共学の)女子学生) ⇔ cold(風邪)
☞ l は筆記体では e に見えることがある.
★ **Misprint** → p. 187

Little Lawrence, **who** was noisy, spoilt child, was running up and down the aisle of an airplane. One annoyed passenger stopped him and said: "Listen, kid. Why don't you go outside and play for a while?"
(幼いロレンスは騒々しい甘えん坊で飛行機の通路を行ったり来たり走っていた. いらいらした乗客が彼を呼び止めて言った.「ねえ, きみ. ちょっと外へ行って遊んでおいで」)

"Farmer Jack's special chicken, **which** lays square eggs, cost him nearly £1000."
"That's an expensive chicken. Can it talk as well?"
"Sure, but it only says one thing."
"And what's that?"
"Ouch!"
(農場主のジャックは特別の鶏を飼っていてそれは四角い卵を産むのだが, 1000 ポンド近く払って買ったものだった.「高い鶏だね. しゃべることもできるのか」「そうさ, だけど一言しか言わないんだ」「それは何だい」「痛い!」)

B. 関係副詞に導かれるもの

先行詞	時を表わす語(句)	場所を表わす語(句)	理由	—
関係副詞	when/that	where	why	how

(1) when に導かれるもの

Father's Day is the day **when** father goes broken giving his family money so they can surprise him with gifts he doesn't need.
(父の日とは, 父親が自分の必要としない贈り物で自分を驚かすことができるように家族に金を与えて, 自分が破産する日である.)

There was a time **when** I could speak Spanish as well as I spoke English. When I was a year old.
（英語と同じくらいうまくスペイン語を話せる時が私にはあった．1歳の時だ．）

Labor Day is a day **when** no one does any.
（労働者の日は誰も労働しない日である．）
☞ Labor Day は9月の最初の月曜日でアメリカ，カナダでは休日．

cf. 次の2例は先行詞または when が省略されたと考えられる例

About the only time the average woman is a good listener is **when** money talks.
（普通の女性が人の話をよく聞くのは金が物を言うときだけだ．）

"Doctor, my husband talks in his sleep."
"Oh, that's not serious. I can give you a prescription that will cure him of it."
"Don't you dare! That's the only time / he ever talks to me!"
（「先生，主人は寝言を言うんです」「それは大したことはありません．治すための処方箋を差し上げましょう」「まあ何ということを．主人が私に話しかけるのはこの時だけなんですのよ」）

(2) where に導かれるもの

The dictionary is the only place **where** success comes before work.
（success（成功）が work（仕事）の前にくるのは辞書の中だけである．）

When you get to the point **where** you really understand your computer, it's probably obsolete.
（自分のコンピューターが本当に分かるところまできた時にはそれはほとんど間違いなく使い物にならなくなっているものだ．）
★ **One-liner** → p. 395

America is the only country **where** a housewife hires a woman to do

her cleaning so she can do volunteer work at the day-care center **where** the cleaning woman leaves her child.
(主婦が掃除のために女性を雇い，ボランティアをするために保育所へ行くとその掃除の女性が自分の子供をそこに預けているなどという国はアメリカだけだ．)

cf. 先行詞が省略されたと考えられる例

Two lawyers were walking along the street discussing a case. One of them said, 'Let's be honest ...' And that's **where** the conversation ended.
(2人の弁護士がある訴訟事件を話しながら通りを歩いていた．1人が「正直に話そう...」と言った．そしてそこで会話は終わった．)
★ **Lawyer** → p. 329

(3) why に導かれるもの

"But give me one good reason **why** you can't marry me."
"I'll give you four. My wife and three children."
(「でも，あなたが私と結婚できない納得のいく理由を1つ挙げて」「4つ挙げるよ．妻と3人の子供さ」)

Husband: Why did you fire my pretty young new secretary? You used to be a secretary yourself.
Wife: That's **why** I fired her.
(「可愛くて若い新しい秘書をなぜくびにしたんだ．おまえは自分が秘書だったじゃないか」「だからくびにしたのよ」)

cf. That's why ___ と **That's because ___** の違いに注意．**That's why ___** は「それが___の理由だ」，**That's because ___** は「それは___だからだ」の意味になる．

Time is a great healer. **That's why** they make you wait so long in the doctor's office.　(Ron Dentinger)
(時は心の傷を癒してくれる．だから医師の診療室では非常に長く待たせるのだ．)
☞ Time is a great healer. はことわざ．

☞ Ron Dentinger (1941-): アメリカのコメディアン・ユーモア作家.

Doctor: I don't think anything's wrong—your pulse is as steady as a clock.
Patient: **That's because** you've got your hand on my watch.
(医師「どこも悪いところはないと思います．脈も時計のように一定です」患者「それは先生が私の時計の上に手をのせているからですよ」)

cf. the reason (**that**) の形もある．
I go on working for the same reason **that** a hen goes on laying eggs.
　　　　　　　　　　　　　　　　　　　　　　　　　　(H. L. Menchen)
(私は雌鶏が卵を産み続けるのと同じ理由で働き続けている．)
☞ H. L. Menchen (1880–1956): アメリカの批評家・ジャーナリスト．

The reason / people blame things on the previous generation is that there's only one other choice.　(Doug Larson)
(人々が物事を前の世代のせいにするのはもう1つしか選択肢がないからだ．)
☞ 自分の世代しか．
☞ Doug Larson (1926-): アメリカのコラムニスト・編集者．

(4) the way, how などに導かれるもの

> "That's a beautiful pleated shirt you are wearing."
> "Those aren't pleats. It's **the way** my wife irons."
> (「あなたが着ているひだの入ったワイシャツ素敵ね」「これはひだじゃないんだ．家内はこんなふうにアイロンを掛けるんだ」)

One woman recently got a divorce because of the housework. She didn't like **the way** her husband was doing it.
(ある女性が最近，家事が理由で離婚した．夫のやり方が気に入らなかったのだ．)

'I grew up with six brothers. That's **how** I learned to dance—waiting for the bathroom.'　(Bob Hope)

(「私は 6 人の兄弟とともに成長した．こうしてダンスを覚えたんだ―トイレの順番を待ちながら」)
☞ 我慢できなくなって跳びはねながら．
☞ Bob Hope (1903-2003): イギリス生まれのアメリカのコメディアン．

A compromise is the art of dividing a cake **in such a way that** everyone believes that he has got the bigger piece.　(Paul Gauguin)
(妥協とは皆が自分が大きい方を取ったと信じるようなやり方でケーキを分ける技である．)
☞ Paul Gauguin (1848-1903): フランス後期印象派の画家．
★ **One-liner** → p. 395

(5) 継続用法：**where** と **when** のみこの用法がある．

A woman was unhappy that she was starting to look like a little old lady. She rushed to a beauty parlor**, where** the usual magic was performed. When she emerged, she no longer looked like a little old lady. She looked like a little old man!
(女性は自分が小さな老婦人になりはじめているのが悲しかった．彼女は美容院へ急ぎ，そこでいつもの魔法が行われた．出てくるともはや小さな老婦人のようには見えなかった．小さな男の老人のようだった．)

They usually have two tellers in my local bank, except when it's very busy**, when** they have one.　(Rita Rudner)
(地元の銀行にはたいてい非常に忙しい時以外は窓口に 2 人いるが，非常に忙しい時は 1 人だ．)
☞ Rita Rudner (1953-): アメリカのコメディアン・作家．

ジョークの常識㉑

★ 教会
　日曜日の教会は大人たちが睡眠不足を解消する場として出てくることが多い．

第22章　副詞節

"**Whenever** I sing I cry."
"Why do you sing?"
"**So** I **can** cry."
"Why do you cry?"
"**Because** I can't sing."
(「歌うといつも泣けてくるんです」「なぜ歌うのですか」「泣くためですわ」「なぜ泣くんですか」「歌えないからですわ」)

> 副詞節は文中で副詞の働きをする節をいう．when, where, if, though, because などの従属接続詞が先頭にきて，**(1)** 時，**(2)** 原因・理由，**(3)** 目的，**(4)** 結果，**(5)** 譲歩，**(6)** 様態・範囲，**(7)** 条件・仮定などを表す．主節の前にも後ろにも置かれる．

cf. (7) 条件・仮定については「第23章　条件・仮定表現」参照．

(1) 時を表すもの

> Chickens are the only animal you can eat **before** they are born and **after** they are dead.
> (鶏は生まれる前にも死んでからも食べることができる唯一の動物である．)

◆ 主な接続語[句]：
　as, after, before, when, every time, whenever, while, as soon as, till [until], once など

(a) as:「＿＿するとき；＿＿するにつれて」
　Politeness today has come to mean offering your seat to a lady **as** you

get off the bus!
(礼儀正しい態度とは今ではバスを降りるときに婦人に席を譲ることを意味するようになってしまった.)

A Zen master stood up to give a lecture. **As** he was about to speak, a bird sang sweetly outside. He immediately sat down saying, "The lecture is over. I have nothing more to add." (Anon.)
(禅僧が講話を始めるために立ち上がった. まさに話し始めようとしたとき, 小鳥が外で可愛らしく鳴いた. 禅僧はすぐに座って言った「講話は終わりました. 付け加えることはもう何もありません」)

Don't worry about temptation—**as** you grow older, it starts avoiding you. (Elbert Hubbard)
(誘惑について心配にはおよびません. 年を取るにつれて誘惑の方があなたを避け始めます.)
☞ Elbert Hubbard (1856–1915): アメリカの作家・出版人.

(b) after:「＿＿した後に［で］」; **before:**「＿＿する前に」
"Mr Maxwell couldn't sleep **after** his wife left him."
"Why? Did he miss her?"
"No, she took the bed with her!"
(「マクスウェルさんは奥さんが出て行ったあと眠れなくなったんだ」「なぜ. いなくなってさびしかったのか」「違うよ. ベッドも持って行ったんだ」)

"What was your mother's name **before** she was married?"
"I didn't have a mother **before** she was married."
(「結婚する前お母さんの名前は何だったの」「お母さんはいなかったよ, お母さんが結婚する前は」)
★ Irish bull → p. 39

(c) when:「＿＿するときに」; **every time:**「＿＿するたびに」; **whenever:**「＿＿するときはいつも」; **while:**「＿＿している間に」
"How old are you, little girl?"

"**When** I'm home, I'm eight, but **when** I'm on the bus I'm five!"
(「お嬢ちゃん，おいくつ」「家では8歳，バスに乗ったら5歳」)

A politician will always be there **when** he needs you.
(政治家はあなたを必要とするときはいつもそこにいるものだ．)
★ One-liner → p. 395

"How was your organ lesson?"
"Fine, and my teacher is so religious."
"How's that?"
"**Every time** I play, he cries, 'Oh, my God! My God!'"
(「オルガンのレッスンはどうだったの」「うまくいったわ．先生とても信心深い方なの」「どういうわけなの」「私が弾くたびに，神よ，神よっておっしゃるの」)
☞ My God!: 驚き，恐怖などを表わす間投詞．

The art of medicine consists of amusing the patient **while** Nature cures the disease.
(医学のこつは自然が病気を治してくれている間患者を楽しませることから成る．)

Whenever I hear about a 'peace-keeping force', I start wondering－if they're so interested in peace, why do they use force?　(George Carlin)
(「平和維持軍」について聞くたびに，なぜだと思い始める．それほど平和に関心があるなら，なぜ暴力を使うのか．)
☞ George Carlin (1987-2008): アメリカのコメディアン．

A baby-sitter is a teenager acting like an adult **while** the adults are out acting like teenagers.
(ベビーシッターは大人のように振る舞うティーンエージャーである，大人たちが外でティーンエージャーのように振る舞っている間に．)

(d) **as soon as** [**the moment** / **the instant** / **the minute**] ＿＿：「＿＿するとすぐに」

Pete:　I'm going to get married **as soon as** I find my opposite.

Hal: Then I'll introduce you tonight to a girl who's good-looking, intelligent, and cultured.

(ピートとハルの対話:「僕と正反対の人を見つけたらすぐ結婚するつもりだ」「じゃあ今夜女性を紹介するよ，美人で，頭が良くて，しかも教養のある女だ」)

The Brain is a wonderful organ. It starts working **the moment** you get up and does not stop until you get into the office.　(Robert Frost)

(脳はすばらしい臓器だ. 起きた途端に働きだしオフィスに入るまでは働きをやめないのだ.)

☞ Robert Frost (1874-1963): アメリカの詩人.

A banker is a fellow who lends you his umbrella when the sun is shining and wants it back **the minute** it begins to rain.

(Mark Twain)

(銀行家とは太陽が照っているとき傘を貸し，雨が降り出した途端に返してもらいたがる奴だ.)

☞ Mark Twain (1835-1910): アメリカの（ユーモア）小説家.

They serve instant food here. You get sick **the instant** you eat it.
(あの店はインスタント食品を出してくれる. 食べた途端に気分が悪くなる.)
☞ instant「即席の」⇔ the instant ＿＿「＿＿するとすぐに」
★ **Pun** → p. 26

(e) **till / until:**「＿＿まで（ずっと）」

"You say the service is bad here! Wait **till** you eat the food."
(「お客様はここのサービスが悪いとおっしゃるのですか. お食べになるまでお待ちください」)
☞ そうすれば本当のサービスの悪さが分かります.
★ **Waiter** → p. 266

Boy: Do you know, Dad, that in some parts of Africa a man doesn't know his wife **until** he married her?

Dad: Why single out Africa?

(少年と父親の対話:「知ってる，お父さん，アフリカには結婚するまで奥さんを知らな

い地域があるんだって」「なぜ特にアフリカを選ぶんだい」)

(f) **by the time**:「＿＿までに」; **now that**:「今や＿＿だから」(→(2) 原因・理由); **once**:「いったん＿＿すると」

By the time most men learn how to behave themselves, they are too old to do anything else.
(ほとんどの男は行儀よく振る舞うことを覚えるまでに年を取り過ぎて他に何もできなくなっている.)

Our generation never got a break. When we were young they taught us to respect our elders. **Now that** we're older, they tell us to listen to the youth of the country.
(我々の世代はほっと息をつく間がなかった. 若い頃は先輩を尊敬しろと教えられた. 今や年を取ってみると国の若者たちの話を聞けと言われている.) (→ (2) 原因・理由)

Marriage is a good deal like taking a bath—not so hot **once** you get accustomed to it.
(結婚は入浴に大いに似ている――一旦慣れればそれほど熱くはない.)

(2) 原因・理由を表すもの

We lost **because** we didn't win.　(Ronaldo)
(負けたのは勝たなかったからだ.)

☞ Ronaldo: ブラジルの元プロサッカー選手.

◆ 主な接続語［句］: **because, as, since, now that** など

(a) **because**:「(なぜなら) ＿＿だから」
　Mother:　Well, Jimmy, do you think your teacher likes you?
　Jimmy:　I think so, mummy, **because** she puts a big kiss on all my sums.
(母「ジミー, 先生はお前がお気に入りと思うかい」ジミー「そう思うよ, 母さん. だっ

て先生はぼくの計算に全部大きなキスの印を付けてくれるもの」)
☞ キスの印は「×」

cf. not A because B:「B だから A というわけではない」の意味になることがある．
A person is **not** overworked *simply* **because** it takes him four hours to do a three-hour job.
(単に 3 時間の仕事をするのに 4 時間掛かるだけでは働き過ぎということにはならない．)

The baby-sitter did**n't** voice an objection **because** the parents were so late, saying, "Don't apologize. I wouldn't be in a hurry to come home either!"
(ベビーシッターは両親が遅れたからといって不服を口にしなかった，そしてこう言った「謝らなくていいです．わたしだって急いで家に帰りたくないですもの」)

(b) as:「＿＿だから」
"Didn't you promise me to be a good boy?"
"Yes, father."
"And didn't I promise you a thrashing if you weren't?"
"Yes, father, but **as** I've broken my promise, you needn't keep yours."
(「いい子にしていると約束しなかったかい」「したよ，お父さん」「いい子にしていなかったらむちでたたくと約束しなかったかい」「したよ，でもぼくが約束を破ったんだから，お父さんも約束を守らなくていいよ」)

(c) since:「＿＿だから」
"I've been misbehaving and my conscience is troubling me."
"I see, and **since** I'm a psychiatrist you want something to strengthen your will power?"
"No, something to weaken my conscience."
(「悪いことをしてきたので良心に悩まされています」「なるほど，それで私が精神科医だから，あなたの意志力を強めるものがほしいわけですね」「いいえ，私の良心を弱めるものがほしいのです」)

(d) now that:「今や＿＿だから」(→ (1) 時)

   Lawyer: **Now that** we have won, will you tell me confidentially if you stole the money?"

   Client: Well, after hearing you talk in court yesterday, I'm beginning to think I didn't.

（弁護士と依頼人の対話：「今や我々は勝ったのですから，内緒でお金を盗んだのかどうか教えてくれませんか」「あなたが昨日法廷で話すのを聞いたあと，盗まなかったと思い始めてます」）

  ★ **Lawyer** → p. 329

(3) 目的を表すもの

> Children used to be let out of school **so** they **could** work—now they are sent there **so** their mother **can**.
> （子供たちは働くために学校をやめさせられたものだった．今は母親が働くために学校へやられる．）

◆ 主な接続語[句]：**so that, lest, in case, for fear** など

(a) so that S can [will など**]** *do*：「Sが＿＿できる［する］ように」

Parking Lot: Where we spend a quarter of an hour searching for a well-situated space **so that** we **can** avoid walking sixty seconds to the mall entrance.

（駐車場：ショッピング・モールの入口まで 60 秒も歩かなくてすむように良い位置にあるスペースを探して 15 分過ごす場所．）

Most children eat spinach **so** they**'ll** grow up and strong enough to refuse it.

（ほとんどの子供がホウレンソウを食べるのは大きくなって食べたくないと言えるほど強くなるためだ．）

(b) lest：「＿＿せぬように」(cf. 堅い表現で文章体で用いる)；**in case**：「＿＿す

るといけないから」; **for fear**:「＿＿しないように」

Monkeys very sensibly refrain from speech, **lest** they **should** be set to earn their livings. (Kenneth Grahame)
（サルが賢明にも口を慎んでいるのは生活費を稼がされないようにするためだ．）
☞ Kenneth Grahame (1859-1932): スコットランドの小説家・児童文学作家．

Customer: Waiter, would you please put the rest of my steak into a doggie bag?
  Waiter: Certainly. Anything else?
Customer: Better put some bread and butter in it too, **in case** my dog wants to make a sandwich.
（客とウエイターの対話：「あなた，ステーキの残りをドギーバッグに入れてくださる」「かしこまりました．他に何か」「バターを塗ったパンも入れてくださるといいわ．家の犬がサンドイッチを作りたいと思うといけないから」）
☞ doggie bag:「（レストランの）持ち帰り袋」

A pessimist is someone who feels bad when he feels good **for fear** he'll feel worse when he feels better.
（悲観論者とはずっと気分がいい時に気分がもっと悪くなることを恐れて，気分がいい時にも気分の悪くなる人．）

(4) 結果を表すもの

> He drank **so** much whisky **that** when the mosquitoes bit him they died of alcoholic poisoning.
> （彼があまりウイスキーを飲んだので蚊が彼を刺すとアル中で死んでしまった．）

★ Tall tale → p. 412

◆ 主な接続語[句]：**so** 〜 **that**, **such** 〜 **that** など

(a) so 〜 that ＿＿：「非常に〜なので（その結果）＿＿」（cf. 〜は形容詞・副詞）
He is **so** mean **that** when he sends his trousers to the laundry, he puts a sock in each pocket.

（彼は非常にけちなのでズボンを洗濯屋に出す時どのポケットにも靴下を入れるほどだ．）

Know him? I know him **so** well **that** I haven't spoken to him for ten years.　　(Oscar Wilde)
（彼を知っているかって．非常によく知っているからこの10年話をしていない．）
☞ Oscar Wilde (1854-1900)：アイルランド生まれのイギリスの詩人・小説家・劇作家．

(b) such ～ that ____：「非常に～なので（その結果）____」(cf. ～は名詞)

He was **such** a bore **that** people used to have parties just not to have him.
（彼はあまりにも退屈な男だったので，皆は彼を参加させないためだけにパーティーをしたものだ．）

cf. that が省略されたと考えられるもの

I drank to his health **so** often / I ruined my own.
（彼の健康を祈って何度も乾杯して私は自分の健康を害してしまった．）

I am **so** busy / I have had to put off the date of my death.
　　　　　　　　　　　　　　　　　　　　　(Bertrand Russell)
（私は忙しすぎるので死ぬ日を延期しなければならないでいる．）
☞ Bertrand Russell (1872-1970)：イギリスの哲学者・数学者・評論家．

The film was **so** bad, we had to sit through it four times to get our money's worth.
（映画はあまりにもひどかったので払った金の元を取るために4回見通さねばならなかった．）

He has **such** a long face, the barbers charge him twice for shaving it.
（彼の顔はあまりにも長いので床屋はひげそりに2倍の料金を請求するほどだ．）
★ **Insulting joke** → p. 97

He was **such** a hypochondriac / he insisted on being buried next to a doctor.

（彼は大変な憂鬱症だったので医者の隣に埋めてほしいと言い張った．）

(5) 譲歩を表すもの

> The employer addressed to the applicant: "We want a responsible man for this job."
> "Then I'm your man," announced the young man, "**No matter where** I've worked, **whenever** anything happened, they always said I was responsible."
> （雇い主は応募者に話しかけた「この仕事には責任感のある人が欲しい」「では私が適任です」と若者は大きな声で言った．「どこで働いても，何が起こったときでも，私に責任があると言われましたから」）

◆ 主な接続語[句]:
　though, although, even if [though], how [what / who / when / where / which]-ever, no matter how [what / who / when / where / which], whether 〜 or など

(a) **though, although**:「＿＿＿だけれど」

Small boys are washable **though** most of them shrink from it.
（小さな男の子は洗いがきく，もっともほとんどの子が縮むが．）
☞ shrink:「(布などが) 縮む」⇔「しりごみする」　★ **Pun** → p. 26
☞ 小さな男の子は風呂を嫌う．

Though God cannot alter the past, historians can.　(Samuel Butler)
（神は過去を変えることはできないが，歴史家はできる．）
☞ Samuel Butler (1835-1902): イギリスの小説家．
★ **One-liner** → p. 395

I'm not a believer in luck, **although** I believe you need it.　(Allan Ball)
（私は運を信じる人間ではない，もっとも君には必要だと思うが．）
☞ Allan Ball (1957-): アメリカの脚本家・映画プロデューサー．
★ **Insulting joke** → p. 97

(b) **even if [though]**:「たとえ＿＿＿だとしても」

"What stays hot **even if** you put it in the freezer?"
"Pepper!"
(「冷凍庫に入れても熱いままの物は何か」「胡椒」)
☞ hot:「熱い」⇔「辛い」　★ **Pun** → p. 26; **Riddle** → p. 64

"You're not a bad-looking sort of fellow."
"You'd say so **even if** you didn't think so."
"Well, we're square then. You'd think so **even if** I didn't say so."
(「君もまんざら悪い顔じゃないよ」「そう思っていなくてもそう言うんだろう」「じゃこれで五分五分だ．僕がそう言わなくても，君はそう思っているんだろうから」)

Even though a number of people have tried, no one has yet found a way to drink for a living.　(Jean Kerr)
(多くの人が試みたが，生活費を稼ぐために酒を飲む方法を見つけた人はまだいない．)
☞ Jean Kerr (1922–2003): アイルランド系アメリカ人の作家・劇作家．

cf. **if = even if**（たとえ＿＿＿でも）の例
　Customer (to sales assistant): **If** my husband doesn't like this diamond bracelet, will you refuse to take it back?
((客が店員に)「主人がこのダイヤのブレスレットが気に入らなくても，返品には応じないでくださいね」)

(c) **however [whatever / whoever / whenever / wherever / whichever]** ＿＿＿:「たとえ＿＿＿でも」

All reformers, **however** strict their social conscience, live in houses just as big as they can pay for.　(Logan Pearsall Smith)
(すべての改革者は，社会的良心がどんなに厳格でも，彼らが支払える程度の大きさの家には住んでいる．)
☞ Logan Pearsall Smith (1865–1946): アメリカのエッセイスト・批評家．

"What makes you so stupid?"
"I don't know. But **whatever** it is, it works."

(「おまえはなぜそんなにバカなんだ」「さあね. でもそれがどうあれ, うまくいってるよ」)

Whenever I meet a man who would make a good husband, he already is.
(良き夫になりそうな男性に会ってもいつも, すでに良き夫になっている.)

Teacher (in geography lesson): Now can anybody tell me where we find mangoes?
Knowing Little Boy: Yes, miss, **wherever** woman goes.
(先生(地理の授業)「さて, 誰かマンゴーがどこにあるか分かりますか」頭のよく働く少年「はい, 先生, 女の人が行くところはどこでもです」)
☞ mangoes ⇔ man goes   ★ 異分析 → p. 375

(d) no matter how [what / who / when / where / which] ＿＿:「たとえ＿＿でも」

No matter how busy people are, they are never too busy to stop and talk about how busy they are.
(人はどんなに忙しくても, あまりの忙しさに立ち止まってどんなに忙しいかについて話もできないほどでは決してない.)
★ One-liner → p. 395

No matter what happens in business, someone always says he knew it would.
(ビジネス界で何が起こっても, 誰かがいつもそうなることは分かっていたと言う.)

Wife: Do you love me just because my father left me a fortune?
Husband: Not at all, darling. I would love you **no matter who** left you the money.
(夫婦の対話:「父が財産を残してくれただけの理由で私を愛しているの」「まったく違うよ, きみ. 誰がきみにお金を残したってきみを愛してるよ」)

A boomerang always comes back to you **no matter where** you throw it. I really want to invent money like that.

（ブーメランはどこへ投げても必ず自分のところへ戻って来る．ほんとうにそんな金を発明したいと思う．）

First Law of Bicycling: **No matter which** way you ride, it's uphill and against the wind.
（自転車走行第1規則：どちらの方向へ乗って行っても上り坂で向かい風である．）

(e) **whether A or B**:「AであろうとBであろうと」; **whether ___ or not**:「___であろうとなかろうと」

Life is like a taxi—the meter keeps going **whether** you are getting somewhere **or** just standing still.
（人生はタクシーのようなものだ．どこかに着こうとしていようがじっと停車していようがメーターは動き続けている．）
★ **One-liner** → p. 395

The most important things in campaigning is sincerity, **whether** you mean it **or not**!
（選挙運動で最も重要なことは誠実さである，本気で言っていようがいまいが．）

cf. 次例は慣用表現．
  Paul: Wonderful news! Our English teacher said we would have a test today **come rain or shine**.
  Saul: What's so wonderful about that?
  Paul: It's snowing.
（ポールとサウルの対話：「素晴らしいニュースだ．英語の先生は雨が降っても照っても今日テストがあると言ったぞ」「それの何が素晴らしいんだ」「雪が降っているぞ」）
  ★ **Irish bull** → p. 39

(6) 様態・範囲を表すもの

> "My teenage son obeys me perfectly."
> "Amazing. How do you do it?"
> "I tell him to do **as** he pleases."

(「10 代の息子は完全に私の言うことを聞く」「驚いたなあ．どうやるんだい」「好きなようにやれと言うのさ」)

◆ 主な接続語[句]：
　　as, like, as [so] long as, as [so] far as, just as ___, so など

(a) **as**:「___のように」
Actual airline announcement:
Feel free to move about **as** you wish, but stay inside the plane till we land.
(実際の機内放送：「ご遠慮なくお好きなように動き回って結構です，しかし着陸までは機内にお留まりください」)
★ Irish bull → p. 39

(b) **like**:「___のように」(＝**as**)
"The traffic officer says you got sarcastic with him." "But I didn't intend to be. He talked to me **like** my wife does and I forgot myself and answered 'Yes, dear.'"
(「交通巡査は君がいやみな態度をとったと言っているがね」「そんなつもりはなかったのです．あの人が妻のような話し方をするので，つい『そうだよ，お前』と答えてしまったのです」)

(c) **as [so] long as**:「___であるかぎり」；**as [so] far as**:「___に関するかぎり」
A psychiatrist is someone who will listen to you **as long as** you don't make sense.
(精神科医とは君の言うことが辻褄の合わない限り言うことを聴いてくれる人である．)
☞ 辻褄の合う話を聴いても商売にならない．

"The politicians in Washington want us to believe that nuclear waste is perfectly safe, **so long as** we're careful where we put it."
"No problem. Let's put it under the White House."

(「ワシントンの政治家たちは核廃棄物はどこに埋めるかに注意しさえすれば,全く安全だと信じさせたがっている」「そんなこと何でもないよ.ホワイトハウスの下に埋めればいい」)

As far as his team's concerned, he's the eternal optimist. He says they can still get promotion if they win eleven out of their last four games.
(彼のチームに関する限り,彼は永遠の楽天家だ.残り4試合中11試合勝てば昇格できると言っているんだ.)

(d) (just) as A, so B:「ちょうどAであるようにBである」

Just as war is waged with blood of others, **so** fortunes are made with other people's money.　(André Suarès)
(ちょうど戦争が他人の血によって行われるのと同様に財産は他人の金によって作られる.)

☞ **André Suarès** (1868–1948): フランスの詩人・評論家.

ジョークの常識㉒

★ **Ethnic joke [humor]**:「宗教・人種・民族・国家・文化などのそれぞれの集団の特徴（と信じられているもの）を揶揄したり笑い飛ばしたりするジョーク」

英語のジョークの世界では，例えば，アイルランド人は非論理的，スコットランド人は吝嗇（けち），イングランド人はよそよそしいということになっている．

日本人はジョークの世界でどう見られているだろうか．

I have no business sense. I just opened a tall men's shop in Tokyo!
（私には商売のセンスがない．東京に長身男性向けの店を開店してしまった．）
☞ 日本人は一般に背が低いと思われている．

Did you hear about the new Japanese camera on the market? When you trip the shutter, it goes crick!
（発売中の新しい日本のカメラのことを聞いたか．シャッターを切るとガッキッと鳴るんだ．）
☞ 和訳不能のジョーク．「カチッ」とか「カチャ」に当たる英語は click．Crick には「筋肉の痙攣」の意味があり，日本人が [l] と [r] の区別がつかないことをからかっている．

第 23 章　条件・仮定表現

Life: A word that has a big *if* in the middle of it.
(人生：その真ん中に大きな「if（もし）」のある語．)

A. 条件を表すもの

If elected, I will win.　(Pat Paulsen)
(選ばれれば勝つだろう．)

☞ If elected ＝ If I am elected
☞ Pat Paulsen (1927-1997): アメリカのコメディアン・風刺作家．

(1) 可能性のある条件

"**If** you are good, Willie, I'll give you this bright new penny."
"Haven't you got a dirty old nickel?"
(「ウィリー，いい子にしていたら，このピッカピカの1セントあげるよ」「汚い古い5セントは持ってないの」)

If you're rich you're an alcoholic; **if** you're poor you're just a drunk.
(金持ちならアルコール依存症，貧乏人ならだだの飲んだくれ．)
★ **One-liner** → p. 395

If you don't drink, smoke or drive a car, you're a tax evader.
(Tom Foley)
(酒は飲まない，タバコも吸わない，車の運転もしないでは，税金逃れだ．)
☞ Tom Foley (1929-2013): アメリカの政治家．

A church notice: There will be a procession next Sunday afternoon in the church ground. But **if** it rains in the afternoon, the procession

will take place in the morning.
(教会の掲示:今度の日曜の午後教会の構内で行進があります.もし午後雨の場合は行進は午前中に行います.)
★ Irish bull → p. 39

(b) 万一の should

"**If** I **should** die, **would** you visit my grave often?"
"Yes, I have to pass the graveyard to go to my hair dresser, anyway."
(「万一ぼくが死んだら,しょっちゅう墓に来てくれるかい」「ええ行くわよ.とにかく美容院へ行くには墓地のそばを通らなければならないんですもの」)

"What would I get," inquired the man who had just insured his property against fire, "**if** this building **should** burn down tonight?"
"I would say," replied the insurance agent, "about ten years."
(「万が一今夜この建物が燃えてしまったらいくら手に入るのですか」と自宅に火災保険を掛けたばかりの男が尋ねた.「そうですね」と保険代理業者が答えた.「だいたい10年でしょう」)
☞ 自宅に放火した場合の刑期は.

(c) provided [providing] ___ (= if):「___であるかぎり」; **unless** ___;
except that ___:「___でないかぎり」
Being ill is one of the greatest pleasures of life, **provided** one is not too ill and is not obliged to work until one is better. (Samuel Butler)
(病気でいることは人生最大の喜びの1つである,もし病気がひどすぎず,良くなるまでは仕事をしなくていいなら.)
☞ Samuel Butler (1835-1902): イギリスの小説家.

It's great to have a genius in the family, **providing** the other members of the family can earn a living.
(家族に天才がいるのはすばらしい,家族の他の人たちが生活費を稼げるならば.)

I never drink **unless** I'm alone or with somebody.
(私は1人のときか誰かと一緒でなければ飲みません.)

★ **Irish bull** → p. 39

An alarm clock in front of a speaker is a good thing, **except that** it wakes up the audience.
(話をする人の前に目覚まし時計を置くのはいいことだ，それで聴衆が目を覚まさない限りは．)

B. 仮定法過去

If youth **knew, if** age **could.**　(Henri Estienne)
(若者が知っていれば，老人ができれば．)

☞ Henri Estienne (1528-1598): フランスの印刷業者・古典学者．

現在の事実の反対の仮定・願望を表すもので，ふつう次の形になることが多い．

従属節（もし…ならば）	主節（…であろうに）
If S + { (助)動詞の過去形 / were [was] } …,	S⁽'⁾ + { would, could, might など } + 動詞の原形…

【注意】1) S⁽'⁾は従属節の主語と同じことも違うことも示す．
　　　 2) be 動詞は S が複数の場合は were，単数の場合は were または was になる．

(1) 現在の事実に反対の仮定：可能性のない条件を表す．

　"**If** you **were** my husband, I'*d give* you poison."
　"**If** I **were** your husband, I'*d take* it."
(「あなたが私の夫なら，毒を飲ませるわ」「僕があなたの夫なら，毒を飲みますよ」)

"I *wouldn't cry* like that **if** I **were** you," said a lady to little Betty.
"Well," said Betty, between her sobs, "You can cry any way you like, but this is my way."
(「私があなたならそんなふうには泣かないわよ」と婦人．ベティ，しくしく泣きながら，

「おばさまはお好きなようにお泣きになればいいのよ．でもこれが私の泣き方なの」）

Little Daughter: Why is father singing so much tonight?
　　　Mother: He is trying to sing the baby to sleep.
Little Daughter: Well, **if** I **was** the baby I'*d pretend* I was asleep.
（幼い娘と母親の対話：「お父さんは今夜はなぜあんなに歌っているの」「歌って赤ちゃんを寝かしつけようとしてらっしゃるのよ」「私なら眠っているふりをしてあげるのに」）

Life *would be* infinitely happier **if** we *could* only *be born* at the age of eighty and gradually approach eighteen.　(Mark Twain)
（もし我々が80歳で生まれ，徐々に18歳に近づくことさえできれば，人生はこの上なくもっと幸せであろうに．）
☞ Mark Twain (1835-1910)：アメリカの（ユーモア）小説家．

(2) 話のための仮定：
(a)「仮に__するとすれば」
　Teacher: **If** Shakespeare ***were*** alive today, he'*d be* looked on as a
　　　　　remarkable man.
　　　Pat: He certainly *would*. He'*d be* more than 400 years old.
（先生「もしシェイクスピアが今日生きていれば驚くべき人だと見なされるでしょう」
パット「確かにそうです．400歳以上でしょうね」）
☞ Pat: Patrickの愛称（アイルランド人に多い名前）　　★**Irish bull** → p. 39

"What *would* you *say* **if** I ***asked*** you to marry me?"
"Nothing. I can't talk and laugh at the same time."
（「結婚してと頼んだら何と言う」「何も．話すのと笑うのを同時にはできないわ」）

Parents are people who always think their children *would behave* **if** they ***didn't play*** with the kids next door.
（親とは子供が隣の子供と遊びさえしなければ常に行儀よくすると思っている人である．）
★ **One-liner** → p. 395

(b) were to *do*: ありそうもないこと・実行する気のないことを仮定する．

Young husband: You must economize! Think of the future—**if** I **were to** *die*, where *would* you *be*?

Young wife: I'*d be* here all right, the question is—where *would* you *be*?

（若い夫「節約しなきゃだめだよ．将来のことを考えてごらん．僕が死んだら，きみはどこに住むんだい」若い妻「わたしはここにいるから大丈夫よ．問題はあなたがどこにいるかよ」）

(3) 現在の事実に反対の願望

| **I wish** S + $\begin{cases} (助)動詞の過去形 \\ \text{were [was]} \end{cases}$ … 「S が＿すれば［であれば］いいのに」 |

【注意】be 動詞は S が複数の場合は were, 単数の場合は were または was になる．

My husband is as strong as a horse. **I** only **wish** he *had* the IQ of one.
（夫は馬と同じくらい強い人です．せめて同じくらいの知能指数があればと思うのですが．）

Andy: **I wish** I *could* stop my wife from spending money on gloves.
Randy: Buy her a diamond ring.
（アンディ「家内が手袋に金を使うのをやめさせられたらいいと思うよ」ランディ「ダイヤの指輪を買ってあげろよ」）

Telegram to wife: HAVING WONDERFUL TIME, DARLING. **WISH YOU *WERE* HER.**
　　　　　　　　　　　　(Signed) *Jonny*

（妻への電報：楽しんでるよ，おまえ．おまえが彼女だったらなあ．ジョニー）
☞ HER ⇔ HERE のスペリングの間違い．I wish you were here. （あなたがここにいればなあ）は旅先からの決まり文句．
★ **Misprint** → p. 187

cf. If only = I wish

A poor starving man walked up to a very rich, fat lady and said: "I haven't had a single meal all week." "**If only** I *had* your will power," replied the lady as she walked away.
(あわれな腹をすかした男がとても裕福な太った女性のところへ歩いて行って言った「1週間ずっと何も食べていないのです」「あなたの意志力があればと思いますわ」と婦人は言って立ち去った.)

C. 仮定法過去完了

If the nose of Cleopatra **had been** a little shorter, the whole face of the world *would have changed*.　(Blaise Pascal)
(もしクレオパトラの鼻がもう少し低かったら世界の全貌は違っていただろう.)

☞ Blaise Pascal (1623-1662): フランスの哲学者・数学者・物理学者.

ふつう次の形になることが多い.

従属節（もし...であったら）	主節（...であったろうに）		
If S＋had＋過去分詞 ...,	S$^{(')}$＋	would / could / might など	＋have＋過去分詞 ...

【注意】S$^{(')}$は従属節の主語と同じことも違うこともあることを示す.

(1) 過去の事実に反対の仮定：可能性の絶対にない条件を表す.

"Doctor," an elderly gentleman, now ninety years old, said, "**If I had known** that I *would* live this long, I'*d have taken* a lot better care of myself."
(「先生」ともう 90 歳になる年配の紳士が言った.「こんなに長く生きることが分かっていたら，もっと身体に注意していたでしょうに」)
★ **Irish bull** → p. 39

"That was a terrible accident. I suppose it knocked you out."

"No—but the doctor said **if** it **had *been*** anyone else, it *would have caused* concussion of the brain."
(「ひどい事故だったな．意識がなくなったんじゃないのか」「いいや，もし他の誰かだったら脳震盪(のうしんとう)を起こしただろうと医者は言ったよ」)
☞ 頭が空っぽだから脳震盪にならなかった．

If Alexander Graham Bell **had *had*** a daughter, he'*d* never *have invented* the telephone!
(もしベルに娘がいたら，電話を発明することは決してなかっただろう．)

If we'*d **known*** we were going to be the Beatles, we'*d have tried* harder. (George Harrison)
(僕らがビートルズになることが分かっていたら，もっと懸命にやっただろう．)
☞ George Harrison (1943-2001)：イギリスのミュージシャン．ビートルズの元メンバー．

"What a boy you are for asking questions," said the father, "I'd like to know what *would have happened* **if** I'*d **asked*** as many questions when I was a boy." "Perhaps," suggested the young hopeful, "you'*d have been* able to answer some of mine."
(「質問ばかりするとはお前はなんて子なんだ．私が子供のときにそんなに質問したらどうなっただろうか知りたいくらいだ」「ひょっとすると，」と末頼(すえたの)もしい息子が言った．「ぼくの質問のいくつかには答えられただろうね」)

cf.「If S＋現在形［過去形］〜, S⁽'⁾＋would have＋過去分詞」もまれにある．
If a thing **is** worth doing, it *would have been done* already.
(する価値があることなら，それはすでになされてしまっていただろう．)

Two economists are walking down the street. One sees a £10 note lying on the pavement and asks, 'Isn't that a £10 note?' 'Obviously not,' says the other. '**If** it **were**, someone *would have* already *picked* it up.'
(2人の経済学者が通りを歩いている．1人が10ポンド札が舗道に落ちているのを見て尋

ねる.「あれは10ポンド札じゃないか」「明らかに違う」と相手が言う.「もしそうなら,誰かがもう拾ってしまっただろうね」)

If I **had** no sense of humour, I *would* long ago *have committed* suicide. (Mahatma Gandhi)
(私にユーモアのセンスがなければ,とっくに自殺していただろう.)
☞ Mahatma Gandhi (1869–1948): インド独立運動の指導者.建国の父.

(2) 過去の事実に反対の願望

| **I wish** S＋**had**＋過去分詞 …:「Sが＿したら[であったなら]よかったのに」|

"And you tell me several men proposed marriage to you?" he said savagely.
"Yes, several."
"Well, **I wish** you *had married* the first fool who proposed."
"I did."
(「そしてあんたは数人の男がプロポーズしたって言うのか」と彼は怒って言った.「そうよ,数人」「じゃあ,最初にプロポーズしたバカと結婚すればよかったのに」「したわよ」)
☞ それがあなたよ.

First fan: **I wish** I'd *brought* the piano to the stadium.
Second fan: Why would you bring a piano to the football game?
First fan: Because I left the tickets on it.
(2人のファンの対話:「スタジアムにピアノを持ってくればよかったなあ」「なぜフットボールの試合にピアノを持って来るんだ」「チケットを上に置いてきたんだ」)
★ Irish bull → p. 39

No one ever said on their deathbed, "Gee, **I wish** I *had spent* time alone with my computer." (Danielle Berry)
(臨終の床で「ちえっ,コンピューターとだけ過ごせればよかったのになあ」と言った奴は未だかつていない.)
☞ Danielle Berry (1949–1998): アメリカのコンピュータープログラマー・ゲームデザイナー.

cf. **If only** = I wish
"**If only** I *had been* born two thousand years ago."
"Why, son?"
"Because there wouldn't be so much history to learn."
(「2000 年前に生まれていたかったなあ」「なぜだい，お前」「こんなにたくさん歴史を覚えなくていいんだもん」)

D. 仮定法を含む慣用表現

(1) if it was [were] not for 〜:「(今) もし〜がなければ」
If it wasn't for Thomas Edison and his invention of the electric light bulb, we*'d be watching* television by candlelight.
(トマス・エジソンと電球の発明がなければろうそくの光でテレビを見ているだろう。)
★ **Irish bull** → p. 39

A couple was having a discussion about family finances. Finally the husband exploded, '**If it weren't for** my money, the house *wouldn't be* here!' The wife replied, 'My dear, **if it weren't for** your money I *wouldn't be* here.'
(夫婦が家計について話し合っていた．とうとう夫が爆発して「おれの金がなければ家だってここにはないんだぞ」すると妻が答えた．「あなた，あなたのお金がなければわたしここにはいません」)

(2) if it had not been for 〜:「(過去に) もし〜がなかったなら」
Father: When I was your age I worked 16 hours a day in this business, seven days a week!
Son: I really appreciate it, Dad. **If it hadn't been for** all your ambition, determination and hard work, I *might have had to do* that myself.
(父と息子の対話:「おまえの年にはこの仕事で 1 日 16 時間，週 7 日働いたんだ」「ほんとにありがとう，お父さん．お父さんの野心と決意と勤勉がなかったら，それを僕自身がしなければならなかったかもしれなかったね」)

(3) **as if [though]** ___:「まるで___のように」

Motorist: Some of you pedestrians walk along just **as if** you *owned* the street.

Pedestrian: And some of you motorists drive around just **as if** you *owned* the car.

(ドライバー「君たち歩行者にはまるで道路の所有者であるかのように歩く奴がいる」歩行者「そして君たちドライバーには車が自分の物のように運転しまくる奴がいる」)
☞ 車の払いが済んでいないのに.

Antiquarian: This vase is 2,000 years old. Be careful in carrying it.

Moving man: You can depend on me, professor. I'll be **as** careful of it **as if** it *were* new!

(古物収集家「この花瓶は 2000 年前に作られたものだ. 運ぶとき注意してくれたまえ」引っ越し業者「任せてください，先生. まるで新品同様に扱いには注意します」)

Pat: While I was going downtown by car this morning, the conductor came along and looked at me **as if** I *had not paid* my fare.

Ruth: Well, what did you do?

Pat: I looked at him **as if** I *had*.

(「今朝電車で町へ行く途中，車掌がやって来て僕がまるで電車賃を払わなかったような目つきで僕を見たんだ」「それであなたはどうしたの」「払ったような顔で彼を見たさ」)

There are only two ways to live your life. One is **as though** nothing is a miracle. The other is **as though** everything is a miracle.

(Albert Einstein)

(生き方は 2 つしかありません. 1 つはまるで奇跡などないかのようにです. もう 1 つはすべてがまるで奇跡のようにです.)
☞ Albert Einstein (1879–1955): ドイツ生まれの理論物理学者.

(4) **but for ～**:「～がなければ［なかったならば］」(= if it was [were] not for / if it had not been for)

There was a report in the newspapers recently about a man who got married so many times, he married one of his ex-wives without realizing it. He never *would have known* **but for** the fact that he recognized his mother-in-law.

（最近，新聞に，あまりに何度も結婚したのでそれとは気づかずに前の奥さんと結婚したという記事が載っていた．義理の母親に気がついたという事実がなかったら，決して前の奥さんとは気づかなかっただろう．）

★ **Mother-in-law** → p. 305

cf. without 〜:「〜がなければ［なかったならば］」(→「第17章 前置詞」J. (18) without)

Somebody asked a professor how science helped the business world. The professor replied, "What *would* the belt business *be* **without** the law of gravity?"

（ある人が教授に科学はビジネス界にどのような貢献をしたかを尋ねた．教授は答えた．「重力の法則がなければベルトのビジネスはどうなっているでしょう」）

★ **Irish bull** → p. 39

"I'm having trouble chewing with my teeth."
"You*'d have* more trouble chewing **without** them."
（「歯で噛むのに苦労しています」「歯がなければもっと苦労するでしょう」）

E. **if** 節が表面に出ないもの

(1) 主語に含まれるもの

"I almost got killed twice today!"
"***Once** would have been* enough!"
（「今日2度も殺されそうになったよ」「1度で十分だったのに」）

★ **Insulting joke** → p. 97

Genuine comment on accident insurance claims form:
Q: *Could* either driver *have done* anything to avoid the accident?
A: ***I could have travelled*** by bus.

（事故保険料請求書の本物のコメント：「どちらかの運転者が事故を避けるために何かできなかったですか」「私ならバスで行けたでしょう」）

A smartly-dressed woman was sitting in an omnibus when a quiet-looking young man, in getting in, accidentally trod on her dress. She talked to him for 10 minutes and wound up by saying: "***A gentleman*** *would have apologized.*" The young man bowed and calmly said, "***A lady*** *would have given* me a chance!"
(しゃれた身なりの婦人がバスの座席に座っていると，おとなしそうな青年が，乗り込む際に，ついその婦人のドレスを踏みつけてしまった．婦人は彼に向かって10分間しゃべり続け，こう言って締めくくった．「紳士ならわびの一言でも言ったでしょうに」青年はおじぎをし穏やかに答えた．「まともなご婦人だったらその機会を与えてくださったことでしょう」)

(2) 副詞語句に含まれるもの

I*'d* give a thousand dollars ***to be a millionaire***. (Lewis Timberlake)
(100万長者になるためなら1000ドル出すだろう．)
☞ Lewis Timberlake (1931–2012): アメリカの経営コンサルタント．

To hear him talk, you*'d think* he begat his own ancestors.
(彼が話すのを聞くと，彼が自分の先祖を産んだと思うだろう．)

With the money it takes to send Junior to college we *could* buy enough comic books to teach him at home.
(息子を大学にやるのに掛かる金があれば家で教えるのに足るだけのマンガ本を買えるだろう．)

George Bernard Shaw, the great British philosopher, was a committed vegetarian. When he met Alfred Hitchcock, of blimp proportions, the latter remarked, "***To look at you***, G.B., one *would* really think there was a famine in England." And witty Shaw replied, "One *would* think you had caused it."
(偉大なイギリスの哲学者ジョージ・バーナード・ショーは徹底したベジタリアンだった．彼が太った体つきのアルフレッド・ヒッチコックに会うと，後者が「G.B.さん，あなたを見ると人はイングランドは飢餓状態だと思うでしょうね」と言った．すると，機知に富むショーは答えた．「人はあなたが原因だと思うでしょう」)

☞ あなたが全部食べてしまった．
☞ George Bernard Shaw (1856-1950)：アイルランド出身のイギリスの劇作家．
☞ Alfred Hitchcock (1899-1980)：イギリスの映画監督．

Wife: The big clock fell off the wall this afternoon. ***A moment sooner***, and it *would have landed* on Mother's head.
Husband: That's it! I'm getting rid of that clock. It's always been slow.
（妻と夫の対話：「今日の午後あの大きな柱時計が壁から落ちたのよ．もう少し早かったらお母さんの頭の上に落ちるところだったわ」「その通りだ．あの時計は捨てるつもりなんだ．いつも遅れてばかりいやがる」）
★ **Mother-in-law** → p. 305

(3) **otherwise**; **or else**:「さもなければ」
"Why do tall people have long arms?"
"Because ***otherwise*** their arms *would*n't reach their hands."
（「なぜ背の高い人は腕が長いのですか」「そうでないと腕が手に届かないでしょう」）
★ **Irish bull** → p. 39

Most of my Irish friends liked to drink to excess, on the principle that ***otherwise*** they *might* as well not drink at all.　(Hugh Leonard)
（ほとんどのアイルランド人の友達は飲み過ぎるのが好きだった，それはさもないと全く飲まない方がよくなってしまうという信条に基づいていた．）
☞ Hugh Leonard (1926-2009)：アイルランドの劇作家・エッセイスト．

It's a good thing there's gravity ***or else*** when birds died, they*'d* stay where they were.　(Steven Wright)
（重力があるのはいいことだ，さもないと，鳥が死んでもそのままそこにいるだろう．）
☞ Steven Wright (1955-)：アメリカのコメディアン・作家．

(4) **It is time S＋過去形**:「もう＿＿＿する時間だ」
We've never had a President named Bob. I think **it's** about **time** we *had* one.　(Bob Dole)
（いまだかつてボブという名の大統領はいなかった．そろそろいてもいい頃だ．）

☞ Bob Dole (1923-): アメリカ共和党の政治家・法律家.

(5) if の省略（→ 第 27 章 倒置 (d)）

ジョークの常識㉓

★ **異分析**（**metanalysis**）: 本来は，ある時代において，例えば a napron（エプロン）が an apron と（誤って）分析されたように，前の時代と異なった分析をされることをいう．しかし本書では，**Pun** の一種として「ある語または語群を駄じゃれのために意図的に異なる分析をすることによって笑いを誘うもの」の意味で用いている．

"Why do hungry people go to the desert?"
"For the sand which is there."
(「腹をすかした人々はなぜ砂漠へ行くのか」「そこにある砂を求めて」)
☞ sand which ⇔ sandwich（サンドイッチ）の駄じゃれ．

"What is the most shocking city in the world?"
"Electri-city."
(「世界で最もショッキングな都市はどこか」「電気市」)
☞ Electricity ⇔ electri + city の駄じゃれ．

To get into show business a girl should know somebody or have some body.
(ショービジネスに入るには女性は誰か有名人を知っているかかなりの肉体を持っていなければならない．)
☞ somebody ⇔ some body の駄じゃれ．

第 24 章　比較表現

Degrees of comparison of "Bad": bad—very sick—dead.
（Bad の比較変化：悪い―重病だ―死んだ．）

◆ 比較変化：規則変化

級　Degree 形の変化	原級 Positive	比較級 Comparative	最上級 Superlative	(注)
―**er**；―**est** 1 音節の語および 2 音節の語の一部	long large hot narrow happy	long*er* larg*er* hot*ter* narrow*er* happ*ier*	long*est* larg*est* hot*test* narrow*est* happ*iest*	① ② ③ ④ ⑤
more: **most** 2 音節の語の多く および 3 音節以上 の語	honest useful important	*more* honest *more* useful *more* important	*most* honest *most* useful *most* important	

(注) 上の表の

① longer [lɔ́ːŋgər], longest [lɔ́ːŋgəst] の発音に注意．

②の類例：fin*e*, wis*e*, tru*e*, nic*e*, rip*e*, brav*e*［e で終わる語］

③の類例：big, fat, thin, wet［短母音＋子音］

④の類例：nob*le*, simp*le*, subt*le*; clev*er*, tend*er*［le, er で終わる 2 音節語］

⑤の類例：earl*y*, heav*y*, bus*y*, eas*y*, prett*y*［子音字＋y］

第24章　比較表現

◆ 比較変化：不規則変化

意味 \ 級	原級	比較級	最上級
よい / よく	good / well	better	best
悪い	bad / ill	worse	worst
遠い	far	farther〔距離〕/ further（その上の）	farthest / furthest
おそい / おそく	late	later〔時間〕/ latter（後者）	latest（最近の）/ last（最後の）
少ない	little	less	least
多い	many〔数〕/ much〔量〕	more	most
年とった / 古い	old	older〔老若・新旧・長幼〕/ elder〔長幼〕	oldest / eldest

(注) further, furthest は「距離」にも用いる.

A. 原級

> I'm **not so** think **as** you drink I am.　(John Squire)
> （わたしや酔っぱらっているほど考えちゃいない.）

☞ I'm not so drunk as you think I am.（君が思うほど酔ってはいない）と言おうとした.
☞ John Squire (1962-)：イギリス出身のギタリスト・画家.

(1) as ～ as ... 「...と同じ程度に～」；not as [so] ～ as ... 「...ほど～でない」
(cf. ～は形容詞または副詞)

　She:　The man I marry must be **as** brave **as** a lion, but not forward; handsome **as** Apollo, but not conceited; wise **as** Solomon, but meek **as** a lamb; a man who is kind to every woman, but loves only me.

He: How lucky we met!

(「わたしが結婚する人はライオンのように勇敢で，しかし出しゃばりでなく，アポロのように美男子で，でもうぬぼれが強くなく，ソロモンの知恵があり，しかし羊のように従順で，すべての女性に親切な男性で，でもわたしだけを愛してくれる人でなければいけないわ」「ぼくたちがめぐり会えて本当に幸運だったね」)

☞ Apollo: ギリシャ・ローマ神話の太陽神．
☞ Solomon: 紀元前10世紀頃のイスラエルの賢明な王．

Politics are almost **as** exciting **as** war, and quite **as** dangerous. In war you can only be killed once, but in politics many times.

(Sir Winston Churchill)

(政治は戦争とほとんど同じくらい興奮させる，そしてまったく同じくらい危険である．戦争では死ぬのは一度きりだが，政治では何度も死ぬのだ．)

☞ Sir Winston Churchill (1874-1965): イギリスの政治家・首相(1940-45, 1951-55).

Doctor: Mr Beazley, that pain in your leg is simply due to old age.
Mr B.: Well, my other leg is just **as** old and that doesn't hurt.

(医師と患者の対話：「あなたの脚の痛みはまったく年のせいですよ」「もう一方の脚も同じ年なのに痛みませんぞ」)

I'm **not as** normal **as** I appear.　(Woody Allen)

(私は見かけほど正常ではありません．)

☞ Woody Allen (1935-　): アメリカの映画監督・作家・俳優．

My wife's cooking is improving. The smoke is **not as** black **as** it used to be!

(妻の料理は進歩している．煙が以前ほど黒くない．)

"Brian! Don't reach across the dinner table for the sugar. Use your tongue!"

"But mom, my tongue is**n't as** long **as** my arm!"

(「ブライアン，お砂糖をテーブルの上に手を伸ばして取ってはいけません。口を使いなさい」「でも，ママ，僕のべろは腕みたいに長くないよ」)
☞ 母親は「取ってくださいと言いなさい」のつもりだった．

Most women are **not so** young **as** they are painted.　(Max Beerbohm)
(ほとんどの女性は描かれているほど若くはない．)
☞ Max Beerbohm (1872-1956): イギリスのエッセイスト・批評家・風刺画家．

(2) 倍数表現：**twice [three times] as** 〜 **as** ...「...の 2 倍 [3 倍] の〜」(cf. **as** ... は省略されることも多い．)

Holiday: A day when Father works **twice as** hard **as** he does at the office.
(休日：父親が会社での 2 倍懸命に働く日．)

"My little brother is one year old and he can walk across the park by himself."
"My dog is one year old and it can walk **twice as** far **as** your brother."
"That's not surprising. It's got **twice as** many legs!"
(「弟は 1 つだけどひとりで公園を歩いて横切れるよ」「僕の犬は 1 つだけど君の弟の 2 倍遠くまで歩けるよ」「そんなの驚かないよ．脚が 2 倍あるじゃないか」)

Movies: The wide screen will only make bad films **twice as** bad.
(映画：ワイド・スクリーンはダメな映画を 2 倍ダメにするだけである．)

A doctor can't persuade a woman to go on a diet **half as** fast **as** last year's bathing suit can.
(医者は去年の水着の半分の速さほどにも女性にダイエットを説得できない．)
☞ 去年の水着を見ればすぐダイエットする気になる．

"Can you imagine anything worse than that solo?"
"Yes, the quartette—it's **four times as** bad."
(「あの独唱ほどひどいものが想像できますか」「ええ，4 重唱ですよ—あれの 4 倍ひどい

cf. 比較級を用いることもある．

"What is a zebra?"

"**Twenty-six sizes bigger than** a A bra."

(「シマウマとは何か」「A ブラの 26 倍の大きさ」)

☞ zebra (= Z bra) ⇔ A bra (A サイズのブラジャー)　　★ 異分析 → p. 375

Exaggeration is **a billion times worse than** understatement.
(誇張表現は控えめ表現より 10 億倍悪い．)

(3) 原級による慣用表現

(a) as 〜 as possible / as 〜 as S can *do*「(S が) できるだけ〜」

Teacher: Tell me, **as** precisely **as possible**, all you know about the greatest English water-colour painters of the eighteenth century.

Pupil: They're all dead.

(先生「できるだけ正確に，18 世紀イギリスの水彩画家について知っていることを全部言ってごらん」生徒「みんなもう死んでます」)

A father phoned the doctor. "Doctor, come quick, we've got an emergency! My little boy has swallowed my golf tees!"

"Okay," said the doctor, "I'll be with you **as** soon **as I can**."

"Tell me what to do till you get here."

The doctor said: "Practise your putting."

(父親が医者に電話した．「先生，すぐ来てください．緊急事態です．息子がゴルフのティーを飲んでしまったんです」「いいです，できるだけ早く行きます」「先生がここに来るまでどうしたらいいか教えてください」医者は言った．「パットの練習でもしててください」)

(b) not so much A as B「A というよりむしろ B」

At his retirement ceremony the boss told him, "The way we see it, we're **not so much** losing a worker **as** gaining a parking space."

(男の退職式でボスは彼に言った.「我々の見るところ, 働き手を失うというより駐車のスペースをもらえるという感じだね」)
★ **Insulting joke** → p. 97

(c) as 〜 as any A「どの A にも劣らず〜」

Passenger: I want to catch the late train to Scotland.

Guard: Take the twelve noon train. That's usually **as** late **as any**.

(乗客「スコットランド行きの遅い列車に乗りたいんだが」車掌「正午のに乗るといいです. 他のどの列車にも劣らずたいてい遅れます」)

☞ late「(時刻が) 遅い」⇔「(適当な時間より) 遅れた」　　★ **Pun** → p. 26

(d) as 〜 as ever「これまでと同じように〜」

The computer is a great invention. There are **as** many mistakes **as ever**, but now it's nobody's fault.

(コンピューターは優れた発明品である. 相変わらず間違いは多いが, 今や誰の責任でもない.)

(e) as far as A is concerned「A に関する限り」

As far as I'm concerned, old age is fifteen years from now.

(私に関する限り, 老齢とは今から 15 年後だ.)

B. 比較級

There is no one alive who is **Youer than** You.　(Dr Seuss)

(君ほど君らしい人は生きていない.)

☞ Dr Seuss (1904-1991): アメリカの作家・詩人・漫画家.

(1) 〜（比較級）（**+than ...**）「(...よりも) 〜」

They told me that as I got **older**, I would get **wiser**. At that rate I should be a genius by now.　(George Burns)

(他人は私に年をとればとるほど賢くなると言った. その調子ならもう天才になっているはずだ.)

☞ George Burns (1896–1996)：アメリカのコメディアン．

It is **easier** to love humanity as a whole **than** to love one's neighbor.
(Eric Hoffer)
(人類全体を愛す方が隣人を愛すより容易である．)
☞ Eric Hoffer (1902–1983)：アメリカの社会哲学者．

The ballot is **stronger than** the bullet. (Abraham Lincoln)
(投票用紙は弾丸より強力である．)
☞ ballot [bǽlət] ⇔ bullet [búlət]　　★ **Pun** → p. 26
☞ Abraham Lincoln (1809–1865)：アメリカ共和党の政治家．第 16 代大統領．

I know I'm getting **better** at golf because I am hitting **fewer** spectators. (Gerald Ford)
(ゴルフがうまくなっているのが分かる．見物人に当てる回数が減っている．)
☞ Gerald Ford (1913–2006)：アメリカの政治家．第 38 代大統領．

"I'm worried about dad. He is so thin."
"Well, just how thin is he?"
"You know how thin you are, and you know how thin I am. Well, he is **thinner than** both of us put together."
(「お父さんが心配なの．とてもやせているんです」「どのくらいやせているの」「あなたと私がどのくらいやせているか分かるでしょ．お父さんったら私たち 2 人合わせたよりやせているのよ」)
★ **Irish bull** → p. 39

The advantage of exercising every day is that you'll die **healthier**.
(毎日運動することの利点はより健康に死ねることである．)
★ **Irish bull** → p. 39

Doctors are amazing. They cure poor people **faster**!
(医者は大したものだ．貧乏人の方を早く治してくれる．)
★ **Doctor** → p. 329

We're **more** popular **than** Jesus Christ now. I don't know which will go first: Rock'n'roll or Christianity.　(John Lennon)
(僕らは今やイエス・キリストより人気がある．どっちが1位かは分からない．ロックンロールかなキリスト教かな．)
☞ John Lennon (1940–1980): イギリスのロックシンガーソングライター．ビートルズのメンバー．

"When it snowed there was **more** snow on our neighbor's yard **than** there was on ours."
"How could that be?"
"Our neighbor has a **larger** yard."
(「雪が降ったら，家の庭より隣の庭のほうが雪が多かったよ」「どうしてそんなことがありうるんだい」「隣の庭のほうが広いのさ」)

America believes in education: the average professor earns **more** money in a year **than** the professional athlete earns in a whole week.
(Evan Esar)
(アメリカは教育の価値を信じている．普通の大学教授が1年で稼ぐ金はプロの選手が丸1週間で稼ぐ金より多いのである．)
☞ Evan Esar (1899–1995): アメリカのユーモア作家．　★ **One-liner** → p. 395

Employer (to job candidate): I hire only married people. They're **less** likely to go home early.
(雇い主が仕事の志願者に:「既婚者だけを雇うことにしている．彼らの方が早く家に帰りそうもないんでね」)

There is only one thing in the world **worse than** being talked about, and that is not being talked about.　(Oscar Wilde)
(話題にされるより良くないことが世の中に1つだけある，それは話題にされないことだ．)
☞ Oscar Wilde (1854–1900): アイルランド生まれのイギリスの詩人・小説家・劇作家．

I had my credit card stolen, but I didn't report it because the thief was spending **less than** my wife did.

（クレジットカードを盗まれたが届けなかった．泥棒の方が家内より使い方が少なかったからだ．）

"It's raining, let's hurry."
"If we hurry will it rain **less**?"
(「雨が降っている．急ごう」「急げば雨が減るのか」)
★ **Irish bull** → p. 39

cf. super**or**（すぐれた），infer**or**（劣った），jun**or**（年下の），sen**or**（年上の）など語尾が「**−or**」の比較級は後ろに「than」ではなく「**to**」がつく．

I believe in equality. Equality for everybody. No matter how stupid they are or how **superior** I am **to** them.　(Steve Martin)
(平等が正しいと信じている．みんなにとっての平等だ．いかに彼らが愚かで，いかに私が彼らより優れていてもだ．)
☞ Steve Martin (1945-)：アメリカのコメディアン・俳優・脚本家．

The wife should be **inferior to** the husband; that is the only way to insure equality between the two.　(Martial)
(妻は夫に劣っているべきだ．それが2人の間に平等を保障する唯一の方法である．)
☞ Martial (40 A.D.-104 A.D.)：スペイン生まれのローマの風刺詩人．

(2) 比較級による慣用表現
(a) the 比較級 〜, the 比較級 ...「〜すればするほどますます...」

"Waiter, I'd like some chicken. **The younger, the better**."
"Good, I'll bring you an egg!"
(「君，チキンを頼みたいんだ．若ければ若いほどいい」「かしこまりました．卵をお持ちします」)
★ **Waiter** → p. 266

"Doesn't it madden you when a girl is slow about getting ready to go to dinner with you?"
"Yes, **the longer** she takes, **the hungrier** she gets."

(「女の子が食事に出掛ける準備でぐずぐずしていると頭にこないか」「くるとも．時間がかかればかかるほど，彼女ますます腹をすかすからな」）

The better a woman looks, **the longer** a man does.
(女性が良く見えれば見えるほど男性は長く見る．)
☞ look「見える」⇔「見る」; does = looks　　★ **Pun** → p. 26

The more argument you win, **the fewer** friends you'll have.
(議論に勝てば勝つほど友だちは減るものだ．）

The more we study, **the more** we know.
The more we know, **the more** we forget.
The more we forget, **the less** we know.
The less we know, **the less** we forget.
The less we forget, **the more** we know.
So why study?
(勉強すればするほど知識が増える．知識が増えるほど忘れることも多くなる．忘れることが多ければ知識は減る．知識が減れば忘れることも減る．忘れることが減れば減るほど知識は増える．じゃあ，なぜ勉強するんだ．）

(b) 比較級 **and** 比較級「ますます〜」

Air travel is a way of seeing **less and less** of **more and more**.
(空の旅はますます多くのものをますます少なく見る方法である．）

Every year women pay **more and more** for **less and less** clothes.
(毎年，女性はますます布の少ない衣服にますます多く支払う．）

As man becomes more civilized, he makes his locks **stronger and stronger** and his defences **bigger and bigger**.
(人間は文明化すればするほど錠をますます強力に，防衛手段をますます大きくする．）
★ **One-liner** → p. 395

(c) not A any more than B / no more A than B「A でないのは B でないの

と同じである」

You can **no more** win a war **than** you can win an earthquake.

(Jeannette Rankin)

(地震に勝てないように戦争にも勝てないのです。)

☞ Jeannette Rankin (1880-1973): アメリカの政治家。アメリカ最初の女性国会議員．

We have **no more** right to consume happiness without producing it **than** to consume wealth without producing it. (George Bernard Shaw)

(幸せを作り出さずに幸せを消費する権利がないのは富を作らずに富を消費する権利がないのと同じである。)

☞ George Bernard Shaw (1856-1950): アイルランド出身のイギリスの劇作家．

"Now, Willie, do have a little courage. When I have medicine to take I do**n't** like it **any more than** you do; but I make up my mind that I will take it, and I do."

"And when I have medicine to take," replied Willie, "I make up my mind that I won't take it, and I don't."

(「少しは勇気を出しなさい，ウィリー．薬を飲まなくてはならないとき，私だってお前と同じで飲みたくないよ．しかし飲むぞと決心したら飲むぞ」ウィリーは答えた「ぼくが薬を飲まなくてはいけないときは，飲まないと決心したら飲まないよ」)

(d) no less A than B「Bに劣らず［と同様に］Aである」

In the mind of the masses superstition is **no less** deeply rooted **than** fear ... (Baruch Spinoza)

(大衆の心の中には迷信が恐怖心と同様深く植えつけられている。)

☞ Baruch Spinoza (1632-1677): オランダの哲学者・神学者．

(e) no more than, no less than など
1) no more than = only

In my life, I have received **no more than** one or two letters that were worth the postage. (Henry David Thoreau)

(生まれてこのかた，郵便料金に値する手紙は1，2通しか受け取ったことがない。)

☞ Henry David Thoreau (1817-1862): アメリカのエッセイスト・詩人．

2) **no less than** ～ = **as many [much] as** ～:「～ほども多く」
Peace has its victories **no less than** war, but it doesn't have as many monuments to unveil.　(Kin Hubbard)
（平和には戦争に劣らず勝利があるが，戦争ほど多くの除幕すべき記念碑はない．）
☞　Kin Hubbard (1868-1930)：アメリカの漫画家・ユーモア作家．
★ **One-liner** → p. 395

3) **no＋比較級＋than**「as＋(反意の)原級＋as」と考えるとよい．（→ 2)）
A hero is **no braver than** an ordinary man, but he is braver five minutes longer.　(Ralph Waldo Emerson)
（英雄は普通の男と同様勇敢ではない，ただ5分だけ長く勇敢なのだ．）
☞　no braver than ～ = as cowardly as ～（～と同じくらい臆病な）
☞　Ralph Waldo Emerson (1803-1882)：アメリカの思想家・詩人．

Wives who drive from the back seat are **no worse than** husbands who cook from the dining-room table.
（後ろの席から運転（を指図）する妻は食堂のテーブルから料理（を指図）する夫と同じようなものだ．）
☞　no worse than ～ = as good as ～「～も同然で」

(f) **no sooner A than B**「AするとすぐBする」
A woman on her first plane trip found herself a nice window seat in a non-smoking area. But **no sooner** had she settled down **than** a man appeared and insisted that it was his seat.
Despite a lengthy argument, she flatly refused to move and told him to get away.
"OK, madam." he said, "If that's the way you want it, you fly the plane!"
（女性は初めての飛行機の旅行で禁煙区域に素敵な窓側の席を見つけた．しかし，席に着くとすぐ男が現れてそこは自分の席だと言い張った．長ったらしい言い合いにもかかわらず，女性は席を移動するのをきっぱり拒否し，男にいなくなれと言った．「いいですとも，奥様」と彼は言った．「それがあなたのお望みのやり方なら，あなた飛行機を飛ばしてください」）

(g) **no longer**「もはや〜ではない」

Father (to teenage daughter): I want you home by 11 o'clock.
Daughter: But, Daddy, I'm **no longer** a child.
Father: I know, that's why I want you home by 11.
(父と10代の娘の対話:「11時までには帰ってほしい」「でも, お父さん, 私もう子供じゃないわ」「そうさ, だから11時までに家にいてほしいんだ」)

(h) **had better**: (**You [He, She] had better** *do*)「＿＿するべきだ」; (**I [We] had better** *do*)「＿＿したほうがいい」

Husband: I hear that fish is brain food.
　Wife: You **had better** eat a whale.
(夫婦の対話:「魚は脳にいい食べ物だそうだ」「あなたはクジラを食べた方がいいわ」)
★ **Insulting joke** → p. 97

"This letter feels kind of heavy. **I'd better** put another stamp on it."
"What for? It'll only make it heavier." (George Burns and Gracie Allen)
(「この手紙ちょっと重い感じだ. もう1枚切手を貼ったほうがいいな」「なんのためなの. そんなことをしたらもっと重くなるだけじゃない」)
☞ kind of ＝ a little (少し, ちょっと)
☞ George Burns (1896-1996): アメリカのコメディアン・作家.
☞ Gracie Allen (1895-1964): アメリカのコメディアン.

(i) **sooner or later**「遅かれ早かれ」

Sooner or later I'm going to die, but I'm not going to retire.
(Margaret Mead)
(いずれ死ぬことになるでしょう, しかし引退するつもりはありません.)
☞ Margaret Mead (1901-1978): アメリカの文化人類学者.

(j) **more or less**「どちらかというと, だいたい」

Congress consists of one third, **more or less**, scoundrels; two thirds, **more or less**, idiots; and three thirds, **more or less**, poltroons.
(H. L. Mencken)
(議会は3分の1のどちらかと言えば悪党, 3分の2のどちらかと言えば愚か者から成り

立っている．そして，3分の3のどちらかと言えば臆病者から．）
☞ H. L. Mencken (1880-1956): アメリカの批評家・ジャーナリスト．
★ **Insulting joke** → p. 97

(k) (all) the＋比較級「それだけなおさら～」

I like a friend **the better** for having faults that one can talk about.
(William Hazlitt)
(友だちがいっそう好きになるのは話題にできる欠点をもっているからだ．)
☞ William Hazlitt (1778-1830): イギリスのエッセイスト・批評家．

Love's like the measles—**all the worse** when it comes late in life.
(Douglas Jerrold)
(恋愛は麻疹のようなものだ——人生遅くなって罹るとなおさら具合が悪い．)
☞ Douglas Jerrold (1803-1857): イギリスの劇作家・作家．

(3) 最上級

Oh, Charlie Brown, of all the Charlie Browns in the world, you are **the Charlie Browniest.** (Charles Schulz)
(おおチャーリーブラウン，世の中すべてのチャーリーブラウンの中で，君は最もチャーリーブラウンらしい．)

☞ Charles Schulz (1922-2000): アメリカの漫画家．

I speak 12 languages—English is **the bestest.** (Stefan Bergman)
(私は12ヶ国語話す—英語がベストですと言えます．)

☞ Stefan Bergman (1895-1977): ポーランド生まれのアメリカの数学者．

(a) the ～est / the most ～

You and I make a great pair. You're **the most beautiful** girl in the world and I'm **the biggest** liar in the world.
(きみと僕はすばらしいカップルになる．君は世界一の美人だし，僕は世界一の嘘つきだもの．)

Q: What ants are **the biggest**?
A: Elephants.
(問「最大のアリは何か」答「象」)
☞ elephants ⇔ eleph＋ants　　★ 異分析 → p. 375

Q: Which ants are the smallest?
A: Infants.
(問「どのアリが最も小さいか」「乳幼児」)
☞ infants ⇔ inf＋ants　　★ 異分析 → p. 375

"Is Mary your **oldest** sister?"
"Yep."
"And who comes after her?"
"You and two other guys."
(「メアリーは一番上の姉さんかい」「そうだよ」「次は誰だい」「君と他の2人だよ」)
☞ after 〜「〜の後に」⇔「〜を求めて」　　★ **Pun** → p. 26

Pupil: I don't think I deserved a zero on this test.
Teacher: I agree, but it's **the lowest** mark I can give you.
(生徒「このテスト0点しかもらえないなんて思いません」先生「その通り，しかしこれが私が付けられる最低点なんだよ」)

I finally met a man who didn't know **the shortest** distance between two points—a cab driver.
(遂に2点間の最短距離を知らない男に会った──タクシーの運転手だ.)
☞ わざと遠回りする．

"I think **the poorest** people are **the happiest**."
"Then marry me and we will be **the happiest** couple!"
(「最も貧しい人々が最も幸せだと思うわ」「じゃあ，僕と結婚してよ，そうすれば最も幸せな夫婦になるよ」)

Jack: Did you hear my **last** joke?

Jill: I certainly hope so.
(ジャック「僕のこの前のジョークを聞いたかい」ジル「確かにそうだといいと思うわ」)
☞ last「この前の」⇔「最後の」　★ **Pun** → p. 26
☞ つまらないジョークは最後にして欲しい．

Paul: Have you heard about Professor Bonkers' **latest** invention?
Saul: No, what's that?
Paul: A waterproof teabag.
(ポールとサウルの対話：「ボンカーズ教授の最新の発明品について聞いたか」「いいや，何だい」「防水ティーバッグさ」)

"My wife has **the worst** memory I ever heard of."
"Forget everything, eh?"
"No, remembers everything."
(「家内は今まで聞いた中で最悪の記憶力の持ち主だよ」「全部忘れるのか」「いいや，全部覚えてるんだ」)

"What is **the most popular** drink in Australia?"
"Coca-koala."
(「オーストラリアで最も人気のある飲み物は何か」「コカコアラ」)
☞ Coca-Cola ⇔ Coca-koala　★ **Pun** → p. 26

"Have you heard that **the most intelligent** person in the world is going deaf?"
"Pardon?"
(「世界で一番頭のいい人が耳が聞こえなくなりそうだと聞きましたか」「何ですって」)
☞ 自分が一番だと思っている．

The most beautiful things in the world are **the most useless**—peacocks and lilies, for instance.　(John Ruskin)
(世界で最も美しいものは最も役に立たない，例えば，孔雀や百合のように．)
☞ John Ruskin (1819–1900): イギリスの評論家・美術評論家．

Of all my wife's relations I like myself **the best**.　(Joe Cook)
（妻のすべての親類の中で私は自分が一番好きだ。）
☞ Joe Cook (1860-1947): オーストラリアの政治家・首相.

Television is probably **the least** physically **harmful** of all the narcotics known to man.　(Christopher Lehmann Haupt)
（テレビはおそらく人間に知られたすべての麻薬の中で身体的に最も害の少ないものだろう。）
☞ Christopher Lehmann Haupt (1934-): アメリカのジャーナリスト・批評家・小説家.

"What kind of house weighs **the least**?"
"A lighthouse."
（「どんな種類の家がいちばん軽いか」「灯台」）
☞ light:「軽い」⇔「明るい」　★ **Pun** → p. 26; **Riddle** → p. 64

cf. a＋最上級＝very＋原級

I've had **a most enjoyable** evening—but not tonight.
(Groucho Marx)
（とても楽しい夕べを経験しました―でも今夜ではありません。）
☞ Groucho Marx (1890-1977): アメリカのコメディアン. Marx Brothers（マルクス兄弟）の中心.
★ **Insulting joke** → p. 97

cf. the second ［third など］＋最上級「2番目［3番目など］に最も～」

Man is **the second strangest** sex in the world.
（男性は世界で2番目に最も奇妙な性である。）

After a complete examination, the doctor told the patient: "Quit smoking and drinking, go to bed early every night, and get up at the crack of dawn. That's the best for you." The man thought for a moment and said, "Frankly, Doc, I don't deserve the best. What's **the second best**?"

(完璧な検査のあと医師は患者に言った。「タバコと酒をやめなさい，毎晩早く寝なさい，そして夜明けに起きなさい。それがあなたにとって最良のことです」男はちょっと考えて言った「率直に言うと，先生，私は最良には値しません。2番目に最良は何ですか」)

cf. even（〜でさえ）を補って考えるべきもの

Look at cows and remember that **the greatest** scientists in the world have never discovered how to make grass into milk.
(乳牛を見て世界の最も偉大な科学者でさえ草を牛乳にする方法をいまだに発見していないことを思い出しなさい。)

(4) 最上級による慣用表現

(a) most を含むもの

Policeman: I'll have to report you. You were driving at ninety miles an hour.
Motorist: Nonsense, officer! I've only been driving for ten minutes **at most**.

(警官「お知らせしなければなりません。時速90マイルで運転していました」ドライバー「バカ言っちゃいけません。お巡りさん。せいぜい10分しか運転していないんですよ」)
★ Irish bull → p. 39

Now that I've learned to **make the most of** life, most of it is gone.
(人生を最大限に利用することを覚えた今や，そのほとんどがなくなっている。)

(b) best を含むもの

Darwinian man, though well behaved, is **at best** only a monkey shaved.　(W. S. Gilbert)
(ダーウィンの進化論を信じるやつは，たとえ礼儀正しくても，せいぜいひげをそったサルにすぎない。)
☞ W. S. Gilbert (1836-1911): イギリスの劇作家・オペラ台本作者・詩人・挿絵画家.

Only a mediocre writer is always **at his best**.　(Somerset Maugham)
(並みの作家だけが常にこの上ない状態でいるのだ。)
☞ Somerset Maugham (1874-1965): イギリスの小説家・劇作家.

An optimist is one who **makes the best of** it when he gets the worst of it.
（楽観主義者は負けると分かっているときに最善を尽くす人である．）

(A letter from a girl of 12 to President Reagan)
To the best of my knowledge there has been no child in space. I would like to learn about being weightless, and I'd like to get away from my mother's cooking.　(Jonathan Adashek)
（（12 歳の女の子からレーガン大統領への手紙）わたしの知る限りでは，宇宙に行った子供はいません．無重力について学びたいし，母の料理からも逃げ出したいんです．）

(c) least を含むもの

　Dit:　I haven't slept for days.
　Dot:　Aren't you tired?
　Dit:　**Not in the least**. I sleep nights.
（ディットとドットの対話：「何日も寝てないんだ」「疲れてないのか」「まったく疲れてないよ．夜は寝てるんだ」）

My wife thinks I'm too nosy. **At least** that's what she writes in her diary.
（妻は私があまりに詮索好きだと思っている．少なくとも妻の日記にそう書いてある．）

(d) last を含むもの

　"My play has been put on the stage **at last**."
　"That's great news."
　"Yes. They cut it up and use it as a snowstorm."
（「ぼくの芝居がとうとう舞台に出たよ」「それはすばらしい」「そうなんだ．すっかりちぎって吹雪に使ってるよ」）

　"Doc, I'm afraid I'm going to die!"
　"Nonsense! That's **the last** thing you'll do!"
（「先生，死にそうな気がします」「バカな．それはあなたには起こりそうもないことです」）

> **ジョークの常識㉔**
>
> ★ **One-liner:**「ウイット・ユーモアに富む寸言・名言」本書にも頻出する．One-liner といわゆる格言・箴言（maxim・proverb）との区別はつけにくい．

第 25 章　否定表現

If two **negatives** make an affirmative, how many **negatives** make a photographer?
(もし2つの否定で肯定になるのなら，いくつ否定があれば写真家になれるのか．)

☞ negative:「否定(語)」⇔「(写真の) ネガ」→ (11) 二重否定

(1) not を含むもの

I took a lie detector test the other day. **No**, I did**n't**.　(Steven Wright)
(先日うそ発見器のテストを受けた．いや，受けなかった．)

☞ Steven Wright (1955–): アメリカのコメディアン・作家．

(a) 普通の用法：動詞・文の否定などに用いる．

"Stop acting like a fool!"
"I'm **NOT** acting!"
(「バカなまねはよせ」「まねなどしていないぞ」)

Policeman:　Did**n't** you hear me yell for you to stop?
Motorist:　**No**, I did**n't**.
Policeman:　Did**n't** you see me signal for you to stop?
Motorist:　**No**, I did**n't**.
Policeman:　Did**n't** you hear me blow my whistle for you to stop?
Motorist:　**No**, I did**n't**.
Policeman:　Well, I guess I might as well go home. I do**n't** seem to be doing much good around here.
(警官と運転者の対話：「君は私が大声で止まれと言ったのが聞こえなかったのか」「聞こえませんでした」「止まれと合図したのを見なかったのか」「見ませんでした」「止まれと笛を吹いたのが聞こえなかったのか」「はい」「どうも私は家に帰ったほうがよさそうだ．この辺では私は役に立たないらしい」)

My wife does**n't** want me to remember her birthday and is disappointed when I forget it.
（妻は私が彼女の誕生日を思い出すのを望まないくせに私が忘れるとがっかりする．）

Sally: Would you punish a pupil for something she did**n't** do?
Teacher: Of course **not**.
Sally: Good, I have**n't** done my homework.
（サリーと先生の対話：「先生は生徒がやらなかったことで罰を与えますか」「もちろん与えないわよ」「よかった．わたし宿題をやってこなかったんです」）

Hotel receptionist (in Spain to Englishman): Are you a foreigner?
Englishman: Certainly **not**! I'm British!
（スペインのホテルのフロントがイギリス人に「外国の方でいらっしゃいますか」「とんでもない．私はイギリス人だ」）
★ **Irish bull** → p. 39

"If you see my wife, tell her to wait for me."
"I do**n't** know your wife."
"Then, tell her **not** to wait."
（「家内に会ったら待つように言ってくれたまえ」「奥様を存じ上げないんですが」「じゃ，待たないように言ってくれたまえ」）
☞ この not は to wait（to 不定詞）を否定している．　★ **Irish bull** → p. 39

Patient: Doctor, these strength pills you gave me are**n't** doing any good at all.
Doctor: Why not?
Patient: I can't unscrew the bottle top.
（患者と医師の対話：「先生，いただいた力をつける錠剤はちっとも効いていませんが」「どうして効かないと言うのですか」「ビンのふたを回して開けられないんで」）
☞ not ... at all「まったく…ない」

(b) not A but B「A ではなく B である」
A wife laughs at her husband's jokes **not** because he is clever **but**

because she is.
(妻が夫のジョークを笑うのは夫が頭がいいからではなく妻がいいからだ.)
☞ not A but B については「第 19 章　等位接続詞」参照.
☞ not because A, but because B については「第 22 章　副詞節 (2) 理由」参照.

(2) no を含むもの

Boss: I don't like 'yes' men. When I say '**no**' I want them to say '**no**' too.
(「わしはイエスマンは好かん. わしがノーと言ったら彼らにもノーと言わせたい」)

Doctor: How is the boy who swallowed the dime?
Nurse: **No** change, Doc.
(医者「10 セント貨を飲み込んだ男の子の具合はどうかね」看護師「変化ありません, 先生」)

☞ change「変化」⇔「小銭」　★ **Pun** → p. 26

There's **no** place like home…after the other places close.
(家庭ほど良い所はない…他の場所が全部閉まったあとでは.)
☞ There's no place like home. はことわざ.　★ **Parody** → p. 199

"When a teacher closes his eyes, why should it remind him of an empty classroom?"
"Because there are **no** pupils to see."
(「先生が目を閉じるとなぜ空っぽの教室を思い出すのでしょう」「生徒が見えないからです」)
☞ pupil「生徒」⇔「瞳(ひとみ)」　★ **Pun** → p. 26

I have what **no** millionaire has—**no** money.
(どの百万長者も持っていないものを持っている. 金がないことだ.)

cf. no＋名詞：名詞の内容を強く否定し, むしろ反対の意味を表すことがある.
A computer once beat me at chess, but it was **no** match for me at

kick-boxing.　(Emo Philips)
(コンピューターがかつてチェスで私に勝った，しかしキックボクシングでは私の敵ではなかった．)
☞ Emo Philips (1956–　)：アメリカのコメディアン．

A woman who got on the bus with ten children was asked by the conductor if they were all her own, or it was a picnic. "They're all mine," she sighed. "And believe me, it's **no** picnic."
(10人の子供を連れてバスに乗った女性が車掌に全部自分の子かそれともピクニックかと尋ねられた．「みんな私の子よ」と彼女はため息をついて言った．「ほんとにピクニックどころじゃないわ」)
☞ picnic「ピクニック」⇔「（否定文で）楽な仕事」　★ **Pun** → p. 26

(3) never を含むもの

> "Why do civil servants **never** talk about their work?"
> "Because they **never** do any."
> (「なぜ公務員は自分の仕事について決して語らないのか」「何もしないから」)

I **never** worry about money. What's the sense in worrying about something you don't have?
(私はお金のことは決して心配しないことにしている．持ってもいないものを心配してどんな意味があるのか．)

　Son:　I saw a black cat in the kitchen.
Father:　**Never** mind. Black cats won't bring bad luck.
　Son:　He's had your dinner.
(息子と父親の対話：「台所で黒ネコを見たよ」「気にすることはない．黒ネコは悪運など持ってはこないんだ」「でもお父さんの夕飯を食べちゃったよ」)

My eyes were **never** good and I have a wife to prove it.
(私の眼は決して良くなかった，そしてそれを証明してくれる妻がいる．)

(4) **neither** = **not** 〜 **either**「どちらも〜ない」

"How about a date?"
"Why, I don't know you."
"I do**n't** know you **either**."
(「デートしませんか」「あら，あなたを知らないわ」「僕もあなたを知りません」)

Father: I'm not pleased with your end of term report, son.
　Son: **Neither** was my teacher, but he insisted on sending it.
(父と息子の対話:「お前の学期末の成績は気に入らないな」「先生も気に入らなかったんだ．でも先生は絶対に成績を送ると言ったんだ」)

"Doctor, I've broken my arm in two places."
"Do**n't** go back to **either** of them."
(「先生，2か所腕を折ったんです」「どちらにも戻ってはいけません」)
☞ in two places「2か所を」⇔「2か所で」

She stepped out of the gorgeous new Cadillac. Terrific body line. The car was**n't** bad **either**.
(彼女は豪華なキャデラックの新車から降り立った．すばらしいボディーライン．車も悪くなかった．)

cf. **neither A nor B**「AでもなければBでもない」；**nor**「(no, not, neverなどの否定語のあとに置いて) もまた〜ない」
Some civil servants are **neither** servants **nor** civil.
　　　　　　　　　　　　　　　　　　　(Sir Winston Churchill)
(公務員の中には使用人でもなければ市民でもないのがいる．)
☞ Sir Winston Churchill (1874-1965): イギリスの政治家・首相 (1940-45, 1951-55).

I'm **neither** for **nor** against apathy.
(私は無関心に賛成でも反対でもない．)
☞ まさに無関心．

Nobody will use other people's experience, **nor** have any of his own till it is too late to use it.　(Nathaniel Hawthorne)
（誰も他人の経験を利用しないし自分自身の経験も手遅れになって使えなくなるまで身につかない．）
☞ Nathaniel Hawthorne (1804-1864): アメリカの小説家．

(5) nobody, no one「だれも〜ない」

"Why don't skeletons like parties?"
"They have **no body** to dance with."
（「なぜ骸骨はパーティーが嫌いか」「ダンスをする身体がないから」）

☞ no body ⇔ nobody　　★ 異分析 → p. 375

My girlfriend phoned me yesterday and said, "Come on over, there's **nobody** home."
I went over. **Nobody** was home.
（ガールフレンドが昨日電話してきて言った．「いらっしゃいよ．家には誰もいないわ」行ってみると家には誰もいなかった．）

Nobody ever died of laughter.　(Max Beerbohm)
（笑いが原因で死んだ人はいまだかつていない．）
☞ Max Beerbohm (1872-1956): イギリスのエッセイスト・パロディー作家．

Tourist:　This is a very dangerous cliff. Why don't you put up a danger sign?
Native:　Well, we did have a sign, but **nobody** fell, so we took it down.
（旅行者「これはとても危険な崖ですね．危険の標識を立てたらどうですか」土地の人「立てるには立てたんです．でも誰も落ちないもんだから，取っぱらいました」）

The trouble with being punctual is that there's **nobody** there to appreciate it.　(Franklin P. Jones)
（時間厳守に関しての問題はそれを正しく評価する人がそこに誰もいないことだ．）
☞ Franklin P. Jones (1908-1980): アメリカのジャーナリスト・ユーモア作家．
★ **One-liner** → p. 395

Everybody wants to live long, though **nobody** wants to be old.
(La Rochefoucauld)
(誰もが長生きしたいと思うが，誰も年を取りたくはないのだ．)
☞ La Rochefoucauld (1613-1680): フランスのモラリスト．警句・格言の作者．
★ **One-liner** → p. 395

"Why didn't the zookeeper bother to lock the door to the lion cage?"
"He knew **no one** would steal a lion."
(「なぜ動物園の飼育係はライオンの檻のドアをわざわざ閉めなかったのか」「だれもライオンを盗もうとはしないことを知っていたから」)
★ **Irish bull** → p. 39

I went to a school reunion the other day, sadly all my friends had become so fat and old **no one** could recognise me.
(先日学校の同窓会へ行ったが，悲しいかな友だちはみなひどく太って老けていたので誰も私だと分からなかった．)
★ **Irish bull** → p. 39

Cop: Who was driving when this accident happened?
Drunk: **No one**. We were all sitting in the back seat.
(警官「この事故が起きたとき誰が運転していたんだ」酔っ払い「誰もしてません．みんな後ろの席に座ってたんで」)

Aunt: Dick, why are you scratching yourself?
Dick: **No one else** knows where I itch.
(伯母「ディック，なぜかいているの」ディック「僕のかゆいところは他の誰にも分からないもん」)
☞ yourself:「自分を」⇔「自分で」

(6) none「何も［誰も］〜ない」; **nothing**「何も〜ない」

> "Three men were under one umbrella, but **none** of them got wet. How did they do it?"
> "It wasn't raining."

(「3人の男が1つの傘に入っていたがだれも濡れなかった．どうやったか」「雨が降っていなかった」)

★ Riddle → p. 64

Patient: Well, what does my brain X-ray show?
Doctor: **Nothing**.
(患者「私の頭のX線写真に何が見えますか」医師「何も」)

★ Insulting joke → p. 97

Teacher: If eggs were twenty cents a dozen, how many would you get for five cents?
Pupil: **None**.
Teacher: **None**?
Pupil: If I have five cents I'd get a bar of toffee crunch.
(先生と生徒の対話：「もし卵が1ダース20セントだとすると，5セントでいくつ買えますか」「1つも」「1つもですって」「5セントあればトフィー・クランチ1つ買います」)
☞ toffee = ((米)) taffy（一種のキャラメル）

A man I knew solved the problem of too many visiting relatives. He borrowed money from the rich ones and loaned it to the poor ones. Now **none** of them come back.
(知人がやたらにやって来る親戚の問題を解決した．金持ちの親戚からは金を借りそれを貧乏な親戚に貸し付けたんだ．今は誰も戻って来ない．)

A lot of labor-saving devices have been invented for women, but **none** have ever been as popular as a husband with plenty of money.
(多くの労力節約の装置が女性のために発明されてきたが，大金を持った夫ほど人気があるものはいまだかつて何もない．)

Hope costs **nothing**. (Colette)
(希望は一切費用が掛からない．)
☞ Colette (1873-1954): フランスの作家．

★ One-liner → p. 395

Doctor: I can do **nothing** for your sickness. It is hereditary.
Patient: Then send the bill to my father.
(医師と患者の対話:「あなたの病気は手の施しようがありません．遺伝です」「じゃあ請求書は父に送ってください」)

"What did you say when you proposed?"
"I was quite frank, I said, 'I am **nothing**, I have **nothing** and I can do **nothing**.'"
"What did she say?"
"**Nothing**."
(「プロポーズしたとき何と言ったんだ」「僕は全く率直だった．『ぼくは取るに足らない男です．財産もありません，それに何もできません』と言ったんだ」「彼女は何と言った」「何も」)

A committee is a group of people who individually can do **nothing**, but together decide that **nothing** can be done. (Fred Allen)
(委員会とは個人では何もできない一群の人々で，一緒なら何もできないということを決める人々である．)
☞ Fred Allen (1894-1956): アメリカのコメディアン．

(7) nothing＋比較級＋than ... / nothing 〜 as＋原級＋as ...:「...ほど〜なものはない」

There is **nothing safer than** flying — It's crashing that is dangerous. (Theo Cowan)
(飛行ほど安全なものはない—危険なのは墜落することだ．)
☞ Theo Cowan (1992-): イギリスの俳優．

Nothing annoys a woman **more than** to have friends drop in unexpectedly and find the house looking like it usually does.
(女性にとって友達に思いがけず立ち寄られて家の中が普段どおりに見えるのを見られ

るくらいいらいらすることはない.）
★ One-liner → p. 395

Nothing is **more** discouraging **than** playing with a golfer who is so good he doesn't have to cheat.
（あまりにうまいのでインチキをしないですむゴルファーとプレーするほどがっかりすることはない.）
★ One-liner → p. 395

Nothing lasts **as** long **as** a necktie you don't like.
（気に入らないネクタイほど長持ちするものはない.）

Nothing is **as** dull **as** a vacation you can afford!
（出費の余裕のある休暇ほど退屈なものはない.）

cf. 次も同じように考えればよい.
　No furniture is **so** charming **as** books, even if you never open them or read a single word.　(Sydney Smith)
　（書物ほど魅力的な家具はない，たとえそれを開くことも1語も読むことがなくても.）
　☞ Sydney Smith (1771-1845)：イギリスの作家・牧師.

(8) nothing を含む慣用表現
(a) nothing like ～「～ほど良いものはない」
　Ken: There's **nothing like** getting up at five in the morning and taking an ice-cold shower and a mile jog before breakfast.
　Bob: How long have you been doing this?
　Ken: I start tomorrow.
　（ケンとボブの対話：「朝5時に起きて，氷のように冷たいシャワーを浴び，朝食前に1マイルジョギングをするほど素晴らしいことはないね」「もうどのくらいやっているんだい」「明日始めるよ」）

(b) Nothing doing.「(強く否定して) 絶対だめだ」
　We are told to live within our income. **Nothing doing**! We may be

poor, but not that poor.
（収入の範囲内で生活しろと言われている．絶対だめだ．貧しいかもしれないが，それほど貧しくはない．）

(c) **nothing but** 〜 / **nothing more than** 〜 「〜にすぎない」（= only）
Always turn to the sports page first. The sports page records people's accomplishments. The front page has **nothing but** man's failures.
（常にスポーツのページを開きなさい．スポーツのページは人々の成果を記録しています．第1面は人間の失敗しか載っていません．）

Happiness is **nothing more than** health and a poor memory.
(Albert Schweitzer)
（幸福は健康と物覚えの悪さ以上の何ものでもない．）
☞ Albert Schweitzer (1875-1965)：ドイツ生まれの医師・伝道師・音楽家．
★ **One-liner** → p. 395

(9) 準否定：1語で否定に近い意味を表す．

> "But how can I be sure that you love me?"
> "Well, I can **scarcely** sleep at night thinking of you."
> "That doesn't prove anything. Papa can **hardly** sleep thinking of you."
> （「あなたが私を愛しているってどうしたら信じられるの」「きみのことを考えると夜もほとんど眠れないほどだよ」「そんなの何の証明にもならないわ．パパはあなたのことを考えるとほとんど眠れないんですもの」）

(a) **few**, **little**（→「第11章　形容詞」D. (1)）
Few of us can stand prosperity. Another man's, I mean.
(Mark Twain)
（繁栄に耐えられる人はほとんどいない．他人ののことだが．）
☞ Another man's (prosperity)
☞ Mark Twain (1835-1910)：アメリカの（ユーモア）小説家．

Advice is something everybody gives but **few** take.

（助言は誰もが与え，ほとんど誰も受け入れないもの．）

Happiness, whether in business or private life, leaves very **little** trace in history.　(Fernand Braudel)
（幸福は，仕事であれ個人生活であれ，歴史にほとんど痕跡を残さない．）
☞ Fernand Braudel (1902-1985): フランスの歴史学者．
★ **One-liner** → p. 395

We know a fellow who, after a physical checkup, was told by his doctor that he was in pretty bad shape: "Too **little** blood in your alcohol stream."
（人間ドックのあと医者に健康状態がかなりひどい，「アルコールの流れに血液が少なすぎる」と言われた男を知っている．）

(b) hardly / scarcely「ほとんど～ない」
　Diner:　Waiter, your finger is in my soup.
　Waiter:　That's all right. It's so used to the heat, I **hardly** noticed it.
（客「君，指が私のスープの中に入っているじゃないか」ウエイター「大丈夫です．私の指は熱に慣れていますから，ほとんど気がつきませんでした」）
★ **Waiter** → p. 266

When I was forty, my doctor advised me that a man in his forties shouldn't play tennis. I heeded his advice carefully and could **hardly** wait until I reached fifty to start again.　(Hugo Black)
（40歳の頃医者は私に40代の男はテニスをすべきではないと助言した．彼の助言には注意深く気を配り，50歳になってまた始めるのが待ち遠しかった．）
☞ Hugo Black (1886-1971): アメリカの法学者．

"Doctor, come quickly!"
"What's the matter?"
"We can't get into our house!"
"That's **scarcely** my concern, is it?"
"Yes, it is. The baby's swallowed the front door key!"

（「先生，すぐ来てください」「どうしたんですか」「家に入れないんです」「そんなことはほとんど私に関係がありませんね」「あるんです，赤ん坊が玄関のカギを飲み込んでしまったんです」）

(c) seldom「めったに〜ない」(→「第13章 副詞」(5) 頻度)

Diner: Waiter, didn't you hear me say "Well done"?
Waiter: Yes, sir; thank you very much, sir. It's **seldom** we get any thanks, sir.

（客とウエイターの対話：「君，私が『ウエルダン』と言ったのが聞こえなかったか」「聞こえましたとも，お客さま．本当にありがとうございます．めったに感謝のお言葉はいただけませんので」）

☞ Well done:「火のよく通った」⇔「よくできた，うまいぞ」
★ Waiter → p. 266

People with good memories **seldom** remember anything worth remembering. (Anon.)
（記憶力の良い人は思い出すに値することをめったに覚えていない．）

(10) 部分否定 not 〜 all [always, every など]：「すべて［いつも］〜とはかぎらない」

Not all men are fools. Some are bachelors.
（すべての男がバカというわけではない．独身者もいるのだ．）

◆ 全体否定と部分否定の違い一覧

	部分否定	全体否定
2人 2つ	not ... both	neither ... not ... either
	どちらも...というわけではない	どちらも...でない
3人 3つ以上	not ... all not ... every	none ... no＋名詞 not ... any
	すべてが...というわけではない	どれも...でない

Anybody who hates children and dogs ca**n't** be **all** bad.   (W. C. Fields)
（子供と犬を嫌う人が誰もがみんな悪い人のはずはない．）
☞ W. C. Fields (1880-1946): アメリカのコメディアン．

"I say, Briggs, don't you ever take your wife out with you in the car?"
"No, I ca**n't** contend with **both** of them."
（「おい，ブリッグス，おまえは奥さんを連れて車で出かけないのか」「出かけないさ．両方とは戦えないよ」）
☞ 車と奥方の両方とは．

Not everybody hates me: only the people who've met me.

(Emo Philips)

（誰もが私を嫌っているわけではない．私に会ったことがある人たちだけだ．）
☞ Emo Philips (1956-): アメリカのコメディアン．

Women do**n't** believe **everything** they hear, but that doesn't keep them from repeating it.
（女性は聞くことすべてを信じるわけではない，しかしそれを口外しないでいることにはならない．）

The first requirement of a statesman is that he be dull. This is **not always** easy to achieve.   (Dean Acheson)
（（立派な）政治家の第一の必要条件は鈍感であることだ．これを達成するのはいつも容易なわけではない．）
☞ Dean Acheson (1893-1971): アメリカの弁護士・政治家．

The dime is**n't entirely** worthless—it still makes a pretty good screw driver.
（10セント貨はまったく価値がないわけではない—まだかなりいいネジ回しになる．）

"If you're not a good little girl you won't go to Heaven. Don't you want to go to Heaven?"
"Well, I've been to the circus, and the automobile show and to

Europe, so I can't expect to go **everywhere**."
(「いい子にしていないと天国へ行けないよ．天国へ行きたくないのかい」「サーカスにも行ったし，自動車ショーも行ったし，ヨーロッパも行ったから，どこへでも行けるとは思えないわ」)

Teacher: You! Did you miss school yesterday?
  Pupil: Yes, but **not very** much.
(先生「君．昨日は学校を欠席したね」生徒「はい，でもあまりそうでもありませんでした」)
☞ miss「欠席する」⇔「なくてさびしく思う」　★ **Pun** → p. 26

No generalization is **wholly** true, including this one.
(一般論が完全に正しいわけではない，これも含めて．)

No one is **completely** worthless―they can always serve as a bad example.
(誰もがまったく無価値というわけではない．いつでも悪い見本として役に立つのだ．)

(11) 二重否定：否定の意味をもつ語が2つ重なると，肯定の意味になる．

Teacher: Sammy, please give me an example of a double negative.
Sammy: I do**n't** know **none**.
Teacher: Correct, thank you.
(先生と生徒の対話：「サミー，二重否定の例を挙げてみて」「なんも分かりません」「その通り，ありがとう」)

☞ Sammyのことばは二重否定ではない．無教養を示している．

A man, who was criticized for not having a Bible in the house, excused himself by saying that there was **not** a word in the Bible that was**n't** in his dictionary.
(ある男，家に聖書を持っていないことを批難されて，聖書にある語の中で自分の辞書にない語など1語もないと言って弁解した．)

Confucius says: "**No** doctor is a good doctor who has **never** been ill himself."
(孔子曰く「自分が病気になったことのない医者で良い医者はいない」)

No work is **im**possible without a committee.
(委員会がなければどんな仕事も不可能ではない.)
☞ 委員会などあるから仕事が捗らない.

A lady is one who **never** shows her underwear **un**intentionally.
(Lillian Day)
(淑女とは自分の下着をうっかり見せたりはしない人である.)
☞ = A lady is one who shows her underwear intentionally.(淑女とは下着を意図的に見せる人.)
☞ Lillian Day (1915-2013): アメリカの小説家・伝記作家・劇作家.

cf. 「三重否定」とでも呼ぶべきもの:無教養を示す.
"Did you study your history?"
"Naw, I **ain't** had **no** time for **nothin'** but my English."
(「歴史の勉強をしましたか」「しなかったよ. 英語以外なんもやる時間なかったよ」)
☞ ain't:(ここでは)have not
正しくは:I have**n't** had **any** time for anything but my English. = I have had **no** time for **any**thing but my English.

(12) 否定に関する慣用表現

(a) can not [never] A without B:「BしないでAすることはできない;AすればかならずBする」

I can **never** pass by the Metropolitan Museum of Art in New York **without** thinking of it not as a gallery of living portraits but as a cemetery of tax-deductible wealth. (Lewis H. Lapham)
(ニューヨークのメトロポリタン美術館の側を通ると必ずそこが現存する肖像画の画廊ではなく所得控除を受けられる財産の共同墓地と考えてしまう.)
☞ Lewis H. Lapham (1935-): アメリカの作家・雑誌編集者.

I am **unable** to pass a theatre **without** wanting to walk in, and

unable to listen to a single word from an actor **without** wanting to walk out again.　(Howard Jacobson)
(劇場の前を通ると必ず入って行きたくなり，俳優の台詞を一言聞くと必ずまた出たくなる．)
☞ Howard Jacobson (1942-　): イギリスのユダヤ系作家・ジャーナリスト．

(b) not [never] A until B:「BするまでAしない；Aして初めてBする」
You **never** really learn to swear **until** you learn to drive.
(悪態をつくことをほんとうに覚えるのは車の運転を覚えてからだ．)

I **never** realized how bad our inflation was **until** I dropped my wallet in the park and got arrested for littering!
(インフレがいかにひどいかを悟ったのは公園で財布を落とすとごみを散らかしたといって逮捕されてからだった．)
★ **Tall tale** → p. 412

It was not until I went on a diet **that** I realized I was a bad loser.
(ダイエットをして初めて自分が負け惜しみを言う人間だと気づきました．)

No man knows how short a month can be **until** he has to pay alimony.
(誰もが慰謝料を払わなければならなくって初めて1ヶ月がどれほど短いかが分かる．)

ジョークの常識㉕

★ **Tall tale:**「おおげさなほら話」ジョークそのものが tall tale と言えるが，その中でも特に絶対にあり得ないバカバカしい話をいう．Elephant joke (→ p. 72) もその一つ．

第26章　時制の一致・話法

My cat can talk. I asked her what two minus two was and she said nothing.
（私の猫はしゃべることができる．2−2は何だと聞くと0だと答えた．）

☞ I said to her, "What is two minus two?" and she said, "Nothing."
☞ said nothing「0だと言った」⇔「何も言わなかった」

A. 時制の一致

(1) 原則

> 主節の述語動詞が過去のときは，名詞節の動詞も自動的に過去，または過去完了になる．つまり，現在→過去；現在完了・過去→過去完了；過去完了→過去完了（変化しない）となる．
>
> 助動詞はそれぞれ，will → would, shall → should, can → could, may → might と変化する．

When I left university I went for several job interviews. At the first interview I was turned down because I wasn't married. The personnel officer *said* that married men **had** much more experience of knowing how to cope if a boss **shouted** at them.
（大学を出るといくつか就職の面接に行った．最初の面接で断られたのは私が結婚していないからだった．人事担当者は結婚している男性はもし上司が怒鳴りつけたらどう対処するかを豊富な経験で心得ていると言ったのだ．）

"Do you know it takes a half dozen sheep to make a sweater?"
"I *didn't* even *know* they **could** knit!"
（「セーター1枚作るのに6頭の羊が必要なのを知っているか」「羊に編み物ができることも知らなかったよ」）

★ Irish bull　→ p. 39

413

"Can you give me a pound for a cup of coffee?"
"But you can get a cup of coffee for 50p."
"I know, but I *thought* you **might** like to join me."
(「コーヒー1杯に1ポンドお恵みを」「しかしコーヒーなら50ペンスで買えるぞ」「分かってます，でもご一緒なさりたいかと思いました」)

I *used to think* that I **could** control the weather, and when I was nine I *said* that I **wanted** snow for Christmas. We got so much snow that year that everyone was trapped in their homes, and I swore never to use my powers again.
(私はかつて自分には天候を左右する力があると思っていた．9歳のときクリスマスには雪が降ってほしいと言った．その年雪が非常に多かったので皆家に閉じ込められた．私は自分の力を二度と使わないと誓った．)

My mother-in-law was kidnapped last week. The kidnappers *said* **if** we **didn't** send $24,000 quick, we **would** have to take my mother-in-law back.
(義理の母が先週誘拐された．誘拐犯たちは24,000ドルすぐに送らないと義理の母を送り返さねばならないと言ってきた．)

☞ 直接話法：The kidnappers *said to us*, "**If** you **don't** send $24,000 quick, you **will** have to take your mother-in-law back."

★ **Mother-in-law** → p. 305

(2) 時制の一致の例外
(a) 現在の状態・習慣

Paul: She *said* I**'m** interesting, brave, and intelligent.
Bob: You should never go steady with a girl who deceives you from the very start.
(ポール「彼女は僕が興味深く勇敢で頭がいいと言ったぞ」ボブ「君をまったくの最初からだますような女の子とだけは付き合うのはやめた方がいいぞ」)

I can now find words in the dictionary much faster than I used to since I *discovered* that the words **are** listed in alphabetical order.

(今では以前よりずっと速く辞書で単語を見つけることができる．それは単語がアルファベット順に並べられていることを知ったからだ．)
★ Irish bull → p. 39

A mailman meets a boy and a huge dog. "Does your dog bite?" asks the mailman. "No," replies the boy. And the dog bites the mailman's leg. "You *said* he **doesn't** bite!" yells the mailman. "That's not my dog," replies the boy.
(郵便集配人が少年と大きな犬に会う．「君の犬は噛みつくかい」と郵便集配人は尋ねる．「噛みつかないよ」と少年．ところが犬は集配人の脚に噛みつく．「君は噛みつかないと言ったじゃないか」と集配人は大声で叫ぶ．少年は答えて「それはぼくの犬じゃないよ」)

Personally, I never go economy class. *Did you know* if you **fly** this way and there**'s** an accident, you **have** to stand up in the life raft?
(個人的にはエコノミークラスで行くことは決してない．もしエコノミーで飛んで事故が起きると救命いかだで立っていなければならないのを知っていたか．)
★ Irish bull → p. 39

(b) 一般的真理（→第1章 1 現在形 A (4)）
A drunk loitering on a street corner is hailed by a police officer. "What are you hanging around here for?" The drunk replies, "I *heard* the world **goes** around every twenty-four hours, and I'm waiting for my house."
(通りの角をぶらついていた酔っ払いが警官に呼び止められる．「なぜこんなところでぶらぶらしているんだ」酔っ払いは答える「世界は24時間ごとに一回りすると聞いたんで家が回って来るのを待ってるんで」)
★ Irish bull → p. 39

When I was a kid, I used to pray every night for a new bicycle. Then I *realized* that the Lord **doesn't work** that way, so I just stole one and asked Him to forgive me.　(Emo Philips)
(子供の頃，毎晩新しい自転車が欲しいと祈っていた．そのあと私は神はそのようにはなさらないと悟ったので，ちょっと1台盗み神に許しを請うた．)
☞ Emo Philips (1956-): アメリカのコメディアン．

Hegel was right when he *said* that we **learn** from history that men never **learn** anything from history.　(George Bernard Shaw)
(ヘーゲルが我々が歴史から学ぶことは人は歴史から何も学ばないことだと言ったのは正しかった．)
☞ Hegel (1770–1831)：ドイツの哲学者．
☞ George Bernard Shaw (1856–1950)：アイルランド出身のイギリスの劇作家．

(c) 仮定法：

He *said* he **would** die **if** she **didn't** marry him and, sure enough, he did—seventy-five years later.
(彼は彼女に結婚できないなら死ぬと言った，そしてやはり死んだ—75年後に．)
☞ 直接話法：He *said* (to her), "I *would* die if you *didn't* marry me."

One man found the key to safe driving for his wife. He *reminded* her that **if** she **had** an accident, the newspapers **would** print her age with the police report.
(ある男が奥方が安全運転するための秘訣を見つけた．彼は奥方にもし事故を起こすと新聞が警察の報告と一緒に年齢も書くだろうと注意したのだ．)

B. 直接話法と間接話法

(1) 直接話法：人のことばをそのまま伝える方法

Theobald walked into the living room and spoke to his father. "Pop," he said enthusiastically. "I've got great news for you." The father smiled and asked, "What is it?" "Remember you promised me $5 if I passed in school?" The father nodded. "Well," said the son, "I'm sparing you that expense this year."
(テオバルドは居間に入って父親に話しかけた．「お父さん」と彼は意気込んで言った．「お父さんにいいニュースがあるんだ」父はほほえんで「何だね」と尋ねた．「お父さんは僕が学校の試験にパスしたら5ドルくれるって約束したのを覚えてるでしょう」父はうなずいた．「あのう」と息子が言った．「今年はその費用を省いてあげるよ」)

I had a blind date. I waited two hours on the corner. A girl walked by, and I said, "Are you Louise?" She said, "Are you Rodney?" I said, "Yeah." She said, "I'm not Louise."　(Rodney Dangerfield)
（ブラインドデートをした．街角で 2 時間待った．若い女性が歩いて通り過ぎるので「ルイーズさんですか」と言った．彼女は「あなたロドニーなの」と言ったので「そうです」と言った．彼女は「わたしルイーズじゃありませんわ」と言った．）

☞　Rodney Dangerfield (1921-2004)：アメリカのコメディアン・俳優．

"Dad, give me a quarter."
"Not today, Son, not today."
"Dad, if you give me a quarter, I'll tell you what the milkman said to mama this morning."
"Here, Son, quick—what did he say?"
"He said, 'Lady, how much milk do you want?'"
（「お父さん，25 セントちょうだい」「今日はだめだ，お前，今日はだめ」「25 セントくれたら今日牛乳配達の人がお母さんに言ったことを教えてあげてもいいよ」「ほら 25 セントやるから早く—彼は何と言ったんだ」「『奥さん，今朝は牛乳どのくらいご入用ですか』って」）

The family had gathered around because old Grandpa was dying.
"Is there anything I can do for you?" said his wife.
The old man raised himself on one elbow and peered at a jag of beer on the table.
"I wouldn't mind a swig of that," he gasped.
"Well, you can't," snapped his wife. "That's for the wake."
（家族はおじいちゃんが臨終のため周りに集まっていた．「何かわたしにできることあるかしら」とおばあちゃんが言った．おじいちゃんは片肘をついて起き上がりテーブルの上のビールのジョッキを目を凝らしてじっと見た．「あれをぐいと飲みたい」と喘ぎながら言った．「あれはだめ」とおばあちゃんはピシャリと言った．「あれはお通夜に要るの」）

(2) 間接話法：人のことばを自分［話し手］のことばに直して伝える方法

I *asked* her **if** she **was doing** anything on Saturday night, and she *told* me she **was committing** suicide. So I *asked* her **if** she **was**

doing anything on Friday night.　(Woody Allen)
（土曜の夜に何かする予定かどうか彼女に尋ねると，自殺する予定だと言った．だから金曜の夜に何かする予定かどうか尋ねた．）

cf. 直接話法：
I said to her, "Are you doing anything on Saturday night?" and she said to me, "I'm committing suicide." So I said to her, "Are you doing anything on Friday night?"

☞ Woody Allen (1935–　)：アメリカの映画監督・脚本家・俳優・作家．

(a) 伝達文が平叙文

I caught him standing in front of the mirror with his eyes closed. He *said* he **was** trying to see what he **looked** like when he **was** asleep.
（彼が鏡の前で目を閉じて立っているのを見つけた．彼は眠っているときどんなふうだか知ろうとしているんだと言った．）

☞ 直接話法：He said, "I'm trying to see what I look like when I am asleep."

He *said* he **hadn't had** a bite in two days, so I bit him.
（彼は「2日間1かじりもしていない」と言ったので私は彼を噛んでやった．）
☞ bit「軽い食事」⇔「噛むこと」　★ **Pun** → p. 26
☞ 直接話法：He said, "I haven't had a bite in two days."

"Waiter, what are these coins doing in my soup?"
"Well, sir, you *said* you **would** stop coming to this restaurant unless there **was** some change in the meals."
（「君，この小銭はスープの中で何をしているんだ」「えー，お客様は食事に何か変化がないとこのレストランに来るのはやめるとおっしゃいました」）
☞ change:「小銭」⇔「変化」　★ **Pun** → p. 26

A young and very beautiful woman was talking to an old school friend.

"My husband tricked me into marrying him. Before we married he *told* me that he **was** a multi-millionaire."
"But he is a multi-millionaire, isn't he?"
"Yes. But he also *said* he **was** eighty-one and in very poor health and I've just found out that he is only seventy and he's in perfect condition."

(若くてとても美しい女性が昔の学校友達と話していた.「夫にはだまされて結婚したの.結婚前には自分が億万長者だと言ったのよ」「でも億万長者でしょ」「そうよ.でも 81 でとても身体の具合が悪いとも言ったの.だけど本当はまだ 70 で健康そのものだと分かったのよ」)

☞ 直接話法：... he said to me, "*I am* a multi-millionaire."
　　　　　　　　... he also said, "*I am* eighty-one and in very poor health."

cf. 下例のように伝達文が（2つの等位節が重なる）重文の場合は and, but の次に that を加えることがある.

A new teacher had a very dirty pupil in her class. At first she didn't know what to do, but finally she sent the boy home with a note to his mother, *saying* **that** he was not clean **and that** he should bathe more often.
The next morning the boy came back to school, and pinned to his dirty shirt was the following note: "Tommy isn't a rose. Don't smell him—teach him!"

(新任の先生にはクラスに非常に汚い生徒がいた.初めのうちはどうしてよいか分らなかったが遂に少年に母親への手紙を持たせて帰した.その手紙には彼が不潔でもっとたびたび風呂に入るようにと書いてあった.翌朝少年は学校に戻って来たが汚れたシャツに次のようなメモがピンで留められていた.「トミーはバラではありません.彼の臭いを嗅がないでください.勉強を教えてください」)

(b) 伝達文が疑問文

"Sam *asked* me last night **if** I **liked** his company."
"What did you say?"
"I *said* I **didn't** know **which** company he **worked** for."

(「サムったら昨日の晩わたしに一緒にいたいかって聞いたのよ」「何て答えたの」「どの会社に勤めているか知らないと言ってやったわ」)

☞ company:「同席」⇔「会社」　★ **Pun** → p. 26
☞ 直接話法：Sam said to me, "Do you like my company?"
　　　　　　I said, "I don't know which company you work for."

I have no luck. A girl stopped me once and *asked* me **if** I **wanted** to have some fun. I *told* her I **did**. So, she sold me a joke book.
(僕はついていない．女の子が僕を呼び止めて楽しいことをしたくないかと尋ねた．したいと言った．すると彼女はジョーク本を売りつけたのだ．)

☞ 直接話法：A girl ... said to me, "Do you want some fun?" I said to her, "Yes, I do."

After receiving a rather poor report card, the boy *asked* his teacher **if** she **would** reconsider his grades, adding, "At home I'm already on the list of endangered species."
(ややお粗末な通知表を受け取ったあと，少年は先生に成績を考え直してくれないかと尋ね，さらに言った「家では僕はもう絶滅危惧種のリストに載っているんです」)

☞ 直接話法：the boy said to his teacher, "Would you reconsider my grades?"

Aunt: I'm sorry, Jack, that you didn't like your gift. Remember, I *asked* you **whether** you **preferred** a large check or a small one.
Jack: But I didn't know you were talking about ties.
(伯母「残念だわ，ジャック，あなたへのプレゼント気に入らなかったのね．思いだしてちょうだい，あなたには大きなチェックがいいか小さなチェックがいいか聞いたのよ」ジャック「ネクタイの話をしているとは知らなかったんです」)

☞ check:「格子じま」⇔「小切手」　★ **Pun** → p. 26
☞ 直接話法：I said to you, "Do you prefer a large check or a small one?"

Little Jimmy had finished his nightly prayer and *asked* me **what** prayers **were**. I *told* him they **were** little messages to God. Quickly he said, "Oh, yes. And we send them at night to get the cheaper rates."

(息子のジミーが夜のお祈りをすませるとお祈りとは何かと尋ねた。それは神様への小さな通信だと教えた。すぐに息子は言った「そうだね。だから料金を安くするために夜送るんだね」)
- ☞ 直接話法：... and said to me, "What are prayers?" I said to him, "They are little messages to God."

A snail was crossing the road when he was run over by a tortoise. A policeman came along and *asked* him **how** it **had happened**. "I don't remember," said the snail. "It happened so fast." (Anon.)
(カタツムリが道路を横切っているとカメに轢かれた。警官がやって来てどんなふうに起こったのかを尋ねた。「覚えてないんです」とカタツムリは答えた「あんまり速く起こったんで」)
- ☞ 直接話法：... and said to him, "How did it happen?"

Somehow, I don't think I'm going to marry my current boyfriend. Last night when I casually *asked* him **how** much money he **had** in the bank, he *said* he **would** have to go home and open the pig to find out.
(とにかく、今のボーイフレンドとは結婚しないと思うわ。昨日の晩何気なく銀行にいくら持っているのか聞いたら、彼ったら帰って豚を開けなきゃ分からないと言ったのよ。)
- ☞ pig = piggy bank：「(子豚の形をした) 貯金箱」
- ☞ 直接話法：... I said to him, "How much money do you have in the bank?" he said, "I will have to go home ..."

(c) 伝達文が命令文

My dentist *told* me recently **to spend** more time with my gums.
(Rita Rudner)

(掛かりつけの歯科医は最近私に歯茎ともっと時間を過ごせと言ったのよ。)
- ☞ 直接話法：My dentist said to me, "Spend more time with your gums."
- ☞ Rita Rudner (1953-): アメリカのコメディアン・俳優。

"Did you reprimand your little boy for mimicking me?"
"Yes, I *told* him **not to act** like a fool."
(「君は坊ちゃんが僕のまねをするのを叱ったか」「もちろんさ。バカなまねをするなと

言ったさ」）
☞ 直接話法：I said to him, "Don't act like a fool."

A young lady went into a bank to cash a large cheque. The cashier *asked* her **to identify** herself, so she took a mirror from her bag and looked into it.
"Yes, that's me all right" she said.
（若い女性が高額の小切手を現金化するために銀行へ入って行った．出納係は彼女に身分を証明することを求めたので，女はバッグから鏡を取り出して覗き込んだ．「はい，確かに私に間違いないわ」と彼女は言った．）
☞ 直接話法：The cashier said to her, "Identify yourself, please."
★ **Irish bull** → p. 39

(d) 伝達文が感嘆文

"Did anyone *tell* you **how beautiful** you **were**—and mean it?
（誰かが君は何と美しい人だと言ったかい―しかも本気で．）
☞ 直接話法：Did anyone say to you, "How beautiful you are!"?

ジョークの常識㉖

★ **Spoonerism:**「頭音転換」**Pun** の一種．同一文中の 2 語以上の語頭音（まれに他の部分の音）が入れ替わってしまう現象．言い間違えた，または故意に言い換えた語句が何らかの意味を持ち，かつそこにユーモアの要素を含むもの．Rev. William Archibald *Spooner* (1844–1930) に由来する．What's-the-difference joke (→ p. 153) に頻出する．

"Give me a well-**oi**led **bi**cycle."（十分油を差した自転車をくれ．）
→ "Give me a well-**boi**led **i**cicle."（十分沸騰したつららをくれ．）

"May I **sh**ow you to another **s**eat?"（別の席にご案内しましょうか．）
→ "May I **s**ew you to another **sh**eet?"（別のシーツにあなたを縫いつけましょうか．）

第 27 章　倒置・強調・挿入・省略

1　倒置

(a) 目的語・補語を強調するための倒置

1) 目的語を強調するための倒置

> **Everything I learned about teaching** I learned from bad students.　(John Holt)
> (教育について学んだことすべてを悪い学生から学んだ。)

☞ John Holt (1923–1985): アメリカの作家・教育(学)者.

"**All I am** I owe to my mother."
"Why don't you send her 30 cents and square the account?"
(「この僕のすべては母に借りがあるんだ」「30 セント送って支払いを済ませればいいじゃないか」)
☞ お前の価値は 30 セント.　　★ **Insulting joke** → p. 97

What he lacks in intelligence, he makes up for in stupidity.
(知性の点で欠けていることを彼は愚かさで埋め合わせている。)
★ **Insulting joke** → p. 97

I once shot an elephant in my pyjamas. **How he got into my pyjamas**, I'll never know.
(かつて私のパジャマの象を撃った。象がどうやってパジャマを着たのか皆目分からない。)
☞ an elephant *in my pyjamas*（私のパジャマを着た象）（形容詞句）⇔ shot ... *in my pyjamas*（パジャマを着て撃った）（副詞句）（→ 第 18 章 句と節）
★ **Elephant joke** → p. 72

Anything parents haven't learned from experience they can now learn from their children.

（親たちが経験から学ばなかったことは何でも，今や子供たちから学ぶことができる．）

2) 補語を強調するための倒置

Blessed is the man who can laugh at himself, because it's a cinch he'll never stop being amused.
（自分を笑える人は幸いである．面白がるのをやめることは絶対にないのは確実だからだ．）

Blessed is he who expects no gratitude, for he shall not be disappointed.　(W. C. Bennett)
（感謝を期待しない人は幸いである，がっかりすることがないからである．）
☞ W. C. Bennett (1900-1979): カナダ・ブリティッシュコロンビア州知事・作家．

Uneasy lies the head that ignores a telephone call at 2 a.m.
（午前2時の電話を無視する頭には不安が横たわる．）

(b) 副詞語句を強調するための倒置

In three words I can sum up everything I've learned about life: it goes on.　(Robert Frost)
（3語で人生について学んだことすべてを要約できる：それは続いて行く，である．）
☞ Robert Frost (1874-1963): アメリカの詩人．

To the small part of ignorance that we arrange and classify we give the name 'knowledge.'
（整理し分類する無知のわずかな部分に我々は「知識」という名前を付ける．）

Of all the noises known to man, opera is the most expensive.
(Molière)
（人間に知られているすべての騒音の中で，オペラがもっとも高価である．）
☞ Molière (1622-1673): フランスの喜劇作家．
★ **One-liner** → p. 395

(c) neither / nor / so による慣用的倒置

"I was in Switzerland on a business trip last week."
"**So** was I."
"I didn't see much of the scenery though."
"**Neither** did I. There were too many mountains in the way!"
(「先週仕事でスイスにいたよ」「僕もだ」「しかしあまり景色が見えなかった」「見えなかったね。山が多すぎて邪魔だった」)

☞ 何を見に行ったのか.

Uncle: I hope, John, you are good children, and always obey your father and mother.
John: We always obey Mamma, **so** does Papa.
(叔父「ジョン，君たちは良い子だから，いつもお父さんお母さんの言うことを聞いてほしいよ」ジョン「僕らはママの言うことはいつでも聞いてるし，お父さんも聞いてるよ」)

Doctor: Say, the check you gave me came back!
Gloria: **So** did my rheumatism!
(医師「ねえ，あなたがくれた小切手が戻って来ました」グロリア「わたしのリューマチもですわ」)

"Can you pay your bill now?"
"No, see me Thursday."
"Thursday I'll be out of town."
"**So** will I."
(「勘定を今払ってくれませんか」「いや，木曜に来てよ」「木曜は町にいないんで」「オレもいなんだ」)

"Why don't you play chess with Gregor any more?"
"Would you play with somebody who cheats?"
"No, I wouldn't."
"Well, **neither** would Gregor."

(「なぜグレガーともうチェスをしないんだい」「君はインチキをする奴とするかい」「いや，しないね」「グレガーもしないんだ」)

There is some consolation in the fact that, even though your dreams don't come true, **neither** do your nightmares.
(夢は実現しないけれど悪夢も実現しないという事実にはいくぶんかの慰めがある．)

The high cost of living is no joke—**nor**, for that matter, is the average joke.
(高い生活費なんて冗談じゃない，いやそう言えば，並みの冗談も冗談じゃない．)

(d) 仮定法：**if** が表面に出ないもの（→ 第 23 章　条件・仮定表現）

Could it think, the heart would stop beating.　(Fernando Pessoa)
(物を考えることができるなら，心臓は鼓動をやめるだろう．)

☞　Could it think ＝ If it could think
☞　Fernando Pessoa (1888-1935): ポルトガルの詩人・作家．

"**Should** this boat sink, whom would you save first, me or children?"
"Me."
(「万一このボートが沈んだら，わたしと子供たちどっちを最初に助けるの」「私さ」)
☞　Should this boat sink ＝ If this boat should sink

Were it not for my little jokes, I could not endure the burdens of my country.　(Abraham Lincoln)
(もし大したこともないジョークでも言わなければ私は国家の重荷に耐えることはできないだろう．)
☞　Were it not for ～ ＝ if it were not for ～　(もし～がなければ)
☞　Abraham Lincoln (1809-1865): アメリカの政治家．第 16 代大統領．

"I apologize for keeping you waiting for so long," the doctor told the patient as he entered the examination room.
"That's OK with me, Doctor. But it might have been better **had you**

seen me while my ailment was its early stages."
(「こんなに長くお待たせして申し訳ありません」と医師は診察室に入るときに患者に言った。「わたしはいいんです，先生．でも病気が初期の段階のときに診てくださっていたら，もっと良かったかもしれません」）

2 強調 （→it ～ that の強調については「第 10 章　It の用法」）

(a) do を使う

> "I dreamed that I had a tough job."
> "Yes, you **do** look tired."
> (「苦しい仕事をする夢を見たよ」「そうだろう，確かに疲れているように見えるよ」）

There are two ways of dealing with the common cold: if you don't treat it, it lasts six or seven days, and if you **do** treat it, it lasts about a week.
(普通の風邪に対処する方法が 2 つある．治療しないと 6，7 日続く，そして実際に治療すると約 1 週間続く．）
☞ いずれにせよ，放っておけば治る．

"Hello, is this the receptionist at the mental hospital?"
"Yes, it is."
"Can I speak to Maurice in Room 327?"
"I'm sorry, sir, but nobody seems to be answering the phone in that room."
"Great! That means I really **did** escape!"
(「もしもし，精神病院の受付ですか」「そうです」「327 号室のモーリスをお願いします」「すみませんが，部屋の誰も出ないようですが」「よかった！ということは俺は本当に逃げ出したということだ！」）
★ **Irish bull** → p. 39

(b) 副詞(句)を使う

Man: Where **in hell** have I seen you before?
Bishop: I don't know. What part of hell are you from?
(男「いったいどこであんたに会ったっけ」主教「わかりませぬ。地獄のどの辺からお出でなされたのかな」)

☞ in hell を単なる強意表現で使ったのに対して、主教は文字どおりに解釈している。

Golfer: I've never played **this** badly before.
Caddie: You've played before?
(ゴルファー「今までこんなひどいプレーをしたことはないよ」キャディー「前にプレーしたことがあったんですか」)
★ **Insulting joke** → p. 97

I was hitchhiking the other day and a hearse stopped. I said, "No thanks, I'm not going **that** far." (Steven Wright)
(先日ヒッチハイクをしていると霊柩車が止った。私は言った。「いえ、結構です。そんなに遠くまでは行きません」)
☞ Steven Wright (1955-): アメリカのコメディアン・作家。

A husband arrived home to find his blonde wife reading his diary. Hurling it to the floor, she yelled: "Right. You've got five seconds to tell me: who **the hell** are April, May and June?"
(夫が帰宅するとブロンドの妻が自分の日記を読んでいるのに気づいた。妻はそれを床に投げつけ叫んだ「いいわ。5秒あげるから言って。April, May, June っていったい誰なの」)
★ **Blonde** → p. 249

Adam (to Eve): Wow, where **on earth** did you learn to kiss like this!
(アダムがイブに「うわあ、いったいどこでこんなキスの仕方を覚えたんだい!」)

"Why **in the world** did you ever write a policy on a man ninety-eight years old?" asked the indignant insurance-inspector.

"Well," explained the new agent, "I looked in the census report and found there were only a few people of that age who die each year."
(「一体なぜ 98 歳の男に保険証券を書いたりしたんだ」と腹を立てた保険調査官が尋ねた。「ええと」新米の外交員が説明した。「国勢調査を調べて，毎年その年齢で死ぬ人はほんのわずかしかいないことが分かったんです」)
★ **Irish bull** → p. 39

Whiskey is **by far** the most popular of all remedies that won't cure a cold.　(Jerry Vale)
(ウイスキーは風邪を治さないすべての治療薬の中で断然最も人気がある。)
☞ Jerry Vale (1930-2014): アメリカの歌手・俳優.

When you get something for nothing, you are probably paying **the highest** price **possible** for it.
(何かをただで手に入れたら，間違いなくこれ以上はない最高額を支払っているのだ。)
☞ ただほど高いものはない.

3 挿入

A cynic is a man who, **when he smells flowers**, looks around for a coffin.　(H. L. Mencken (Attrib.))
(冷笑家とは，花の匂いがすると，周りに棺桶(かんおけ)がないかとさがす男である。)
☞ H. L. Mencken (1880-1956): アメリカの批評家・ジャーナリスト.

We forget all too soon the things **we thought** we could never forget.
(Joan Didion)
(我々は決して忘れるはずはないと思ったことをあまりにもすぐ忘れる。)
☞ Joan Didion (1934-　): アメリカの作家.

A wise man is one who is smarter than **he thinks** he is.
(賢い人とは自分が思っているより頭の良い人である。)

My diseases are an asthma and a dropsy and, **what is less curable**,

seventy-five.　(Samuel Johnson)
（私の病気は喘息（ぜんそく），水腫（すいしゅ），そしてもっと治りにくい，75歳だ．）
☞ Samuel Johnson (1709-1784): イギリスの詩人・批評家・辞書編纂家．

"I've been sleeping fine, Doctor, since I attended your lecture on insomnia."
"Great. And did you enjoy the lecture?"
"No, but, **as I said**, it cured my insomnia."
（「先生，先生の不眠に関する講演に出て以来よく眠っています」「それはすばらしい．それで講演はおもしろかったですか」「いいえ，申し上げた通り，それで不眠が治ったのです」）

An egotist is one who, **reading a book and not understanding something in it**, decides it is a misprint.
（自惚（うぬぼ）れ屋とは，本を読んで何か分からないことがあると，それは誤植だと決めつける人である．）

The one thing that unites all human beings, **regardless of age, gender, religion, economic status or ethnic background,** is that, **deep down inside**, we all believe that we are above-average drivers.
（年齢，性別，宗教，経済的地位または民族的背景に関わりなく，すべての人間を結びつけるものは内面の深いところで我々はみな自分は平均以上の運転者であると信じていることである．）

A sociologist is someone who, **when a beautiful woman enters the room and everybody looks at her**, looks at everybody.
（社会学者とは，美しい女性が部屋に入ってきて皆が彼女を見るとき，皆を見る人である．）

You can understand people better if you look at them—**no matter how old or important or impressive they may be**—as if they are children. For most men never mature; they simply grow taller.
　　　　　　　　　　　　　　　　　　　　　　　　(Leo Rosten)

(人々をよりよく理解するためには，もし，どんなに年取っていても，重要人物でも，堂々としていても，彼らをまるで子供であるかのように見ることだ．というのは，ほとんどの男は決して成熟しない．ただ背が伸びるだけだ．)
☞ Leo Rosten (1908-1997): ポーランド出身のアメリカのユダヤ系作家.

A wise school teacher sent this note to all parents on the first day of school: "If you promise not to believe everything **your child says** happens at school, I'll promise not to believe everything **he says** happens at home."
(賢い学校の先生が学校の初日にすべての両親に次のような短い手紙を送った「もしお子さんが学校で起こったとおっしゃることを全部は信じないとお約束いただけるなら，わたくしも家庭で起こったとお子さんがおっしゃることを全部は信じないとお約束いたします」)

4 省略

> Why is "abbreviation" such a long word? (Steven Wright)
> (「省略」がなぜこんなに長ったらしい単語なんだ．)

☞ Steven Wright (1955-): アメリカのコメディアン・作家.

(a) 語句の繰り返しを避けるための省略

1) 名詞の省略

She served him blended coffee—**yesterday's** and **today's**!
(彼女は彼にブレンドコーヒーを出した——昨日と今日の．)
☞ yesterday's (coffee) and today's (coffee)

"You're the last man I ever expect to marry."
"**How many** are there ahead of me?"
(「あなたは結婚したいと思う最後の人よ」「僕の前に何人いるの」)
☞ How many (men)

2) 動詞の省略

Adversity makes men; **prosperity, monsters.**

（逆境は人を作る，繁栄は怪物を作る．）
☞ prosperity (makes) monsters

Everyone complains of his memory, **no one, of his judgment**.
(la Rochefoucauld)
（誰もが自分の記憶力を嘆くが誰も判断力を嘆かない．）
☞ no one (complains) of his judgment
☞ la Rochefoucauld (1613-1680): フランスのモラリスト．警句・格言の作者．

A politician thinks of the next election; **a statesman, of the next generation**.
（政治屋は次の選挙を考え，政治家は次の世代を考える．）
☞ a statesman (thinks) of the next generation

They were a well-matched couple as both of them were madly in love —**she with herself**, and **he with himself**.
（彼らは2人とも猛烈に恋をしていたので似合いのカップルだった―彼女は自分に，彼も自分に．）
☞ she (was madly in love) with herself, and he (was madly in love) with himself

"Madam, you've put too many stamps on this letter."
"Oh dear, it won't go further than I want it **to**, will it?"
（「奥さん，この手紙に切手を貼り過ぎですよ」「あらまあ，届いてほしい所より遠くへは届かないのね」）
☞ I want it to (go)　（→「第14章 不定詞」(7) 代不定詞）

3) 補語の省略

"Are you the oldest in your family?"
"No, silly. Daddy **is** (　　)."
（「子供の中では一番年上かい」「違うよ，バカだな，お父さんだよ」）
☞ Daddy is (the oldest); family「家族」⇔「子供たち」　★ **Pun** → p. 26

A wife told her husband, "Be an angel and let me drive." He did and he **is** (　　)!

第 27 章　倒置・強調・挿入・省略　　　　　　　　　433

（妻は夫に「お願いだから運転させて」と言った．彼はそうしてそうなった．）
☞ Be an angel and ～「お願いだから～してちょうだい」
☞ He did and he is = He let her drive and he is an angel.
　He is an angel.（彼は天使である）ということは今は天国にいるということ．

"So that is a popular song he's singing?"
"It was (　　) before he sang it."
（「じゃあ彼が歌っているのはポピュラーソングなんだね」「歌う前はそうだったんだ」）
☞ It was (popular)

He recently finished his last book. At least people hope it is (　　)!
（彼は最近最後の本を書き終えた．少なくとも人々はそうあってほしいと思っている．）
☞ it is (his last book)

(b) 副詞節における「主語＋be 動詞」の省略

> Housework can kill you if (　　) done right.　(Erma Bombeck)
> （家事はまともにやったら死にますよ．）

☞ if (it is) done right
☞ Erma Bombeck (1927-1996)：アメリカのユーモア作家．

When (　　) angry, count four; when (　　) very angry, swear.
　　　　　　　　　　　　　　　　　　　　　　　　　(Mark Twain)
（腹が立ったら 4 つ数えろ．非常に腹が立ったら悪態をつけ．）
☞ When (you are) angry; when (you are) very angry
☞ Mark Twain (1835-1910)：アメリカの（ユーモア）小説家．

Our body cells renew while (　　) asleep. If only our wallets could do the same.
（身体の細胞は眠っている間に新しくなる．財布も同じことができればなあ．）
☞ while (we are) asleep

If (　　) reelected, I will promise to fulfill all the promises that I made in the last election campaign.

（再選されました暁には，前回の選挙運動中にいたしましたすべてのお約束を実行いたしますことをお約束いたします．）
☞ If (I am) reelected　　★ **Politician** → p. 329

Frequent naps prevent old age, especially when (　　) taken while (　　) driving.
（頻繁に居眠りすることは老化を防ぐ，特に運転中には．）
☞ when (they are) taken while (you are) driving
☞ 居眠り運転で若死にすれば老化は避けられる．

あ と が き

　編著者ほぼ 30 年来の念願の書がやっと何とか仕上がった，というのが本音です．本書は東京書籍の高校英語教員対象の小冊子『高校通信東書英語』に「英文法にジョークを利用して」と題して 1981 年 11 月号から 1989 年 6 月号まで断続的に 31 回続いた連載記事が基になっています．しかし定年退職後に集めたジョークの方がはるかに多いかもしれません．そのせいか，教室では使いにくいものが増えていったような気がしています．

　編著者はジョークを「常識からの逸脱」と考えています．物事を等身大で語らない，言いかえると，大きいものは過剰に大きく，または過剰に小さく，小さいものは過剰に小さく，または過剰に大きく語るのがジョークの常道です．誇張された形で本音が見えるとも言えるでしょう．そして，そこから人生の真実が見えてくるところにジョークの面白さがあると思っています．

　1982（昭和 57）年度以降，高校の英語科目から「英文法」がなくなりました．しかし教室から英文法が消えるはずはなく，結局，副読本・参考書・問題集はむしろ増えました．新たに「オーラル・コミュニケーション（OC）」という科目が設置されましたが，「オーラル・グラマー（OG）」などと呼ばれて，「OC」の授業は「英文法」の授業のままという教室が特に大学を受験する生徒の多い学校で見られました．また，2013（平成 25）年度から大幅に科目編成が変わりました．もちろん「英文法」という科目はありません．しかし英文法の授業は当然行われています．またそれは当然のことだと思います．英文法をきちんと身に付けずに英語を正しく理解［発表］することはできないからです．

　お読みいただいて，ジョークはそれほど大したことを笑っているのではないことを理解していただいたのではないかと思っています．ビジネスの現場などで英語のネイティブの人が冗談を言い合っているなら，分からなくても一緒に笑えばいいのです．なぜ笑ったのかなどと尋ねられる心配はありません．逆に，覚えておいたジョークの一つも披露すれば大受け間違いなしでしょう．

　「まえがき」にも書いたとおり，見本原稿としてある章だけをメールで送ったつもりが，その時点での全原稿を送ってしまったことが，本書出版という「間違いの喜劇」を産んだのかもしれません．その意味でも出版部部長 川田 賢氏に感謝

しなければなりません．

　また，出版の可能性もはっきりしない段階で原稿を読み，「◎（非常に面白い）」「○（面白い）」「△（面白くない；あまりよく分からない）」「×（つまらない；分からない）」とほとんどすべてのジョークに印をつけてくれた筑波学院大学の卒業生である土生都直哉，滝本麻由（旧姓鈴木），根本佑治，櫛田ひかる，の 4 君に感謝したいと思います．

参 考 書 目 （アルファベット順）

[英文法書]

安藤貞雄（2005）『現代英文法講義』（開拓社）

江川泰一郎（1982）*A New Approach to English Grammar*（東京書籍）

江川泰一郎（1991）『英文法解説　改訂三版』（金子書房）

伊藤健三・廣瀬和清（監修）萱原雅弘・佐々木一隆（1999）『大学生のための現代英文法』（開拓社）

松川昇太郎（1966）『新英文法概要』（清水書院）

大塚高信・中嶋文雄（監修）（1982）『新英語学辞典』（研究社）

芹沢　栄（1958）『表覧英文法』（有精社）

安井　稔（1996）『英文法総覧　改訂版』（開拓社）

[辞書・学習参考書]

飛田茂雄（編）（2000）『現代英米情報辞典』（研究社出版）

豊田一男・山本敏子（編）（1997）『トリム英和辞典』（研究社）

瓜生　豊・篠田重晃（編著）（1993）『全解説　頻出英文法・語法問題1000』（桐原書店）

山岸勝榮（編）（1997）『スーパーアンカー英和辞典』（第3版）（学習研究社）

[ジョークに関する本]

安部　一（1984）『英語で笑え―アメリカン・ジョーク入門』（ジャパンタイムズ）

古家　淳・ロバート＝ジュペ（2002）『耳で聴きたい英語の名文』（雷鳥社）

郡司利男（1966）『英語熟語笑辞典』（英友社）

郡司利男（1982）『英語ユーモア講座』（創元社）

郡司利男（1982）『英語なぞ遊び辞典』（開拓社）

郡司利男（1984）『ことば遊び12講』（大修館書店）

晴山陽一（2004）『すごい言葉―実践的名句323選』（文藝春秋）

晴山陽一（2008）『英語ベストセラー本の研究』（幻冬舎）

速川和男（1985）『英語ユーモア教室―ニガテな英語が好きになる！』（ライオン社）

東森　勲（2011）『英語ジョークの研究―関連性理論による分析』（開拓社）

広永周三郎（1980）『英語のしゃれ』（太陽出版）
広永周三郎（1986）『対訳　アメリカのジョーク』（太陽出版）
岩間直文（2003）『すぐに使える英語のジョーク150』（丸善）
小林章夫・ドミニク-チータム（2005）『イングリッシュ・ジョークを愉しむ』（ベレ出版）
丸山孝男（2002）『英語ジョークの教科書』（大修館書店）
丸山孝男（2005）『英語脳はユーモア・センスから―ビジネス・日常会話に役立つジョーク集』（ベストセラーズ）
丸山孝男（2007）『英語ジョーク見本帖』（大修館書店）
丸山孝男（2011）『アメリカの大統領はなぜジョークを言うのか―名句・迷言・ジョーク集』（大修館書店）
毛利八十太郎（1957）『ジョーク集成』（研究社出版）
森　浩二（1980）『英語のジョーク―実用英語』（創元社）
森　浩二（1980）『英語のジョーク2』（創元社）
村松増美（1998）『私の英語ウォッチング―話題のことば・気になる世相』（ジャパンタイムズ）
中野清治（2009）『英語ジョーク快読のススメ―ジョークがわかれば、言葉も文化もわかる』（開拓社）
ピーターセン，マーク（1988）『日本人の英語』（岩波書店）
ピーターセン，マーク（2010）『日本人が誤解する英語』（光文社）
里中哲彦（2000）『英語の迷言・放言・大暴言』（丸善）
里中哲彦（編訳）（2004）『1日1分半の英語ジョーク―ネイティヴ・スピーカーも思わず吹き出す！』（宝島社）
里中哲彦（2010）『英語の質問箱―そこが知りたい100のQ&A』（中央公論新社）
杉田　敏（1990）『杉田　敏の英語落書帖』（日本放送出版協会）
杉田　敏（1999）『最新アメリカジョーク事情―インターネット版ジョークが映す現代アメリカ』（DHC）
杉田　敏（2004）『人生を考える英語―名言・迷句このひと言196』（プレジデント社）
トミー植松（2001）『トミー植松　パーティー・ジョークを楽しもう―英語ユーモア社交術』（丸善）
豊田一男（2003）『英語しゃれ辞典　Punctionary』（研究社）

Arnott, Stephen & Haskins, Mike (2004) *Man Walks into A Bar* (Ebury Press)
Bayan, Rick (1994) *The Cynic's Dictionary* (Hearst Books)
Beeching, Cyril Leslie (1990) *A Dictionary of Eponyms* (Oxford University Press)
Berle, Milton (1989) *Milton Berle's Private Joke File* (Crown Publishers)
Bonham, Tal D. (1981) *The Treasury of Clean Jokes* (Broadman Press)
Connolley, Mat (2004) *butter comes from butterflies* (Random House Australia)
Copeland, Lewis & Faye (1965) *10,000 Jokes, Toasts & Stories* (Doubleday)
Esar, Evan (1978) *The Comic Encyclopedia* (Doubleday)
Fecthtner, Leopold (1973) *5,000 One and Two Liners for Any and Every Occasion* (Parker Publishing Company)
Fields, Marty (1999) *Marty Fields' Takeaway Jokes* (New Holland Publishers)
Goldstein-Jackson, Kevin (1977) *The public Speaker's Joke Book* (Elliot Right Way Books)
Greene, Mel (1999) *The Greatest Joke Book Ever* (Avon Books)
Grothe, Mardy (2004) *Oxymoronica* (HarperCollins)
Humes, James C. (1995) *The Wit & Wisdom of Winston Churchill* (Harper-Perennial)
Jarski, Rosemarie (2004) *A Word from the Wise* (Ebury Press)
Jarski, Rosemarie (2006) *The Funniest Thing You Never Said* (Ebury Press)
Jarski, Rosemarie (2008) *Dim Wit* (Ebury Press)
Jarski, Rosemarie (2010) *The Funniest Thing You Never Said 2* (Ebury Press)
Kelly, Rosanna & Pakenham, Eliza (1999) *The Little Book of Wit & Wisdom* (Parragon)
MacHale, Des (1996) *"Wit"* (Prion)
MacHale, Des (1997) *More "Wit"* (Prion)
MacHale, Des (1998) *Yet More "Wit"* (Prion)
MacHale, Des (2011) *Dublin Wit* (Mercier Press)
MacHale, Des (2011) *Wittypedia* (Prion)
McNeely, Scott (2011) *Ultimate Book of Jokes* (Chronicle Books)
Meiers, Mildred & Knapp, Jack (1980) *5600 Jokes for All Occasins* (Avenel

Books)

Metcalf, Fred (2001) *The Penguin Dictionary of Modern Humorous Quotations* (Penguin Books)

Metcalf, Fred (2003) *The Penguin Dictionary of Jokes* (Penguin Books)

Mieder, Wolfgang & Kingsbury, Stewart A. (1994) *A Dictionary of Wellerisms* (Oxford University Press)

Phillips, Bob (1989) *The Best of the Good Clean Jokes* (Harvest House)

Picering, David (2006) *Penguin Pocket Jokes* (Penguin Books)

Pollack, John (2011) *The Pun Also Rises* (Gotham Books)

Price, Steven D. (2006) *1001 Funniest Things Ever Said* (Lyons Press)

Rosten, Leo (1996) *Leo Rosten's Carnival of Wit* (Plume)

Rudin, Helen (ed.)(1984) *Jokes & Riddles* (Waldman)

Sherrin, Ned (1995) *The Oxford Dictionary of Humorous Quotations* (Oxford University Press)

Swan, Jonathan (2007) *Man Walks into a Bar 2* (Ebury Press)

Swan, Jonathan (2010) *Man Walks into a Bar 3* (Ebury Press)

Tibballs, Geoff (2006) *The Mammoth Book of Jokes* (Carroll & Graf)

Tibballs, Geoff (2012) *The Mammoth Book of Jokes 2* (Robinson)

Weekes, Karen (2007) *Women Know Everything!* (Quirk Books)

Weisberg, Jacob (2001) *George W. Bushism* (Fireside)

Wilkerson, David (2011) *Booklover's Book of Jokes, Quips & Quotes* (The British Library)

Woolard, George (1996) *Lessons with Laughter* (Language Teaching Publications)

Woolard, George (1999) *Grammar with Laughter* (Language Teaching Publications)

Auntie Lou's Quotes: Soft, Strong and Not Too Long (2012) (Prion)

Reader's Digest (1997) *Laughter, the best medicine*

Reader's Digest (2011) *Laughter Really Is The Best Medicine*

Reader's Digest (2012) *Laughter The Best Medicne @ Work*

Reader's Digest (2012) *Laughter The Best Medicine Those Lovable Pets*

索　引

1. 「文法用語」は五十音順，その他はアルファベット順で並べてある．
2. 数字はページ数を示す．

【文法用語】

［あ行］

意志未来　20

［か行］

過去(進行)形　13
過去完了　61
過去完了進行形　62
過去分詞　237
可算名詞　99
仮定法過去　364
仮定法過去完了　367
関係代名詞　330
関係副詞　341
冠詞　170
間接話法　417
感嘆文　44
完了不定詞　220
疑問詞　32
疑問文　27
句　306
強調　427
強調構文の it　150
継続用法　338, 345
形容詞句　308
形容詞節　330
形容詞の語順　155
原級　377
原形不定詞　222

現在完了　57
現在完了進行形　60
現在分詞　230
5 文型　47
固有名詞　113

［さ行］

再帰代名詞　126
最上級　389
使役動詞　222
指示代名詞　128
集合名詞　106
従属接続詞　306
受動態　65
準否定　406
状態動詞　3
省略　431
助動詞　73
所有代名詞　120
親身の we　123
節　306
先行詞　330
選択疑問文　29
前置詞　267
前置詞句　309
相互複数　106
挿入　429

［た行］

代不定詞　219

代名詞　119
単純未来　19
知覚動詞　225
抽象名詞　111
直接話法　416
定冠詞　174
等位接続詞　313
倒置　423
動名詞　250
動名詞の意味上の主語　260
独立所有格　123

［な行］

7文型　55
二重限定　335
二重前置詞　301
二重否定　410
人称代名詞　119

［は行］

比較級　381
比較表現　376
否定表現　396
否定命令文　42
付加疑問文　30
不可算名詞　108
付加詞　55
不規則動詞　14
副詞　188
副詞句　309
副詞節　346
普通名詞　99
物質名詞　108
不定冠詞　170
不定詞　200
不定代名詞　131
部分否定　408

分詞　230
分詞構文　243

［ま行］

未来（進行形）　18
未来完了　63
未来完了の代用　60
名詞　98
名詞句　307
名詞節　321
命令文　40

【ジョーク関連語句】

Absent-minded professor　320
Black humor　118
Blonde　249
Boner　46
Bushism　169
Doctor, Lawyer, Politician　329
Elephant joke　72
Ethnic joke [humor]　361
Goldwynism　56
異分析　375
Insulting joke　97
Irish bull　39
Jewish mother　312
教会　345
Light-bulb joke　139
Misprint　187
Mother-in-law　305
One-liner　395
Parody　199
Pun　26
Riddle　64
Spoonerism　422

Tall tale 412
Tom Swifties 229
Waiter 266
What's-the-difference joke 153

【構文・成句】

do は動詞の原形, *done* は過去分詞を示す.

[A]

according to 267, 303
a Ford 173, 174
after school 185
(all) the＋比較級 389
alphabetically speaking 248
an Edison 174
a pair of 104
apart from 302
as 〜 as 377
as 〜 as ever 381
as 〜 as possible 380
as 〜 as S can *do* 380
as far as 360
as far as A is concerned 360, 381
as if [though] 371
as long as 359
as of 303
(just) as A, so B 316, 360
as soon as 348
as well 316
as well as 316
at best 393
at *one*'s best 393
at home 185
at last 394

at least 394
at most 393
at war 185
avoid *do*ing 252

[B]

be about to *do* 218
be being *done* 70
be busy *do*ing 266
be going to *do* 23
be supposed to *do* 219
be to *do* 218
be used to *do*ing 266
because of 302
belong to 4
beside *one*self 128
Biologically speaking 248
both 〜 and … 314
by bus [plane / subway / taxi] 184
by far 198, 429
by *one*self 128
by the time 350

[C]

cannot [can never] *do* too 〜 84
cannot have *done* 83
cannot help but *do* 264
cannot help *do*ing 264
cannot [can never] A without B 411
catch 〜 by the arm 182
catch 〜 *do*ing 235
come *do*ing 232
come rain or shine 358
compared to 304
consider *do*ing 252
consist in *do*ing 255
consist of *do*ing 255

[D]

day after day　185
demand that S+*do*　228
door to door　184
due to　302

[E]

each other　135
either A or B　318
enjoy *do*ing　252
〜 enough to *do*　216
escape *do*ing　252
even if [though]　356
every+複数名詞　135
every time S+V　348

[F]

feel 〜 *do*ing　235
feel like *do*ing　263
find 〜 *do*ing　235
find 〜 *done*　240
finish *do*ing　253
for ages　59
for fear S+V　353
for *one*self　128
forget *do*ing　259
forget to *do*　259
Frankly speaking　248
from generation to generation　184
from 〜 to ...　276

[G]

Generally speaking　248
get+*done*　69
get 〜 *done*　242
get 〜 to *do*　212

go *do*ing　233
go on *do*ing　255

[H]

had better　388
happen to *do*　215
have [has / had] been *done*　71
have 〜 *do*ing　243
have 〜 *done* [*do*ing]　241
help 〜 *do*　225
help 〜 to *do*　225
hear 〜 *do*　226
hear 〜 *do*ing　234
hear 〜 *done*　240
here and there　310
hit 〜 in the face　182
hit 〜 on the head　182
How about ... [*do*ing]?　38
How come ...?　38
hundreds of　102

[I]

I wish S+had+*done*　369
I wish S+was [were / (助)動詞の過去形]　366
if it had not been for　370
if it was [were] not for　370
in case S+V　352
in case of　304
in class　185
in *do*ing　262
in front of　303
in hell　428
in itself [themselves]　128
in no hurry　55
in order to *do*　216

in spite of　304
in spite of *one*self　128
in terms of　304
in *one*'s twenties [thirties]　102
in the world　428
insist on *do*ing　255
insist that S+*do*　228
instead of　304
A is to B what C is to D　326
it goes without saying　265
it is ～ for ... to *do*　144
it is no use [good] *do*ing　264
it is ～ of ... to *do*　145
it is ～ that S+V　146
it is ～ that [who] S+V（強調）　150
It is time S+過去形　374
it is ～ to *do*　143
it occurs (to ～) that S+V　148
It seems (to ～) that S+V　148
It takes [costs] ～ to *do*　147

[J]

Judging from [by]　248

[K]

keep *do*ing　233
keep ～ *do*ing　236
keep ～ *done*　240
keep ～ from *do*ing　261
keep on *do*ing　255
kiss ～ on the cheek　182
kiss ～ on the forehead　182
kick ～ in the stomach　182

[L]

laugh at　69

leave ～ *do*ing　236
let ～ *do*　223
Let's [Let us] *do*　42
listen to ～ *do*　227
listen to ～ *do*ing　236
look for　10
look forward to *do*ing　266
look ～ in the face　182

[M]

make ～ *do*　222
make ～ *done*　241
make the best of　394
make the most of　393
make up *one*'s mind　60
many a　167
may as well *do*　88
may have *done*　87
may well *do*　88
might as well *do*　90
might have *done*　90
mind *do*ing　253
miss *do*ing　253
more or less　388
must have *done*　92

[N]

need *do*ing　258
need ～ *done*　241
needless to say　209
neither A nor B　400
Never mind!　43
next to　305
no less than　387
no less A than B　386
no longer　388
no matter how [what / who など]　357

no more than　386
no more A than B　386
no sooner A than B　387
not A any more than B　386
not as [so] ～ as …　377
not A because B　351
not ～ but …　316, 397
not ～ in the least　394
not only ～ but (also) …　315
not so much A as B　380
not that A but that B　317
not A until B　412
nothing ～ as+原級+as …　404
nothing+比較級+than　404
nothing but=nothing more than　406
nothing doing　405
nothing like　405
now and then　310
now that S+V　352

[O]

of no avail　309
on account of　302
on earth　428
on doing　262
on strike　55, 309
once in a while　310
one another　136
one ～ the other　132
outside of　302
owing to　302

[P]

pass away　62
pat ～ on the shoulder　182
practice doing　253
prevent ～ from doing　261

propose that S+do　228
put off doing　253

[Q]

quite a few　165

[R]

recommend that S+do　229
regardless of　305
remember doing　258
remember to do　258
resist doing　254
Roughly speaking　248
run over　69

[S]

see ～ do　225
see ～ doing　234
see ～ done　240
seem [appear] to do　214
shake hands with　106
Shall I [we] do?　21
should have done　79
smell ～ doing　237
so as to do　216
so ～ as to do　217
so ～ S can [will] do　352
so ～ that …　353
so to speak　209
some ～ others　134
some ～ the others　134
sooner or later　310, 388
speaking of　248
spend ～ doing　237
start with　2
stop doing　254

stop to *do*　254
strictly speaking　248
strike ～ on the head　182
such ～ that …　354
suggest *doing*　255
suggest that S+*do*　228

[T]

tell [ask / want など] ～ to *do*　210
thanks to ～　305
That's because S+V　343
That's why S+V　343
the+形容詞　180
the+比較級～, the+比較級…　384
the moment [instant / minute] S+V　348
there is [are] ～　48
there is no *doing*　265
to be frank with you　209
to be honest　209
to be sure　209
to begin [start] with　209
to make a long story short　209
to tell (you) the truth　209
to the best of *one*'s knowledge　394
too ～ to *do*　215

try *doing*　259
try to *do*　259
turn off　11
twice [three times] as ～ as …　379

[U]

upside down　310

[W]

want ～ *done*　241
watch ～ *do*　227
watch ～ *doing*　235
weather permitting　249
Were it not for ～　426
When it comes to *doing*　265
whether A or B　358
whether A or not　358
Where am I?　36
Why don't you *do*?　37
Why not *do*?　37
worth *doing*　263
Would you like to *do*?　74
Would you *do*?　74
would rather [sooner] *do*　75

【編著者紹介】

豊田 一男（とよだ かずお）

1938年東京生まれ．東京教育大学文学部卒．1962年から28年間，静岡県・東京都の公立高校4校，筑波大学附属高校勤務．その後，筑波短期大学，筑波女子大学，筑波学院大学を経て，筑波学院大学名誉教授．大塚英語教育研究会元会長．高校教員時代から，高校英語教科書編集に参加．現在，英語のジョークを楽しむ会（Joke-Loving Club）（略称JLC）企画運営委員．

主な著書：『ニュースクール英和辞典』（共著，研究社，1988），『トリム英和辞典』（編著，研究社，1997），『英語のとびら』（全3巻）（共著，日本書籍，1993），『英語しゃれ辞典 Punctionary』（研究社，2003），『わかりやすい英語教育法』（共著，三修社，2009），『わかりやすい英語教育法（改訂版）』（共著，三修社，2013）

ジョークで楽しむ英文法再入門
English Grammar through Jokes

編著者	豊田 一男
発行者	武村 哲司
印刷所	萩原印刷株式会社

2015年6月28日　　第1版第1刷発行©

発行所	株式会社 開拓社

〒113-0023 東京都文京区向丘1-5-2
電話 03-5842-8900（代表）
振替 00160-8-39587
http://www.kaitakusha.co.jp

ISBN978-4-7589-1309-6　C0082

JCOPY　〈(社)出版者著作権管理機構　委託出版物〉

本書の無断複写は，著作権法上での例外を除き禁じられています．複写される場合は，そのつど事前に，(社)出版者著作権管理機構（電話 03-3513-6969，FAX 03-3513-6979，e-mail: info@jcopy.or.jp）の許諾を得てください．